PATRICK SYMMES writes about Latin American politics, globalization and Third World travel for a number of magazines, including *Harper's*, *Outside*, *Wired*, *Condé Nast Traveler* and *GQ*. In his book *Chasing Che*, he retraced the journey Che Guevara made in 1952 through South America that later became the subject of the film, *The Motorcycle Diaries*.

Praise for *Chasing Che*

'Patrick Symmes is the ideal journalist: he gives you the information clearly and when you need it. He also gives your imagination something poetic to leap from.'

Los Angeles Times

'Symmes unearths the man behind the legend and discovers for himself some of the suffering that so affected Che.'

Time Out, New York

'Unsentimental and funny, this book combines the spiritedness of a gonzo journalist with a serious reporter's sense of purpose.'

Publishers Weekly

D0881679

Also by Patrick Symmes

Chasing Che

Fidel Castro and his Generation –
From Revolution to Exile

PATRICK SYMMES

ROBINSON
London

For my mother, who encouraged all my ventures,
great or small, wise or foolish.

Constable & Robinson Ltd
3 The Lanchesters
162 Fulham Palace Road
London W6 9ER
www.constablerobinson.com

First published in the UK by Robinson,
an imprint of Constable & Robinson Ltd, 2007

Copyright © Patrick Symmes 2007

The right of Patrick Symmes to be identified as the author
of this work has been asserted by him in accordance with the
Copyright, Designs and Patents Act 1988.

All rights reserved. This book is sold subject to the condition that it
shall not, by way of trade or otherwise, be lent, re-sold, hired out
or otherwise circulated in any form of binding or cover other than that
in which it is published and without a similar condition including
this condition being imposed on the subsequent purchaser.

A copy of the British Library Cataloguing in
Publication Data is available from the British Library.

ISBN: 978–1–84529–000–9

Printed and bound in the EU.

1 3 5 7 9 10 8 6 4 2

I want to leave today for the island of Cuba, which I believe to be Japan . . . The Indians . . . say it is very large and has people there with one eye in the forehead, as well as others they call cannibals . . . I also understand that, a long distance from here, there are men with one eye and others with dog's snouts who eat men.

—*From the logbook of Christopher Columbus*

CONTENTS

LIST OF ILLUSTRATIONS

Every effort has been made to trace the holders of copyright. In the event of any inadvertent transgression of copyright please contact the author via the publisher.

Portrait of Colegio de Dolores taken in 1941.
(*Courtesy of Lundy Aguilar.*)

Fidel Castro and friends at the scene of his fist fight with José Antonio Cubeñas.
(*Courtesy of Padre José Maria Patac, S. J.*)

The Jesuits gathered in the school's upper patio.
(*Courtesy of Padre José Maria Patac, S. J.*)

A page taken from a Dolores yearbook.
(*Courtesy of Miguel Llivina.*)

José Antonio Cubeñas, Ceferino Catá, Sócrates Pinto, Guillermo Martinez, Alcides Nuñez and Fidel Castro pose for a publicity shot for a locally made health tonic.
(*Courtesy of the Center for Cuban Studies.*)

José Antonio Cubeñas.
(*Courtesy of the author.*)

José Antonio Roca.
(*Courtesy of the author.*)

ACKNOWLEDGEMENTS

I would like to thank Beth Segal for her constant support, Elizabeth Hightower for her scalpel, Tom Miller for his compass, Annie Dillard for her binoculars, and the Canadian stranger for his cash. Many Cubans contributed to this book informally, and they have been given pseudonyms when necessary.

Lastly, this book would have been impossible without the kindness and cooperation of the men from Dolores and their families. Pepín Bou, Lundy Aguilar, David, Arturo, and Kiki de Jongh, Pedro Haber, José Antonio Cubeñas, Roberto Mancebo, Miguel Llivina, Alberto Casas, Jorge Segura, Ceferino Catá, José Antonio Roca, Bernardo Souto, Balbino Rodríguez Romero, Juan Sotus, and many others opened their homes, archives, memories, and passions to me. Any failings in the result are the fault of the author; any successes are theirs.

CUBA 1959

Havana

Varadero

Cárdenas

PINAR DEL RÍO HAVANA MATANZAS

Playa Larga

Santa Clara

LAS VILLAS

Cienfuegos

Escambray

Bay of Pigs

Trinidad

Sancti Spiritus

Isle of Pines
(Isle of Youth)

Caribbean

FLORIDA
USA

Hialeah Miami

THE BAHAMAS

Florida Keys

Straits of Florida

CUBA

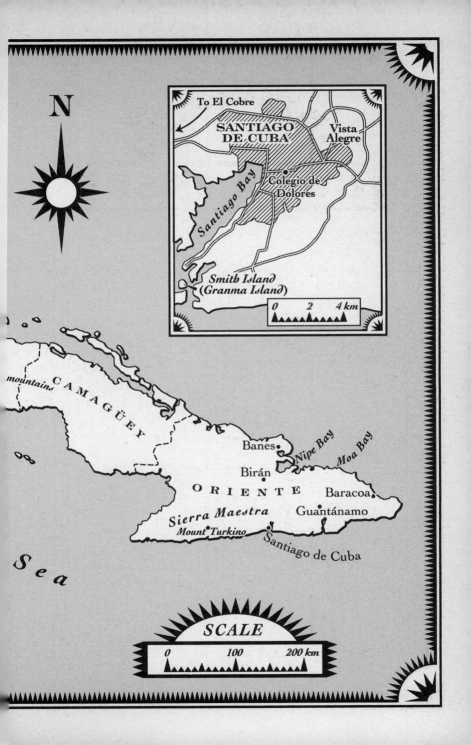

1

MIAMI SPRINGS

'THIS HAS BEEN A DIFFICULT YEAR for the sad ones,' Pedro Haber said, but before he could continue, there was a metallic purr, which grew quickly into a feedback loop. The sound squawked over the ballroom, a room full of wrinkled men in brown suits and ageless women in immovable bouffants. Pedro tried to continue. He said, 'Four who regularly attend these reunions have fallen, God has them in all his glor –'

But he was cut off now, fatally. The screech made even a busboy put down his bread rolls and cover his ears. A devilish *skeeeeeeeTWAAAAAAAAAweeeeeeSKEEEEE* refracted off the rented glassware and then ricocheted off the golf club plates, a piercing white noise like a fax machine in your head. Old hands rose, trembling, searching for hearing aids.

Pedro, class of '59, stood calmly and stared at the microphone. One more betrayal in a lifetime of disappointments.

SKWEEEEEEEEEE-BWAAAAAAAAAA-SOOOOOOOOOO.

Pedro ran the reunions because he was the most stalwart, reliable and capable of the men from the old days. But this was exactly why he disliked being called on to manage things, yet again. He was a friend to everyone. He did nothing to deserve this. Stress was bad for a man his age. But duty was duty: at 64 years of age, he was one of the younger men in the room.

Unplug. Fiddle with knobs. Move cables. Start over. Forget to replug. Replug. Readjust knobs. Tap tap. 'Can everyone hear me?' He was back in business. But nobody, all night, could handle the microphone. Not even the singer.

Pedro Haber didn't actually start by saying that it was 'a difficult
year for the Sad Ones'. He had said that it was a difficult year for
the Dolorinos. The phrase is rooted in *dolor*, meaning 'pain, ache;
sadness, grief'. When Pedro said *los Dolorinos* it sounded like all of
those things, a world of aching and grieving for the ones who
suffer. But it had another meaning, for these were the men who,
as boys, came from a happy place. Dolores was their old school,
the Catholic academy, run by Jesuits. The Colegio de Dolores
where they had all met, had been their boarding school in eastern
Cuba once upon a time. The sadness had come later.

Everyone in the room, from the busboys on up, spoke the twin
languages of this nation-within-a-nation. But not everyone is
naturally ambidextrous, and thought and speech leapt between
Cuba and the United States. At the far right of the room, near the
entrance, was a special table reserved for VIPs and the guests of
honour. Pedro Haber and I were sitting here, and the accents and
vocabulary at this table were a mixture of proper, upper-crust
Castilian Spanish and plain American English. Two places over to
my right was Pedro Roig, a Dolores alumnus and Bay of Pigs
veteran, who was now head of TV Martí in Washington.
Immediately on my left was Lundy Aguilar, retired from his
professorship at Georgetown University, where he had taught
European history to a young Bill Clinton. And directly across the
table was the Reverend Father Juan Manuel Dorta Duque, one of
the last surviving teachers from the old school in Cuba. He was a
Jesuit, or more properly, a member of the Society of Jesus,
perhaps the most influential of all Catholic orders. Dorta Duque
was 82 years old, retired but still living in a Jesuit *residencia*. He'd
first come to Dolores in 1951, after Fidel left, but the school was
awash with alumni who remembered him and Jesuits who'd
taught him. One of the survivors of Fidel's affections, Lundy
Aguilar, was sitting at the table a few feet away.

TWO LANGUAGES, TWO MINDS, a Cuban inside every
American. Even here, at their own high school reunion, among
their very own, they were unmoored, adrift, their homes, lives,
even their manner of speech, all without footing.

Cuban exiles are on a journey that cannot be finished in one lifetime. This 200-mile transmigration of the soul is at once irreversible, and incompletable. The survivor suffers from temporal confusion, at once in eastern Cuba in 1941 and in Miami Springs in 2005. Equally at home in a lost Atlantis, that mythical Cuba from 'before', and in the Dade County real estate market. What difference between the old Santiago de Cuba, in the long-ago Republic, in a time of youth, privilege and revolution, and this old age of wrinkled faces at a golf club near Miami International? Weren't these the same people? Like a snail, the exile carried his home along.

The phrase *los Dolorinos* harked back to a starting point, before any expulsion from any garden. The Colegio de Dolores was the leading school of Cuba's second city, Santiago, the best education available in eastern Cuba. The richest gathering of the richest part of Cuba, a school of the chosen few. All Pedro Haber had meant, what he truly said, was that they, the Dolorinos, had lost yet more friends. Four had fallen from the ranks, this year. For this room of aged Cuban exiles, locked in an actuarial competition with Fidel Castro himself, attrition was a difficult subject.

The reunion was held in late September, the middle of a very bad hurricane season. There had been 11 inches of rain in a month. The water table was up to the grass. It had rained again this morning, hard. Low clouds scudded over the golf course, lit up brightly by the ground beacons of Miami International, by the strip malls along the Le Jeune, and by the floodlights of an industrial park across the road. Turbulent and wet, the clouds passed without releasing drops, for now. Black patches of night sky winked in and out.

The old Dolorinos and their wives had started arriving en masse at 7 pm, most of them not just on time for the cocktail hour, but early. Over the next hour heavy American cars kept rolling into the lot, and then the progression of aged legs across the street. The grass lawn of the country club would slowly hiss as someone explored the possibility of taking a short cut. A dress shoe came back out of the grass with a sucking sound. A high heel stabbed an indentation in the lawn that began to fill with runnels of silt. The click of heels on brick soon followed. These men and women, averaging somewhere in their early sixties, cut no corners. Moving slowly, often supporting each other, they made right-angle turns on the brick walkways, which were uneven and slicked with algae. The men wore a mixture of brown and black suits, or sometimes the formal tropical shirts called *guayaberas*, long-sleeved and embroidered. The women had formality and reserve. (It wasn't their reunion, of course; Dolores was a boys' school.) Or maybe the women had, in their upright carriage, just the composure required by cream gowns and structured black cocktail dresses, by shoulder wraps of the very gauziest pastels. Their hair was stiff. Usually short, a tropical reality, but fixed in uplifted constructions. Their lips and eyelashes were lacquered with precision. Even on the men, every hair was in place – brushed back, Brylcreemed, ordered and clipped. No straggling locks, or dissenting cowlicks: all was order. You had to draw the line somewhere and this was it: neatness of tonsure was a way of fighting back, of defending civilization against the barbarians.

The banquet hall of the Miami Springs Country Club is called the Legends Room, but it isn't very big. There were 105 people in there by 8 pm, and most of them were talking, a raucous atmosphere of jokes, bragging, disbelief, laughter, shouts, argument and monologue, all of it bouncing off long tables of rented glass and dull knives. The crowd was slightly faded, prone to thick glasses and hearing aids, but they were functional, still able to dance, and to argue. The men touched each other constantly, putting a hand on another's arms, pressing a shoulder in their grip, even clutching one another's lapels in a kind of menacing embrace. They wore pins in those lapels, showing off their allegiance to political movements, their qualifications as survivors of various disasters, their enlistment in Masonic lodges, the Elks, Lions, Odd Fellows and Rotary, or ethnic allegiances, sporting clubs, religious leagues, cultural groups, charitable drives, and other such bulwarks against the loss of everything. Ariel Dorfman, a Chilean, said that an exile had only two possessions, the language of his birthplace and the 'keys to a house that no longer exists'. Cubans are joiners, filling their pockets with new things.

On the way into the Legends Room, the door charge was $5, collected as a donation to the welfare fund for impoverished alumni of the school. For that money you received a printed programme for the reunion event. It listed the speakers, and featured page after page of pictures, old shots of the Colegio de Dolores and of the students of past days, and shots of the landmark buildings of Santiago and the surrounding region.

In America, someone is always standing by to sell you your history, so more of the same photography was available for sale at the back of the room. Two women in icy competition were selling similar arrays of souvenirs and memorabilia related to Cuba. Photographs and paintings. Antebellum cigar box labels. Stamps of the old Republic of Cuba. Tickets from the Spanish lottery. Coins. Most of it was fake.

They both had maps for sale. One, a reproduction of early Spanish cartography, showed Cuba in outline only, with the interior a blank unknown, a paradise of the imagination. Even in such an old map, you could see what Cubans always claimed to see, the island shaped like a sleeping alligator, snout to the west and the long thin body stretching out to the east, with the tail tucked back under the body to make the stubby shape of Oriente province. It mapped out well enough. Medallions around the borders of the old map showed the four winds, and the native peoples in their imagined costumes. There were modern maps for sale, but not too modern. The most recent maps were still fanciful in their way, also decorated around the edges with symbols of an imagined Cuba. Thatched bungalows. The old capitol building in Havana, now abandoned because it looks exactly like the US capitol. An American navy ship was shown steaming past eastern Cuba, while up north some seventeenth-century natives paddled canoes. In the interior of this Cuba, hokey peasants on carts with huge wheels rolled up the middle of the island, passing schematic palm trees.

In the south, somewhere near Grand Cayman, was a legend which said: THIS MAP HAS BEEN CREATED TO PRESERVE THE MEMORY, KNOWLEDGE, AND PATRIOTISM OF THE YOUNG CUBAN IN EXILE. And next to that was a list of 'facts' about Cuba, including the statement that 'Three fourths of all Cubans are white, of Spanish descent,' which wasn't true in whatever past being mapped here, and certainly isn't true today.

These were charts to a Cuba that didn't exist, that hadn't, couldn't, and wouldn't exist. Yet they were accurate in their way, as charts of the peculiar mental geography of Cuba in exile. Whether printed in great detail, framed and placed on a wall in a home, or distributed on disposable placemats in Cuban diners, these special maps for exiles show only and always a Cuba of six provinces, the original Spanish imperial demarcations dating back to the days of the conquest. From west to east these six were Pinar del Río, Havana, Matanzas, Las Villas, Camagüey and Oriente. Almost everyone here at the reunion tonight identified themselves as being Oriental, an easterner, from around the region that surrounded Santiago de Cuba. There were a few Havana people here, because there were always Havana people. But no matter who you were, wherever you came from, when they asked you your place of origin, you answered with one of those six old names, the province.

That was Cuba, but that isn't Cuba. Oriente didn't exist any more. Fidel Castro had literally redrawn the map, turning the traditional six into a new 14. The old provinces and identifications were blown up and replaced with rational borders and, sometimes, names commemorating Castro's own life. Part of the beloved old Oriente province was broken off and renamed Granma province, because Castro had run his boat *Granma* aground there. How could an exile say he was from such a place? The old Isle of Pines, where Castro had served jail time, had been split off to make a province called the Isle of Youth, contractually dedicated to education. Who could acknowledge such things?

They didn't sell accurate road maps either. Never mind if Castro had built a new highway down the middle of Cuba, or that a better map would reveal all the satellite housing cities and rural polytechnic universities that had sprung up across Cuba. Nobody was going to that Cuba. The less accurate the map the better.

I browsed through some copies of old photographs of Santiago, with men in straw hats, and views of the bay, or the old Bacardí rum factory. Next down the table was a Havana telephone guide from 1959. This old phone book, full of period illustrations and corporate optimism, was the single best-selling item at the Cuba Nostalgia Fair, a memorabilia mart that drew 30,000 people to a convention centre in Miami once a year.

The same brisk commerce was available the rest of the time from dozens of shops around the city: an endless supply of Cuban flag paintings, regional histories, and posters of Elián, the five-year-old who had washed up in Florida after his mother drowned while rafting to America. Elián, sent back to his father after an apocalyptic custody battle, was now the sacred child of exile, often portrayed as though lifted across the waves on a dolphin's back. Just yesterday, driving along Calle Ocho in Little Havana, I'd counted four stores in 17 blocks that specialized in manu-factured memories of Cuba. The latest, Havana To-Go, featured 'Made in Manzanillo' T-shirts. The owner wasn't even Cuban.

I'd already bought myself a copy of the 1959 Yellow Pages there on Calle Ocho. I'd spent ten years reporting on Cubans, but I knew nothing about Miami, only Havana. I knew the street grid of Nuevo Vedado in the dark, but the highways of Dade County left me confused and frightened. I'd been to Cuba a dozen times, often for a month at a stretch; I'd been to Miami half as often, sometimes for as little as a few hours. The Cubans I knew were in Cuba.

Flipping through the pages of the phone book was seeing Cuba through the wrong end of a telescope. Distanced, and rendered small by misunderstanding, the Cuba of this vision was perfectly useless as a guide to anything but the imagination of the Miami Cubans. The photographs in the ads showed a Havana where the avenues were crowded with commercial signs, bustling with banks, airlines, department stores, liquor promotions, society institutions and cheap entertainments. For a Cuban phone book the amount of English was startling: Westinghouse, General Electric Cuba, Eagle Electrical Specialties, Mercury Air Cargo, Orkin, Nelson, Singer. The commercial dominance ran on and on. But the Cubans had their pride too, like the Tropicana, listed

under 'cabarets' as the '*Night-club más bello del mundo!*' There was a
full-page ad for an efficient-looking bus company, with seven
departures a day for Santiago, all the latest models. Waiting now
for the cocktail hour to end, I flipped through the Havana
restaurant listings for 1959, which made me sad.

The first call to sit for dinner was ignored. The phone book had
a White Pages listing as well and, idly killing time, I looked under
C and found this:

Castro, Raúl – 14 no. 109 Mnao – 29–4770

That's to say, Raúl Castro, Dolores class of 1947. There was no
listing in the phone book for his brother, Fidel Castro '42. The
1959 edition of the Havana phone book would have been put
together during 1958, a year that Fidel and Raúl spent fighting in
the mountains of eastern Cuba. Apparently they had kept their
phone service turned on while overthrowing the government.

The Cuban-American poet Orlando Ricardo Menes warned
against nostalgia. He wasn't addressing the phone book directly,
but a man he met who painted sunsets of Havana, the kind of
sunsets where the clouds are underlit, the sea blue and calm, palm
trees obscure the foreground and, at rear, a Cuban flag ripples
from the battlements of the old castle, El Moro. Such pictures
were for sale everywhere in Miami. Ricardo Menes cautioned the
painters:

My Cuba collapsed from corruption, greed, and violence.
Idyllic memories are merely a jeweled noose.

At the second call for dinner, a few people actually sat down,
mostly us outsiders. There were a few Cubans here who weren't
from the old school. After Dolores had been closed by the
Revolution, it had been recreated in Miami, but not as Dolores.
The students-in-exile had been merged with the pupils of two
other exiled Jesuit schools at a new campus in Florida. But the
new school kept the name of the largest, the Colegio Jesuitico de
Belén. Belén had always been a sister school to Dolores, and the
student bodies were intimately tied together – many Dolores
students, including Fidel Castro and Lundy Aguilar, had attended

Belén at one point – but also rivals. Belén was Havana, Dolores was Santiago. So the Legends Room was full of a confusing mix of Dolores alumni, some old, some young, some graduates from Santiago, others from Belén in Havana, with younger ones from Belén in Miami. So as usual a bunch of people from Belén and Havana had shown up to dominate everything. Half a century ago the Dolores boys had felt like hicks when they showed up at Belén, transfer students lost in the huge school building in the bustling capital. Now at their own high school reunion half the people were from Belén.

A third call to sit for dinner, this time with the lights flicking off and on, but people just kept talking. Ten minutes went by, the waiters squawking haplessly at clots of Cubans engaged in furious rounds of hand-shaking, exchanging addresses and bits of old news, wrapping up old stories and starting new ones. After fifteen minutes the head of catering came out, clapped his hands furiously, and marched around the rooms shouting '*Damas y caballeros, por favor.*' Slowly, people began to pry apart, to exchange business cards, to release lapels and sit. Pedro Haber now reached the microphone, and began to flick switches on the sound system.

Disorder bubbled along pleasantly for the rest of the evening. Through dinner, and the scheduled remarks, and the events, and even the prayerful invocation, a few people kept talking loudly at the back, or wandering around shamelessly shaking hands. There would be a great crash during a speech, when some unruly person, attempting to pose for a disposable camera, tripped over a chair and brought down a tablecloth full of plates. Craggy old faces kept popping up from the long tables, waving to each other, signalling or passing notes, no different than the behaviour in the Dolores lunch room a lifetime ago.

One of every ten Cubans have fled the island since Castro's Revolution. They have scattered to the four corners of the globe. There are Cubans in Burundi and Bilbao, Mexico City and Manhattan. Several thousand live in Australia. But the capital of exile is certainly Greater Miami. In a diaspora of more than a million Cubans, 833,000 are in Florida. That ratio was reflected in

the Legends Room. A few determined men had made the long
slog to this dinner, coming from Houston or Los Angeles or
Puerto Rico. They were the exiled exiles. And there were a few
who, even though they lived in Miami, were strangers here. One
short, wrinkled man in glasses, standing alone, told me he had
attended the Colegio de Dolores for only one year, in the 1950s.
He didn't know anyone here but had come to the reunion
anyway. Dolores had been the most prestigious school in eastern
Cuba, an honour to attend. The idea of Dolores still drew him.

The attendees from outside Miami were self-selected by
enthusiasm, even more than the local crowd. They were the
most delighted, the loudest, the most prone to interrupting
anything for photographs, the first to pass business cards, the last
to sit down. While dinner was finally being served, a thoracic
surgeon from Texas jumped the gun, stepping to the microphone
and turning it on before anyone had quite realized what he was
doing. He introduced himself to the crowd at a blasting volume,
announced that he was about to tell a funny joke, and then took a
piece of paper from his jacket and unfolded it.

'I'm sorry for speaking in English,' he said.

'*Habla Español!*' a woman at the VIP table shouted.

The surgeon opened his mouth, closed it, and stared at the
room. 'I apologize for speaking English,' he said again. And,
weaker: 'The joke has to be told in English.'

He'd done more than slip up, or break form. He'd betrayed
something by turning his back on the old language and preferring
the new. He might as well have said the unspoken into that
microphone: *We aren't really Cubans.*

Nobody here was Cuban, any more. Exile had to remake
them, separate and change them. Nobody had expected to spend
the rest of their lives abroad, like this, but they had, and Cuba had
gone on living the decades without them. The exiles might have
been born in Cuba. They might be Catholic, and speak Spanish,
and have Cuba engraved in their hearts. But they weren't the real
Cubans any more. Nine out of every ten had stayed. That was
Cuba, over there. The Cuba of memory and old phone books
was something different. Cuba was soldiering on without these

people, and the exiles had gone through defeats and abandon-
ments, stranded in other places with the tide receding from them,
never to carry them home.

Were they Americans? Some were citizens, certainly. But exile
is defined by leaving, not arriving. You drifted a line whose
course went only away, leaving you between worlds and languages, neither here nor there. Neither one nor the other. How
could you be a Cuban if you didn't live in Cuba? How could you
be an American if you still lived, in your head, in Cuba?

For years I had visited with a Cuban exile in New York, a
barber who had lost the natural confidence of Spanish without
ever gaining an equivalent fluency in English. He had become a
stranger in his own mouth, suffocated by the transition. For the
older exiles, too long in Cuba to fully leave it and thus never fully
at home in America, language was a perilous landscape freighted
with subtle signifiers. They heard their children flitting from
English to Spanish between syllables, and saw their grandchildren
stare dumbly when asked a question in Castilian. Even the older
people, at ease in English, would see their abilities fade with the
years, their mind leading the way back to Cuba.

The surgeon was a rare exception. Maybe he'd been isolated
among English-speakers in Houston, because he'd gone so far
into English he couldn't come back. The woman who shouted
Habla español was sure he had abandoned them all.

So the doctor from Houston told his unauthorized story, in
English. A migrating bird meets a cow, and later a cat, and large
piles of cow shit are mentioned. After three iterations, the doctor
reading from his creased paper, it ended, to silence.

'And that is the story,' the surgeon said. Silence. 'The moral of
the story, which is the point, is, not everybody who shits on you is
your enemy.' He sat down to polite applause.

The business of the evening now flowed on quick heels. With
roast beef on our plates, Pedro Haber stood up and set the
microphone to screeching, whining and peeling. Eventually, with
the technical problems sorted out, he began his remarks on the
four fallen comrades from Dolores, and the difficult year of the
Dolorinos. He kept it all moving, though, and after a quick prayer

of invocation from Father Dorta Duque, Haber didn't miss a beat, moving straight into the business of handing out honorary plaques.

Pedro Roig, a neat, wiry man with white hair, leapt up from the VIP table to receive the first. TV Martí, which he ran, was a television station funded by the US government, and staffed by Cuban exiles. Broadcast from an aircraft in the Florida Keys, TV Martí offered 'free' television – the full spectrum of news, sports, weather, and entertainment – to captive Cubans. But it was a signal to nowhere. The 90 miles distance from the Keys to Havana was simply too great for television transmission. I had never met anyone in Cuba who had seen the channel. It was a purely theoretical station, a bit of heated rhetoric hurled into the ether. Yet year after year, an alliance of anti-Castro congressmen and exile influence workers managed to keep federal funding for TV Martí. Even if no one could see it, they argued, the mere fact of its existence was vital. Free television was supposed to give heart to the enslaved Cuban population. Cutting the funding would be nothing less than giving in to Castro. Sustaining an illusion of that size was award-worthy.

Then Lundy Aguilar got up, with a bashful smile for an old man. At the podium he was not exactly steady, but then he'd never been an athlete. Lundy, class of '44. Nearing 80, he was small, bent, skinny as ever, now, as always, a model of self-control. As Haber described it, the plaque was presented in honour of Lundy's achievements as an illustrious professor, a newspaper columnist known even in the 1950s, a philosopher of liberty, a member of distinguished academic bodies, campaigner for democracy and liberty, both before and after the Revolution. He'd done all the things other people only talked about. He'd known and rejected Castro. He'd protested for democracy, and then fought the new tyrant. His predictions – that the Revolution would produce a tyrant, the tyrant would drive them out, and that realism was the only answer – had fallen on deaf ears, but they had come true. He was still at it, publishing occasional articles in the *Miami Herald*, or the *Diario Las Américas*, and knocking out weekly internet postings on liberty, or history, or the God of

Marxism, or Stalin, or Castro as a salesman, auctioning off Cuba. This habit of pouring out commentaries and publishing revelations was common enough among Cubans – ubiquitous, even – but Lundy was different. His friends actually did call him the Prophet. Sustaining a realism like that, among Cubans, was award-worthy.

There were also five plaques for five men, all from one extended family, ranging in age from their seventies down to their twenties. The grandfather had gone to Dolores in Santiago, the sons to Belén, first in Havana and then Miami, and now the youngest generation was at Belén, and had known nothing else but Belén, and Florida. Dolores was too far gone to matter, but the lineaments, the Jesuit strictures, were the same. The family achievement was endurance. The youngster had his hair gelled into spikes, but the same Windsor knot as his grandfather.

Sitting down again, Lundy looked tiny, and especially boyish, fondling his plaque, smiling easily, and talking with the Reverend. Dorta Duque leaned forward, tilting over the table in his high white collar, and asked Lundy where the rest of the survivors from his own class, the boys one year ahead of Fidel, were. There had been only 13 students in Lundy's class.

'Four or six should still be alive,' Dorta Duque suggested.

'No, father,' Lundy said.

'Three?'

'No, father.'

'Two?'

'No, father. Only one,' he said. 'I am the only one left alive.'

TRAGEDY IS STALE NEWS to Cubans, and the evening slid right into farce. The music was bad, loud and popular. A baritone dressed entirely in black, even to the dye in his mustache, pressed some buttons on a karaoke console. Instrumentals erupted, and he began to belt along to *son* standards, the soul music of Cuba. He was effective. The combination of the music, and his striving, melodramatic voice pushed to breaking, was deafening. But many of the people in the room were already partly deaf, and these were Cubans, so the small dance floor filled up before the midpoint of the first song. Couples in their fifties and sixties danced with the easy flow of people who have spent decades together on the floor. Many of them had been dancing together for half a century; the divorce rate was minuscule. There was a mambo, danced cheek to cheek. And a *son*, a classic Beny Moré number. And then a cha–cha–cha, with everyone chanting along, as happy as children to be shouting it out, throwing their hands into the air: '*Cha cha CHA!*' More dancers piled in, taking the last spots on the parquet dance floor, and then filling up the carpet around the edge. Then a conga line, invented by a Dolores man.

It was real dancing, blessedly unselfconscious, everyone bumping elbows, turning, their butts colliding, men calling out to one other, cutting in, reclaiming partners, and starting over with the next song. It wasn't 9.30 yet. Between tunes the crooner would ruin the mood by pressing buttons, so that tape screeched backward and forward as he looked for different tracks, or he might accidentally knock his microphone into one of the speakers, for another thunder and yelp of feedback. But then there would be a tune, a voice, and the dancers picked right up.

The route to the bathroom was lined with black and white pictures of golfers: Arnold Palmer, Sam Snead, Jack Nicklaus, Jackie Gleason, and 1950s faces I didn't know. A sign taped on the wall said, in quick handwriting, DOLORES REUNION – LEGENDS ROOM. At the urinal, two Cubans took the spaces on either side of me, and began to quiz me while relieving themselves. Was I Cuban? No, Irish from Virginia. What was I doing here? Looking for people from the old days, I said. To tell their stories.

They volunteered their stories. Although they had never met until standing at these urinals, they had both attended Dolores in the 1950s. And, they said, the old days were nothing compared to what they had been through since. One guy was 'in agriculture', he said. The other interrupted to say that he was also in agriculture. The first had a farm near Tampa. Oh, really? The second had a farm in Nigeria. Well, the first man came to Miami with nothing, he said, and built up a whole agricultural business, from farming and packaging to transport and added value, all from scratch. Amazing, the second man said quickly, because he himself had come to America with nothing, not one cent, and had supported his entire family and their extended clan by simultaneously opening a medical practice and starting a ranch in Venezuela. The first man cut in: he was growing five kinds of root vegetables in commercial quantities, including a very profitable manioc crop.'*Muy rentable*,' he shouted at one ear. The second man shouted at the other ear: over in Nigeria he'd crossed Holsteins with the African cattle, and they were getting 10,000 gallons of milk a day.

'Well,' the first man said, zipping up. 'I didn't know anything about farming, but with this exile, we have to do what we can.'

We all washed up, but they pursued me toward the Legends Room, insisting that I write about them. Under cross-examination, the second man admitted that he had a plan to produce 10,000 gallons of milk a day in Nigeria. As I walked to the VIP table, he yelled out, 'But we really taught that bastard a lesson!'

I knew not to ask who he meant. *That bastard*. The name missing from the mailing list of this high school reunion. He was here, of course, if only because he was rolled up and hiding in my pocket all along. Only when the party began to wind down, around 10.15, did I clear away some strawberry shortcake and unroll the print, a particularly large copy of the picture that had brought me here. Twenty people were soon gathered around.

Again, no need to ask certain questions. They remembered the building. Not just the men, who had been students there, but their wives, some of whom had seen it for themselves, as visitors back in the girlhood of their 1940s or 1950s, and others who had merely encountered a thousand stories and snapshots in the decades since. The photograph was a straight shot of the entire student body at the Colegio de Dolores, taken the fall of 1941. Two hundred and thirty-eight boys in uniform, lined in eight ranks, the youngest at the bottom, the oldest at the top. Around the edges of the frame were glimpses of railings, mudejar archways, tall doors and white-washed walls. I pointed out where Lundy Aguilar, 15 years old then, was standing, holding the school flag.

There was another face in this picture, a ghost face, missing from the room we stood in, but somewhere there on the paper. I saw a few people bend in to look for it.

Discussion died out as people fell into an intense scrutiny of the wide panorama, with a mounting suspense and frustration. Fear of success matched by a fear of failure. But they had to know how close they stood.

It always gave people a shock when they finally recognized him. The uniforms made everyone look indistinguishable, but once I put the nail of my pinkie across his open, round face, his raked-back visage, that cocky gleam in his eye, there was a collective gasp. It was him. Third row down from the top, fifth from right. A tall boy, with his head tilted back. Instead of a necktie, like the boys on either side of him, his collar was open.

Him. A wilful, wild little man, 14 years old.

'It's him,' a woman said. A man in a grey suit took out his glasses, cleaned them with a purple cloth, put them on, and studied the picture.

'Look at that son of a bitch,' he said.

But I couldn't. I couldn't look at the man whom Guillermo Cabrera Infante called 'Cyclops', the terrible giant who ruled over his own island. You go blind from staring directly at the sun. Better to turn away. Let the eyes adjust to something else, whatever is in the shadows. There was more than one man in Cuba. And more than one boy in Dolores. His history was not the sum total of Cuban history.

Some thought he was a messiah, others a criminal worse than Stalin, but I myself was not even sure he existed. Was he a real creature, or a myth that walked? Once, in Havana, I had stood as close to him as the VIP table was to the microphone, close enough to see his hands trembling, but was he real? It wasn't possible for one man to have done everything in Cuba, no matter what the television in Havana and the radio in Miami said. There had to be larger forces at work, a river of decisions and actors, accidents and intentions, to shape the bends of generations. One life – even one long, century-spanning life – was not enough. One alloy in the Cuban tragedy was this willingness to believe that it was all him, for good or ill. Cubans were gullible, Lundy

Aguilar had once warned, for they 'believe in no one and believe anyone'. They grasped for bitter heroes.

He, the other he, whose name tasted like ashes in their mouths, liked it that way too. A personalized history, full of his actions, his glories, his insight. The enemies of Cuba were *his* enemies, who despised and demonized *him*. He constantly talked of assassination plots, which equated the killing of the Revolution with the killing of him, personally. His enemies sometimes did him the courtesy of getting caught with .50 calibre sniper rifles, proving the equation.

But there were other men. You could draw a frame around any collection of Cubans, really. Any picture of 238 boys would make a reference point, a control group for Dr Castro's experiment. Why not find them, scattered to the winds?

By 10.30, when the crowd was done fingering the photograph, and pressing stories, emails, business cards, accusations, phone numbers, advice, and obsolete addresses in Hialeah and Camagüey upon me, there were only a few stragglers still on the dance floor. A woman of about 60 danced toward me, took my hand, and pulled me on to the dance floor, and then wrapped me in an inebriated hug. As we danced in this embrace, sashaying slowly around the floor, my nose was buried into the airy confection of her hair. The stiff hit of hairspray woke me right up.

'Remember,' she shouted up at me, leading me in circles. 'We are 99 per cent Republicans. Put that in your book!'

The only thing that all Cubans agree on is that they are, each of them, completely reasonable, and that everyone agrees with them.

But the real figure is 80 per cent.

LUNDY'S HOUSE LAY OFFSHORE, hove-to like a wise sailor on the security of Key Biscayne. The next afternoon, with the wet storm weather blown out by fierce winds, I paid a dollar for the toll and drove out the long causeway, leaving behind Miami. The road rose up, becoming a long white bridge, the blue of Biscayne Bay to my right, dotted with wind surfers, and the skyline of downtown Miami behind, on the left. It was Sunday and cruise ships were outbound, nosing through the enclosed bays like white buses. The road swooped down to the brief Virginia Key, and then the long, flat island itself:

> *You said you'd bring to me*
> *Biscayne Bay*
> *Where the Cuban gentlemen sleep all day.*

The road ran through parkland, where crabgrass grew up through sand, and past the old Winter White House of Richard Nixon. Key Biscayne runs five miles, sticking out from the side of Miami, a low barrier island that shields the city itself from hurricane swells. The highest point on Key Biscayne is a pile of landfill, built up beside the sewage plant. The island looks so low, so flat and featureless, that a stiff roller from the Gulf Stream could surge through the mangroves and submerge the whole thing briefly.

The beaches out here were poor, by Miami standards, and smelled of sulphur. That, plus the dollar toll on the causeway, served to keep most people out. Seldom visited, with only a few hotels, it was a prosperous residential neighbourhood. As I drove into what passed for the centre of town, I saw that the parking lot of the Key Biscayne Yacht Club was filled to overcapacity.

Lundy Aguilar's house was on a side street, off a side street. It was a modest but valuable one-storey ranch, with slatted louvres on the windows, and royal palms growing in front and back. It was nestled in a tight row of similar houses. Lizards, mostly alive, dotted the road and driveway. Vera, Lundy's wife of 50 years, sent me into the living room to wait for him.

Lundy had taught European history at Georgetown University, but his was no dry and academic affection. He wallowed in history like a boy in a mud bog. He collected and painted toy soldiers for a hobby, and these were laid out on three bookcases beside the white armchair where I waited. On the left, the shelves supported 25 lancers and hussars of the Napoleonic infantry, the men in huge bearskin hats, with each little pom-pom painted red. These were facing an equal number of English Life Guards, their swords and breastplates gleaming in hand-daubed silver. Their

French and British standards were accurate, and all the figures mounted on small black stands. Below that were 54 more soldiers – a platoon of the Black Watch, with some skirmishers out front, and an assortment of Wellington's officers on horseback. The bottom shelf had more of the same.

Down the middle row there were soldiers from Cuba, from the war of two names. To the Americans this war was called the Spanish American War, best remembered for the neat charge up San Juan Hill in 1898. But that was not Lundy's war: the figures here were mostly Cuban fighters from what he and other Cubans called the War of Independence. This was a struggle, fought with interruptions over 30 years, that was all but over by the time the Rough Riders arrived. In this conflict, the enemy soldiers – the Spanish troops – still looked, in miniature, much like the Napoleonic soldiers that had proceeded them. They wore an imperial uniform of white breeches, epaulettes, and flashy belts. But the shelves were mostly taken up with something new on the battlefield. The Cuban fighters were a ragtag bunch fighting under a new red, white and blue flag. These toy rebels wore wide straw hats, and rough peasant clothing. Some were barefoot. Their cavalry were the *mambises*, the irregular squadrons of Afro-Cuban men, who fought only with the sharp edge of their machetes. So this was an insurgency, a people's war. A liberation struggle. No Americans on this shelf, or the lower ones.

Over on the right, the last three shelves were divided among an oddball assortment of Vikings, French knights, samurai, brass cannons, and finally some Americans: a squad of Confederates, and a few disordered Yankees. Below that were the Romans, apparently in hand-to-hand mêlée with some Ottoman janissaries. A few Cossacks were rushing in. Saxons occupied the bottom shelf, along with a dozen crumbling leather books.

Lundy came in, stooped, but spry and lean. He smoothed his hair and sat down in a white armchair, close by his battalions. Above and behind him on the wall there was an antique sword crossed against a kind of small blunderbuss. He told me right away that he had known Fidel Castro for five years at Dolores, and then four more years at the University of Havana. They were only 14 months apart in age; Lundy was older, and had been a calendar year ahead of Fidel.

'I didn't like Fidel,' Lundy said. 'We were friends, but we never became close.' But at a small school with 238 boys spread across eight grades, those of similar ages were thrust together, inevitably intimate in some way. The school was also too small to tolerate division: there were, Lundy said, no cliques, or separation by social class, the way he saw later at Belén, the bigger and more socially sensitive sister school. At Dolores, everyone was pulled together by proximity, and pushed together toward something larger. The school had a mission.

'The Jesuits were the vanguard of the Catholic Church,' Lundy explained. 'They were born in Spain, and the order grew because the founders believed in studying science, that the kids in the Jesuit schools should know what the scientific movement was doing. In Cuba, when you reached a school of the Jesuits, you felt that you were in the avant garde.'

After a long talk, we went into the back of the house. There was a small nook, between the bathroom and the TV room, which had been curated into a kind of memory chamber. There were trophies, and bits of antique armour, but mostly there were photographs from the old days, whether that meant Cuba in the 1940s and 1950s, or America in the 1960s and 1970s. The biggest of the photographs was the same one I had shown around at the reunion, a broad black and white panorama of the student body at Dolores in the fall of 1941. The 238 boys line up, the whole student body of boarding and day students. It was Lundy, of course, who had first given the shot to me.

Even this, which was my original, was a copy of a copy of a large-format negative. Multiple generations had smudged the faces, softening the lines of the eyes, smoothing out the clothing, draining the shadows of detail. Scratches, a tear, and several spots of mould on an earlier print were all faithfully reproduced here.

The picture showed the boys in the patio, as they called the school's inner courtyard. It was split into upper and lower sections by a wall, which was topped with a black iron railing. Most of the boys, six full rows, were arrayed below that divide, and ranked by age. The teenagers stood with their backs to the wall, while down at the very front, seven-year-old boys in stiff uniforms sat on tiny chairs, some of them unable to touch the ground with their shiny black shoes.

Up behind the iron railing was a different group. Just two rows, a mixture of class leaders, special honorees, members of the band, and assorted flag-bearers. Lundy pointed himself out in this group, dead centre, between the Cuban flag and the large standard of Dolores itself, which had blue and white stripes with a field of Jesuit heraldry, the pole topped by pom-poms and a gilded halberd. The standard of an army. 'There I am, holding the flag,' Lundy said of his 16-year-old self. 'Taking notes on everything with my eyes.'

His academic achievements and good conduct had won him the privilege of carrying the flag. He was recognizable, in the print, chiefly from his cavernous cheeks and the spacing of his eyes. He had dressed that day in the full uniform that they rarely wore: black shoes, white trousers, a dark blue blazer over a white shirt, with a white Sam Browne belt running up and over the left shoulder. Like all the boys, even the tiniest, he wore the visored officer's hat, whose broad white crest was fronted with the Colegio de Dolores seal over a black hat band.

Lundy wore a solid dark necktie; the other 237 boys wore a variety of ties, striped or solid, and a small number, like Fidel, were tieless. He was one row below Lundy, but on the other side of the railing. Fifth in from stage right, his shoulders brushed with the folds of blue and white flag. The wide lapels of his shirt were thrown open to reveal a bit of chest. He wore his hat thrown back, and held his chin high, staring right into the camera with a sense of purpose. The boys around him looked in every other direction. You could project arrogance on to the way his hat was cocked, if you wanted, but this was simply a 14-year-old boy.

Lundy waved at the photo vaguely. The boys were not from the elite, he said. Not a true elite. Cuba never had an upper class in the European sense, and there were only a few boys at Dolores who could claim an important Spanish name, or old money. What Cuba had was a few super-rich people, often of new fortune and dubious background, and a relatively large middle class. Most of the boys at Dolores, Lundy said, were sons of professionals, or of businessmen, or came from poorer families that strove to produce professionals and businessmen. As a whole, Lundy suggested, the boys at Dolores were less concerned with intellectual attainment than with the usual adolescent concerns of sport, and getting into a university. The parents were mostly interested in getting their boys established in a good career. 'Most of them,' Lundy said, pointing again at the picture, 'didn't go on to study history or law. They went on to be physicians, or engineers. They were not analytical types. I was in the other category, a kid reading history all the time.'

Lundy's son and namesake now crowded in behind us. Named Luis Aguilar, he was known as Lou, and had the same rangy, lean face as his father. In his mid-forties, wearing a white T-shirt, Lou was a screenwriter in LA. But he was fed up with Hollywood, and was spending more and more time in Miami, living with his parents. Born in Cuba, he'd left that island before he could form any memory of it, and had grown up in Florida and Washington DC, making a living from the English language. But Cuba, even at the remove of imagination, had impressed itself in his form. It was Lou's generation, the hybrids, the first Cuban-Americans, who had a kind of Baby Boomer affinity for *Made in Manzanillo* T-shirts and declarative nostalgia. The older Cubans had known the real thing, so it was usually the young who needed the replacement. In polling data, the younger Cuban-Americans generally held more liberal views than their parents, but were also far less realistic about Cuba. Untempered by any actual experience, their views lacked proportion. Lou, hearing his father mention the young Fidel, interrupted.

'He's worse than Hitler,' he said.

'Well,' Lundy said. 'Not really. He's not a Hitler.'

'Dad, he —'

'He didn't make a holocaust,' Dad said.

Although Lou himself didn't believe his own words, the comparison was common enough. On the seething AM bands of South Florida you could hear Castro compared to Hitler, or

Stalin, or Pol Pot, or Ceauşescu, or Mao, every week. A few people even said that Castro was *worse* than Hitler, because he was just as bad, yet had never been defeated, or driven from power. There was always someone, somewhere, to make that argument.

But they didn't talk that way in the house of a historian, a man of Jesuitical balance. Lundy frowned at his son and went off to sit in his office. A few minutes later, I found him there, laughing. 'Me!' he said. 'Defending Castro!' But it was true, he repeated, the Cuban dictator was no Hitler.

He sighed. 'That doesn't mean I wouldn't like to kill him,' he added, mildly. 'But as a historian, I have to be as objective as possible. I define myself as a sceptic, a humanist, a man from the Renaissance. A person who asks questions, who looks for everything.'

That was, as clearly as I ever heard it put, the Jesuit education model in a nutshell. Lundy had been Jesuit all the way: he'd started with Jesuit teachers at Dolores, and had spent a 30-year career teaching at Georgetown University, another Jesuit institution. He was one of the best educated people I have ever met, and I had to ask him: had so much love of history, so much study of nuance, so much reading, prepared him for what happened? For the Revolution? For this?

He was still, a long time. Finally he swung his face side to side, as if exhausted. He had been naive, he said. Despite his own doubts, some of them voiced in the newspapers, he hadn't quite realized what was going to happen, not until it was too late to stop it. The moment he first saw the future, he said, was 'on the third or fourth day of the Revolution', meaning the third or fourth day of January, 1959. Castro was triumphant, but hadn't even reached Havana yet.

'I went into the centre of Santiago to see some people,' Lundy said. The city had never been taken by the rebels, but when the old regime collapsed they moved in immediately. Santiago was the home base of many of the guerrillas, and full of supporters. It was the scene of the greatest rebellion, and the widest repression, under the old government. And by the third or fourth day of that new year, and era, Santiago was in an ecstatic uproar, delirious, the streets full of people, and every hour bringing some new celebration. Castro was driving toward Havana, slowly, and the criminals, the torturers, and the corrupt were being caught and punished. Swept up in the mood, Lundy went that morning to see 'some people'.

The first was a man, described by Lundy as 'a mulatto who had worked with Raúl Castro'. The fellow had been an underground courier for the guerrillas, and would certainly know the latest news. Lundy arrived at his house, excited by walking through the city, with a huge smile on his face.

'Professor,' the courier said. 'Nice to see you. Are you celebrating all this?'

Lundy stood there, grinning. 'I thought you intellectuals were more intelligent than that,' the man said. 'Don't celebrate, professor. These kids only know the whip. It's going to be a government of the whip. The only thing they know is the machine gun and the whip.'

Un gobierno del fuete? A government of the whip? Nonsense. Castro's platform was there for anyone to see: constitutional law, free elections, more schools, and independence from foreign meddling. What machine guns? The mulatto was crazy. But that phrase stuck in Lundy's head. *A government of the whip.*

That night it happened again. He was heading to a party at a friend's house. A wealthy friend. As he walked along, seeing the city lit up, full of banners and music, reconciliations and reunions, Lundy's mood soared, and he whistled the official hymn of the rebels. Even today, the sound of that anthem is 'very moving', Lundy confessed, and in 1959 he was enthusiastically tweeting it through the streets as he reached the house. A gardener was watching the door. Lundy knew him.

'You are whistling the hymn of hunger,' the gardener said.

Castro was parading toward Santa Clara, uncontested at this point, but the gardener said he already knew what would happen when the rebels reached Havana. 'If those guys win power,' he said, 'hunger will come to Cuba.'

Those were 'the people who told me first', Lundy said now. The first to have the gift of foresight. 'Not that I didn't have my doubts,' he added. History has few examples of good revolutions.

And just from knowing Fidel Castro, Lundy had some doubts about his character.

Lundy had doubts about the character of *all* Cubans. In an article called 'El Profeta' he had warned a visitor that Cubans lived in a permanent state of contradiction:

> Don't try to get to know them, because in their souls they live in the impenetrable world of dualism. Cubans drink happiness and bitterness from the same cup. They make music from their weeping and laughter from music. They take jokes seriously and make everything serious a joke.
>
> Never underestimate Cubans. The right arm of Saint Peter is a Cuban and the Devil's best advisor is also Cuban. Cuba has never produced a saint nor a heretic. But Cubans pontificate among heretics and blaspheme among the saints. Their spirit is universal and irreverent. Cubans believe in Catholicism, Chan-gó, in charades and horoscopes all at the same time. They will appeal to your gods and make fun of your religious rites. They don't believe in anybody and they believe everybody. They will never give up their illusions and they never learn from their delusions.
>
> Don't argue with them, ever. Cubans are born inherently wise. They don't need to read, they know everything. They don't need to travel, they have seen everything. The Cubans are the chosen people . . . chosen by themselves. They pass among lesser peoples like a ghost passing over water.
>
> Cubans are characterized individually by their sympathy and intelligence and as a group by their shouting and passion. Every one of them carries the spark of genius and no geniuses are tolerated. That's why is it easy to reunite Cubans, and im-possible to unite them.

'El Profeta' had been written in 1986, and the article swiftly became Lundy's most successful, widely reprinted, translated, taped up in Cuban diners, put under glass in waiting rooms, or pinned to bulletin boards. His self-mockery tapped some frustration among a people gradually getting used to failure, to

the idea that they were not going to defeat their enemy, that they
were not going home, that they were here, in this exile, to stay.

I asked Lundy what had happened to the boys in the photo, as a
whole. He shook his head. 'That is a melancholy question. The
casualties are already very high. That was 50 years ago.' He
repeated his conversation with Dorta Duque the night before. I'd
been sitting between them, listening as they talked, but some
stories need retelling, and Lundy carefully repeated his dialogue
about the number of survivors in his class. Six? Four? Two? *I am
the only one still alive.* But now Lundy broke into a smile and
added, with relish, 'and I am still a-smiling'.

Most of the other boys from Dolores – the whole body of 238
– had scattered after the Revolution. 'Of 12 or 13 in my class in
Dolores,' he said, 'only one stayed in Cuba.' They had gone
everywhere – from Florida to Venezuela, the Dominican Republic to Puerto Rico, and were found in Mexico, Toronto,
California, even Australia. One 'boy' from the photograph was in
a Dade County trailer park. Another was at the desk of the
president in Havana.

'Try to find José Antonio Roca, in Spain,' he said. He picked
out a figure in my print of Dolores, a long face, just next to his
own. Roca was also carrying a flag, the blue and white banner of
Dolores, emblazoned with a Madonna and heraldic knights and
castles. Lundy said that Roca had nearly been killed while
working underground for Castro during the Revolution. He
was a dentist now.

'And this is Pepín Bou,' Lundy added, looking at another face.
'He lives right here on Key Biscayne. A few blocks from here. But
this fellow, I think is dead. And Juan Grau, there, he was a Bacardí
guy who lives in Mexico now. He went hiking in the mountains
with Fidel a lot. Enrique Hechevaria is here somewhere. Maybe
Arturo de Jongh is here somewhere, I can't see. He lives in Miami.'

He spoke as if Miami was some distant place. Maybe from
retirement, with the causeway and the toll, it was. Everything you
needed was right here on the mangrove flats of the Key. Winn
Dixie and La Carreta Cuban Café. Catholic schools and churches.
Old friends, and ambulance service. Views toward Cuba.

Cubans always joked that the great thing about Miami was how close it was to the USA. And if Miami, on the mainland, was already that way, more Cuban than American, more banana republic than magna carta, then wasn't this doubly true for Key Biscayne, floating offshore, detached from other worlds? You could close your eyes out here and smell your own Caribbean youth, and then open them to find better plumbing and more asphalt. Not everyone on the Key was Cuban, but Spanish was the idiom of the island, and there was a familiar brine on the wind. At night, lying in bed, you heard the same dry clatter of palm leaves that appeared in your dreams.

Lundy's office was a corner room, right off the front door. It was generous in size, but shrunken by a chaos of books, which filled two walls of shelving top to bottom, and were stacked everywhere. Everything was piled up with papers and files and more books, most of it lying at cross angles, yet the position of everything was known, the piles organized by subject, or project, or cause, or passion. Boxes filled the floor space, most of them empty. Lundy and Vera needed a simpler place to live, he admitted, an apartment, rather than a house with lawn care and leaking roofs. And, Lundy explained with quiet awe, their house was worth a lot of money. He'd been a poorly paid freelance writer and an academic for most of his life, but here in the sunny markets of Florida real estate was a shot at the exile dream, the replacing of one lost world with fortune recouped, a gift restored to the next generation. They didn't have an exact plan for moving yet, but they would sell the house, soon, and he was getting ready to box things up.

As Lundy, already tired from hours of talk, ushered me out of the office, I asked about a line buried in his résumé. Slipped in among the entries on education, publication, and career was a reference to 'some not very successful attempts to ship arms to the anti-Castro resistance'. What did that mean?

Lundy waved me silent. He dug into the alluvial deposits on the desk, emerging with a sheet of white paper and a black ballpoint pen. He drew a small crocodile in one corner, with its tail tucked under its back feet; Cuba, in overview. Then he made a larger, hasty sketch of eastern Cuba, marking Santiago de Cuba, Manzanillo, the Sierra Maestra, Guantánamo, and so on, all in a few seconds. Concentrating, he filled in more details of Oriente: some swamps in the south, and then a big bay on the north side. He couldn't remember the name of the bay, he said.

Nipe, I told him. It had to be Nipe Bay. But Lundy was lost to this world. His hand now came down from the top, drawing a slow, unsteady line that wiggled down and hit Nipe Bay. The line smudged out there, the pen rubbing back and forth. Then he sketched in three other lines, quick arrows that darted in from the east, touching different points along the coastline.

'We only went four times,' he said, handing me the map. 'The spring of 1961.'

He wouldn't say anything else, at all. He simply packed me off, pushing me out of the office and, for a little old man, doing it with dispatch. I was out the door before I had even looked over the map.

As I stood there on the lizard-bedecked driveway, looking at the four lines on the white paper, Lou came over. He was the screenwriter of some commercially released B- and C-grade films, *Dark Queen*, *Sisters of Sin etc*. We had known each other, very slightly, for years.

'You know he has Alzheimer's,' Lou said. 'Right?' I didn't know.

'Yeah, he's losing it,' he said of his father. 'He's shot,' he added, with a chop of the hand. 'He's done.'

MOST OF THE HOUSES on Key Biscayne looked the same – one-storey ranches and bungalows in earth tones, with long roof overhangs to keep the rainy season at bay. It was only a few blocks to the house of Pepín Bou, one of men Lundy had mentioned. Lundy had given me the address, but he had specified that I should pay no attention to the house number. Instead I was to watch for three big palm trees crossing trunks. Indeed the trees, unusually tall and thick for palms, were visible from a block away.

Pepín wasn't surprised to see me, although I hadn't called. The old Cuban way remained in him: people made social visits, stopped by, dropped in, made rounds, and called on each other, rather than called each other. An unexpected visitor was the best kind. I mentioned Lundy and he invited me in. We sat in a dining room that ran across the back of the house, looking through glass doors at a small pool.

He was tall and very pale for a Cuban, the pinkest of men, with fine hair that was white-blond in his youth and now entirely white. His real name was José, but Josés were so common that they had to be separated by nicknames. For no reason at all, Josés are usually called Pedro. But at Dolores there were already so many Josés that the usual nicknames – Pedro, and then Pepe, and even Pepíto – were already taken. On arrival at the college he was thus given the nth derivation, Pepín, to differentiate him.

I asked him why I hadn't met him at the reunion of Dolores alumni in Miami Springs. 'I went to a few of those,' he said. 'You go to those reunions and you don't know who anyone is, and the ones who were there last year are dead. Personally, I find it depressing.'

Pepín was from Oriente, the son of a Santiago engineer. He described his childhood there as privileged, especially in comparison with the squalid life of the black sugar cane cutters who were the main workforce in the province. Like a lot of boys from Dolores, he had gone on to the University of Havana with Fidel, and this personal connection had gotten him mixed up, against his will, in the early days of the Revolutionary government. While quietly plotting his escape, he'd double-crossed Raúl Castro, and one of his last acts in Cuba had been to lie calmly and at length to Che Guevara.

He'd left alone in 1961 'with nothing', Pepín said, and then corrected himself. 'All I had was a dime.' His family had already abandoned the country, and Pepín left behind their house, their possessions and money. Even the luggage had been trimmed down at the last minute, by regulations that governed the number of pairs of underpants they could carry out of Cuba. At the airport the Revolutionary militia had confiscated the gold band of his watch. But in mid-air, halfway between Cuba and Miami, an Englishman on the plane had taken pity on Pepín.

He'd given him an American dime, just enough money to make a phone call.

We went into the kitchen and he rooted around in a drawer, and then another drawer. He checked between the blender and the refrigerator, but it wasn't there. He looked under a pile of bills and found it. It was hard to lose: the dime, blackened with age, was encased in a block of clear lucite, four inches wide by six inches tall, and two inches thick. He set it out on the coffee table, upright, a tombstone for everything that had been lost. Or perhaps it was the reverse. Maybe the dime was a memorial for all that had been regained. The house. The family. The job. The friends. The pool in back.

I mentioned the photograph of all of them together in 1941. 'This one?' he asked, and went into the next room and brought out a framed copy. He'd gotten it from Lundy years ago.

He flipped the frame, carefully, and there on the back were two dense columns of ballpoint writing. Sixty-five names.

Pepín's sister was married to another one of the Dolores boys in the photograph, a fellow called Alberto Casas. 'He made this list when he was here in the house one night,' Pepín said. 'He has a phenomenal memory, a really incredible memory. He knows all the faces. He has it all up here,' he said, touching his temple. 'You should talk to him.'

Alberto was a wild man, Pepín said, grinning. He lived down in Puerto Rico now. 'His family had the biggest cattle farm in Cuba,' Pepín said, 'and now they have the biggest cattle farm in Puerto Rico.'

I stared at the list. Everything that had happened to Cuba since 1941 had happened to, through, or among them.

Of course, you couldn't find them *all*. Out of 238 boys in the picture, Alberto Casas had identified just 65, and some of those were only partial names, or were followed by question marks. There were a lot of nicknames ('Fatso' Rabelo, 'Little Rocket' Festari, or just 'Basquito'). Even I recognized some of the names. The Bacardí boys were here, scions from the rum dynasty, a family that also ran Santiago politics. And, of course, a couple of Castro brothers.

The 65 boys were listed by row, left to right and back to front. The names were a file of diminutives and oddities, from Sócrates to John. There were many brothers. The boys who had died were marked with a demure EPD, meaning *en paz descansa,* or rest in peace. The Castro brothers were both followed with the notation that they were '(HP)', or Sons of Whores. A couple of names – just a couple – were already marked 'Miami' or 'PR'. The fate of the rest was speculation.

Pepín snorted when I asked where they were. '*Se fueron,*' he said, waving a hand at the glass doors, the pool, Biscayne, the world. They'd scattered. Most were in Florida, elsewhere in the Caribbean, maybe Europe. For sure other parts of the US. Even Australia.

Any still in Cuba? 'No,' he said.

But he didn't know that. That was Cuban thinking. To believe that everyone had decided the same as you. To believe there was only one right answer. If you had left Cuba, then everyone should have left.

Cuban thinking exists to make Cuban reality tolerable. The Revolution had used a dull knife to make a deep and ragged cut through Cuba. People had been tossed to one side or the other, divided by timing, flights of persuasion, accidents, the seductions of power, or the terrors of it. The only rule was that every family, every city, every group, and every institution in Cuba had been divided against itself. There was no reason the Colegio de Dolores should be any different.

As he let me out Pepín began to acknowledge this very complication. He had insisted that none remained in Cuba, but now he recalled that there was still one. A Dolores alumnus *was* there, apparently. Some Miami friends had visited Cuba recently, and had shown him a video they shot. They'd filmed all over Santiago, capturing the old places that Pepín remembered. The Parque Céspedes at the centre of town. The Cathedral. The harbour. The old Bacardí distillery. At one point they had visited the church in Vista Alegre, the swanky neighbourhood where most of them had grown up. Pepín remembered seeing an old timer in the film there, a Dolores alumnus. He

couldn't remember the fellow's name. 'Maybe Llanez, or Lla-
nova,' he said, and shook his head. 'Llibino. Or Yoruba or
something.'

He tried on a few more names, and then said, abruptly, 'No. I
don't know. But even if I did know someone who was still there,
I wouldn't know him, you know what I mean?'

2

THE COMPANY

DAWN IS the childhood of time. Even on a crocodile-shaped, tropical island, prone beneath heat spells and doldrum humidity, time still has its small moments, the chill intimations that come before consciousness, arriving in the soft separation of blackness from the not-black, the division of silence from the not-quite-silent. Beauty is tied to decay; time counted when it is gone. Every day in the tropics starts with disillusionment. The cool and transient moment before. Before light. Before day. Before the riot and rot of all days. Cubans are expelled from Eden 365 times a year.

In the arrival of real day, between their waking at 6 with that first light, and their rousting by the 7.45 bell for mass, the world comes to Dolores in the form of noise and light. For the sleeping students the first sounds only seem loud because they stand alone. The quiet shifting of a blanket. The slide of a drawer. Then these domestic sounds seem even quieter as new sounds insist on attention. In the distance now comes the broken-throated cry of a rooster, and then the consequences of motion, of city life: footsteps, bells, doors, voices echoing up, first from within the school's own courtyard, and then from the street. The first car passing through the rectangular plaza outside, the long, tree-shaded block that slouched downhill toward the harbour. Then the sound of shutters rolling up on the stores around the plaza, and a ship's horn in the harbour, long and soft, and then the hard-throated cries of the first food vendors, carrying their baskets or pushing small carts up Herredia Street out back. Each vendor has a particular chant that is the first music of the day, a little song of commerce. Called *pregones*, these are simple rhymes and catalo-

gues of goods, salted with double entendres. *Ice ice ice*, someone
shouts in a husky, all–day voice. *Keep cool at a good price.* Or, *Fruits
pineapples mango and yes, gentlemen, papaya too, you know you like it.*

Cuba is sprawled out across the sea, lazy, long and ripe, a
continent more than an island, almost half the land and people of
the whole Caribbean, its vast planes of thick topsoil divided up by
small, sharp ranges of mountains. A shape-shifting island, a little of
everything, with something everywhere. Out in the farthest east,
on the black sand beaches of Baracoa, you stare down a raging
Atlantic; in the west, beyond Pinar del Rio, orchid-fringed
mountains reach for Central America. Cuba is big and, by
tradition, wealthy and powerful. It alone is free of the crippling
smallness of scale that V.S. Naipaul blamed for stifling the
economies and crimping the minds elsewhere in the Caribbean.
With the biggest cities and busiest harbours in that round sea,
Cuba feels itself at the crossroads of the world; there is none of the
isolation that Derek Walcott lamented as the defining tragedy of
island life.

At 746 miles long, Cuba is still unmeasurable. The land mass, a
long and recumbent crocodile of 47,000 square miles, is less a
nation and more an approximation. Twisted, multi-limbed,
bumpy, and wrapped in sub islands and archipelagos, Cuba is
actually composed of either 1,600 or 4,000 islands and islets,
depending on how you count them. The northern and southern
coasts are fringed with strings of islands, called 'gardens', which
include everything from big islands covered with forests, farm-
land, towns and swamps, down to tide-shaped *cayos*, spits of sand
barely higher than a storm wave. The *cayos* are always in motion,
whether eroding slowly over decades, or disappearing, relocating,
and rebuilding in a single hurricane. Cuba crawls, too slow to
track, the idea of one known country supplanted by the sugges-
tion of a reigning consensus that can be expressed only on
obsolete maps.

Columbus set the course for all these misapprehensions. After
passing smaller islands, he touched down in Cuba, in Oriente,
perhaps at Baracoa, on 27 October 1492. Arawak Indians told
him that the island was inhabited by a race of one-eyed giants,

who ate human flesh and had the snouts of dogs. It was this report – one-eyed giants – which Guillermo Cabrera Infante would take literally almost half a millennium later, when he insisted that Castro himself was the Cyclops, the terrifying monster who stalked the island. But Columbus, no novelist, disdained their words, and thought he knew better: this big land mass in front of him was, at last, the mainland of the Orient, a land of fabled riches and grandiose palaces, not of monsters. He wrote a letter to the 'Great Khan', a title and address that had been obsolete for more than a century, and dispatched it into the interior with two men. These were not diplomats or princes, but below-decks sailors, chosen because they spoke Hebrew and Greek. They returned after two days, having found neither the Khan, nor China, nor India. Columbus was some 10,000 miles short of his goal; if his theory about a sea route to Asia had been correct, he would have starved to death. But chance favoured him, and he was made Admiral of the Ocean Sea for discovering what he continued to insist was 'the Indies', even when he began to suspect otherwise. He spent the rest of his life extolling the beauty of Cuba, and exaggerating the richness of what he had found on the greatest of islands.

In the history that followed, few who touched Cuba did any better. The island exerted a magical grip, a dream of fortune glittering under blue skies and palm trees. By 1941, when the boys at Dolores were waking up to their world, that old Cuba of the conquest, of one-eyed giants and gentle Arawak people, had been sublimated into a folk memory, the original story of a time before, of paradise won and lost. The pearl of the Antilles they saw around them now was nothing so rustic or mystical, but a bustling nation, coursing with the profits available during a time of war in Europe and Asia.

This Cuba was a society in flux, reaching for its democratic high point, but also unbalanced and divided. In Havana, in 1941, the Communist Party of Cuba was a legal organization, feeble but full of bureaucratic Marxists and academic revolutionaries. They divided Cuban society into three rigid social classes, each with its diligently differentiated subgroups and categorical imperatives. At the top was a ruling class, itself composed of two separate subclasses. The first, and most obvious, was the tiny, plutocratic elite in Havana, whose fortunes, and therefore power, often came from big businesses, or inheritance, or Europe. Out in the rest of the country, the ruling class was a broader and more uniform group of Creoles, the white, Spanish-descended planters. Their power and wealth usually came from gigantic land-holdings, often preserved generation after generation, even across centuries. This provincial elite depended on the land, which is to say on the rain and the sun, but also on the size of the American sugar quota, and on the availability of cheap, tractable labour. Although politics could do nothing about the weather, it could arrange the rest neatly.

Below them was a middle class, small, but still bigger than was found in most of the rest of Latin America. The number of telephones and automobiles per capita lagged behind only Argentina and Venezuela, the traditional powerhouse economies. Cuban cities were filled with professionals. This native class of intelligentsia was enhanced by a large flow of immigrants from Europe and the United States during the 1920s and 1930s, who brought talent and resources to fuel the economy.

And then, *los humildes*. The poor were millions, a majority distributed everywhere from the wide plains of Santa Clara to the nooks and crannies of the harbour towns. They were day labourers in the stockyards of Matanzas, and the sons of slaves who farmed tiny plots in the Guamán mountains. Above all, the poor were beholden to the system of big agriculture. At the very bottom of Cuban society was the thing that held Cuba up: the *macheteros*, the cane cutters, an army of starvation-wage victims who moved in great waves through the countryside, hopping from plantation to plantation, doing dirty, dangerous, exhausting labour in the hot sun. In any given place the *zafra*, the cane harvest, lasted for only about 120 days. Most *macheteros* could string together employment for barely six months of the year. Hunger was common, malnutrition chronic. The per capita intake of calories (2,800 a day) looked sufficient on paper, but there is no average between rich and poor, and by 1941, amid a stable and expanding market for sugar, the average consumption of meat was actually falling in Cuba. The poor simply could not afford it: they lived on rice, beans, and especially the empty calories that come from gnawing on a stalk of sugar cane. As Che Guevara later pointed out, leaving children to starve for several months each year, with nothing but *guarapo*, the weak juice from crushed cane, to survive on, was all the justification anyone needed for a revolution.

The extremes of wealth and poverty were striking, and therefore deliberately evaded in the consciousness of Cuba's elite. The state schools and hospitals were pathetic, with little budget and few facilities, but still, they could say, the University of Havana was one of the greatest schools in the Americas. Peasants in the countryside had to travel to a city to have any hope of treatment in one of the very few public hospitals, but still it had to be mentioned that Cuba had some of the best doctors in the world. Havana might be ringed with shanty towns, but it was the most advanced city in the Caribbean, the envy of a hundred islands. In the countryside people were rotting from the inside out on a diet of cane juice, but epic fortunes had been made in slavery, sugar, alcohol, gambling, corruption, hotels, and even hard work, and Cuba gleamed in the sun.

The classes could be divided up almost indefinitely – lumpen and proletariat, petit and grand bourgeois, vanguard and exploiter – but one thing was always the same. In memory, no matter how it had been, the sun was always shining, the sky blue, the palm trees swaying in a breeze. It didn't matter what lies were told by the statistics, or even memory, because everything was always perfect in the old days, by definition. Even the weather.

EVERYTHING GOOD AND BAD IN CUBA comes from the east, from Oriente. Santería, the syncretic, Afro-Cuban religion that marries Roman Catholicism to the demigods of West Africa. *Son*, the infectious Cuban rhythm blending the Spanish guitar and the drum with the liberation of jazz. Slavery and sugar cane, which were planted together in the fertile plains of Oriente. The New World itself, which was born when Columbus set foot on the sands of Oriente and found, instead of his one-eyed monsters, a land of 'exceeding riches', with a population so gentle they could be enslaved 'by 50 men with swords'.

Something about Oriente invites exaggeration. It is the hottest part of Cuba, the most mountainous, the first settled and the earliest to achieve glory and shame. Santiago (named 'de Cuba' to differentiate it from the one in Spain) was founded in 1515, by Diego Velázquez. That was only one generation after the Muslims were driven out of Spain; just one generation after the Jews were expelled. There were men present at the founding of the city who had known Columbus himself, and the 1515 date was so early that it rooted Santiago more in the European Middle Ages than the New World that was to come. Santiago was the first capital of Cuba, reigning for 40 years before eventually losing out to Havana, an insult never forgotten. The city served as a kind of Jerusalem to the Americas, spreading the new faith of conquest, and the new tongue of Castilian. Cortéz had sailed from the harbour of Santiago to conquer the Aztecs in 1518. The gold and silver of the Incas had all passed back through the ports of Cuba. Sugar cane, one of the world's greatest cash crops, was first introduced in Oriente; soon thereafter the first slaves were imported into Cuba, landing at Santiago in 1554.

In Oriente, it was enslavement that produced sugar, and sugar that produced great fortunes, and great fortunes that led to a flowering of culture. Cuba's great champions of liberty were from Oriente, and the real, original Cuban revolution was seeded here, when the generals Máximo Gómez and José Martí landed to begin their war of independence from Spain. A few years later, Teddy Roosevelt and his Rough Riders came ashore in Oriente, conquering San Juan hill, just outside Santiago. The great names of Cuba – Bacardí, Castro, Desi Arnaz – are Oriente names.

In the early 1940s, Santiago de Cuba was a city of just 200,000 people, compared to Havana an intimate city, folded inside its ring of hills. Santiago was far from the rest of Cuba, but joined by sea to other cultures and influences, with a more Caribbean feel than the capital. The people of Santiago described themselves as more passionate, fiery, or ardent than the materialistic Habaneros.

Santiago people spoke quickly, dropped their Rs, and larded their speech with foreign words. Bahamian English drifted up from the harbours; Yoruba and Hausa terms had been imported with the slaves, who were still being landed, fresh from Africa, right up until abolition in 1870. Both French and Haitian Creole were heard in the streets of Tivoli, a quarter of Santiago settled by thousands of refugees from the 1791 slave revolts in Haiti. (These immigrants were about one-third white, one-third free blacks, and one-third slaves belonging to the first two groups.) In the early twentieth century black Jamaicans arrived in Santiago, taking jobs in the harbour and bringing words and a dance – the limbo – that became part of city tradition. In 1941, with a war in Europe driving Cuban agriculture, the need for common labourers had grown so acute that a new generation of Haitians was being brought in to cut cane.

Cuba had little of the formal racial segregation found in America, and Santiago was even less rigid than Havana. Away in the big capital, Cubans were influenced by the racial codes imported by North Americans. But in Santiago there was a less formal détente. Race mattered in Santiago, deeply. It was the blackest city in the blackest region, the Afro-Cuban metropolis *par excellence*, but Santiago was still ruled by whites, and the divisions were there, if hidden. Whites preferred to think of Santiago as a city with 'easy' or 'warm' relations between races, but that was because blacks and whites knew their separate places and kept to them. After an obscure political conspiracy in 1913, white mobs had lynched blacks, a demonstration of power not lost on Afro-Cubans. They knew the clenched fist behind white Santiago's easy ways. Black Cubans had to channel their energy into achievement and survival within their own community.

Still, in the Cuba of 1941, racial mixing occurred routinely in a variety of ways that would have been unacceptable, or even illegal, in the United States. In a country and city with people of every possible shade, a routine colour bar was impractical. Inter-racial marriages were disapproved of, but not unknown, and 'good' blacks were admitted to some elite schools and institutions, even as they were systematically excluded from the best social

clubs. In politics, alliances reached across colour lines, so that in
Santiago during the 1940s, the mayor was Justo Salas, a black who
was elected chiefly with the support of the white middle class, and
who defeated a white candidate supported chiefly by blacks.

Sugar was grown all over the island, but the two greatest belts
of cane ran across Oriente province. One was on the interior, or
western, face of the Sierra Maestra mountains, and the other, the
greatest in Cuba, flowed across the rich soil of the north,
wrapping itself around the Bay of Nipe, and enveloping Birán,
the town where the Castro family lived. These cane lands were
among the most profitable possessions in Cuba, and the wealth
they generated flowed through Santiago. Oriente also had the
richest mineral deposits in Cuba – iron ore in the Sierra Maestra,
just to the west of Santiago, along with manganese and copper.
Rich strikes of chromium, cobalt and nickel had been found in
the north-east.

The largest of the old Spanish provinces, Oriente was never
large enough to contain the egos of people who lived there. To
live in Santiago was to walk tall, if slowly. Residents absorbed, by
osmosis, the enormous pride of the city, the geocentric presumption that age confers superiority. All Cubans were in agreement
that their island was the jewel in the crown of the Spanish
Empire; that it was the centre of the modern Caribbean; the
most progressive and enlightened of all island nations. This lunatic
self-regard reached even greater heights in the east, and was
distilled to an essence in Santiago, where it occupied the thoughts
of everyone, from Santiago's oldest families, with their triple-
barrelled surnames, to those who had no surname at all. White or
black, poor or rich, the Santiaguero insisted with a straight face
that fruit is riper, the sun stronger, the women more passionate,
the politics more sincere, the talk more profound, the cemeteries
more grand, even the night darker, than elsewhere in Cuba.
Oriente folk insisted that not only was Cuban music the best
music in the world, which everyone already knew, but Oriente
was the source of the best of Cuban music.

Even when they were excited, Oriente people could be smug,
and complacent. In the middle of raging parties they would shout

at the musicians, *todo está inventado ya*, or, *no hay nada que inventár!*
There is nothing left to invent. Everything has already been
invented. They meant this as encouragement.

THE COLEGIO DE DOLORES, preparatory academy and
boarding school, emerged from sleep a self-contained community, enclosed behind high walls, and sealed against the outside
world by a pair of tall, flat-topped doors that were locked with a
heavy iron key at night. The doors seemed huge, looming over
the tallest boys, high enough even to accommodate the Virgin of
Fátima, a statue on a bier that was carried through the doorway on
the shoulders of a dozen boys every 18 January. Despite a few
such public events, it was only the boys and the families of
Dolores who came inside, not the rest of the world. There was a
division. Inside the walls were an elect. Outside was the world
that would be led.

The physical plan of Dolores was simple and typically Spanish:
a regular rectangle constructed around a courtyard, whitewashed,
with high ceilings and arched galleries. But the true shape of
Dolores was hard to fathom, since the grid of exterior streets
pressed the building into the side of one of Santiago's many hills.
Looking at the school from outside, on the nearest tree-shaded
plaza – named the Plaza Dolores, of course – it seemed to be a
two-storey building with unusually tall windows, but there were
actually three storeys on this, the downhill side, and an irregular
fourth storey added on to the back, to compensate for what was
swallowed below by the encroaching hillside.

While blue-grey still ruled below, that fourth floor was the first
to feel the touch of direct sunlight, which came peering over a
slanted roof of curved red tiles. Boarding students lived one level
down on the third floor, in shared rooms. There were only 22 of
these *internos* living in the school, full-time enrollees who ate all
their meals at Dolores, slept and woke within the walls, and were
entirely captive of the school's educational climate. These boys
were all from other parts of the province, sent in by their parents
to make sure that rural life or small town limitations did not keep
their children from rising within Cuban society, whether that rise

was achieved through merit, or a superb Jesuit education, or connection to the most prominent families of eastern Cuba, or all of the above.

The *internos* slept two or three to a room, with brothers normally housed together. Sleeping in the communal and monastically quiet atmosphere of a religious institution, they went to bed early and often woke up long before required, stirred from the blackness of slumber by the first hint of sound, the first, most subtle changes in the darkness. The late risers would certainly be provoked by the growing noises, the daylight peering into the upper storeys.

Before the 7 am breakfast, every *interno* was expected to make his bed, order his room, wash up, gather books and shine shoes. The bathrooms were communal, a crowd gathering at the end of the corridor to clean face and hands, brush teeth, wet and tame hair from ardour to order. Then the remaining minutes before 7 were for preparing their homework and school books. On normal days, they dressed in any white trousers, and a light-coloured shirt with the sleeves rolled down. Dark neckties were expected, but not required. With this, the common outfit of day-to-day education, they didn't have to wear their dark blazers, or don the hated officer's caps, which were big white things with stiff black visors, heavy and hot. Nor the awkward Sam Browne belt of white leather that was difficult to clean, hard to adjust, and annoying to don or remove. That outfit – the formal uniform – was reserved for feast days, days with important visitors, days with academic ceremonies, or the special public days with theatrical performances, oratory competitions and school pageants. There are a lot of feast days in Catholicism, and a few of the Jesuit fathers loved to see their boys dressed up in military perfection, so the formal outfit was liable to be evoked at the slightest opportunity.

There were many sets of brothers within the walls, triples and doubles, genetic repeats that kept the school intimate and familiar in the most literal sense. The three Castellvi brothers, the three Tercias, and the three Ravelos. Then there were David, Arturo and Kiki de Jongh, with their unusual last name for old-fashioned Oriente. Their grandfather, a Dutch physician, had emigrated to Curaçao in the service of the Netherlands army, then followed a Cuban woman to the island in the early 1900s. His three grandsons, though born and raised in Cuba, full of Oriente pride, were creatures of many worlds. Catholic, but of Jewish heritage. Cuban, but of Dutch origins. Spanish-speakers, but with an English-speaking, American-educated father, and their own private language at the school, the encrypted chatter of Papimiento, a lingua-franca of the Netherlands Caribbean that mixed Dutch, Spanish, English and Arawak words. The three de Jonghs were day students, who lived in a big house with many servants, and had cars. They looked as similar as three pennies.

And there were the Castros: Ramón, the gangly eldest, dark-haired, one of the tallest boys in the school but destined to never shine with brilliance. Ramón made little impression on people: he was a conformist, first born, certain to inherit the land and fortune his father had cultivated. He was interested mainly in agricultural equipment and sports. Then Fidel, almost as tall as Ramón, with a round face and pale grey-blue eyes that, combined with his rapidly increasing height, made him a natural standout on a dark-eyed island. A second son, he would inherit only his father's determination. He was in constant conflict with the old man, which both of them seemed to enjoy.

And then Raúl, the odd man out. Raúl was short, and darker skinned than Ramón or Fidel. His face little resembled that of his older brothers. His eyes were almost Chinese, and only a fool would ever mention aloud at Dolores the rumour that he was really fathered not by Ángel, but by a Chinaman in Birán. In the small world of the Oriente elite, such a thing would preclude an advantageous marriage.

Bad reputations were hard to shake. The three Casas brothers, for example, were known troublemakers. There was Américo, Lorenzo and Alberto. Their grandfather had built up the largest dairy farm in eastern Cuba, or so people said, and they had 500 milch cows. Every boy in the school knew that the milk on the breakfast table was Casas milk, in Casas bottles. Friends of the brothers would make legendary trips to the family plant, a state-of-the-art dairy on the outskirts of Santiago, filled with roaring machinery and hay, vacuum tubing and rubber hoses, refrigeration and steaming manure, obscenely huge animals and foul-mouthed men who somehow, in an orchestra of chaos, produced truckloads of clinking glass bottles delivered to the entire network of city streets. A playground beyond all playgrounds.

A boy raised this way, as a prince in a rustic empire, could say no. Alberto Casas said no. He had already compiled the worst disciplinary record at Dolores. There were infractions for speaking out of turn, for stubbornness, for mocking the Jesuits openly, for fighting with other students. But Alberto had recently broken with his regular offences, for the worse. His older brother had asked him to pick up something at the hardware store during the day: four boxes of .22 calibre bullets. These are the kind of tiny bullets used for target shooting. There was nothing unusual about this; Cubans have an almost American affinity for guns, and for the idle occupations of target shooting, wandering around in fields looking for birds to shoot, and blasting tin cans. Alberto bought the bullets during his lunch break, but when he returned to Dolores he was stopped at the front door by a hissing voice.

'Alberto Cathath, what are you carrying?' It was Padre López, the chief disciplinarian. Alberto told him what he had: four boxes of bullets.

López looked in the bag. 'For carrying bullets in school,' he said, 'you are sentenced to detention until 6 pm.'

More unfairness! Alberto erupted: 'You teach us to tell the truth and that's what I told you!' He shouted up at the Padre's face. 'I didn't lie and say it was candy in the bag!' He announced he would take the issue right to the Padre Prefect.

For arguing, López extended the punishment to a full week. Six pm detention every evening.

Alberto went into the detention hall – a dreaded, second-floor room all the way back on the right – for that first afternoon. There was nothing to do for more than two hours except read stupid books, do homework, and make faces whenever Padre López looked away. Alberto was used to spending his afternoon roaming the dairy, looking in on 'his' cows and pursuing his whims. Now he stewed. He already knew the detention hall well and hated the hours here. His friends had gone home. Even the *internos* were more free than he was, a day student trapped in the building. He was supposed to sit here, studying and suffering right through the afternoon heat until 6 pm.

López was old, weak, and slow moving. He spent all his time sitting down scowling at Alberto. López was a toothless tiger, and when he turned away that afternoon, just for a moment, Alberto jumped up, climbed from his chair to a desk, and yanked open the tall window shutters. Before the padre could even stand up, Alberto leapt on to the sill, and threw himself out the window. It is a second-floor window.

It was a long way down to Herredia Street, but the rise of the hill cut the distance somewhat, and though he hit very hard, Alberto had the elasticity of youth. He rolled, got up and, with the cry *Alberto Cathath* trailing after him, vanished at a run into the city.

Before mass the next morning, Father López was waiting on the front steps. 'You are expelled,' he said, when he saw Casas. But another Jesuit was there, and quietly overrode the verdict, sending Alberto into the school.

For Alberto, this little victory was almost worse than defeat. He was infuriated by the unfairness of López, by his punishments, and by the absolute power of the administration, even when it overruled those punishments. So furious that Alberto plotted quietly to expose this injustice. Working with friends and the school mimeograph machine, he printed up a little newspaper, a revival of a student paper called the *Dolores Critic* that had died of indifference some years before. Alberto wrote the articles dealing with the unfairness of discipline and the hypocrisy of the school. He even managed to run off some copies before the Padre Rector saw one. After reading the *Critic*, he confiscated the issue and ordered the mimeograph locked away.

Alberto noted this down. There was no justice in his small world.

UP HIGH, where the morning sunlight first struck Dolores, the school looked like a perfectly regular construction. On the third floor, the short sides of the rectangular layout were lined with four arches, each directly echoing the four doors of the four bedrooms there, each used as a dormitories by three or four boarding students. The longer sides of the floor held a dozen arches, and a dozen more small rooms.

But the pleasing symmetry of life on the third floor began to dissolve as sunlight slipped down below. The second floor was less regular, with the arches misaligned against the entrances to classrooms, and a few doors that were taller and wider. The classrooms were airy, with the high ceilings and tall windows necessary to purge the Santiago heat. The classrooms were lined with appropriate exhibits of educational value. There were rooms decorated with maths tables, or diagrams of plant circulation, but, aside from the science lab, the greatest fun in the building was the Museum of Cuban Birds. The second classroom on the right was lined with dark cabinets that went almost to the ceiling. Behind the glass were dozens of stuffed and mounted birds from the shores and peaks of the island, as well as a few mounted fish and a small stuffed shark to round out the picture. Atop the cabinets were paintings of the rest of the animal kingdom. The natural history classroom was likewise lined with cabinets of rock samples, plants, insects and a few more birds, all under the stern gaze of a portrait of Ignatius Loyola, the founder of the Jesuit order, high overhead. The science classroom was even more transporting than the stuffed birds: here were an assortment of antique but effective telescopes, Bunsen burners, and a large cabinet dedicated to the wonders of electricity, complete with a tiny generator for delivering experimental jolts.

Down at the bottom, the whole idea of order gave out. Entering from the Plaza Dolores, the first floor began with a lofty ceiling near the entryway, which opened out quickly to the courtyard. Here the arches made Moorish *pasillos,* the shaded walkways. But the *pasillos* seemed to erode: as they ran away, they buried themselves into the hillside that backstopped Dolores, remaining dark all day but also airless.

To accommodate the rise of this steep city, the large courtyard itself had to be stepped, divided by a six-foot wall into lower and upper patios. That wall, topped with an iron railing, was an obstacle to every sport, but there was still enough room on the lower patio for stickball, and the wall itself served as mount for one basketball hoop, with the boys playing a short-court game back and forth between the wall and a hoop mounted near the chapel.

An obstacle to sports, the wall was a gift to ritual. The students would stand and face it for assemblies, to receive instruction, and to hear proclamations. A proscenium arch would be erected for plays and pageants. The oratory contests would be presented here, with boys learning the bombastic tone and clenched-fist style of declamation. They would put on plays here, choral works, and, where the railing provided a jumping off point, it was an irresistible place for showoff contests.

This, of course, was where the boys lined up for the school photo, which was made annually, by the same photographer, during a special assembly in midmorning, while the courtyard was still in shadow. The boys dressed in their gala uniforms, the blue blazers and white officers' caps. On the lower half of the courtyard, rows of chairs and then a bleacher were set up. Two men arrived from Foto Mexicana, the high-society studio of Santiago. The photographer was an anonymous technician; it was the brand name that mattered. Cubans, who conceded little glory to other countries, associated Mexico with artistic genius; in the 1930s that 'revolutionary state' was crowded with painters, sculptors, muralists and photographers. Foto Mexicana was the choice of the elite, and the studio's trademark – a rosette stamp on the lower right corner of a photo – appeared in the shots taken at country clubs, all the leading schools, at wedding celebrations, and in official church portraits.

There were commercial landmarks all around the Foto Mexicana studio: El Encanto, the gleaming, air-conditioned department store, and La Muñeca, where the boys from Dolores (and all the other parochial schools in Santiago) bought their uniforms. Foto Mexicana was the chronicler of this world, of the best of Santiago, and when they came to Dolores it was not merely to shoot the entire student body, but to continue with the students broken down into separate classes, with individual portraits of the graduating seniors, the student Brigadier who supervised each Division, and of the various *dignidades*.

After arriving in the courtyard, the Foto Mexicana technician would prepare for work by first draping a black cloth around his neck, a kind of velvet cowl that was a badge of office for photographers. He would stand with his back to the basketball hoop, directing an assistant – a young bull, to carry the equipment – as he fetched first the heavy wood tripod, then the big box camera itself, usually a large format Dearborn from Chicago. Then he brought in the film: a special suitcase packed with individual 8 × 10 negatives, each sheet of film pre-loaded into a 'slider', a metal frame that would deliver it into the camera itself. Even a negative this big would have to be printed at double size to produce a clear shot of such a big group.

And then – only then, once the camera was prepared – would the students themselves appear, led by the *reguladores* into their rows, with the Jesuits, standing behind the camera, directing and demanding. It was essential to work quickly. In the front, the smallest and youngest boys, just seven years old, were arrayed on folding chairs, 33 across. Some of them were too small to touch the floor with their toes. Each row older and bigger, until, in the last row of bleachers, standing with their backs to the wall, the oldest and biggest. Then, behind them, looking down from the railing of the upper patio, two more rows of boys. These were the *dignidades*, the student leaders, including flag-bearers like José Antonio Roca, and Lundy Aguilar. Fidel Castro stood below them, stage right. His brother Raúl was two rows down from him.

It was the morning of a bright day, but the sunlight striking the top of the walls had not reached down to the patio yet, which remained in shadow. The white stucco rising on all sides, however, served as an ideal reflector, softening and bouncing back the sunlight, brightening faces and filling in dark areas around the eyes. The photographer, who made such pictures on an everyday basis, would have known without calculating that there was no need for additional lighting, and could estimate from experience that the lens aperture should be wide, and the exposure fast. Just one-sixtieth of a second, so fast that not one face out of 238 would blur with movement. But he would calculate the exposure anyway, with a light meter, to verify his instinct. The shutter speed and aperture would both be set on the lens itself, by moving tiny sliders.

He then stepped behind the camera, facing the ground glass, the image. The camera had a long accordion bellows, which stretched between two standards or frames. Bending down to focus, he flipped the black monk's cowl over his head with a practised gesture, dropping it over the camera top, concealing himself in darkness. Now it was possible to study the image on the ground glass clearly, looking at it from a couple of inches away. He would fiddle with the bellows, drawing the image into sharp relief, then check that the frame was filled, moving it in or out, slightly, and refocusing. After these swings and tilts, there were only a few seconds for the difficult art of *scheinflug*, or matching the focus plane to the natural tilt of the composition. The boys at the bottom of the frame were much closer to the camera than those at the top, eight rows back, so the front standard had to be tilted to match, using a small gear. And then the overall focus had to be reset, so that every face was equally crisp. Foto Mexicana made its money by selling copies of the pictures to every family represented; even one boy out of focus was a lost sale.

After popping the cloth up and back behind his neck, he stood up and raised his hands like a conductor, to draw their focus. *Everyone hold still.* Now the clock was ticking.

He stuck out a hand and was given, by the assistant, a slider, the metal film-holder. Maybe he would throw the cowl over himself and the camera one last time, to check the focus, compulsively, because the slowest thing was to rush the job. But he had to stand, in the end, because you couldn't take a picture with this kind of camera while looking through the lens. With a slam, he would rack the film-holder in, depositing the negative in front of the ground glass, and then reach forward and throw a toggle to close the shutter on the lens. Probably standing beside the camera, still focused more on the boys than his machine, he would pull the slider out, leaving the film naked. *Look here*, he would say, loudly, pointing to the lens. *Not at me.* And then click. Just a simple, light pressure on the shutter switch. It was over in a sixtieth of a second.

The slider, now empty, had a tab that was black on one side and white on the other. One colour meant exposed and the other unexposed, although which meant which was up to the individual photographer, a matter of habit when loading film. Now he would reverse this tab, shove the slider back into the camera, and yank out the larger film-holder, entire, with its encased and protected negative. This he would exchange, instantly, with his assistant, who passed him a new one and stored the old one away in the case.

When shooting small groups, the photographer's rule of thumb was one frame per subject, but that wasn't possible with a group of this size, since even the most disciplined children will quickly lose their patience and begin to move. With large groups there is about a minute, or 90 seconds at most, to finish such a job. Three or four exposures would be enough, but a professional would do six in that time, perhaps, just to be sure. It wasn't necessary to bracket the exposures or change anything; exposure could be fixed easily in the printing process. But multiple shots gave some proof against blurred and blocked heads. Even one obscured child could lead to complaints from angry parents. So, in roughly 90 seconds, a steady rhythm: bang, reload, bang, reload, bang, reload. At some point the photographer would notice that the boys were wavering, losing their focus, so he might make a commanding reminder, halfway through: *If you can't see me, I can't see you.*

Bang, reload, bang, reload. Most photographers couldn't resist checking the focus one last time, ducking back under the velvet cowl to verify that all was sharp, before putting in a last negative and clicking the shutter on one last shot. About two minutes after it started, all the negatives were tucked away, sealed in the Foto Mexicana suitcase, and the Jesuits would clap with satisfaction and release the boys.

BEFORE HE TOUCHED THE BELL, Lundy had it easy. He was rail-thin, knock-kneed in his white trousers, already wearing a long face at age 13. Aguilar had a preoccupied mind and a love of books. A day student, he tried to read even as he walked to school each morning, even though he sometimes strode right into lamp posts, or mailboxes. Pleasing to his parents, and to the Jesuits, he was bathed in extraordinary freedom for an adolescent boy. Every day, he would wake up in his own home, in his own time, make his own bed, and dress himself without consulting his parents. They even let him prepare his own breakfast, as he wished. His father, by day a grave supervising judge in the criminal courts, was at home tolerant and even indulgent, for little Lundy excelled at many things, and could not be found guilty of much. Lundy's mother trusted him. The boy was diligent, punctual, thorough, and could seemingly do no wrong. Even the Jesuits, who were always generous with praise, gave special credence to this oddly serious 13-year-old boy.

Having eaten or not, as he wished, Lundy hit the streets of Santiago around 7.15, and began his daily ramble through the noble city. Although the Aguilar family had Oriente roots going way back, Lundy had lived his early years in central Cuba. Until the age of seven, his whole world had been that small cow town outside the larger cow town of Santa Clara. The land there was all flat plain, cowboy country, with some sugar cane, lines of royal palms, and little else. That village had close horizons – familiar faces everywhere, a few dirt streets churned only by horses' hooves, and a special welcome everywhere for the son of the town judge. But the lack of spectacle, of variety and new things was what had driven Lundy into books. He devoured stories of history, of adventure and travel, of the conquistadors and buccaneers, of early Cuban heroes and of desperate battles between cavalrymen and Indians. When his father was promoted to Santiago, Lundy began to walk to his new school every day in a kind of rapture, convinced he had stepped into the pages of his true life at last. The voluptuous hills of the city were gifted with sudden vistas, and surprises lay around every corner. Tramcars! Woolworth's! Air-conditioned buildings! (And so many of them!) Ships' horns blasting in the harbour. Immigrants. Foreigners. Two hundred thousand Cubans in every walk of life. The stores were packed with American toys and European fashions. This was the genuine city where the conquistadors in Lundy's books had once strode about in armour, plotting their departures for new lands. Santiago was big and energetic, just like the *Nueva York* shown in movies. He knew that he was walking through his kingdom, and that Santiago stood at the centre of the world.

No matter how many times he walked to the Colegio de Dolores, year after year, there was always something to see. It was only six blocks, up the never-flat streets, through the Plaza Dolores and then, just past the chapel, up the stairs and inside the two tall thin doors. You could vary the route, watch the cars, poke into shops, pass the houses of friends, sit on benches, talk to children and adults, watch strangers, see projects and works in progress. You could see something, always. You could take it all in.

THE JESUITS had made Lundy a *regulador*, one of the class officers charged with keeping order among his own age group, making sure that everything happened on time. But Lundy was not just another of the two dozen *reguladores*; he was a flag-bearer, the boy who stood at the very centre of the school photos, who marched in front at parades. As the most punctual and well regarded of all the *reguladores*, he was given the special duty of sounding the assembly bell for mass, literally ringing in the school day.

His badge of office was the wristwatch, given to him as a prize by the Jesuits for his combination of good grades, punctuality and diligence. All the boy had to do was keep one eye on that watch. In the early dawn he could dawdle on the hills, or choose to go around another way, through some back street, or stop to talk to another student, although he rarely saw other students until he reached the school itself. Whichever way he went, he had to keep an eye on the hands. That was the trust that came with the watch: with diligence came power, and with power responsibility. The model student was a clock spring turning steadily toward a larger goal.

In his *Constitutions*, Loyola suggested that students should be contemplative and focused during any activity that was not specifically evil. Any ordinary task, even studying, could be done for the glory of God if it was done with intention. Loyola had an almost Buddhist obsession with careful observation, attention to present reality and reasoning from careful apprehension and imagination. The Jesuits themselves were taught to have no will – they vowed to 'go where the Pope sends me' dead 'as a corpse' to their own desires – but they taught students to strengthen their own willpower and to be contemplative, to excel. The students at Dolores were given a maxim, 'ask everybody everything every day', and the teachers were guided by the rule, 'a minimum of precept, a maximum of practice'. Biology was to be taught not just by textbooks but also by the handling of animals, working in a laboratory and hiking expeditions in the Sierra Maestra. Even a maths class was designed to be engaging – for the youngest boys at Dolores there were numbers games posted on the walls, and cubes and triangles to play with on their desks.

For the Jesuits time was of the essence. Dolores was located on Calle Reloj, Clock Street. In colonial times, the presence of a church here had meant the ringing of hourly bells, to keep the faithful on *hora inglesa*. The school displayed time everywhere, in the classrooms and on the walls, in the dormitories and the dining room. There were clocks, and bells, boys with ordinary wrist-watches, and then special boys with special wristwatches, given to them expressly for keeping everyone else on time. The Jesuits tried to think about the very long term, as if centuries were minutes, but they also insisted that minutes be treated like seconds, caught and used before they flew away. *Hora inglesa* means 'English time', which is to say, on time. Punctuality was a double good: symbol of diligence, and maker of it.

But these were boys, after all. Some as young as seven, scared and lonely, in their first months of schooling. Others were older, confident veterans who felt at home, teenagers who had spent more nights in this building than they had anywhere else, even in their parents' homes. But they all shared the dangerous habit of drifting off, as if time didn't matter and childhood was forever, adolescent energy rocketing into young adulthood. Their natural state was the reverse of the Jesuit ideal: children drew out the minutes, and made time itself into another servant. That was what the bell, and the *regulador* were for: to keep everyone on *hora inglesa*, following the orderly life within these walls, and then without them.

At half past seven most mornings, Lundy would turn the corner on the Plaza Dolores, sweep up the short staircase and enter school. The *internos* had finished their breakfasts and scattered. He might stop to read the notices, but soon he would be on the second floor, checking his watch against the office clock and taking possession of the hand bell. It was brass, with a thick clapper and a wood handle. At 7.44 he went to the railing overlooking the courtyard and watched his watch. When the second hand swept past the top, he threw his hand down, and up, down and up, harder and harder:

Bam bam bam bam bam bam bam.

Seven times, or 17 times, as many and as loud as he could get away with. It made every kid jump. They had 270 seconds to get to their places.

Those seconds, starting every day at 7.45, were the prelude to holy mass, and then classes, and they were the most frenzied minutes of the day. The bell set a machine of 238 gears in motion. Boys came out of every doorway in the school: the bathrooms, the classrooms, the dining room, the chapel, the dormitories, the science lab and the offices. Scores of late or skylarking boys came crowding in through the front door all at once, a wave of children that met with a smaller number of boarding students tumbling down from the third floor. The courtyard began to fill up, and dawdlers jumped the steps two at a time. Single-digit boys, the seven- and eight-year-olds, were pushed around and mixed in among those twice their age, everyone trying to sort into lines by age, prodded by *reguladores*. With seconds to go, amid muffled collisions and play shoves, 238 boys formed up, the military drill crescendoing to a sudden and practised perfection. Nine files across the patio. The youngest and oldest students were always fewest in number, while the middle grades often had 16 or 20 or even 25 boys each.

When the three minutes were up, and everything ready, the sudden stillness was undercut by tiny murmurs, encrypted bursts of insult, arrangement and gossip:

'Tonight, Fatso.'

'Move it, Leadbutt.'

'Did you?'

'Shut up, moron.'

'Moron!'

Then the black-robed Jesuits themselves, sweeping in among the snaking lines, straightening postures, squaring shoulders. The last slackers would be chased into file by a few syllables of over-articulated Castilian:

Quick. Hurry up. Keep quiet.

And for the blabbers and fidgety, just the sharp, attention-getting interrogative: *And you?*

The routine was the same: everyone was called to attention, gave a military salute – sometimes accompanied with a goofy face – and then the long lines would begin to snake through the courtyard, beneath the gallery and through a side entrance into the chapel attached to Dolores. The youngest boys marched in front and took seats in front; then the next class, and the next, in order, pushed from behind, a *regulador* policing each group, keeping them moving, until the pews were full. In the space of 15 minutes – exactly 15 minutes – the 238 students had remade themselves into one.

Dolores was a military academy without weapons. The Jesuit order is explicitly based on a military structure. Their founder, Ignatius Loyola, was a hardened Spanish soldier who lost a leg to a French cannon ball during the siege of Pamplona in 1521. After making an unexpected recovery, Loyola dedicated himself to religion, conceiving a new religious order, his 'Society of Jesus', that would mirror the administrative efficiency, scientific modernism, and dedication to mission of a trained European army. The head of the Jesuits, residing in Rome, is called the General. The worldwide structure is divided into provinces, each run by a 'Provincial', a military title. All the way down to the student *reguladores*, the Jesuit way was structure, order, attentiveness. Everything in its right place, on time, clean, neat. Focused. Disciplined. Modern.

At eight o'clock *hora inglesa*, they stood in the pews, watched by some three dozen instructors and staff. About half of the adults were Jesuits, in their high collared robes, black wool on most days, but white linen as a concession against the hottest weeks. The other half were civilian teachers, in the uniform of the Cuban middle class: wide, short neckties, light-coloured suits, gleaming shoes. Teachers and students alike faced front and clasped their hands together, and waited. At 8.01, when the priest rose, the assembled body fell still and silent. The day had begun.

ALBERTO CASAS HAD GROWN UP TO MARRY Pepín Bou's sister, Hortensia. In 2003 Pepín told me that the couple were living in Puerto Rico, and though he had given me a number it was surprisingly hard to get Alberto on the telephone, and even harder to keep him on it. He lived in San Juan, the biggest city, but on most days he kept to the habit of a lifetime, rising before dawn to travel out into the countryside where he had his pastures.

Over the course of a year I did reach Casas, sometimes. I might catch him on his cell phone, as he stood in a field under the summer sun. But the conversation would be intermittent, frequently interrupted by the yelling of cowboys as they moved a hundred head through a gate, or Alberto himself would begin shouting at some recalcitrant beast, bovine or human, and hang up in an obvious emergency. Or I'd reach him at home at 7.30 in the evening, and he would plead that he had just walked in the door, 'covered in mud', and needed a shower. He was 75.

When we did talk, it was as Pepín had said: Alberto did all the talking. Standing in a pasture once, he spent the whole call denouncing Puerto Ricans and all things Puerto Rican, the 'collective cowardice' and 'corruption' of their politics, the ruined society they had made. He poured indignation into the cell phone until his battery died. After twelve months of these exchanges I flew down to Puerto Rico to see him.

The island was an alternative vision of Cuba, a could-have-been theory brought to life. Seized by the Americans at the same moment as Cuba, it was never released, but openly annexed. Now it was a Caribbean society where English and Spanish were intertwined, where the people held American passports and took convenient domestic flights to New York but were grown from the same rootstock as the Cubans, the same African and Spanish elements. Casas held them in contempt for this very thing: they were like the Cubans, but had never had the strength that Cuba did. Not the strength to resist the Spanish, nor to resist the Americans. Even the Cuban exiles had come in here and taken the place over, he said.

But Puerto Rico, with all its faults, had to make do, for it was as close as a Cuban exile could get to home. The historic heart of the city, Old San Juan, was puny compared to Old Havana, but it did have the same star-shaped fortresses along the harbour, the same step-through doorways and pastel houses. Out in the countryside the conditions for cattle were the same as in Cuba. The language and social arrangements all echoed what I had seen in Cuba, but with American highways and brands everywhere.

I had picked a cheap beach-front hotel out of a guidebook, and after checking in I walked the few steps to the beach, which was wide and lovely, with a few men in tiny bathing suits lounging around. I was planning on spending the entire weekend with Alberto, touring his farm and meeting over meals with various Dolores alumni he knew in Puerto Rico. But when I called him, Casas immediately barked that there was an emergency. A relative in the Dominican Republic was sick, and he was leaving that very night. Before I could say anything he announced that it was now or never: he would be at my hotel in 30 minutes.

He strode into the lobby half an hour later looking every bit the *guajiro* in a short-sleeved shirt and straw hat, his face bronzed by the sun, his rough hands like slabs. He was enormous, a barrel-chested man with a sagging belly below, and big shoulders spread wide. His head was the only delicate part of the man, set with intense, darting eyes and washed with lively expressions of all kinds. He'd rounded up one friend on short notice, Juan Sotus,

Dolores '48, a quieter, less animated character who arrived in a blue blazer.

Long before, Casas had described himself on the telephone by telling me, 'I'm trouble, and I always have been. I'm a bad mix of Yon Wayne and Clint Eastwood.'

Now, as we sat down at a plastic table under an awning, he started right in, talking right over the efforts of his friend, Sotus, to add comments, and ignoring the slow parade of guests, mostly skinny men, mostly from New York, mostly in the very tiniest bathing suits. Alberto didn't look left or right as he launched into stories about Dolores, cackling gleefully as he recalled working out a way to muffle the alarm on the emergency exit at the rear of the school bus. When the bus pulled up to school each morning, he would stifle the alarm, open the back door, and lead a stealthy jailbreak, four or five boys dropping from the back of the bus unseen and scattering to avoid mass. 'There was a lot of that,' he said, pleased. 'I wasn't the only one.'

I went to the bar and bought three *daiquiri naturales*. Carrying the white plastic cups back, I noticed that the hotel had a lot of rainbow flags. The flyers on the table next to us were for gay nightclubs. But Casas didn't notice, then or later. He made his own weather.

Almost as soon as I sat down again, Alberto jumped up so hard he slammed the table, splattering the drinks. 'Squeeze this,' he said. He made a muscle. 'SQUEEZE IT!'

I did. He was almost twice my age, and his bicep was double the size of my own. Hard as a cannon ball. He'd spent his whole life outdoors. At 18, he'd been put in charge of operations at the family dairy. It hadn't been, as other alumni claimed, the very largest cattle ranch in Oriente; no, it was merely the second largest dairy operation in the province. And his current ranch, here in Puerto Rico, wasn't the very largest on the island, as friends in Miami had told me. It was the second largest feed lot operation.

When I asked if he'd gone on, like so many Dolores kids, to the University of Havana, he scoffed. 'I went to *la universidad de acosta*,' he said. 'THE SCHOOL OF HOW YOU SAY HARD KNOCKS HA HA HA!'

Happily deprived of further education, Alberto had instinct and field savvy in place of philosophy. He could reduce the twentieth century to two sentences ('Cuba was the *querida*, the woman, of the US. When Castro kicked out American corporations, the war was on.') that were impossible to dispute.

A big man knew something of appetite. For decades, the conflict over Cuba had flowed from that possessive desire, that need to dominate, to have a *querida*. Alberto was Cuban, and emphasized his credentials as a nationalist and a patriot. He was quick to condemn Batista and the disgraceful American meddling of the 1930s and 1950s. But he had never believed that Castro was really on the side of Cuba. All he remembered of Fidel was enough: the older brother of the pesky Raúl, Fidel was a domineering presence in the patio, always with a high opinion of his own judgement. As Fidel and Raúl led the guerrilla war in '57 and '58, Alberto sat out the conflict, minding his cattle. But Casas was wealthy, and when the Revolution came he needed no prophets to tell him what the future held. He bolted in February 1959, earlier than Lundy the Prophet, earlier indeed than anyone I had ever met. He was allergic to authority.

Alberto had barely touched his daiquiri. He told me, unconvincingly, that he didn't waste his time thinking about Dolores, or the old days. He said he mostly thought about Puerto Rican life, Puerto Rican business, and Puerto Rican politics. He'd become a leader of the cattlemen's association here, and a lobbyist for all the agricultural importers, and had redirected his ire from various idiots in Cuba to various idiots in Puerto Rico. He had a weekly radio show which he used to denounce the current government, whoever it was. He mocked the Cuban exiles who talked about the past too much. There was a special beach in Puerto Rico, Alberto said, which was known as Used to Have Beach, because it was full of Cuban exiles who sat on their butts all day, talking about what they used to have in Cuba.

At Dolores, Alberto's discipline troubles were entirely the fault of the Jesuits, he explained. He praised the Jesuits enthusiastically, for about ten seconds, and then talked for ten minutes about how awful some of them were. Dolores was full of 'unbearable priests',

Alberto said. They were narrow-minded, unfair, disagreeable, smelly, authoritarian, unreasonable, and were, he finally concluded, nothing but 'a little Gestapo'. He mocked their lisping Spanish accents, the way they called him 'Alberto Cathath'.

A Gestapo? I asked. Wasn't that a little strong?

'A GESTAPO!' he shouted. He smiled as he talked, a provocateur enjoying some psychic revenge. The worst of them all was Father López, the head *vigilante*, who was responsible for discipline, but Alberto also denounced the rector, Father Pedro, at length, and the Jamaican Jesuit, Father Tremble, and would have gone on scourging priests if Sotus had not interrupted him, successfully for once.

'Most of the Jesuits are buried now in the Dominican Republic,' Sotus said, soothingly, trying to tamp down his friend's ardour. When the Jesuit teachers had been forced to leave Cuba, many had settled in Jesuit schools elsewhere in the Caribbean, particularly the Dominican Republic, living 'without possessions', sacrificing for the betterment of the world.

Like many lifelong friends, Sotus and Casas shared a mutual contempt. Sotus revered the memory of Dolores, the priests, and the close-knit school feeling. His own background was 'from the docks', he said, but he wasn't a wharf rat or sailor. His family had *owned* three of the main docks in Santiago, as well as farms. He mentioned the sleepiness of Santiago, and said the momentous event of their childhood had been the opening of the concrete Central Highway in 1932, which sped a flood of commerce into the city, and created easy contact with Havana for the first time in 400 years.

Alberto rolled his eyes when he saw me taking notes on this. 'Don't write about him,' he said, waving a dismissive hand at Jorge. 'His brother is the one you should write about.' Juan's older brother, Jorge, had been 'the James Dean of the family', Alberto explained. Indeed, Jorge Sotus had participated in many of the key events of the Cuban Revolution. He'd joined the urban underground, rising to the rank of captain. He had led sabotage missions and had fought in a failed uprising in Santiago in 1956. Jorge Sotus had later been trusted with large amounts of cash and sent on gun-buying sprees in the US and Central America. An early dissident, Jorge had died in Miami. Juan, by contrast, had stayed out of the war, living quietly, keeping his head down. The anti-romantic survivor.

When I showed Alberto and Juan the 1941 school photo, and the list of names attached to the back of it, written in Alberto's own handwriting, they both studied it intensely. Pepín had said that Alberto recognized more of the faces than anyone else alive. 'It's true,' Alberto announced, 'I have a phenomenal memory. And every time I look at the photo I remember someone new I didn't remember before. My memory is superb.' To prove it he leaned forward and flipping back and forth between the front and back of the photo, began adding names to the list.

'Rolando Cisneros,' he wrote in his neat Dolores cursive, followed by the notation 'Miami?'. And then Evaristo Tercilla. Ceferino Catá. Renee Fernández. It had been several years since he had made the original list for Pepín. Now he updated the old names, writing 'passed away', in English, beside Juan Asganio. For some reason he switched to Spanish, writing 'EPD', or *en paz descansa*, next to Eduardo Marmul, Adolfito Dangillecourt Bacardí and Felipito Fernandes de Castro. Jacky Fioc was 'NY' and Jongo Ramirez Cisneros was 'Balt. physician'. John Grist was 'Argentina?'. Rocky Festari, known in a bilingual pun as *el cohetito*, the little rocket, had passed away in Santiago recently. Fatso Rabelo was in Cuba, along with Kiki de Jongh and Charles Magrans, who was a doctor, a nephrologist. I'd find José Antonio Cubeñas in New York, and José Antonio Roca in what Alberto inscribed as VA./Spain.

Despite his low opinion of Dolores, and his insistence that he rarely concerned himself with the past, Alberto still met, frequently, with his old friends from the school. There were a half dozen *antiguos alumnos* in Puerto Rico, and they got together '*a menudo*', informally. They ate a big meal and just hung out, Alberto said. But he disliked the reunions in Miami, which weren't really Dolores reunions at all, he explained. 'When we talk about the old alumni of the Jesuits, and we get together here, we are 100 per cent Dolorino,' he explained. 'But when they have the reunion in Miami, there are all these people from Belén. That doesn't interest me. I'm 100 per cent Dolorino and will always be 100 per cent Dolorino.'

Before leaving to catch his flight for the Dominican Republic, he asked me who else I would interview. I mentioned some names from the old days, many of them taken from his own list. Others I would find as I could. He grew uncharacteristically quiet. 'Any you speak to,' he said, 'tell them of me.'

I had allowed time to tour Alberto Casas' dominions, so I spent the rest of the weekend roaming around San Juan, idly, killing time, just as I would in Cuba. Crime is much higher in San Juan than in Havana, guns are more common, unemployment and drugs are both chronic, and police corruption is an ongoing scandal. The hoteliers urged me not to go out exploring the city, especially at night, but I had to know how the city compared to Havana, its ancient sibling. I prowled the old city centre, which was indeed very like Old Havana, but smaller, and without the rich layer of 1930s and 1940s architecture. Cruise ship customers flooded into the bars and restaurants, but only for a few hours around dinner. In the afternoons and late at night, it was dead quiet.

Out in the rest of the city, in the folds between the huge beach-front hotels and the *casería* housing projects, there was good food, but even the waiters warned me not to come back to their restaurants like this, alone, at night. Even though Puerto Ricans are American citizens, many spoke to me as if New York were an impossible distance away, a longing that could never be achieved.

The flight home was just the opposite of a return from Cuba. The exit from Havana was slow and bureaucratic, hours of paperwork and searches in the airport, with increasingly hostile questions. ('Why do you come to Cuba so often?' they said, and I erased their doubts by saying, like everyone else, 'I have a woman.') The trip home from Cuba was expensive, passing through more airports, and third countries, usually overnighting somewhere, often flying ridiculous routes, heading north to Canada and then doubling south again, or going west to Mexico to turn around and head east, via Charleston, before going north.

And then, on re-entry to the US, more lines and paperwork, and either evasion (the careful management of deceptions, the juggling of passports, the hiding of rum and cigars) or admission (an automatic red circle around the word CUBA, called out of line, inspection of credentials, quizzing, confession, confusion, supervision, the production of rum and cigars) at the desk. Either way, I would be waved through, exhausted, two days after setting out.

But in San Juan, all I needed was my driver's licence, a cheap ticket on American Airlines, and three hours later I was standing in the domestic lounge in a New York airport. That was life without the drama of Cuban politics.

A few weeks after getting home, I called Alberto. We laid plans to continue the interviews, to eat *a menudo*, to visit the ranch. But just a couple of months later, when he was working in the fields, early, the habit of a lifetime, he felt faint. By nightfall he was in a hospital, diagnosed with a fast-moving bronchial infection, and it killed him within a week.

MORNING UPON MORNING, week upon week, fall, winter and spring, year after year, the same. The bell at 7.45, crying out *bam bam bam bam bam bam bam*. Then assembly. Lines. The march. The pews. And mass: from 8 onward, a crowded 15 minutes of joint prayer, homily and ritual, finished off with a question. On some saints' days, mass was extended to an hour to allow for extra readings and studies on the martyrdom, achievements, famous sayings and moral example of the particular man or woman being celebrated. But on most days it was just 15 minutes, the quickest part of the school day.

It was repetition, rather than length, that mattered. The Church needed to remind people. Despite its status as the official faith of Cuba, Catholicism had always had a weak grip on the island, and its people. Although more than 90 per cent of Cubans described themselves as Catholic by baptism, cultural allegiance, or self-definition, a full 75 per cent said they were not practising, and only 2 per cent of all Cubans were regular churchgoing Catholics who took the sacraments on a regular basis.

The Church still had a long reach. In the first decades of the twentieth century there were hundreds of societies for Catholic laymen, which gave the Church a powerful auxiliary wing, and allowed Catholic influence to reach into many spheres of Cuban life, through ecclesiastical societies for the Virgin of Fátima, Our Lady of Charity, the Blessed Sacrament, and the Virgin of Loreto. The business and professional communities rallied in civil associations like the Knights of Columbus, the Legion of Christ, and Catholic Action.

As a whole, the Cuban Church taught the faithful to seek justice and to reform society, but not through political action. The emphasis was instead on the realm of personal behaviour, on morality and relations with others. It was fine to feed the poor, as the actions of Cuban priests often showed, but it was wrong to ask why they were hungry. The Church did not challenge the established authorities of Cuban life, or the precepts of capitalism. The traditional tripartite alliance in Latin America – landowner, military officer and priest – held sway here too. There was no Vatican II yet, no Liberation Theology, no 'preferential option for the poor'. The Church was imbalanced, disconnected from the roots of society by its attachment to the ruling class. Catholic schools, charities and outreach projects were disproportionately located in Cuba's cities, and often concentrated in well-to-do neighbourhoods. Although there were many examples of the Church reaching out to the poor, during the first half of the twentieth century the Cuban Church was politically conservative, and tied closely to the elite. One reason for this was that the Cuban Church was hardly Cuban at all: out of 681 priests on the island, only 125 were actually born there. The vast majority were Spaniards. In the late 1930s, these European men were often sympathetic to the 'order and progress' promised by new rulers, like Franco and Mussolini, who came to power in poor, politically divided Catholic countries. Franco was an explicit champion of the Catholic Church, who vowed to smite its enemies and punish the radical anarchists and Communists who had persecuted and even executed priests during the 1930s.

Fascism was on the rise, but in the fall of 1941 there were two very different wars raging across the surface of the earth. The Nazi war machine had already flattened Poland, Holland, Belgium and France. Air war raged over London; U-boats were on the offensive in the Atlantic, and were beginning to appear in the Caribbean, striking British and Dutch oil tankers right off the coast of Cuba. The Japanese, already in control of much of China, had signed a new tripartite alliance with Hitler and Mussolini. Yet at Dolores the subject of this global fighting rarely came up, for it was grim, distant and politically sensitive. In history class, the war they were studying was the Trojan war. But there was little doubt which side most of the instructors identified with. Sometimes a Jesuit at the blackboard would let slip a comment about 'the wonderful job that Mussolini is doing, putting all the people to work'.

It was another war that occupied the time and thought of students and instructors. Relentlessly, in class and after it, in instruction and conversation, they discussed the other war, the real war, involving a conflict more profound, more subtle, and even more widespread than maps in the newspaper indicated. This war, the real war, was the struggle between the legions of Christ and the armies of Hell. This perpetual, supreme conflict was being fought today and tomorrow, here and everywhere, a struggle for the free will of each and every human being, in all places and at all times. The Jesuits were governed by one of Loyola's central maxims, the urge to 'find God in all things'. Even the humblest activities could be bent to the glory of God. As they sat at their desks, walked to school, even as they played sports or ate their meals, they were troops in an eternal cause. The war in Europe was a sideshow.

The children were grouped into three 'Divisions' by age. The oldest, Lundy's group, were known as *mayores* and the younger students were called *segundos* or *primeros*.

Discipline was rarely needed during line-ups, or any other time. It was usually a matter of applying layers of chiding, gentle wisdom, confinement in the *sala de disciplina* after hours, and the occasional bout of physical persuasion. Tugging on ears, slapping boys on the head, and threatening them with a ruler were not unheard of. The Jesuits were inventive. Two boys who antagonized each other, routinely and endlessly, were ordered to climb up to the *solar*, or sun room, that made a kind of fourth floor, and fight it out. They were left alone, and did fight, but it was one of the hottest days of the school year, and the *solar* was like an oven. It took only minutes for the boys to return, reconciled.

In a culture of conformity and a setting of middle-class aspirations, there was little need for such forceful measures, however. Most of the boys would be brought into line with nothing more than a glare, or a lisping *¿Qué pasa?* from one of the Spaniards. Few children dared to keep talking when hushed.

EVEN IN RELIGION, Cubans spoke in their particular dialect of doubled language. The central fact of life at Dolores was an orthodox Catholicism of the most traditional kind. The day began with mass and ended with prayers before bedtime – an envelopment of Christianity that was emphasized in Dolores yearbooks, which showed reassuring pictures of the clean, slick-haired, knock-kneed *internos* in neckties, caught praying at their bedsides at night by Foto Mexicana, or shown filing in and out of the chapel, or preparing for First Communion, the symbolic entry into adulthood and enrolment in the faith.

First Communion was something Dolores boys yearned for. At 7, they were issued a book with a green cover – the Catechism, the first ritual of the faith. (For the similar but less significant Confirmation, at 13, they received a red book.) Everything they needed to start life as an adult was between those green covers. The Catechism was a set of questions and answers, a book of fundamental principles of the faith to be memorized backwards, forwards, inside and out. The Hail Mary. The Apostles' Creed. The Litany of the Blessed Virgin Mary. The Act of Contrition. Sanctifying Grace. The Ten Commandments. The Seven Virtues. The Seven Sacraments. The Seven Deadly Sins.

At 7 they began practising for the Communion ritual, marching to the assigned pew, forming a queue, and appearing at the railing. Instead of wine, the actual blood of the Lord, they received a sip of water. Instead of a holy wafer, the actual flesh of Christ, the priest placed a tiny slip of rice paper on their extended tongues, which they had to swallow. Despite these rehearsals, it wasn't always possible to prevent nervous boys at First Communion from choking and spitting up a soggy holy wafer right there at the railing, in front of everyone.

Becoming a Christian, joining the body of the Church at First Communion, was a proud moment. But it was also an entry into a secular adolescence, and by Cuban tradition First Communion meant something practical: money. It was normal for relatives, neighbours, and the various people caught in a family's tight web of social networks, to donate small amounts of cash, which added up to a boyhood fortune. At Dolores, with so many wealthy families, the boys knew they would come in for a serious windfall. In *Waiting for Snow in Havana*, Carlos Eire describes a similar party for a kid known as Sugar Boy – one of the Fanjul kids, heirs to Cuba's greatest sugar fortune. Sugar Boy was showered with opulent gifts, including toys flown in specially from New York. In the middle class there were fewer such bonanzas, but as First Communion approached, it meant special parties at somebody's beach house, or the steady arrival of toys, or of a peso pressed into a small palm, or of jingling coins, including American nickels, sprinkled in their pocket. First Communion meant ice cream, and a trip to El Ten Cent for the latest American gizmos, for airplane models and battleship games and bins of toy soldiers, entire cowboy outfits with cap guns, balsa gliders and squirting bou-tonnières. Maybe the boy and his friends would be treated to a double-header at one of Santiago's air-conditioned movie thea-tres.

On the actual day of Communion the families dressed in their best clothes, and the boys were paraded through the streets in new white suits, with shopkeepers and even passing strangers handing them coins, and cheering them on, the proud families marching behind, the boys greeted with applause, kisses, and little gifts of money everywhere they went. As they drew in toward Dolores there was a growing set of embraces, the families of the prominent coming together in Clock Street in common celebration. Santiago was a small city, the elite even smaller; they could often assemble themselves into one viewfinder. Santiago's main newspaper, *Diario del Oriente*, often ran news photos of events like Communion at Dolores, showing the Jesuits in 'casual' poses with the boys, smiling at the front door, greeting people, or Clock Street filled by a hundred men in straw hats, a sea of linen.

Communion was merely the apogee of a calendar stuffed with Catholic scheduling. With more than 4,000 saints in the Catholic panoply, every day in the year was associated with several. There were too many to memorize, but the boys were expected to be familiar with all of the important ones. Francis of Assisi was especially beloved, the patron of animals and small children. The boys liked the exciting Teresa of Lisieux, too – the patroness of pilots and foreign missions. San Cristobal protected travellers; Santa Gertrudis the teachers. Saint John the Apostle was invoked to watch over printers, editors, book-binders, and all others in the line of scribes. Saint Martin, a black martyr of Peruvian origins, was always noted in Santiago because he was the patron of anyone of mixed race, and there were endless more patrons to learn, protecting conquistadors and fiddlers, altar boys and carnival workers, bald men and the youth of Mexico, those who needed rain and those who needed protection from rain, the royalty of France and girls living in the countryside, those who overslept and those who bottled champagne. It was more than anyone could absorb, and daily mass at Dolores was too brief to do more than mention a saint a day.

Occasionally, in the quick moment after the recitation of these heroes and martyrs, with their amazing powers to affect others, the boys would hear a darker note slip into the homily. Just once in a while, they would hear the priest denounce not just the usual sins, but new things. Superstition, he might say. Foolishness. Fortune-telling. *Brujería*, the practice of witchcraft. *Obscurantism*, the priest might say, and mention the official Catholic position against 'criminal anthropology' – whatever that was.

When mass ended, these adult words floated away on the

sunlight of the patio, carried by the chaos of 238 voices. The bell for classes rang, and good Catholic boys were not troubled.

BY WITCHCRAFT, *Obscuratism* and Criminal Anthropology they meant the Religion of Black People, or Santería. What you oppose defines you, and in Cuba, Catholicism attacked Santería because they were so close, as close as black beans and white rice. Santería is the Way of the Saints, an Afro-Cuban cult built around venerating the Catholic saints held up to the boys of Dolores, but done in a very different way, often at night, amid drumming and cigar smoke and rum. The saints were also called different names, and summoned for different purposes, and attended by different people (though often as not, the followers of one cult would be seen at rites of the other). The Catholic Church claimed the high ground by attacking this low faith, the religion of the common people, as witchcraft, the work of Satan, a dangerous nocturnal creed of criminals and the ignorant. They denounced Santería bitterly because it was bigger, more popular, more influential, than Catholicism itself.

Santería is a veneer of Catholicism laid over half-remembered African faiths. Principally Yoruba in its origins, and known formally as the Rule of Ocha, it was widely practised in Cuba, especially in Oriente, where there was a strong black majority. To Santeros, the pictures of Catholic heroes like Santa Bárbara and Martín de Porres were familiar from the church on Sunday, but had other meanings. The Catholic saints were portals, entryways into the complex reality of a universe crowded with gods and demigods, malevolent spirits and shape-shifting divines.

Christ became the face of Obatalá, guardian of the unfinished creation. Ogún, the patron of hunters and blacksmiths, was a drunkard who appeared in the guise of Saint John the Baptist. Yemayá, the blue goddess of the seas, was also Our Lady of Regla, the Catholic patroness of Havana harbour. Oshún, the yellow-clad beauty who represented erotic love, was twinned with the Virgin of El Cobre, the crucial symbol of eastern Cuba with a shrine just outside Santiago.

In the white precincts of central Santiago and in the big houses of the Vista Alegre neighbourhood, Santería was derided by day, but often consulted by night, a balm in moments of private desperation.

This was hypocrisy, but centuries of slavery and repressive politics had taught Cubans to be expert at *doble cara*, 'two-faces', the practice of saying one thing and doing another, of keeping two separate and even contradictory truths in place at the same time. *Doble cara* allowed opposition and loyalty at once, dissent and conformity side by side. You could aspire to democratic rule and then work for the latest tyrant; you could practise Holy Roman rituals on Sunday and the next night have a fortune told, a love affair arranged, or a trial influenced, amid cigar smoke, turtle bones and chicken blood.

For white, middle-class kids, Santería was the faith of the house maid, of the gardener or chauffeur.

Even good Catholics peered into its shadowy realm from time to time. If the priest denounced the old African rites during mass, then how many mothers of boys at Dolores blushed, having sought out fortune-tellers and arrangers of love affairs? How many fathers had laughed at the Rule of Ocha, or one of the other parallel and Africanized cults, but then covered their bets by leaving a lottery ticket at the Catholic shrine of El Cobre, with a muttered appreciation of the good fortune that Changó or his rival Ogún might allow them? How many professed the doctrine of the Universal Church, and then refused to cut down a kapok tree because it was foolish to offend Iroko, the resident spirit?

NOTHING ABOUT THE BOYS of Dolores was typical or average. Dolores was a Jesuit school, one of three on the island, and by design the Jesuits and their students stood apart. Santiago had several good private schools, run by the Christian Brothers and other orders, as well as academies for girls, like Sagrado Corazón, which was run by nuns but applied the same educational principles as the Jesuits. But there was only one top school, and it was Dolores. To be a Dolores boy was to walk through the Plaza Dolores as if you owned it, and to step right past students in the uniforms of other *colegios* without comment. Dolores acknowledged no equals.

The Colegio de Dolores was imbued with Loyola's original impulse to forge a new Catholic vanguard. For this mission, the sons of the elite were a fine fit. The wealthy and powerful families of Santiago were themselves determined to accomplish the same goal of training their children to rise up in life. For the Jesuits, choosing the wealthy and the elite was not enough. Wealth was fine, an old name was good, but the larger cause needed talent. A boy who showed academic skill, and who demonstrated potential, was too fine a prize to turn away, even if his father was humble, his name unknown. The school gave places to families that could not afford them, so that a department store employee's son like José Antonio Roca sat beside a landowner's scion like Fidel Castro.

The exception was race. Dolores was a segregated school. Black students, no matter how intelligent, were excluded by a social dictum enforced by white families to protect their own privileges. At the country clubs, restaurants and schools that served the elite, white was the only colour that counted. In the 1940s, Dolores was no different.

But Cuba had always known an amorphous racial climate, not of blacks and whites, but grey areas – or brown ones. For centuries, Cubans have lived in the reality of a mulatto society, acknowledging a wide spectrum of skin tones with frank language unknown to the north. This vast middle ground was comprised of mulattos, but mulattos themselves are unselfconsciously described as octoroons, or white mulattos, or dark whites, or clear octoroons, or creole. Blacks are labelled by shade: 'congo' (pure black) or 'blue black' or 'red black' or 'black like a raisin' or 'black-haired' (meaning nappy), all of which denoted subtle differences along the spectrum of Africanness. Even whites were also rated on a scale of whiteness, ranging from the dark-haired *gallegos* ('Galician', meaning of Spanish descent) like Fidel Castro, on up to *claros*, the palest Cubans, like white-haired Pepín Bou, or the Dutch-Cuban de Jongh brothers, with their translucent skin. And of course anyone with even a touch of indigenous blood (rare in Cuba) or any type of Asian background (much more common) was bluntly labelled *chino*. (A current joke held that Cubans were half-white, half-black, and half-Chinese.) With so many gradations, Cubans could use the subtlest signals to convey colour, like dragging two fingers over the back of their hand, to indicate that someone was 'marked', or coloured.

Even a segregated institution like Dolores had to live within such subtleties. Formally, it was a white school. Yet even a quick glance through early yearbooks reveals a sprinkling of students with skin that was not just olive, but downright dusky. Black and white photos don't reveal everything about skin tone, of course, but that was the point: Cubans weren't living in a black and white world. Colour was one factor, divided into a hundred shades, and then cross-indexed with other social indicators, like wealth, religion, speech, clothing and behaviour. So the school excluded blacks, and nominally mulattos, but then who were those few boys, smiling, neat, eager, gleaming out of the yearbooks? Was someone at Dolores supposed to separate mulattos from octoroons, or grade forearms? If a family was Catholic, middle-class, properly behaved, and their boy had talent, who would pry into the secrets of a family's past?

The Jesuits were already considered radically, dangerously progressive on social issues, by the standards of orthodox, official culture in 1930s Cuba. Racially, they preached the brotherhood of man and equality before God. Economically, they drew heavily on the middle class who made Cuba work. Educationally, they opened the doors of their schools to admit, if not a cross-section of Cuban society, at least a wide sample of the middle and upper classes. That made the students at Dolores typical not of Cuba, but of the people who ran it: the powerful, the rich, the talented and the useful. And they were typical of the future, too, for it was their generation of young, frustrated, middle- and upper-class boys that would shape, through its internal feuds and frustrations, the Cuban Revolution. And for the boys from Dolores, this would often become a family affair, splitting brother from brother. Fidel Castro would use, and eventually consume, his own family, his own cousins, and neighbours, his relations by marriage, and those who he knew through schooling, first from

Santiago, and later from Havana. He would use Dolores when he needed it — to protect him physically, or politically. And in turn those who helped him would join the ranks of the regretful.

Whether bred, recruited, or raised, these boys were from an elite, and part of a world that rested on an overhang, unstable, dangerous, blind to the world below it. Locked behind their high walls, the Dolores boys were also invisible to that larger world, meant to be separated out of it, in order to shape it. Dolores fulfilled this mission, albeit disastrously for itself. It did make rulers, of two; it made the rest, across decades, into survivors.

Not everyone endured: some withered, here or in exile. But the most common sight, a lifetime later, would be a man, surrounded by his family, who had survived hardship and loss, and re-established himself with an astonishing degree of consistency, true to his education, profession and religion, and the memory of a place that will never come again.

Some of them would even become the elite they were meant to be, wealthy in business or industry or agriculture, leaders in medicine and academia. Just not here, in what they were told was their city, and their Cuba.

THE DAY STUDENTS lived in an expansive world the boarding students could hardly credit. Every single day, often for hours at a time, they got to wander in the wider life of city streets. At night they had the deep comforts of a kitchen table, a mother, many generations, strangers and neighbours. When they returned to school each morning they were full of stories, chronicles of new things.

But at 8.20, the end of morning mass, these incoming day students were reminded that much of what mattered at the school occurred after they left, during the long closed hours of the afternoon and night. The most important rivalries and friendships were cemented, the longest arguments begun or ended, and the strangest stunts were all carried out after hours, among the *internos*. It was these 'prisoners' who caught glimpses into the private lives of the Jesuits. It was all those *interno* brothers, whispering at night, who ferreted out the secrets, and plotted the most ambitious projects.

The Mass over, same long lines of boys now uncoiled from the chapel, spilling in reverse into the patio and the surrounding courtyards, but with a rapidly decaying order that quickly dissolved. The boys had ten minutes until class, ten minutes to organize themselves and their books, ten minutes to visit the bathroom, ten minutes to engage in the all-important gossip about what had happened overnight, who had pulled what stunt, and gossip. Boys rushed upstairs and back down, and the last stragglers, the three or four cheats every day who had skipped mass and snuck out the back of the school bus, now came darting inside, hoping to dodge in the front door when no priests were looking, and often, thanks to the chaos, succeeding. For ten minutes, everyone tried to move and talk at the same time.

Lundy arrived early one morning, rang the bell for mass, joined in the assembling of the lines, marched in, listened dutifully for 20 minutes, and then, like all the boys, exploded into the courtyard looking for novelty and *chisme*, gossip and jokes. A crowd of *internos* was in the courtyard, nervously flicking a ball back and forth. They were were debating who was the most valuable player on the school basketball squad. José Antonio Roca was the real star; he had scored 61 points against La Salle, a school record. Everyone should vote for him.

The boys in the courtyard flipped the ball about, nervously, and switched to debating which game they should play – a basket shooting contest, or a real pickup basketball, or stickball, or catch, or anything they could think of.

Lundy had no part in this. He was a *zurdo*, a klutz, and rarely participated in the great cleaving contests of *besból* and *futból* in the courtyard. And the *reguladores* were never exactly popular. Lundy was the uptight kid with the prize wristwatch and the job of keeping them all on schedule. So he usually retreated into his books, soaking up Sir Lancelot, or the ambush of Pizarro by his own men, or went to the second floor, to the office. On his way upstairs that day, eyes always roaming, he glanced at a bulletin board full of notices. There was a letter tacked up there. Written across the top of the paper it said: THE WHITE HOUSE, and then WASHINGTON, DC.

You didn't need to understand English to know those words. It was addressed to a 12-year-old-boy at the school Lundy didn't know.

'Who,' he asked a passing boy, 'is Fidel Castro?'

The session bell rang before he could get an answer. It was a charmless electronic buzzer that had none of the antique pride of Lundy's hand-wrung school bell. It was 8.30. Time for history, geography, Spanish literature, grammar, Greek or Latin, mathematics or biology, depending on the boy or the day. Time to work.

THE WHITE HOUSE HAD WRITTEN in reply to a letter from Fidel which is still in the National Archives in Washington. Castro wrote it on official school stationery filched from the office after hours. COLEGIO DE DOLORES, it says, over the number of a post office box in Santiago de Cuba.

Fidel wrote in English, but not very good English. The 12-year-old used brackets to indicate where he was substituting a Spanish word for an English word he didn't know. His handwriting, however, was excellent. The school taught the Palmer method of penmanship, a regimented system which produced floral cursive lettering and highly ornamented words on tightly ruled lines. Fidel's cursive was nearly flawless, but he made one major mistake right at the start. He misspelled the name of the recipient:

Santiago de Cuba
Nov. 6 1940
Mr. Franklin Roosvelt
President of the United States

My good friend Roosvelt
I don't know very English, but I know as much as write to you.
    I like to hear the radio, and I am very happy, because I heard in it that you will be President for a new (periodo)
    I am twelve years old. I am a boy but I think very much but I do not think that I am writing to the President of the United States.

Turning the page, Fidel had continued on the back, his English degenerating quickly:

> [I]f you like, give me a ten dollars bill green american, in the letter, because never, I have not seen a ten dollars bill green american and I would like to have one of them. My address is:
> Sr. Fidel Castro
> Colegio de Dolores
> Santiago de Cuba
> Oriente, Cuba
>
> I don't know very English but I know very much Spanish and I suppose you don't know very Spanish but you know very English because you are American but I am not American. (Thank you very much)
> Good by. Your friend

Then the signature, worthy of a nobleman. Fidel produced a swirling, picturesque rendition of his name that was a work of art, or at least nerve. The abbreviated first name – just 'F' – was overlaid by a vast 'C', and at the end of *Castro* the final 'o' came back to cross the 't' and link the letters. The signature was so ornate that he wrote his name one more time, in plain print, to make sure they got it: *Fidel Castro*

It looked wonderful. But perfection is beyond even the most determined boy, and Fidel undercut his own effort by adding a sloppy, and apparently hurried, postscript:

> If you want to make your sheaps, I will show to you the biggest (minas) of iron of the land. They are in Mayarí, Oriente Cuba.

That was it, a page and a quarter.

It is worth noting that Castro's writing wasn't the only writing on the paper. If you turn the letter on its side, there is a second hand, in pencil. There, along the margin, are just two words, in the large and firm writing of an adult. An adult at the US State Department. All it said there was, 'Castro, Fidel'.

Here was the first entry in what would become a very long file.

DURING THE MINUTES BEFORE LUNCH, Lundy returned to the letter from the White House. 'Who,' he asked again, 'is Fidel Castro?' He had met the three Castro brothers, certainly, but which was which? They were *internos*, and Lundy didn't know them. Ramón was older, Fidel and Raúl younger.

'That one,' someone said, and another: 'That's him. There.' Different boys all pointed to the courtyard, to a tall boy in a crowd.

Fidel, the tall one. A round face. Arched eyebrows. A Roman nose, and the pale skin of a *gallego*. Lundy wasn't timid. He was a year older than Fidel Castro, and a year ahead of him, and also a *regulador*, a statesman in the world of teenagers. He went straight up to Fidel and blurted out, 'I didn't know you had written to Roosevelt.'

'Yeah, well,' Castro said. 'He won the election. But the Americans are assholes. I asked for ten dollars and they didn't send me a cent.'

They shook hands, and stared at each other. 'This is phenomenal,' Lundy said.

Castro chatted greedily. He had a high, soft voice, almost feminine. But he was a comfortable speaker, his natural disposition polished in the declamation contests at Dolores, where they were judged on rhetoric, pacing and the stentorian tone favoured by great Cubans. They learned practical things for the contests: how to speak without notes, use a microphone, stand in the light. Fidel enjoyed an audience, even in the patio.

He disclaimed any great achievement, and then began referring to it as if he'd heard personally from the President of the United States, rather than a correspondence office. In fact, he explained to Lundy, he was quite upset with Roosevelt. The American had also ignored Fidel's offer of good Cuban iron. Everybody knew that Oriente had not just lots of iron, but the best quality too. How could you build a fleet of battleships without iron from Mayarí?

They would come to know each other too well. They overlapped for five years at Dolores, both of them star pupils and school leaders. Then they overlapped again at the University of Havana, earning law degrees. So a connection that endured for 20 years began there, with the letter. The two boys quickly discovered some mutual enthusiasms, and had a brief and intense friendship. They both loved stories about the conquistadors, they discovered. Geography class was a favourite for both, and they shared their detailed plans for travelling the world. They even agreed on some career goals: the best life was to be a famous explorer, and an adventurer, and also a great man of history.

Dolores had film nights, parties that drew in families and day students like Lundy to join the *internos* in watching films that were projected from an RCA Victor machine on to a sheet draped on a wall. Lundy and Fidel sat through several films together. The selection was usually whatever was cheapest to rent, like dreadful Mexican cowboy movies, full of singing heroes, dumb villains and bad lighting. Lundy ranked films in a way that was common among Dolores boys. Mexican cowboy films were the worst, worse even than films with kissing. There was a middle ground – thrillers, war movies – and then at the top there was one kind of film above all others, the Hollywood Western. The outfits, horses and guns were the same as in the Mexican films, but these were bigger, more glamorous movies, expansive, with clean sunshine, dirty heroes, and thrilling escapes. John Wayne and Gary Cooper were real men. If film night had included one of these great works of art, then the boys would be ecstatic afterward, lingering in big knots, talking wildly. They would rechoreograph the gunfights, re-enact the ambushes, and stage the sudden overturning of villains and heroes all over again, laughing all the while.

But Lundy noticed that Fidel never joined in. When Lundy asked why, Fidel told him, 'The wrong side won.' He didn't like the American cavalry. It was the Indians who were brave, who were underdogs, who'd been beaten down by power.

THE UNITED STATES HAD INVADED Cuba in 1898 with the usual mixture of noble sentiment and grasping self-interest. The struggle had already been under way, intermittently, for decades, and was portrayed in American newspapers – then in the heyday of their yellow journalism – as a heroic battle between the native freedom fighters of an island paradise and the corrupt overlords imposed by a cruel European tyranny. Newspaper cartoons depicted Spanish soldiers as bloodthirsty rapists who crushed Cuban liberty – usually depicted as a dusky maiden in Greek robes – under their boot heels. American sympathy was so strong that gunrunners and mercenaries – the 'freebooters' – who served the Cuban rebels were treated as heroes. The *New York Tribune* sent a novelist, Stephen Crane, to describe one of these gunrunning missions. When the small ship, laden with ammunition, caught fire in the Straits of Florida, Crane and the crew fled in a crowded dinghy, barely surviving their time adrift. Crane's thinly fictionalized account of the sinking, 'The Open Boat', became the most famous short story in American literature, and added a patina of glamorous risk to the profitable business of feeding weapons to the Cuban insurgency.

Even in the midst of popular emotion, the American government did not lose sight of what was really at stake. Presidents as far back as Thomas Jefferson had dreamed of annexing Cuba. With its combination of rich agricultural lands, marketing opportunities and slave society, Cuba was a coveted target of annexation for American planters. In the mid-1800s Spain rejected American overtures to buy the island, and by the 1890s, Cuba was routinely portrayed as a natural dependency of the US. By the time war broke out, this ambition was veiled behind a frenzy of sentiment, but Mark Twain outed it, calling the Cuban intervention a 'pathetic comedy' in the service of building a new empire.

By 1898, the Spanish had been locked in a brutal, scorched-earth conflict for three years, and were on the defensive, secure in the cities but unable to dislodge the wild Cuban cavalry, the *mambises*, who raided the countryside, burning crops and bringing the country to a halt. It was then that America intervened suddenly, and with overwhelming force, annihilating the Spanish navy off the coast of Oriente. This cut off the beleaguered Spanish infantry (including Fidel's father, Ángel Castro, a quartermaster) from all hope of reinforcement, resupply, or withdrawal. Then more than 17,000 American troops, including the horseless troop of Wyoming ranchers, Manhattan aristocrats, and plains Indians known as the Rough Riders, landed in Oriente. Aided by Cuban rebels, the American expedition engaged in several showy but small battles (only 268 Americans were killed or wounded in action; 14 times that many fell to disease) and soon had Santiago surrounded. The war lasted 113 days and, just as Twain predicted, brought not just Cuba but Puerto Rico, the Philippines and Guam under US control, creating an instant American empire from the dregs of a once-Spanish globe.

After the Spanish surrender, the new order of things became clear almost overnight. The American commander in Santiago refused to allow Cuban rebels to march in his victory parade. In fact, the rebels were not even allowed to enter the city to *watch* as American troops marched through the streets. The Cubans were then excluded from the peace negotiations, which were held in Europe, with Spain and the US negotiating between themselves.

The United States ruled Cuba directly for only three years, disclaiming all imperial ambitions while setting up a system that ensured American domination for decades. American businesses rushed in, investing $30 million in just a couple of years. United Fruit quickly bought almost 2 million acres of farmland, at 20 cents per acre. A Wall Street syndicate bought out the Havana street car company. American tobacco and timber companies moved in. By 1901, American business controlled 80 per cent of Cuba's mineral exports.

Reform of the *latifundio* system of huge estates was long overdue, but the rules introduced by the American government had the effect of turning Cuba into a giant cane field, supplying sugar to America under a new system of annual quotas. Throughout the economy, American interests dominated at the expense of Cuban business, so that Americans won the contract to pave Cuban streets, and did it with old paving stones from Boston, rather than new ones from a Cuban quarry.

In 1903, the United States refused to leave Cuba until the new government signed the Platt Amendment, which guaranteed America's 'right to intervene for the preservation of Cuban independence'. This was a legal fiction to cover standard policy. As early as 1822, US troops had made repeated landings in Cuba to hunt pirates. In 1825, British and American troops staged a joint landing at Sagua La Grande to chase more pirates, and the US Marines returned later that year. The policy of intervention was on display in the 113-day war of 1898, and again after 1903, when US forces nominally withdrew from most of Cuba. They returned in 1917, landing to protect the usual 'American interests' and to secure wartime deliveries of sugar at favourable prices. (The troops remained for two years.) A huge naval base at Guantánamo was granted to the US 'in perpetuity', and through the 1920s, a series of pro–American presidents were selected from the ranks of the elite. America was particularly identified with the dictatorship of General Gerardo Machado between 1925 and 1933, a time of brutal assassinations and open warfare among political gangs. Various currents of opposition to both Machado and the US meddling finally coalesced in an uprising by the ABC, an opposition movement rooted in the upper classes of Cuba, but in a broad popular alliance with radical students and Communists. The hated Machado was finally ousted in August 1933, and on this occasion President Roosevelt broke form by refusing to send American troops ashore to intervene directly. But the US navy was sent to 'demonstrate' off Cuban shores, and Roosevelt engaged in a new, more subtle form of intervention, encouraging Cuban militarists to oppose and undermine the new government. After just 17 days, this liberal and well-intentioned administration was overthrown by a new military coup, which Roosevelt welcomed. Although the Cubans now rescinded the Platt Amendment, Roosevelt had shown that direct intervention was no longer needed. Ambitious Cubans could be counted on to protect American interests.

Machado's sudden and violent downfall in Havana brought down many, including, at distant Dolores, one of the most popular of all the boys in the school, a boy named Desiderio

Alberto Arnaz y de Acha. He was the scion of an aristocratic family that had once owned large portions of California, and which had ruled over Santiago de Cuba for at least a generation. Desiderio's father had been the youngest mayor in Santiago's history, and in 1933 had just taken up a seat in the Cuban senate, as a supporter of Machado's party. And Desiderio's uncle was the head of the Santiago police force.

At Dolores, these prominent connections meant far less than the popularity Desiderio derived from playing guitar in the patio, or singing with a high, clear voice during the school's religious pageants and festivals. It was good to be one of Desiderio's friends. The family had a real estate empire around Santiago, including an old family home just six blocks from the Parque Céspedes, and also a brand-new house up in Vista Alegre. They had three farms in the countryside, and (best of all, from a boy's perspective) a summer home out on exclusive Cayo Smith, the resort island sitting in the throat of Santiago Bay. Desiderio, a member of the Dolores swim team, sometimes brought his team-mates out to Cayo Smith before a big meet. They would train by swimming halfway around the island in the morning, watched over by family retainers in a speedboat. In the afternoon they would return and swim the second half.

This life of privilege came to an abrupt end that August. Those who hated Machado hated his cronies, and a mob tore through Santiago, lynching some Machado supporters in front of their homes. The Arnaz clan – source of mayors, senators and police chiefs – was next, and as the mob came up the street toward their house, a family servant hastily bundled Desiderio into a car and fled. The frustrated mob looted the home, smashed the piano, tipped over another family car, and eventually set the building on fire, before moving on to sack the Moncada army garrison, setting it too on fire. Attacking Moncada, the symbol of military authority in Santiago, was a practised gesture in any rebellion.

Within days, Desiderio was living in Miami with his father. Unlike Machado's more quick-fingered associates, the Arnaz clan did not manage to leave Cuba with any money, and at 17, Desiderio took up manual labour, shovelling and sorting cracked tiles, and cleaning restaurants. He soon found that singing in restaurants was less onerous work, and earned $5 a night for playing his guitar. Even in Florida, Cuban music was still a novelty, an ethnic curiosity. On New Year's Eve, desperate to entertain a bored crowd, Desiderio grabbed a conga drum and began parading through the tables, imitating the rhythmic marching at Santiago's carnival. Urging people to follow him around the room, Desiderio thus invented the conga line, which soon became a national craze, launching his career as a band leader. Shortening his name from Desiderio Alberto Arnaz y de Acha to just Desi Arnaz, he conquered New York and eventually Hollywood, where he met the red-headed comedienne Lucille Ball.

The marriage of this popular American actress to an exotic entertainer was a tabloid sensation, and Lucille Ball shrewdly realized that the new medium of television was the perfect way to convert this public fascination into a 'reality show' about her life. Ball designed a sketch comedy about a famous actress who marries a zany Cuban. During rehearsals, she discovered it was much funnier if she was portrayed as just an ordinary, talentless American housewife, always *trying* to crash the showbiz career of her Cuban husband.

Lucy – and her 'Ricky' – became the show that made television, number one in the ratings for four of its six years, and still at number one when it went off the air in 1957, just as another Cuban was launching his bid for the top. In his despicable autobiography, *A Book*, Arnaz catalogued the whores he slept with, and basically took credit for inventing Cuban music, but he said his only regret was never graduating from high school.

THE PLATT AMENDMENT WAS GONE, but America remained, a set of people, rules, incentives, finances, and values which were new on the island. Before 1898, the Cuban elite had prided themselves on their conservative values and Catholic traditionalism, and they had remained loyal to Spain later than any other country in the Americas. But the arrival of American soldiers was only the beginning.

The American military government had two obsessions. One

was draining swamps. Cuba was portrayed as unhealthy, a festering, backward country ruined by disease. The army set about ditching and draining, and spewing new regulations about sewers and trash removal. The Platt Amendment was really a list of strict hygiene standards for Cuba; failure in any category could lead to American invasion. One of the enduring symbols of the American presence was the arrival of mosquito screens. Cubans had always made do with nets over the bed, or with no protection beyond a breeze or the smoke from a fire. Open windows were a part of Cuban social custom, a form of transparency that encouraged long chats at the *reja*. But the Americans built their houses back from the roads, and slapped fine mesh netting over every window. You couldn't see them, or speak to them. They thought Cubans were dirty.

The other American project was an outburst of educational reform. The age of compulsory education was raised from 9 to 14. The island was divided into school districts, with school boards, and parent-teacher committees. The reforms benefited many students, but the elite in Cuba had rarely cared about the many. The American government did work closely with Cubans in designing the new system, but it still altered fundamental notions of Cuban identity, taking away even the nominal role of the Catholic Church and substituting a secularized American model. The reforms were administered by a Cuban, but a Cuban chosen by the Americans. (Almost a hundred years after it happened, José Antonio Cubeñas could still identify why this man alienated the traditional families in Santiago. 'He was a Cuban,' he said, 'but a Jew. The people did not want that.' When I pressed him on this point, Cubeñas pressed back. 'An *atheist* Jew,' he said. A real Jew might have been acceptable; a secular one was not.)

The reforms thus drove a counter-tide, in which Cuba's elite and the increasingly large middle class withdrew steadily into religious schools, away from (Protestant) American values, Jews and other threats. Dolores grew quickly during the first decades of the century, growth that brought with it funds and connections. But the rise of elite schools came with an attendant failure of public ones: in the 1930s, the private system enrolled three times as many pupils in all grades as the public system. The gap was even more severe in high school, where there were 1,181 private ones to only 21 public ones. Society had decided that any education beyond reading, writing and arithmetic was presumably wasted on *macheteros*. About 30 per cent of Cubans were illiterate. This wasn't as bad as the figures of 50, 60, or even 90 per cent claimed by Cuban officials in the 1990s, but it was terrible enough, and it did call for a revolution.

THAT WAS ALWAYS A POPULAR IDEA IN CUBA. There were revolutions (failed, attempted, sometimes successful, always loudly declared) in the 1860s, 1870s and in 1895. There were attempted revolutions in the 1920s, and then in 1933 there was the street revolution which overthrew the hated Machado. Like the 1959 revolution, the one in 1933 had been driven from below by a broad, populist uprising against corruption and dictatorship, before being diverted into the hands of a military man.

Sergeant Fulgencio Batista was that careful man. Batista was part of the military clique that displaced the original civilian government just 17 days after Machado's overthrow. Batista originally had no gripe other than getting a pay rise, and no constituency other than the military, but as he elbowed his way to the top of the new government, he found it convenient to have allies. He grabbed at the rhetoric of the social movements at hand, declaring himself a revolutionary and a progressive, a nationalist and a patriot. Staying behind the scenes at first, he picked a reformist politician, Ramón Grau, to be the new president, invited students and leftists into the government, and made fine speeches. Batista soon figured out what he really wanted – another pay rise – and within a year he forced Grau out, assuming the presidency himself so that he could extract giant bribes. He kept the Cuban legislature intact, however, which was dominated by a reform movement, and introduced a series of social programmes designed to undercut the claim that he was just a power-mad soldier. He infuriated America by instituting a fifty-fifty employment law that reserved half of the jobs in any US-run enterprise for Cubans. He placed the first Cuban price quotas on the sugar crop, forcing the Americans to pay a stable rate. And he launched the first national campaign against illiteracy, a 'civic-military' campaign that used teachers from the army and was funded by the military budget. Between 1936 and 1940, the Batista government constructed 1,100 new schools. Although the programme was not sustained for long, and did not reach every part of Cuba, illiteracy dropped by about 10 per cent.

Bohemia, Cuba's leading magazine, called the literacy campaign progressive and commendable, but Batista's revolution was really just a screen of convenience, cover for his increasingly brutal and corrupt rule. He used martial law to crush pro-democracy strikes in 1935 and, despite his avowed nationalism, the 1930s are known to Cuban historians as the 'era of puppets' because of the way Batista sent a rotating cast of political hacks to receive instructions from the American ambassador, Jefferson Coffery, and Sumner Welles, FDR's trouble-shooter on Cuba.

Resentment of American meddling and lingering Spanish influence fed another round of patriotic reforms to education. In 1939 the government imposed a curriculum on all schools, public or private, religious or secular. It mandated 228 school days on the calendar, with classes beginning on the first Monday in October and running through to the middle of May, with a full month following for intensive examinations. Grades were issued on a 100-point scale. Scores under 59 received a 'Disapproval', a category that meant suspension was imminent. A score between 60 and 70 earned 'Approval', while 70–79 meant 'Good' and 80–89 was rated 'Very Good'. Anything over 90 meant *Sobresaliente*, 'Superb' or 'Excellent'. Regulations detailed the total number of hours of chemistry, mathematics, natural history, Cuban history, civics and psychology necessary to graduate.

The patriotic urge peaked the next year, when the New Constitution came into effect. A consuming issue of Cuban politics for several years, the New Constitution, promulgated in 1940, gave Cuba one of the most liberal and idealistic political systems in the world. They studied its terms in civics class at Dolores the next year, where the boys were instructed in the details. On paper, Cuba was now a broadly enfranchised democracy, with an array of civil, religious, and economic freedoms enshrined in law, and an explicit government mandate to create social justice. Society was to be remade, especially in schooling, where the New Constitution demanded: 'All education, public and private, shall be inspired by a spirit of Cubanism and national unity, tending to form in the hearts of students a love for the country, its democratic institutions, and all those who fought for both'.

That meant specific lessons blaming the US for many of Cuba's problems and, more awkwardly for Dolores, lessons that blamed the Catholic Church for supporting the Spanish side in the War of Independence. The New Constitution also altered not just what was taught, but who could teach it: 'In all teaching centers, public or private, the teaching of the literature, history, and geography of Cuba, as well as of civics and the Constitution must be done by teachers who are Cubans by birth and with textbooks by authors that have that same character.' Since almost all the teachers at Dolores were Spaniards, that meant new Cuban instructors, and new Cuban textbooks, to go along with the new lessons. A Spaniard couldn't even teach geography now.

There was a far graver problem: the new curriculum also mandated an expansion of high school to include a fifth year. Dolores, already straining at the seams with over 200 students, and scrambling to accommodate new staff and lessons, was unable to absorb an entire new grade. Not only would the boys have to endure an extra year of high school, they would have to do it somewhere else. For Lundy, Fidel, and part of each class, that meant Belén in Havana, the largest Jesuit school. Dolores students saw Belén as a rival; now they would be boarding students there, submerged in a far bigger student body, amid a city and people they didn't know. Even their diplomas would come from Belén, as if Dolores had disappeared. It soon would.

THE NEW CONSTITUTION OF 1940 was the result of a broad public push to oust the squalid and transparent Batista.

Finally, abandoned even by the United States, he agreed to step down, and in 1942, Carlos Prío won what many consider to be the cleanest elections in Cuban history. The elections, and the marvellous constitution with its noble claims, were the high-water mark for democracy in Cuba, and the boys at Dolores were raised in an era of revolution and hope. When they recalled the ideal Cuba, this was it, the early 1940s, the old Republic, a time before time.

There was hope and stability in that exciting time, but what impresses us more than our own adolescence? Cuba was still deeply broken, perhaps more so with such open ideals. The prosperity, the rebirth of democracy, seemed wonderful, but in crucial ways the new democracy of 1940 was weightless, a shell. Society was too divided, the reality of Cuban politics too hypocritical. The lofty goals were in the hands of democratic institutions – political parties, legislature, press, judiciary and the police – rotted by corruption. With Batista in retirement, little changed in practice. Cuba was hemmed in by its homegrown culture of *amiguismo*, or economic and political 'friendships'. Connections opened all doors, and patronage and favouritism determined success. *Amiguismo* generated enormous cynicism in Cuban society. Advancement depended on who you knew. Position was more important than profession. By squeezing power and decisions through the hands of a few, *amiguismo* choked the economic and political air out of Cuba. It was an inheritance of the corrupt Spanish colonial system, but thoroughly Cuban as well, and would never disappear, even under the coming Revolution.

American companies in Cuba promised a change from that, a way of life built on equality, open dealing and fairness. One hundred and fifty thousand Cubans worked directly for American companies around the island. These people often adopted American educational practices, cultural values, styles of dress, and even names. (In Banes, the capital town of the sugar region where the Castro family socialized, common names for Cuban children included Tony, Betty, Nelly, Mike and Walter.) Cubans were becoming more and more American on the outside, but an

aspiring middle class quickly discovered that acting American did
not translate into real equality. Americans kept the best jobs for
themselves. Even when Cubans rose up to equal footing with
Americans, they often found the foreigners were getting paid
more for doing the same job. Cuban professionals rarely rose
above the status of clerks, even when they were more qualified
than their US superiors. And Americans, along with other
foreigners and the richest Cubans, lived literally and metaphori-
cally apart from the mass of islanders, screened behind walls, air-
conditioned, and shielded from accountability.

Americans didn't come to Cuba for equality. First there was
political dominion, then the economic advantage. And always,
there was the social opportunity. For tourist or expatriate, Cuba
was an escape from whatever social strictures and mores governed back home. Decade after decade, in tourism advertising,
Hollywood films or Irving Berlin songs, the island was portrayed
as a land of sensual adventures, a place to indulge forbidden
urges without limit or care. The reality for visitors and expats –
endless rounds of boozing, some mob-run gambling, and dis-
count sex – was hidden behind 1940s silence and euphemism,
but everyone knew what was really happening. Hemingway
was rude enough to write it down. What foreigners wanted
from Cuba, one of his characters confessed, was 'cheap whores
who can fuck'.

The dollar was like a diplomatic passport. An American in
Cuba could get away with almost anything. That knowledge
crept from the drunken streets at midnight into the hot noon,
where Cubans and Americans, in their business and their personal
relations, looked at each other across a gulf.

Cynicism and hypocrisy were the adders in this garden. Bribery
and violence controlled politics. Although it was popular to
blame Americans for the crushing failure of promise in the
1940s, the rot was Cuban. The promise of the 1930s and
1940s evaporated, slowly, without notice. In 1952, the old tyrant,
Fulgencio Batista, suddenly attempted a coup. Cubans would not
fight for a democracy that was fraudulent and weightless, not even
President Prío, who departed quietly.

IN HUNDREDS OF SCHOOLS IN DOZENS OF COUN-
TRIES, the Jesuits taught to the same standard. In the 1940s
and 1950s, the student in one place knew that his comrades in
another were undergoing a virtually identical curriculum of
academic and spiritual challenges. Jerry Brown, a graduate of a
Jesuit school in California, had gone on to be the governor of
California, where he had gained some insight into the way
Jesuit values affected the lives of political men, whether Cuban
or American. Brown was still in politics, serving as the Mayor of
Oakland, California, when he told me about the Jesuits and his
own history with Castro. Oakland, on San Francisco bay, was
one of the only places in America where a politician gained
votes by posing for a photograph with Castro. Brown declared
Oakland a sister city to Santiago de Cuba and began shipping
relief packages of medicine and supplies to Cuba. He flew to
Cuba himself and met with Castro for four hours. As usual,
Fidel said nothing about his own background or education, but
in their discussion of global affairs, Brown saw that the Jesuits
'certainly had an impact' on shaping Castro's mind. The Jesuits
taught their students 'to bring change in the world. The
Ignatian thing is to win the world for Christ.'

Brown described the religious ideology of the time. 'This was
before Vatican II,' he said. 'There was only one model of Catholic
education. The model that was around for 400 years. The
emphasis was on willpower, subduing the passions, getting a
broad historical framework, and an integrated view of the world.
This was not the age of postmodernism. This was the age of
structure, of the Catholic story, of God's will, of the emphasis on
nonmaterial values.' Castro 'was trained to look at material
possessions with a certain jaundiced eye. He would not be
troubled, or as troubled as folks in the developed world are,
by the lack of material success and possessions in socialist Cuba.'

Brown described the frequent workshops and retreats that all
students of the Jesuits underwent. The children were expected to
build a communal spirit together, by living collectively, separated
from regular society, day after day. At Dolores, these retreats were
held in a Santiago mansion, or at La Fortaleza, an imposing hilltop

house on the far side of the bay. At all these multi-day events, Brown explained, the students were governed by a monastic schedule of early rising, reading, quiet study, discussion groups, and then testing on the *Ignatian Exercises*, a book of catechistic questions and answers about the Church. At night, during the retreats, the students would read pages from a book called *Rules for Thinking with the Church*. This was a guide to keeping your mind disciplined, turned toward the work of God. The method it advocated was straightforward: total and unquestioning acceptance of the teachings of the Church, no matter what. Complete unity with the institution. The Jesuit brother was to be as dead to his own desires as a corpse, Loyola famously declared.

'The Church sets a certain line, and a certain dogma,' Brown said, 'and you have to go along with it.' Paraphrasing Loyola himself, he added: 'If the wall looks white, but the Universal Church says it is black, you see it as black, and you say it is black, and you believe it is black.' This absolute loyalty was echoed in the Communist Party, Brown noted, with its regimented cadres, its insistence on uniformity of thought, and its need for total compliance.

The most crucial of all the Jesuit retreats, Brown said, was 'The Meditation on the Two Standards', a climactic three-day session where older students were confronted with a stark choice. The 'Two Standards' referred to battle standards. These were the flags of war carried by two armies, the followers of Christ on the one hand, and the legions of Hell on the other.

Brown pointed out however that Castro had violated some crucial Jesuit values in his great crusade. Despite their reputation for conspiracies and love of power, the Jesuits 'are on one level a humanist organization', Brown noted. 'Castro could take a lesson from that.' And when Castro struck out to overthrow the Batista government, and then overthrow the society that had created it, he may have been acting from a Jesuit urge for reform and justice, but he was taking it in the wrong direction. The Jesuits taught personal, not political, revolution, Brown explained. 'The whole idea of revolution comes from a Christian idea of reform . . . but with the reformation of the soul. It's a reformation within your life.' Under Castro, 'that idea got extended outward to all of society, which was not the Jesuits' idea, and not Jesus' idea, and not St Paul's idea either. They were talking about a personal, individual reformation. So the idea that revolution is played out, not against the individual soul, but in society, is not the Christian idea at all.'

'The Jesuit thing is the next world,' Brown said. 'Castro is the essence of this world.'

ACCORDING TO A DOLORES YEARBOOK, the truly modern education rested on the moral lessons of Catholicism and on this broad curriculum of advanced academic studies, especially a frank acceptance of the principal scientific methods of measuring, comprehending and interpreting the world around us. But the 'complete intellectual formation' of the students depended not just on the 'splendid laboratories' for chemistry and biology classes, but also the other activities that Loyola believed could be used to glorify God. These included a scientifically based regimen of sports, gymnastics classes, arts and music programmes, and 'excursions to the mountains'.

There were plenty of mountains to choose from. The Jesuits believed in the virtues of strenuous hiking, and there were regular trips from Dolores all throughout the Sierra Maestra, intended to train more than the body. Hikes were an extension of botany and biology lessons, opportunities to collect butterflies and birds for the school's small museum on the second floor. Something as simple as a fern could be a tool of learning. It wasn't enough to say that a fern was a fern. Look at two plants by the path, the Jesuits would ask: how were they similar, and different, and why? Colour? Structure? Fruits and flowers? What did minute inspection with the eyes, ears and fingers reveal? What about soil type, and the advantages of rainfall?

It was like that later, when the students were taken hiking along the fortifications on San Juan hill. This was the spot, just outside Santiago, where the Americans had fought a sharp engagement with the Spaniards in 1898. The Rough Riders had taken one hill, but the Americans had been repulsed in other places along the line. Pointing to one such spot, Fidel said, 'This is where we defeated the Americans.'

'What do you mean we?' Lundy replied, mystified. 'The *gallegos* did it.'

For most Cubans, the enemy in that battle was the Spanish army, the imperial power occupying the island. 'We' would refer to our side, the Cubans, and those fighting with us. Cuban rebels and American troops were battlefield allies. But Fidel saw it the other way around. The Americans coming up the hill were the villains, not the Spaniards defending it.

Either he was being true to his father's service in the Spanish army, or he was already focused on the future, on a larger conflict. It was the Americans who dominated the sugar business in Banes, the agricultural capital of Oriente. It was Americans who dominated Cuba. It was Americans who dominated Latin America. It was no different at movie night. Instinctively, at the root of his being, Fidel sided with the Indians. Anyone who confronted that enemy, who opposed the American colonizers, whether in the past, present, or future, was heroic.

On hikes, Fidel liked to be first up the trail. Second tallest in his class, barrel-chested, he had discovered the joy of being good at baseball and basketball, of physical power and skill, of victory. Fidel had arrived at Dolores already tough, with the body of a farm boy, and day hikes and longer camping excursions became part of his training regimen. He volunteered for every hike, and became an organizer of them, carrying the Dolores pennant up the slopes of Mount Turkino, at 6,500 feet the biggest peak in Cuba, with a long line of students and brothers stretched out behind him. Month after month, year after year, the Jesuits showed him the secondary peaks that ran along the entire east coast of Cuba, and the main towns and smallest villages through the mountains. They hiked trails to the most remote sections of the range and saw, hidden throughout the most obscure corners, the mountain people, the poor and the crushed, the black, brown and white peasants who scratched yucca from tiny plots, or tended someone else's pigs. These people lived almost within sight of Santiago but it was another Cuba, a place where illiterate and impoverished people lived in fear of the local landlords, the rent collectors, and the corrupt police and army who backed them up.

Ignatius Loyola believed that a student's task was to stand before another reality, something completely new, alien, or unrecognizable, and, centring his attention, begin to study, comprehend, judge and come to conclusions. The worst mistake was to refuse to look carefully, to deny yourself that comprehension. A Dolores student couldn't help but study these two utterly different Cubas, each destined to torture the other. When the hikes ended at a trail head, with a ride back into Santiago, and up through the Parque Céspedes, toward school again, was it possible to ignore the differences? Or was it necessary to see them reconciled?

After the San Juan hill hike, Lundy and Fidel began to spend less time together. Lundy found him hard to like: Fidel was showy, a big talker, always promising big stunts. Their intimacy had lasted only months, just some film nights and walks in the hills. But they would orbit the same institutions for decades to come. As students at the same university, they would come to opposite conclusions on the role of violence in politics. They could not even agree on the lessons of Cuban history, or which side was defending the future in the Cold War. Eventually, a single piece of newsprint – mere words – would separate them for good.

AT THE RELATIVELY EARLY HOUR OF 11.15 AM the boys laid down their pencils for the midday break, a full two hours off. It was traditional in Cuba, and particularly in hot Santiago, to take these long lunches. The city boys – all those who had walked to school – were allowed to set out again, heading home for their meal. The *internos* remained behind, with a group of half-board students, making a colony of more than 40 kids. They put away their books and reported to the long, high-ceilinged dining room before noon. They gathered at tables, this time sorted not by class and Division, but by age and affinity, choosing their own seats and alliances. José Antonio Cubeñas, Ceferino Catá, and Joaquín Herrera usually sat together.

A lifetime later, Dolores alumni recalled the lunch menu in all its numbing routine: fried eggs, rice and plantains, sometimes with potatoes or beans, and always with strong coffee laced with milk and sugar, even for the youngest boys. (Sick boys were sometimes given a popular commercial 'tonic' that basically consisted of vitamins in red wine.) There was no meat on Friday, but there also was no meat on most other days. The cooking was the main reason that almost 200 of the boys at Dolores went home for lunch every day.

After the meal there came the long recess that was often the high point of the day for the understimulated *internos*, who now had the extra companions they would miss so badly at night. They had, depending on the day, one hour or 90 minutes. Recess could mean almost anything: games, naps, study, long chats with the brothers, reading comic books, even brief walks outside the building. The Jesuits tried not to structure the break, but they were mostly Spaniards, and had a European obsession with soccer. They often tossed out a soccer ball at recess, with subtle or not so subtle encouragement to organize games. But left to their own devices, the boys organized scratch games of basketball, or baseball. The latter was really stickball, a game built for small dimensions and obstacles, easy to play in the street, a patio, or even inside a room.

Once day when the lower patio was occupied, Fidel organized a recess game of stickball atop the *aljibe*, the cistern, or water tank, whose strong cement cover formed the small upper platform of the patio. Santiago had long dry spells in the summer, and neighbours were allowed to draw from the reservoir inside. The boys could stand, run and play safely atop the *aljibe*, so they assigned home plate to the foot of a small spiral staircase leading up to the second floor, with first, second and third distributed around the walls. They had a real baseball bat, but used a *fufa*, a 'ball' made of bottle caps taped together. A *fufa* 'didn't go anywhere when you hit it', Cubeñas recalled later, but flew crazy, ricocheting off the walls and ceiling, and taking unexpected bounces. Cubeñas was one of about 35 boys watching from the railing over the cistern when Castro came to bat. He swung three times, and he missed three times.

Struck out! On a *fufa*! The jeering was instant. Laughter all around.

Castro looked up, and in the same gesture hurled the bat, hard and high. It flew up and struck Alcides Nuñez in the right arm. Somehow the blow dislocated his shoulder. Castro hadn't been aiming at Nuñez specifically – they were friends who had tried to form a volleyball team at Dolores – which only made it worse. As the crying boy was helped to the infirmary by a few students, Cubeñas leaned over the railing.

'Animal!' he taunted Castro, below. 'Beast!'

'Don't mess in what's none of your business,' Castro shot back.

'It is my business,' Cubeñas said. 'We are all together here.'

With everyone watching and waiting, Cubeñas had no idea what to do, so he said, 'Either you come up, or I am coming down.'

To his horror, Fidel began climbing the circular stairs. Castro looked pale, but he came on, his fists clenched.

As soon as he reached the first floor they attacked each other, windmilling punches. Cubeñas threw Fidel down, jumped on top of him, and began fending off Castro's punches with his left while delivering several with his right. When he raised his right arm for another blow the arm would not come down: Father Sánchez, a Basque, was holding it.

'What are you doing!' he bellowed, and dragged Cubeñas back, separating the boys. Fidel stood up. They faced each other, their chests heaving, red-faced with effort, as Sánchez yelled at them. Cubeñas didn't hear the words. The crowd of boys fled, dispersed by the priest, and Fidel and José Antonio both were led off. They were to spend a few hours in the *sala de disciplina*, but Castro managed to get out of the school and ran around the corner to a city bus stop where no one could see him leave.

The volatile and violent man within the boy Castro had been

emerging slowly, always with consequences. As a child at his first small rural school, he had argued with teachers and fled the building when criticized. When he was still not a teenager, Fidel had threatened to burn down his father's house if he wasn't sent to a boarding school. A brief stint with a private tutor – really a foster home – in Santiago had been a disaster, with Fidel, Ramón and Raúl running wild, dirty, unruly, rough and full of coarse country manners and speech. By all accounts, the more toughness and confrontation Fidel showed, the more his father respected and favoured him, and Ángel Castro set a pattern of promoting Fidel out of trouble. First the boys were rewarded with two years at the boarding school run by the Christian Brothers in Santiago, and then Ángel sent them up the hill to Dolores. Fidel had flourished at the school, finally getting the recognition his bright mind deserved, but the fight with Cubeñas, which lasted only seconds, marked a turning point. Soon Fidel would be gone.

At first, there was no change. A few days after the fight, Fidel boldly walked up and sat down at the lunch table where Cubeñas and his friends were eating. Castro sat catty-cornered from José Antonio, completely ignoring him, and began eating. Lunch was the usual fried eggs. The salt was sitting in front of José Antonio. Fidel hadn't asked for it, and wouldn't. Herrera made an exaggerated signal with his eyes, looking from José Antonio to the salt, and then at Fidel.

'Salt,' José Antonio said, reaching across the table with a long, bony arm.

'Thanks,' Fidel said.

That was as much reconciliation as they would ever have. José Antonio believed there was a change after that, not just in his relations with the young Fidel, but in a general queering of the school's atmosphere. It wasn't unknown for boys to fight, but this had been a sharp, fast combat between two of the bigger, most athletic boys at the school. Although inconclusive, the fight had shown one thing nobody at Dolores had ever seen before: Fidel, vulnerable. Fidel, not so much beaten as shown to be beatable. Everyone had seen him knocked down.

At the start of the fall semester, the 1942–43 academic year, Fidel was gone. After five years at Dolores he had transferred to Belén, in Havana. Lots of Dolores boys were headed that way eventually. Lundy Aguilar was one of many who took his new fifth year of high school at Belén. For many Santiago families, the social connections at the larger Jesuit school in the capital were too advantageous to miss. It is easy to see this move as another promotion for the Castro family, Fidel climbing up from rural schoolhouse in Birán, to the Christian Brothers, to Dolores, and now to Belén. But José Antonio thought the real reason Fidel had left was obvious. The thrown bat and subsequent fist fight had made him look simultaneously threatening and weak to other students. He was 'exposed', José Antonio said. Fidel had to see himself, and had to be seen, as the top boy at Dolores. And if he couldn't have that, if the students in the patio saw him on the ground, then he would go somewhere else.

After the fight – in the first days at the lunch table, and in the long years after, at the University of Havana, and on through their twenties, they engaged in a wary dance. José Antonio's family had land, money and connections, and in the 1950s Fidel would approach his old antagonist, feigning affection, asking for things, favours that could not be taken by force. During the war years, it was a steady plea, delivered in letters from the mountains: help me, José Antonio. Help us with money. Help us with information. Send us support. Let us use your farm and your people. Do us this one favour.

But maybe it was really José Antonio who had changed that day, not the atmosphere at the school, or Fidel. Maybe it was José Antonio who saw something to scare him off, something in the way Fidel had come up the circular stairs at the start of that fight, afraid but determined. Something in the way Fidel had gotten back up from the ground as Cubeñas was hauled away by the Basque father.

Fidel kept coming, with fists or friendship. Even a one-time enemy was a potential ally, a person to be won over again, reconverted. Always, year after year, right through the 1940s and 1950s, Fidel kept pressing José Antonio, gently, for support, friendship and the necessities of wartime. And always José Antonio withdrew. He smiled, he spoke nicely, and then he withdrew. To the extent possible, he avoided Castro, especially later. He put off answering Castro's letters, or sent back messengers with warm but vague, and even evasive, replies. He did the minimum, strategically avoiding any more outright ruptures with Fidel, avoiding another fight or confrontation. Fidel was a dangerous combination, a bit of a bully, a bit of a dominator, weak enough to pick on the weak, strong enough to fight when cornered. To be his friend would be even more dangerous than to be his enemy.

What Fidel had learned, on the other hand, was that he could take a beating.

AFTER THE LONG DOUBLE BREAK of lunch and then recess, classes restarted at 1.30. There were just two sessions in the afternoon, often geography and history. Late one hot afternoon in the spring term, the boys in the front of the geography class were listening, still working, but some in the back were forgetting themselves, drifting off or goofing – whispering, passing notes, wasting their whole lives.

The geography teacher got angry. This in itself was memorable. The Jesuits could be cold and arbitrary, but they rarely showed a temper. This one pinched a few ears and let fly with an angry lecture. You boys are just drifting through life, he said. You will amount to nothing. There wasn't one among them, not even the best, who lived up to his potential. They didn't even know how to employ the most powerful of all their senses, he said. Did they even know which sense that was?

The boys waited. José Antonio Cubeñas raised a hand. 'Sight?' he asked.

No. Other boys volunteered. Touch?

No. Taste?

No.

Was it smell? Boys were curling out their fingers now, counting the senses, but the geography instructor only shook his head.

'There is a sixth sense,' the father said. 'The sixth sense is common sense.'

Duh. The boys groaned with disappointment.

Enrique Hechevaria piped up from the back. He stood right next to Fidel in the school photo. Fidel wasn't even in the room, but at this point, after his letter from the White House, and his fights and stunts, he was the best known student at Dolores. 'Padre,' Hechevaria offered, 'you know Fidel has seven senses.'

'Well then he's not using at least two of them,' the priest said.

Bzaam, the bell rang for the end of the day. Cars had been lining up in Clock Street since before 4 pm, and the Dolores bus had ground up the hill, muttering black smoke from a stovepipe exhaust. At 4.15 the doors flew open and more than 200 day boys fled. In the street there was a hot and chaotic unwinding of the day, a mix of fathers, sons, priests, professional drivers, mothers, brothers and layabouts. Dozens of boys herded on to the Dolores bus, a blue and white embarrassment that was painted COLEGIO DE DOLORES over the windows, and across the engine cowling, in case anyone doubted who was inside. The bus ran two miles uphill to Vista Alegre, the new suburb where more and more elite families lived.

Only a few boys travelled by car. Some were scooped up by a dad returning from work, but the wealthiest families dispatched a uniformed driver in a gleaming American car. The most spectacular car usually belonged to the Bacardí family, who seemed to always have at least one boy in Dolores. The very youngest of all the Bacardí boys, Facundo, climbed into the family car in Clock Street one afternoon, but never reached home. Later, the family received a ransom note: Facundo had been kidnapped. The police quickly identified the kidnapper, who turned out to be the most obvious suspect, the chauffeur himself. After a few days, officers hunted down the chauffeur's hiding place, where they freed Facundo and shot the driver dead.

The killing was not untypical of police methods in Santiago at that time. The kidnapping of a child was a heinous crime; the Bacardí clan was powerful and wealthy. Perhaps officers thought they could please and cultivate the Bacardís, but the act backfired. The driver had not resisted arrest; he had simply been shot down in cold blood. Rumours spread that the powerful family had ordered the murder. To clear their name, the Bacardís insisted that the officers be put on trial, but the policemen were acquitted and the incident left a bitter taste in Santiago, leaving the impression that police – and perhaps the wealthy – could get away with killing the lowly. After that, the threat of kidnapping convinced more parents to pick up their own children at school, and the number of cars in Clock Street grew, more people waiting outside the building, jockeying for space, parking and double parking, tooting horns to divide the crowd as Dolores exhaled the last day students, noisily.

The *internos*, of course, stayed right there. There were few escapes for them. Lundy did remember seeing Ángel Castro out front a few times, picking up his three boys at the start or end of a semester, or liberating them for an afternoon during a rare business trip to Santiago.

Ángel was a hick. Birán was tiny; even from Banes, the sugar industry headquarters, the glories of Santiago, the cosmopolitan world of Lundy's parents, the world of a professional class in a busy port city, the life of Enramada and clanging tramcars, of the law courts and social clubs and Cathedral socializing, was infinitely far away.

Banes did have its own claim to fame: it was not just any sugar town, but the very heart of the richest sugar cane belt on the island. Sugar was Cuba: an eighth of Cuba's entire land mass was planted in cane, with more than 400,000 people dependent on the business for direct employment. Sugar accounted for about a quarter of the nation's income, and some 80 per cent of its exports. The crop planted in 1940 would produce a harvest of 2.5 million tons of sugar, a poor harvest by historic standards, but still larger than the 2.2 million tons produced in 2004.

If sugar meant wealth, it also meant Americans. Banes, the social centre to which the Castros aspired, was a largely American town, over half of it built from scratch for the employees of United Fruit, the greatest of all sugar companies. Cubans liked to gawk at this privileged American section, with its queer new houses, set too far back from the street. The Americans looked like ghosts as they moved around in the distance, behind their mosquito screens. They didn't learn Spanish. They created their own social clubs, and met only with the richest, whitest Cubans. But it wasn't easy to gawk at the new side of Banes; the police would chase away any Cubans who loitered in what was called 'America Town'.

Sugar was a good way to get rich. United Fruit controlled huge sections of the countryside all through the region, either directly, through its ownership of hundreds of thousands of acres, or indirectly, through its control of men like Ángel Castro. Ángel got rich off United Fruit, but he didn't start out that way. He was not just a *gallego*, in the Cuban sense, meaning anyone from Spain, but an actual Gallego, a person born in Galicia, the north-west corner of Spain. Wet and achingly poor, green and stony, Galicia is the Ireland of Spain (literally, since Gallegos and the Irish share Celtic culture and even DNA). Galicia produced hard men: in 1941 the new Spanish führer was Francisco Franco, himself a Gallego. (A generation later, Franco, an unrepentant fascist, would admit his admiration for Fidel Castro, simply because he was a tough leader of good Gallego stock.)

Ángel had the hardness of his flinty land. He had come to Cuba as an illiterate mercenary, paid by a wealthy Spaniard to fill his place in the army. A quartermaster in the cavalry, he'd handled supplies, not a weapon. Despite being on the losing, European, side in the Cuban War of Independence, he liked what he saw of the island. This was a big country of rich soil and cheap labour. A man could establish himself. Ángel went back to Spain only long enough to collect a bride. Once married, he emigrated to Cuba, settled in Oriente, in the fields around Birán. Most of the land in this, the heart of the Cuban sugar belt, was controlled by big foreign – that is, American – companies. Ángel started with a small farm he worked himself, but his land was surrounded by the fields of United Fruit. He ingratiated himself with the Americans, and became a labour boss, a supplier of *macheteros* to neighbouring ranches. The *macheteros* followed the harvest from farm to farm under Ángel's direction, as he reaped the benefit of supplying their labour to the truly wealthy. A man like Ángel Castro had to be an enforcer, able to mobilize impoverished men to work in brutal conditions for long hours and criminally low pay. It took a heart of stone, a corrupt soul, and a long whip. The many members of the Castro clan who now live in exile have fought in court about just how bad Ángel really was. Fidel's daughter in Spain has said Ángel was a rapist and murderer, while Fidel's sister in Miami defended Ángel (with a libel suit) as an honest man. But certainly he was a rough man, a provincial, and typical of what was wrong with Cuba. Fidel has described his own father as an 'exploiter'.

Was Fidel himself innocent? When some imported Haitian labourers at the Castro farm went on strike, refusing to cut cane at the pay rate offered, Ángel (and, according to some accounts, the teenage Fidel) rode in among the Haitians on horseback, beating them with the flat of a machete. Ángel Castro supplied more than 10,000 blades (cane cutters) to United Fruit and other big land-owners. The *zafra*, and therefore the economy of Oriente, would come to a halt without him.

Ángel had his own big ranch now – one of the bigger ones in Oriente – and he liked to claim that he had expanded it by going out at night and moving the fence posts of his neighbour, United Fruit. He also claimed to have taken tractors from the company simply by slapping a different colour of paint on them and driving them away. Underneath this amiable front, the jolly forwardness, was a man used to giving orders, tough enough to dominate even those who carried sharp blades every day. He beat his employees, and paid them in coupons redeemable only at his own store. He grew rich in a dirty business.

He'd be waiting by his car in Clock Street on rare afternoons, ignoring the other fathers and chauffeurs. Although barely educated, he was a Spaniard and believed in the inherent superiority of Spaniards, of European culture and people. He approved of the Jesuits on this basis alone, their wool robes and Hapsburg lisps a reminder of home. On the few days that Ángel was there on Clock Street, waiting,

Fidel and his brothers were able to have a bit of escape, an exception to the routine.

But that was a rare day for any *interno*. Far more often, the 22 boarders watched from inside as their classmates dispersed on foot, by car, by bus, in chaos and good cheer, amid clouds of exhaust. By 4.30 almost everyone would be gone. The front doors of the school would swing shut. Before dinner, the unlucky souls in detention would be let out of the *sala de disciplina* and skip off. Most children did homework in the late afternoon, before another dull meal in the now quiet dining room. The tropical night stole in suddenly while they ate. In the dark 22 boys would climb up to their third-floor rooms, the younger students on the left, the older on the right. By 9 pm everything was quiet, but for the hushed sound of the Jesuits, who moved about the building at will, crossing the dark courtyard, or climbing up to the fourth floor. There was a final round of business when, under stern adult eyes, the *internos* had to kneel and pray before getting into bed.

Sometimes the night was enlivened, with a movie, or perhaps a birthday party for one of the boys. The Jesuits would produce a cake, and gather all 22 boys to watch the blowing out of the candles. Then the cake would be divided up into thin slices, an exciting moment for any boy. The used candles would be gathered up and set aside, ready for the next birthday.

3

DAYS OF FIRE

THE PARADE WAS TWO HOURS late, but nobody in Santiago cared. Maybe I was the only person in Santiago to even *notice* that the parade was two hours late. For Cubans, inured to long lines, never-ending delays, and decades without difference, the longer this night took to get started, the better. In ancient Santiago this night was different from all other nights. The first night of Carnaval. The first party of Cuba's week of parties.

In the twenty-first century, an era often called post-Communist, Castro's Cuba was still, among other things, a life sentence to boredom. Numbing routine, endless anomie and empty conformism. The exceptions to this flat lifescape were rare, treasured even more in anticipation than in the event. So the later they started Carnaval the better. The more disorganized the better. It only meant that the party would run later. Communist Party logistics were a tribute to the Lords of Misrule.

There was always time, in Cuba. Time for thousands of ordinary people, black, white, brown, to gather along two designated blocks of a broad avenue, time to have some beer, minutes to flirt, and still more time to wander. Occasionally there was a half hour set of music, somewhere on a back street. Sometimes even by a live band. So people would wait, then dance like crazy for a few songs, and then, when it was over, they would stand patiently, without worry, ready for whatever happened next, whenever it happened. Equanimity is, in Cuba, a survival adaptation.

July in Santiago de Cuba. The hottest time, in the hottest place. Santiago drops down over rolling hills, toward the long, twisted bay where Spanish sailors had found shelter from the winds.

Ringed by volcanoes, the bay was a heatsink, immune to even the faintest Haitian breezes.

Life adapted. Santiago people are famous for walking slowly, which is really saying something for Cubans. It was so brutally infernal during the long July afternoons that no one moved in the city during midday, or worked much at all, or even talked. Walking was swimming, the moist air parting around you. On stepping into one of the city's mercilessly air-conditioned hotels, my sunglasses would frost over. Only at night did the drama of mere existence ease.

Two hours so far, waiting for the parade, and only now, just after 10 pm, was the temperature down to merely hot, not hell itself. It was merely humid, not the ocean of daytime. You only sweated when you moved. The wind, or lack of wind, was maddening. A breeze fluttered for a few minutes, tantalizing, and then shut off. In the stillness hundreds of Cubans began fanning themselves. Then the breeze erupted again, hot and hard, hurling up the dust generated by the growing crowds, rattling plastic bags in the gutters, pushing scraps of paper in circles. Then nothing.

Although I had been to Cuba seven times in the last eight years, this was my first night in Santiago. I had always lingered in the west, in Havana and the tobacco fields of Pinar del Río, or come no further than the central plains, Santa Clara, Trinidad, the Guamán mountains. There had always been nooks to explore – Sancti Spiritus and Matanzas, Varadero and Cienfuegos – long before I could reach Santiago on the miserable buses or the immobilized train system. But somewhere in Santiago there were a few lingering examples of that small minority, the Dolores boys who had never left. And that was enough to put me that very morning on a rusting, oil-dripping Ilyushin–18, a Warsaw Pact-model that first saw service in 1965. The four turboprops stained the tarmac with oil at Havana; as we flew, bumping and bouncing eastward toward Santiago, they trailed smoke. I had taken a room at the only hotel available and had bought a $5 ticket to Carnaval.

Anyone who showed up at Carnaval with a 'ten dollars bill green American' was assured of two seats in a bleacher reserved for hard-currency customers. The result was that the white bleacher, elevated on a platform and looking right into the maw of the arc-lit asphalt that would be parade central, was filled with foreigners only. (The exception was a pleased Cuban TV crew who were allotted free seats and also drink tickets.) In the bleacher there was a very excited French couple on my left, and some German photography enthusiasts beyond them. Then on my right I had Sócrates, a retired diplomat from Mexico, with a friend from home, José. Both of the Mexicans were in their sixties, but they were feeble old men, liver-spotted, wrinkled, almost trembling. Like most people at Carnaval they were already drunk. Sócrates sat in his chair, twisted around backwards, his face searching vainly for the waiter who would fetch us cold drinks.

'Five dollars is a good price,' Sócrates said in English. He'd been stationed at the embassy in Washington for some years, and spoke like an honorary American. For $5 we each got a lawn chair, packed immovably tight against those to right and left in a row of 40. Because the waiter was so slow, Sócrates recommended that, like him, I should order two daiquiris at once, enough to tide us over.

Right across the avenue was another bleacher, entirely for Cubans. But that bleacher – the only other set of seats for the whole of Santiago on the first night of Carnaval – had been filling up, over the last two hours, with very important comrades. It was the bleacher for the Carnaval judges, but there were also Carnaval officials, and non-Carnaval officials, and families and friends, and *maimbe*, the high-ranking civilians, in an invisible system of patronage. Except for the 200 there, all Cubans – thousands already, the crowd growing steadily – were standing, a long and deep line of the public at large, running up both sides of the next long block, and contained behind tall hurricane fencing.

Even I knew that the parade would run behind schedule. I had arrived half an hour after the announced start and had still been among the first to claim a seat. From the front row, I'd been staring up the four broad lanes of the Avenida Victoriano Garzón for two hours, expecting a parade the whole time. The bleacher filled in, parade marshals stood around frowning, the strong TV lights, hung from cranes overhead, came on, and the crowd grew, thousands and then thousands more.

The overwhelmed waiter finally pushed down our row. Sócrates, José, and I ordered a pair of daiquiris each. The breeze blew steadily for a few happy minutes, and I discovered that if I remained perfectly still, I could feel my face drying, then my arms, and eventually even my shirt. But the wind died, and seconds later beads of sweat were running down my back.

Two and a half hours. If I was going to sweat even without moving, then why not move? 'I'm going to find the parade,' I told Sócrates. I gave him money. 'Keep my drinks for me.'

'A very good idea to go for a walk,' he said, making no effort to rise, and then mimed stashing two daiquiris under my chair.

I slid under the railing and dropped five feet down to the asphalt of the Avenida. A parade marshal glared but did nothing more, so watched by thousands of pairs of eyes I marched up the middle of the avenue, alone, toward the city centre. The parade had to be out there somewhere.

Pressed up against the hurricane fencing were children, a first short row of expectant faces, and behind them, in second and third rows, were their parents, their relatives and neighbours, faces blank. The only excitement was further back, where hundreds of teenagers milled about on the dirt lawns of several grey prefab apartment blocks. The kids in their faded American T-shirts of hip-hop stars and basketball heroes were shuffling and dodging around in flip-flops, an ambling juvenile version of the old Spanish *paseo*, hundreds of kids circling back and forth, talking, looking, posing, circling again. People dressed for the heat, in either short skirts or shorts, and the girls in the briefest of shirts, with many boys in none at all.

During Carnaval the state opened its taps, and beer flowed out. Most adults were carrying the evening's chief accessory, a plastic kitchen jug. Translucent, worn from everyday use on the table, these cheap pitchers in faded yellow, tepid green and dull blue had two uses. When they were full, you could drink for an hour. And when they were empty, you could turn them over and beat out applause, or rhythm. A profane plastic *batá* drum.

A short tanker truck, which looked like it would normally carry pesticide or soup, came grinding up the avenue, passed me, and stopped at a row of palm-thatched stalls, where it decanted hundreds of gallons of beer through a fat green hose.

According to a map in the paper, the parade would start in the city centre, and the theoretical dancers, floats and musicians would climb up the old Enramada Street, juke their way through the Plaza of Martyrs, and then come marching up the wide Victoriano Garzón toward us. Three intersections along the route, each about a kilometre apart, had been closed off with steel railings, and converted into plazas where people could gather to watch. After ten minutes of walking through empty blocks, I reached the first of these cutouts, which had a stage and a big set of speakers. A band had just finished playing. The whole space was ringed with vendors, all using identical little wooden carts to sell food that I had never seen in Cuba before: cookies, roast corn, fried and sugared *churros*, popcorn and roast pork sandwiches.

The beer was bad, and warm, but it cost 12 cents a litre. And they charged by the litre: everyone in line had that plastic jug filled, precisely. Other one-man kiosks were selling *aguardiente*, the rough firewater that is a precursor to rum, distilled only once. Clear, cheap, and dangerous, it was sold by the shot in paper cones. Everyone nipped it straight down; no sense waiting for the unwaxed paper to soak through. Many people had been drinking since morning, and some were already sitting on the kerb, cross-eyed and painless.

The shortest line, with only five people in it, was at the booth selling genuine rum in genuine plastic cups. The kiosk was a little stand, three feet wide and two deep. Three men were fitted into this space, nervously measuring out exact shots into the cups.

It was awkward in another language: *How much does it go?*

He held up four fingers.

I counted out $4 and handed it over. He stood still for a moment, eyeing me, and holding the money. Then he conferred

with the other two men, an encrypted exchange of whispers.
They all nodded, and he handed me the bottle.

Four dollars *a bottle*. They laughed when they saw this notion
dawning on my face, but they took the bottle back with good
grace, and returned my four dollar bills, and then accepted instead
an American quarter, which was the price of one shot. They gave
me a generous, unmeasured pour, real rum, double-distilled, oily
with potential.

Carnaval is a time of reversals, of masques and deceptions, of
master and servant trading places. Even the Cuban government
throws off restraints here. Beer was gushing; there was all the clear
liquor you could drink, and cheap; and salted in among the
alcohol vendors were a dozen one-man kiosks selling pork
sandwiches. The sandwiches were tiny, but at less than 50 cents
apiece the hardworking vendors couldn't make them fast enough,
their hands glistening with fat as they sliced at a golden pig,
layering slivers of grey meat, quivering white fat, and crisp skin on
to buns. It was a terrible sandwich, unless you'd just had a big shot
of rum.

Here in the plaza were two things completely uncharacteristic
of Cuba: calories, and enterprise. Only 2 or 3 per cent of Cubans
are self-employed, or 'self-accounting' in Marxist parlance. In
the lean times of the early 1990s the government had allowed a
few people to open tiny, one-person businesses like these
sandwich carts. As long as you hired no one else, it became
legal to be a language tutor, a dog trainer, a flat-tyre repairman,
or a carpenter. These people, paid at market rates, were soon
making more per month that the 97 per cent of Cubans who
remained state-employed. Even this was restricted to 118 jobs,
most of them menial and tightly licensed. The self-accounting
are a threat to a system built on mass control. *Granma* denounced
the self-employed as 'piranhas' and Fidel Castro was particularly
irritated by the few private restaurants that operated in people's
homes, vowing to shut them down several times. When he
grumbled during a six-hour speech that there was too much
'wimpiness' in Cuba, his aides knew just what to do: tax
inspections and harassment shut some restaurants, and the labour

ministry banned magicians, masseurs and jewellery makers. The sandwich men have their assistants – usually a wife – hidden behind a wall, for fear of being classed as an employee.

Santiago has been destroyed by earthquakes many times, so it doesn't look as old as it should. The low houses are unlit, struggling to stay upright, full of makeshift rooms and improvised electrical systems, the walls daubed with faded and irrelevant slogans celebrating forgotten heroes. The small 1930s office buildings are what passes for modern in Santiago, except for the rare and titanic state buildings, like a hulking sports complex visible off in the western darkness, an immense modernist box, lifeless, imposing, the front lawn spiked with a piece of Socialist Realist art like a tank trap. Here on the avenue the only sign of life was a single shop, still lit up hours after closing. It was a dollar store and, despite the protests of a security guard, a crowd of women pressed against the glass, pining for the frozen meat, cold beer, baby clothes, kitchen appliances and shampoo inside.

The avenue topped out at the Plaza of Martyrs, which was dark and quiet, but ringed with people, sitting patiently, fanning themselves. There was no music. People told me they hadn't seen or heard the parade, but they weren't concerned either way.

I could see down the steep hill into the city centre. Enramada ran down by El Ten Cent, past the old hotels, past the Parque Dolores and the radio station where Fidel made his first address to the nation, down past the old, dark movie theatre, and the new Communist Party headquarters. Eventually it dropped past the Bacardí factory, its red brick arches now stripped of the bat medallions seen on bottles from around the world. Here Enramada expired on the waterfront flats, a wasteland of rail tracks and crumbling customs houses, where wet rats scurried through the miasma.

I didn't go down. The one business operating on the plaza was selling cold drinks. It was a filthy state shop with a staff of 12 young men in white paper caps. One fed sugar cane into a hand mill; one turned the mill; a third caught the juice; a fourth poured it into cups; a fifth carved ice, which a sixth put into the cups, while a seventh rang it up, and an eighth served it. The other four watched.

America! they shouted, when they found out where I was from. America! The magic land.

As I walked through the Plaza of Martyrs, girls approached with the usual offers. *Don't you want a friend, handsome?*

Or, *Are you lonely?*

Or just, *I want to make love to you tonight.*

Where are you from? they called out. *Take me with you, my love.*

As I finished the last sip of my sugar cane juice I heard a distant crash of drums, followed by the blaring of horns. It was coming from back up at the top of the Victoriano Garzón. Somehow the parade had gotten around behind me.

For a dollar, a pedicab driver huffed, puffed and sweated his way up the hill, and he dropped me off just in time for Sócrates to hand me two cold daiquiris. The first drummers, formed into a rectangle, came banging their way into the light.

ELEGGUA WAS IN THE HOUSE. The Santería god of destiny, wearing red and black, inaugurated the evening by marching down the avenue, waving a sceptre and greeting the crowd, before passing beneath our raised bleacher, the swaying fringes of his jester's cap almost brushing my big toe.

The parade was erupting out of a side street. Apparently there hadn't been enough fuel to drive the floats up through the whole city, neighbourhood by neighbourhood, as traditional. So they had assembled near the finish and were only going to cover the last two blocks of the official route. Hundreds of marchers came hurrying out of the staging area around a corner, formed up in ranks, and then, with a blast of a whistle, the first 'school' had suddenly picked up its feet and begun marching. Their drum corps, sounding a plain walking rhythm, included dozens of snare, base and conga drums, along with the improvised drums that were the signature of the Santiago Carnaval. My favourite was a dozen young men, all shirtless, who banged in perfect rhythm on brake cylinders, rusted old Ford and Buick parts. Struck with a metal rod, the brake cylinders gave a high pinging back beat to the looming madness. There were no introductions, explanations, or declarations. It just happened, all at once.

Each school represented a neighbourhood or an organism, the latter meaning a workplace, school, or association of some kind. The first school had about a hundred marchers. On reaching the arc-lit section of the roadway, the drum corps broke into a new routine, and the marchers took up a new step, the distinctive, three-forward-and-one-to-the-side manoeuvre that Desi Arnaz, with a conga tucked under his arm, had converted into a nightclub phenomenon. As the school passed through the first block, people on the hurricane fences took up the beat on their plastic jugs, but this was all anticipation: at the entrance to our block the school came to a new halt, gathered its momentum, and then, with a burst from a whistle, exploded at a run into the final block. Sócrates shouted his approval, and the French couple took a picture.

There must have been some pattern or purpose to what followed, but that theory eluded me. A dozen men, women, boys and girls – divided into those groups – broke in every direction at once, making spiralling lines and curving patterns, screaming, leaping, spinning and dodging, turning back on themselves, and all the while, in the middle of this chaos, came inexplicable sights. A pair of abominable snowmen, in outfits made entirely of white chicken feathers, skipping. Someone dressed as a giant sea horse. A group of ancient women, with canes and thick glasses, dressed entirely in white but for their richly coloured necklaces, who ambled through the careening formations as though heading to the corner store, not even looking up from their gossip. Groups of girls in track suits, doing karate. A man – apparently it was a man – inside a suit made entirely of old paint cans, scores of them, so that he waddled along clanging and banging. And Eleggua, wandering freely, waving his sceptre, always the first presence, always unimportant in himself. Eleggua initiates any ceremony involving rituals of Santería, not because he is great – he is a little god – but because he is an intermediary, a cross between Mercury the Messenger and an Apache trickster, stirring up trouble as he meddles in human affairs. As the 'opener of doors', his interventions determine your destiny in life, but he is unreliable. He has been known to forget

his missions, to get drunk and fall asleep, or to spend the evening
flitting about in the form of an owl, looking for innocent girls to
impregnate.

In this religion of the powerless, the great deity and supreme
creator is Olofi, who long ago lost interest in this puny world,
leaving it in charge of his successor, the white-clad Obatalá, the
embodiment of truth, justice, wisdom and peace (although he has
been known to share Eleggua's liquor, with disastrous consequences). But even he is removed from human affairs; the real
orishas, or deities, who control life are the thundering brothers,
Changó, the lord of fire, war, drums and virility, and Oggún, the
patron of blacksmiths. And to reach these and any other figures,
like the crucial Ifa, the lord of divination, it is Eleggua who must
be summoned first, with drums. Eleggua is a trickster and lord of
pranks, a lover of fun, and a shape-shifter who is almost impossible
to define. All Santería gods are made of overlapping, even
contradictory identities, but Eleggua is the most slippery, a fool's
fool, who sometimes appears to be a black man from one side and
a white man from other, so that no one can see him clearly.
Deception is part of Santería: Eleggua is male but really female,
powerful but weak, crucial but frustrating, with always another
layer of truth hidden from all but initiates.

Eleggua is Cuban, but of direct African descent. Yorubas in
eastern Nigeria worshipped Legua (or Legba), a guardian of the
crossroads, the place where wrong turns change fate, and
the traveller could encounter strangers, foreigners, enemies,
even the devil in disguise. Unlike in the United States, the
slave-owners of Cuba made little effort to suppress African culture
and language, and imperfect knowledge of the old gods survived,
generation after generation. Slavery did break the recitation of
family lineages that stood at the centre of Yoruba faith, and the
strong priestly caste was supplanted in the New World by
decentralized 'societies', groups of believers from one plantation
or town. In Africa, possession by an *orisha* was rare, even for high
priests; in Cuba anyone could fall into a trance, or *éré*, even at a
birthday party. Legua of Nigeria became, with the corruption of
time, Eleggua of Cuba, the keeper of the crossroads now

associated with doorways. And, in league with the official Catholic imagery that served as Santería's covering, he took on the outer identity of the Child of Prague. Cubans seek from Eleggua what we all seek: safe passage, and fateful choice.

With his blessings in place, the pace increased. The stylized chaos of the first school gave way to a new rival, another hundred people dancing in ecstatic energy down the full width of the avenue. In front of the judges they expanded into the patterns of an American marching band, but with better dancing. The costumes were better, too: men in broad buccaneer hats and shimmering shirts, Carnaval queens in long yellow gowns trailed by attendants, a King waving kindly from beneath the parasol – a plastic beach umbrella – that was his symbol of office, and attended by a whole Royal Family of ecstatic boys and girls. More boys banging more drum sticks on the brake cylinders of more old Chevies. At another point a school of 'Jamaicans' came through, who were of course Cubans from the waterfront, where Jamaican immigrants had settled generations ago. The female Jamaicans flipped their skirt hems; the men wore straw planter hats and had billowing, ruffled sleeves, and they all came down the avenue doing the limbo, and singing in English as best they could, *leembo leembo la, leembo leembo la, da musi gaw may yew leembo, leembo leembo la.*

The main difference among the schools seemed to be their colour schemes, the next one favouring solar yellows and the one after dotted mostly with hot pink, and the following one white. Everyone was slathered in sequins, dancing wildly, and some women had their hats piled high with Carmen Miranda-sized piles of plastic fruit. A glowing girl came forward to be presented to the judges, four attendants helping spread out her velvet cape, decorated with sequins that showed Uncle Sam, running for his life as a locomotive labelled THE REVOLUTION RETURNS bore down on him.

Men in tin-foil helmets. Cowboys. Break dancers. African tribesmen. On and on, for three hours, the women gyrating their hips, the men leaping and banging. Capes, banners, more dancers. There were big papier-mâché heads, called *mamaroches*. The *mamaroches* were traditionally caricatures of Santiago's leading citizens, and inside the giant heads the anonymous marchers would belt out ribald songs about the powerful. Tonight there was nothing more risqué than animals and space aliens, painted emerald and turquoise, and seven poorly made dwarves who looked vaguely familiar.

Passion makes the powerful nervous. Carnaval was banned by the Spanish government of Cuba in 1669, but it proved irrepressible and was re-legalized in 1743. The authorities put the *mamaroches* on a government payroll in order to control them, but it didn't work, and in 1815 a decree banned Carnaval once more, citing the moral and physical damage caused by the mixing of classes, and parade-goers who 'take the liberty of insulting anybody with indecent songs and offensive sayings'. Carnaval was revived again decades later, but still feared by the government as a time when slaves, using the chaos of the festival, could escape. Later it was said that anti-Spanish rebels, hidden behind Carnaval masks, were moving freely, passing messages, and even launching attacks. This was exactly what Fidel Castro did, timing his first attack on Batista for the dawn following this Carnaval's first night.

Well after midnight, in a kind of finale, the floats appeared. These were huge contraptions of lights, glitter and dancing girls, pulled along by old Soviet tractors. The tractors were themselves disguised under wide skirts of fabric, so that the driver's head and the exhaust pipe were the only things visible above a slowly moving box. Each float vied to be more outlandish than the last, and the biggest was the green and silver one from Cristal, Cuba's favourite beer, which was covered with dancing girls dressed in no more than a dozen rhinestones each. They gyrated on platforms, furiously jiggling their butt cheeks at the judges, their green, blue and silver feather headdresses swaying wildly.

Social control was still on the agenda. In the usual management-by-shortage, it was the government that doled out cloth, sequins, tin-foil, tractors, generators, fuel and permits. Where once private beer companies had sponsored floats, now government beer companies sponsored the floats. Where Spanish officials once tried to control the lyrics, now the block committees vetted all routines, ruling out caricatures, silencing the *mamaroches*.

Same dog, the Cubans say, new collar.

WHEN I HEADED HOME at 3 AM, the crowds were thronging in the avenues, people drunk enough to need no music for dancing. Children wove wildly through the night, the beer wagons and pork carts still doing a brisk business. Two men staggered into each other accidentally and fell into a hopeless, inept fist fight, unable to even see what they were swinging at. A man lay on top of a woman in the bushes, groping her as she pleaded. I overtook a slow-moving Cuban couple just as the woman, in high heels, hunched down in the gutter, pulled up her tube dress, and let loose a heavy stream of urine. 'Don't look!' she shouted.

At my hotel, a tall red and grey monstrosity that was about five minutes old, a Toyota taxi was just pulling away. It stopped suddenly, backed up, and the window on my side came down.

'Patricio!' Sócrates shouted. He was sitting in the back seat, with a girl on each side of him. José was up front. Sócrates leaned out the window. 'Where are you going my friend? The party is just getting started!'

I demurred, but he wouldn't hear of it. 'Come with us,' he insisted. 'Alina here will move over'.

'A-*lyyyy*s-sa,' she said, and slapped him on the back of the head.

That wasn't my last obstacle. The doorman, wearing the long wool coat and top hat of an English footman, was astonished to see me alone.

'Sir,' he said, in a confidential tone. 'Don't you need a *chica*?'

THE ATTACK CAME TWO HOURS LATER, long before the blue-black dawn, as I lay asleep, twisting and trembling against the arctic chill of the hotel's centralized air-conditioning. The assault had been carefully timed for 5 am, the hangover moment.

The insurgents broke from cover and rushed at the Moncada garrison en masse, shouting *Long live the Revolution!*, or so the newspaper said. The news media, the only defenders of the barracks this time, were a little sleepy, and fired back only with their camera flashes before gently surrendering.

Fifty years to the day after the original 26th of July assault in 1953, the attackers were dewy Cuban boy scouts, Young Pioneers in their short pants and red kerchiefs. The Moncada barracks was exactly the same – the battle damage from 1953 had been repaired by Batista, and then painstakingly recreated by Castro, down to redrilling each bullet hole – but the targets this time were the attackers themselves. Although membership in the Young Pioneers was mandatory for all Cuban children, it was a special honour to be picked for this event. The children had stayed up all night, meeting in the actual farmhouse that Fidel had used, where Party officials spoke with them about making a deep personal commitment to the Revolution.

Which side were you on? The people? Or the enemies of Cuba? Were you really, truly, committed? Were you bound and determined to put your life in the service of the country? The best Young Pioneers later joined the Union of Young Communists, a finishing school that fed its most committed members into the Communist Party, the vanguard itself. So this nocturnal retreat at the farmhouse was an opportunity, a path toward that future. Would they take it? There was only one answer. The boys had been bused down to the city, dropped in a parking lot at 4 am, and then given their cue.

The real 1953 attack wasn't so organized. About 80 men had left the farmhouse in a grab-bag of vehicles, using four different routes into Santiago they had not rehearsed. Many of the volunteers were from small towns in western Cuba, and got lost in Santiago's twisting streets. With just three dozen men, and more courage than wisdom, Castro launched the attack anyway, riding on the sideboard of a car as it rushed the Moncada just before dawn. The guards fired, surprise was lost, and the thousand army troops sleeping in the barracks had time to wake up, routing the assault. Many of the wounded or captured rebels were tortured, and then summarily executed.

There was one Dolores alumnus killed. Renato Guitart, a

graduate from 1948. Although he had arrived at Dolores after Fidel left, Castro was already known for political activism, and by 1952 he was famous as a congressional candidate known for his radio speeches against Batista. Just 22, Guitart joined the rebels out of pure idealism, and died that morning in the first volley of a war that has, according to Castro, never ended. In the thick of the fighting, Raúl and Fidel Castro both came through without a scratch.

For the survivors, there was a mad dash to escape. The Moncada fortress was located just 850 metres from the Colegio de Dolores, and for Fidel and Raúl, fleeing was no problem, for they knew every alley. Fidel ducked into one safe house, later transferred to another, and by that afternoon was in the country-side. Raúl stayed hidden in the city.

BACK IN MIAMI, Pepín Bou had dimly recalled the name of a Dolores alumnus who'd cropped up in some video. Yivena, or Yivera, or Llivina, he had said. Something like that. 'Even if I did know someone who was still there,' he'd said, 'I wouldn't know him. You know what I mean?'

For the alumni outside Cuba, those still on the island were an unwelcome reminder that not everyone had made the same choices. But it was simple enough to find such a person. A telephone shop just off the Parque Céspedes had a phone book that was several decades out of date (not a reproduction, this time, but an actual 1980s phone book). In the stasis of Cuba, these never became obsolete. I flipped through the 'Y's without luck, but quickly spotted a likely candidate under the double 'L's: LLIVINA, MIGUEL.

He answered the phone himself. 'Oh, Lundy,' he said when I mentioned that name. 'OK. He was a good friend of my sister.' When I identified myself as an American writer, he switched into English and invited me over. He gave me his unromantic address, which was 15 No. 3, in Vista Alegre.

He didn't ask why I was calling. There was only one reason a foreign journalist would come looking for him. He was Dolores class of 1953, and that was as close as he had brushed up against history.

The remote location of my hotel, a brutalist tower on the northern outskirts, was now an advantage. The Vista Alegre neighbourhood was nearby, and his address was a short walk. I started over in the late afternoon when the sun had dropped toward Havana and the old trees on these quiet streets cast shadows out into the avenue to shelter me.

Fifteenth Street was just beyond a traffic circle where six different streets and avenues collided, dividing the lower, older, narrower portions of Santiago from the ring of more spacious suburbs. On the higher side of that split were the stately mansions and elite neighbourhoods of the old days, still valued residential properties. A few of the old mansions had been converted into businesses. The first I passed was the Maison de Moda, a fashion centre. It had a catwalk equipped with lights in the yard, and two bars and a restaurant. At night the *jineteras* (prostitutes) were lined up three deep at the entrance, waiting for the chance to escort a foreign man into the restaurant. Off to the east a few hundred yards was the San Juan Motel, a classic American motor lodge predating the Revolution. On a subsequent visit to Santiago, I caught the maids at the San Juan stealing my soap and shampoo.

Many of the boys from Dolores had lived in Vista Alegre, which was a brand-new suburb in the 1930s, hardly developed, high above the city on a breezy hilltop. Although little had been built here in the last half century, the neighbourhood still had a modern feeling compared to the rest of Santiago. Down below, the houses were Spanish in style, with interior courtyards, and were separated from narrow lanes by sidewalks only two or three feet wide, all you needed in the era of horse carts. In Vista Alegre, the streets were wide, for automobiles, with grassy medians and wide sidewalks. The houses, often made of cement, were set back behind lawns, many of them overgrown with thorns and waist-high weeds. The former gardeners and servants, declared masters in 1959, had lain down their tools. So had many owners, although the houses were usually passed on to relatives. A few abandoned homes had been converted into *cuarterías*, smaller apartments made with plywood dividers. Two dozen unrelated people could end up living in one house, the old living room split in half, the bedroom partitioned, even the hallways or a porch split up to make tiny bedrooms. But most houses in Vista Alegre still seemed to be in private hands, often occupied by a solitary old person who had been there for half a century. And sprinkled around the neighbourhood were discrete government businesses offering services most Cubans never used: travel agencies, special commissaries, foreign exchange offices and joint-venture bureaucracies in great mansions. I stopped at a small dollar store, unmarked and almost hidden, in what had once been an art nouveau home. In a powerfully air-conditioned room, accompanied by the beeps and dings of a state-of-the-art cash register, a Cuban family with fat children ransacked the coolers for ice cream and sodas. I had never seen obese children in Cuba before.

Next door, a Lada pulled into the breezeway of a house, disgorging a young white man in a short-sleeve Madras shirt and khakis, the uniform of the Yummie, or Young Upwardly Mobile Marxist. Clutching a leather folder, he went inside and locked the door. Next door was an older Spanish house, with Corinthian columns, a cracked facade and a crumbling roof. The lawn was split between waist-high weeds and a failed crop of corn.

Miguel Llivina was waiting on his porch. The house, shaded by a large tree, was the same one he had grown up in, the same one he had left every morning in the 1940s to catch the blue bus to Dolores. He pounded the walls with his flat palm, to show me how thick they were. Santiago was known as the Land of Fire, he explained, which referred to more than the heat, or the ardent character of its people. The city was surrounded by extinct volcanoes, which still let loose with tremblers. There had been a serious earthquake in 1932, so Llivina's father had built this house to survive even a solid shake from the Land of Fire, with only one storey and chicken wire laid inside the walls as a reinforcement against cracking.

We sat in the sweltering living room. The heights of Vista Alegre were normally breezy – that is why the wealthy settled here – but the weather was still, wet and merciless. Along with Carnaval, the Land of Fire also had, every July, the Days of Fire, a nocturnal celebration of the heat itself, marked by bonfires in the poorer neighbourhoods. Heat appealed to the people of Santiago. It defined them, it justified their self-image as *ardiente*, fiery souls with uncontrollable passions, both personal and political.

I had arrived at Miguel's sweaty, and we both remained confined to our seats (an armchair for me, the sofa for Miguel). It was an Eisenhower living room, with louvred windows and lounge furniture that had been lovingly tended for decades. We stayed motionless during the hour of conversation. He was wearing slacks, loafers and, despite the temperature, a blue dress shirt with the sleeves buttoned at the cuffs. His hair was almost all white, with just a dusting of the black of his youth.

When I asked about Dolores, Miguel turned in his chair, reaching unsuccessfully for something on a bookshelf. He called for his son, who took a thick pile of documents from the shelf, passed them to his father, and then sat in an armchair matching my own, by my side. He was middle-aged and wore shorts and a velour sport shirt. His name was also Miguel — 'Doctor Miguel Jorge Llivina Lavine' his card said, 'Subdirector of the Center for Educational Studies'. He was coughing when he sat down, and the coughing occasionally burst into harsh fits. Rocking back and forth on his cushion, he cradled an ashtray in his lap, listening to his father and smoking between rounds of phlegm.

He scanned the faces of the very youngest boys in my school photo, trying to pick himself out, but could not settle on one face, first seeing himself to the left, then the right. He flipped through his own yearbook and pointed out his photo from '52, standing among ranks of the oldest boys. He wore a double-breasted navy blue blazer, white pants, and the tightly knotted tie that Fidel had disdained for his own posing. Miguel's hair was slicked back, even and shiny, and his face was smooth and round; he'd been chubbier as a teenager than he was today.

When I showed him Castro's face in the old photograph, he said, 'And here is Uncle Paco.'

Uncle Paco? Was that one of Castro's nicknames? 'No,' Llivina said. He'd made it up on the spot. Uncle Paco was just a jumble of syllables to substitute for a more dangerous word. Llivina looked at the image of Castro, the small round face under the railing. 'He's dressed a little *déshabille*,' he said. 'Not like the others. A bit messy.'

Despite keeping his Dolores yearbook close at hand for 50 years, Miguel said he was not romantic about the old Cuba. Outside the walls of the school there had been a harsh reality. He volunteered that there were a million illiterates in the country-side, and recalled the desperately poor *campesinos* of Oriente, surviving on sugar cane and bits of *tasajo*, the scraps of dried, salted beef of the worst quality, imported from Uruguay. 'There was equality, and no equality', Miguel said. 'The poor in Cuba were a huge class. Public health was in bad shape. Only a minority had access to it. In the *campo*, there were no hospitals. The state hospitals didn't have enough budget. People had to travel to the city for help.'

The middle class was in a better situation. 'In the forties and fifties the middle class in Cuba was bigger than in many countries in Latin America,' Miguel noted. Indeed, two-thirds of the population could claim to be middle-class, by some estimates, a figure unparalleled in the region. They had access to good schools like Dolores, private health insurance companies, and the *sociedades mutuales*, cooperatives that offered inexpensive doctor visits. As bad as rural poverty could be in Cuba, Miguel recalled with a shudder his visit to Mexico during a summer break at Dolores. 'In Mexico, there was a rich class, and then a huge poor class. The middle class was much smaller than in Cuba.'

The priests at Dolores had taught them to look at these problems, not away from them, Miguel said. The education had been excellent, and rigorous, focused on preparing them for their special obligations as future leaders of Cuba. His only complaint was that the school, with its strong religious teachings, was lacking in 'rationalism'. (Fidel Castro agreed, telling Frei Betto that the school had 'negative influences . . . such as the non-utilization of rationality, that is to say, the non-development of reasoning and feeling.')

The pages of the yearbook were soft, and Miguel pointed out

the entries on the radio club, and on the basketball team, both of which he had joined. He particularly remembered the outings to the surrounding hills – the famed nature walks where Fidel had absorbed the topography he would use in 1957. Miguel lingered over a picture of Facundo Bacardí, the six-year-old heir to the rum and political dynasty, whose kidnapping had been the most exciting thing that had ever happened at Dolores, Miguel thought. A close second was the military coup on 10 March 1952. All classes were abruptly stopped that day, and the students ordered to assemble in the courtyard. Far away in Havana, Fulgencio Batista had just shoved his way back into power, ending Cuba's experiment in liberal democracy and throwing the beloved 1940 Constitution in the trash. Most of the Jesuits, Miguel said, were sympathetic to General Franco, the strutting little strongman who had fought to victory in the Spanish Civil War, imposing a system of crypto-fascism on Spain, crushing leftists, and restoring the Church to power. But Batista was no Franco, and this was not Spain. The Padre Prefect assembled the students in their usual formations in the courtyard, and spoke quickly, condemning the coup, denounced Batista, and warning the boys to go home immediately, in case political trouble spread to Santiago. When Miguel finished telling this story, his son snorted.

'Father, no,' he said. 'Objective conditions did not permit this.' Miguel the Younger was an expert on the history of education in Cuba, he explained. He worked at the ministry of education in Havana, where he designed the curriculum for teachers' colleges – training the trainers, as it were. He was a Communist Party member, one of the 7 or 8 per cent of Cubans formally enrolled in the machine, and well versed in the Party's practice of constructing secure walls out of language. No teacher at Dolores, he explained, could have condemned Batista. The old system of education in Cuba had been 'crude, irrational', he said, using the same language as his father, and Fidel. It was a system designed to preserve the interests of the elite, he said. The Jesuits had to serve that monolithic interest, which meant they had to support Batista.

By contrast the Revolution had 'massified' a 'conductive model of pedagogy. Of what does this consist?' Rhetorical questions were the only safe questions. Words themselves were dangerous, to be handled at a distance: he spoke of planification, and massified pedagogy. A fit of severe coughing tore into him, cutting off words and even breath. He wheezed, choked, and then, forcibly silenced, rocked back and forth in the chair, smoking.

Miguel the Elder disagreed now, quietly. Dolores had progressive aspects. The school even 'had negroes, up to a certain point', he said.

'Three!' his son shouted.

They were both right. During the 1940s Dolores had edged away from segregation, allowing a few exemplary black students though only in auxiliary classes. By 1955 it was more integrated than American public schools.

Blacks 'didn't have the social position' to attend the school, the father explained, a little defensively. 'Or the money.'

Miguel himself had enough of both to go straight on to the United States after graduation. He enrolled as a freshman at another great Jesuit institution, Georgetown University in Washington DC. He'd entered the school of foreign service there, hoping to become a Cuban diplomat or an international businessman, but in the end he'd gone home, and become a certified accountant in Santiago.

During four years in Washington he'd learned fluent English, which he tried to demonstrate. But it had been half a century. His pronunciation had decayed so badly he only confused me. But in Spanish his native ease helped old memories to the surface. He recalled the names of bars and streets around the campus in Washington, and remembered crossing to Virginia and climbing on the earthen embankments that had been part of a Nike missile battery once. I had clambered over the same embankments as a teenager, just a few miles from my home.

In the same easily accessible stack of documents he had a photo of himself lounging in his Georgetown dorm, and another of a snowball fight with some other Cuban students, all of them dressed in natty jackets and ties for this novel experience. Miguel sorted through his sheaf of documents and pulled out a *Directorio de Antiguos Alumnos del Colegio de Dolores*.

The Directory of Old Alumni was the last of its kind, published in 1956, with listings and addresses for 3,300 graduates of Dolores reaching back to the founding in 1913. According to its prologue, the booklet had been compiled to satisfy a natural curiosity about Dolores, and 'the situation and influence on national life of the alumni who passed through its doors . . . to view, as in a panoramic vista, the works and influence of the College in the national life'.

This was of course my own purpose. Here was the control group. Brother divided from brother, roommate from roommate, neighbour from neighbour, to their scattered fates. What was continuous, from the past to this future? And what had ruptured? Everything? Or nothing? Was even this event, the shattering Revolution, incapable of breaking what had come before? Which vanguard was stronger?

Everything had been so neat, before it unravelled. Here was Pepín, his early life summarized in the Directory under his proper name, which Miguel read out:

> Bou, Leonard José Roberto 1940–47
> New Orleans
> Chemical Engineer

Then under C were the Castros, their maternal name misspelt, the Ruz turned to Ruiz:

> Castro Ruiz, Ramón 1939–41
> Colono

That was the eldest, Ramón. 'Colono' was an antique term for someone with a large plantation, which is what he would have inherited without his brothers' interference, a position of power. In Cuba, where words had two sides, *colono* was also street slang for a bootlicker, or a flatterer.

Miguel wouldn't even read the next entry under 'C'. He looked at it and then handed the booklet back to me. 'Here is Uncle Paco,' he said. It read:

Castro Ruiz, Fidel 1937–42
Abogado
Calle 23 No. 1552 Vedado Habana

After that was:

Castro Ruiz, Raúl 1939–45
Calle 23 No. 1552 Vedado Habana

The two brothers were living at the same address, in Havana. Fidel, a lawyer, was a candidate for the Cuban Congress in '52, at least until Batista staged his coup. Raúl had no occupation other than shadowing his brother.

There were four Bacardí boys at the school at one time or another, among them:

Bacardí, González José Rafael 1945–51
Vista Alegre

And of course, my host was listed:

Parajon, Miguel M. Llivina
15 No. 3 Vista Alegre 41216

I asked Miguel what had happened to the boys in the alumni guide, and the boys in my old photograph. 'The first ones to leave, the vanguard, were high-class people,' he said. 'They were afraid of the confiscations, of the nationalizations of businesses, and industry, and of their land.' They often assumed that any privileges and property they lost by departing Cuba could be restored by the next government. But there had never been a next government.

'Those who leave the country today come from a different

class,' Miguel continued, 'and are leaving for different reasons. Over 40 years, the exodus has continued and even increased sometimes. But those early people had other ambitions.'

Not everyone had gone, even if most had. He dug around in his papers and gave me an address in what he called the 'Jamaican' neighbourhood, down on the flatlands adjacent to the harbour. There was a man there who organized help for the few Dolores alumni who remained in Santiago, making sure they had food and clothing in their old age.

'His name is Segura,' Miguel said. 'He is older than I am. Jorge Segura. Same years as the Commander.'

THE BIG HOUSE was the main hotel of Santiago, at least symbolically. It was located right on the central plaza, the Parque Céspedes. Built in 1914, its real name was the Casa Granda, and it had a baroque facade that was whitewashed to a blinding purity in the Santiago noon. Babe Ruth and Joe Louis had stayed here, when men wore neckties to breakfast, but now European and Canadian men in flip-flops and wife-beaters were packed into the terrace bar, overlooking the square, all day from midmorning until it closed near midnight. The cans of beer were warm, expensive and slow to arrive, but there was nowhere else in the city to sit, drink, look at the view and talk with girls. Or more accurately, to sit, drink and ignore the girls. The men were Italians, Germans, Dutchmen, Brits and Quebecois, Jamaicans and Bahamians, Americans and Mexicans, but aside from a token effort at saying hello, even those who spoke Spanish didn't bother to talk with their Cuban women. It wasn't about talking. Anyway the women's stories were always too sad or transparently false to earn compassion from the defeated men who came on vacation here. The clients were usually working-class, the kind who took orders at home and came to Cuba to give them. They paid for volume, not quality.

Santiago was still the second city of Cuba. The population had more than doubled since 1940, to around 500,000 people, but the city itself had not expanded much, the people being crammed into the same infrastructure, or stacked in the functional apartment towers that were dropped into vacant lots. It was a remarkably compact jurisdiction, with people crowded into the mudejar houses in the centre and virtually no suburban sprawl beyond the art nouveau of Vista Alegre. Drive out of Santiago and in just ten minutes you would be looking at it, whole, in the rear-view mirror. The laid-back, Caribbean feeling of the city was also intact, but a lot of the isolation had faded. The main highway down the middle of the island was eight lanes wide now, though unpainted, and it was quicker than ever to reach Santiago.

The Big House was at the centre of everything, next to the finest old social club, across from the most ancient sites, and overlooking the park, where *jineteras* circulated. The Cubans say, *if you want to eat fish you have to get wet*, and these girls didn't conceal their intentions. Their revealing outfits typically began with absurdly high platform sandals, rose up with a pair of black lycra pants that had windows laddered along the outside of the leg, and then summited an enormous backside, the butt cleavage enhanced and enforced by thong underwear. Spandex tops and huge quantities of crude makeup completed the package. I simply couldn't stand it. The girls flitted about in the park, intercepting any likely lads headed for the Big House, and the more ambitious ones strolled back and forth in front of the stairs to the hotel, eyed mercilessly by a security guard charged specifically with keeping them out. Any Cuban woman was welcome in the hotel, of course, as long as she had a specific foreign man inviting her inside. In a gesture at fairness, Cuban men were actually allowed to enter the terrace with their girlfriends too, although they were humiliated by having to show the guard that they carried enough US dollars.

There was nothing to do during the afternoon, so I sat in the shade of the balcony like the other foreign men, killing time until night, drinking shamefully bad daiquiris, fending off advances, and watching the *jineteras*, the lucky ones, sit in silence with those they had just met. Descending to the Parque Céspedes, the ancient plaza where the conquistadors had paraded, I sat on a bench and befriended a young braggart who advised me on the

superiority of Santiago, although he immediately admitted that he
had never seen anything else. He'd never even been to Havana,
he admitted. But there was no reason to go to Havana, for
Santiago was better. He explained that Cuba itself was the
'greatest country in the world for culture, for education, for
advancement, in science and sports. There is no music in the
world that is not based on Cuban music. This is the most beautiful
country.'

He'd been to other countries?

'It doesn't matter,' he said. 'Everyone knows it is the most
beautiful. Christopher Columbus said so.'

The plaza was bustling, a crossroads of tourists snapping
photographs and young Santiagueros in search of excitement.
The benches were nearly full, and couples strolled around the
outer edge of the square, knots of girls walking with linked arms,
and grinning boys pursuing them. Children swerved past the
fountain in miniature automobiles, pulled along by parents haul-
ing on a rope. A steady stream of ambitious women – teenage
girls, usually in pairs – approached me and made excuses for
conversation. ('Do you know what time it is?' 'What's your
name?' 'Where are you from?') Some, assuming I spoke no
Spanish, turned to my new friend and asked who I was, and
why I was alone. He defended me, which left me time to study
the tattoo of a marijuana leaf on his left shoulder, so crude it must
have been done with a sewing needle. This was as far as rebellion
went in Cuba: smoking dope was one of the only escapes, a way
of dropping out mentally, of becoming a passive non-participant
in the heroics of Cuban history. Unlike imported cocaine, which
was vigorously suppressed by the Cuban police, marijuana was
grown in Cuba, right in the same mountains where Castro and
the guerrillas had fought, and couldn't be eliminated. Weed
wasn't exactly tolerated – this fellow had been harassed by the
police, he said, just for sporting the tattoo – but you could get
away with it. For young people, those who were struggling *en
fuego*, living the street life of girls, pimps and cash, trading sex or
whatever they had for a few dollars, marijuana was the least of
their problems.

As if on cue, there was a shout, screams, and then a roar of people running. A fight had broken out on the far side of the plaza, and people were rushing toward it, not away. We stood on the benches and watched as a couple of young toughs went at it, windmilling punches with their right hands as they used their lefts to grasp and spin each other around. Faces lined the balcony of the Big House, but in less than a minute a flying squad of police officers burst through the crowd, ripped the boys apart, and threw them into the back of a van in handcuffs. People applauded the arrest, and then went back to parading through the Parque Céspedes.

'It's not possible to live here,' the boy on the bench told me. 'We can't survive like this.' He detailed the common problems of life – not enough to eat, not enough to drink, not enough real jobs or useful education, too many *comemierdas*, literally 'shiteaters', interfering in what was none of their business. 'Even if you work you don't have enough to survive,' he explained. 'I get paid seven *fulas* a month at my job,' he said, using the slang for a US dollar. 'I give one to somebody who I owe money. Then I spend one on something to eat. The girls won't pay any attention to you if you don't have money, so you have to invite them for a beer, which costs a dollar up there,' he said, pointing to the Big House. 'One for you, one for her. Plus something to eat for her. So that's all the money. By the time I get home in the morning, what do I have left for my wife, and my baby? Nothing.'

He raised his hands, palms out, in disbelief. What could be more unreasonable than that?

More girls came by. What's your name? *Pepa*, I said. That was what the *jineteras* called all their clients. Where was I from? *Yuma*, the slang for America.

During the next pause the fellow asked me a question I hadn't expected. He wanted to know about the September 11 attacks in America. 'We couldn't believe it when we saw it,' he said. The TV news in Cuba wasn't always 'complete', he explained carefully. Was it all true? Had it really happened like that?

Even Castro had been struck mute, for once. He'd led tens of thousands of Cubans to the American mission in Havana to present a wreath. Finally, something that could transcend enmity, uniting Cubans with their official enemy.

But such talk was pointless in the Parque Céspedes. The night had come on. The miniature cars went around and around. The girls continued to walk past, looking for their own way to escape this world. *Where are you from? What's your name?*

Pepa Fula de Yuma, I insisted, but the joke was lost in mistranslation. They couldn't understand me. A foreigner was a rich man, always. Why come all the way to Cuba if you didn't want to drink beer, make love, and then get something to eat?

FOTO MEXICANA HAD TAKEN out advertising in the same Dolores yearbooks that were filled with its own work. The ads listed their address, which I'd found quickly on Enramada, about 10 minutes from the school. El Ten Cent was still across the street, with the Woolworth's sign, but empty.

Enramada, one of the oldest streets in Cuba, was still lined on both sides and overhung with commercial signs that predated the Revolution, a thicket of rusty, burned-out 1940s neon and peeling placards in 1950s typefaces. Signs had replaced the bower of tree branches that had given the street its original name (meaning literally 'enbranched') in the 1600s. The streets were the oldest things in Santiago, still known by their folk names – Clock Street, Branched Street, Barricade Street. The old Cuban Republic, and then the Revolution, had slapped new names on them. But people still spoke the original names, the memory of centuries.

Like every business in Cuba, Photo Mexicana was long gone. The studio was listed in the yearbook at José A. Saco #310, which was the ignored official name for the street everyone called Enramada. The address was a hotel school now, where a few rooms were rented to Cubans and the staff were in training to work at first-class tourist hotels, the island's only real industry now. The dull yellow building was clean and bustling, for hotel school was a glamorous, coveted slot in Cuba, leading to jobs around foreigners, with fringe benefits like better food, tips, free shampoo and soap. I knew a man who had paid a bribe of $300 to get his son into a hotel school like this.

From Enramada, it wasn't far to the Colegio de Dolores itself. The school was easy to find, right on the Plaza Dolores, its facade already familiar to me from photographs. As usual in Cuba, the decades seemed to have had no effect on the outside of things. It was after 5 pm when I traipsed up through the Plaza and stood in front of the big front door on Clock Street, which was shut. I rapped twice and felt the door move; it wasn't locked. As I was about to peer inside, it opened a crack and a man, leaning backwards in his chair, said, 'Can I help you?'

I'd forgotten to prepare a cover story, and so blurted out the truth: I was interested in the history of the school. Could I see it?

He was a genial man, the kind who rescues Cuba from disaster. He shook his head no, but then he opened the door wider, and I caught a glimpse of the interior, the high ceiling of the entryway, the arched galleries, and the courtyard opening beyond. Just as it was before, perhaps. But he wouldn't let me in. I pleaded in a slow, good-natured way, asking just for a peek, making small talk about how far I had come, but it was to no avail.

After he was done rejecting me, I waited. Cubans always have time. He finally said, 'Where is your home?'

America, I said, and left the word dangling. He explained that the school, which is what it still was, would be closed during Carnaval. The students would return on Monday, five days from now. Surely I could talk to someone then. Why didn't I try coming back on Monday?

The Plaza Dolores was quiet already, the day winding down, darkness coming on. I popped into a bar just across Clock Street, and brooded over a $1 Cuba Libre, alone with the bartender, wondering what to do with myself for five days.

More time cost more money, and I was burning through a limited supply of cash in a country where credit card transactions were impossible for Americans. There was a cash machine farther downhill on Enramada, tucked into an entryway that the bank shared with the shiny new Communist Party headquarters for Santiago.

A Canadian tourist walked up, withdrew some American dollars (the only currency available), and then watched in amusement as I tried the same. FUNDS NOT AVAILABLE, the machine said, unable to process my American card. This electronic enforcement was one of the only effective measures in the entire fantasy of the US trade embargo, and it wasn't that effective (via the internet I soon had a debit card that worked in Cuba).

Just an hour later, I ran into the Canadian at a restaurant. He offered to lend me $400 on the spot. We walked back up to the Party ATM, and a moment later he handed me the green bills American, taking only my promise to repay him.

'YOU NEED A LIBRARY CARD,' the guard at the Biblioteca Provincial explained. Santiago's main library was spread through the upper floors of an old commercial building a couple of blocks above the Parque Céspedes, between Saint Faith and Slaughterhouse streets. I marched up the hill on a hot afternoon to see if the library had, among its vast holdings, the old newspaper of Santiago, the *Diario de Oriente*. It was this paper, the voice of Cuba's richest province, that had faithfully recorded the events of life at Dolores in the 1930s and 1940s, running photographs of school pageants and detailing graduations and victories by the school's baseball team. And it was the *Diario*, which had allegedly carried an approving item about the young Fidel's strikebreaking escapades back on the family farm. Several Dolores boys had mentioned the article, but in America, no one carried back copies of this provincial newspaper, not the Library of Congress, the New York Public Library, or the great archival collections of Miami and Tampa universities. I thought I could spend a few days in the Biblioteca Provincial reading back copies from 1940 and 1941. But the guard didn't care what I wanted. 'You need a library card or you can't come in,' he said. After a few minutes of loitering by the door, I waylaid a staffer returning from lunch, and she went off with a message. She never returned. Eventually, bored of my pleading, the guard assigned someone to escort me upstairs.

There was a high-ceilinged reading room on the second floor,

with yellow light and the sweetly acid smell of fermenting paper.
A team of students were assembling huge piles of manila folders,
part of a study project on Cuba's economic reforms in the 1970s.
A librarian finally appeared to tell me that they would love to let
me read old newspapers, but first I needed a library card. And for
that I needed a *responsable*.

Responsable, the Responsible One. A dreaded word in Cuba.
Everyone had to belong, had to be incorporated within some
piece of the system and placed within its chain of responsibilities.
You couldn't get a library card; you had to apply through your
responsable. This was doubly true for foreigners, who had to
'pertain' to some 'organism' before they could undertake any
kind of official contact in Cuba.

For a decade I had been scrupulously careful to avoid having a
responsable. I had avoided contact with Cuban authorities in all
their guises, arriving on tourist visas, never asking permission, and
avoiding examination. I tried to fly beneath the radar, switching
passports and mumbling my way through immigration, disguising
myself as a common tourist. If I overstayed my visa, I played
dumb (what visa?). On the ground, year after year, I relied on
personal contacts and street reporting whenever possible. When
official interviews were necessary I tried to bluff my way in the
door, often successfully. Government functionaries in Havana
were usually less guarded than those in Washington.

Although it was certain that I had an entry somewhere, in some
government file, this strategy of shady imprecision, wheedling
and flattery, false names and switched-up paperwork, had always
been enough to keep me more or less untraced, an exception,
outside the system of control and monitoring for foreigners on the
island. And I wanted to remain that way, *irresponsable*. But here at
the provincial library I was rubbing up against the socialist need to
organize, regulate, categorize, control, channel and document.
There could be no exceptions.

The librarian suggested that I try making Santiago's official
Historian of the City into my *responsable*. I went down past the
Parque Céspedes to the address she gave me, where I was refused
entry to a building. The guard agreed to send my passport in, and

after half an hour in the doorway I was let inside, stepping over a
Spanish door into a cool, cobblestone corridor. It was a lovely old
building with a small courtyard, built around a fountain. Nothing
had been modernized. The doors were old, dark wood, elabo-
rately worked. The courtyard was open to the sky, not roofed
with dirty glass and aluminum like so many improved buildings in
colonial Lima or Bogotá. The ochre walls were interrupted by
arches, much like Dolores, that formed shaded galleries. There
was a red tiled roof overhead, higher on the uphill side by an extra
floor. Following instruction I went up the open stairway, and as I
climbed, a view over the bay opened up, with El Cobre, the
Catholic shrine, visible on a hillock more than ten miles away,
and then beyond that, the peaks of the Sierra Maestra, pointed
and heavily forested. The mountains were either grey-black or
flat green, depending on whether they lay beneath cumulus or
sunlight.

The Historian of the City was out, but her deputy, a jovial,
round-bellied intellectual named Omar, had been curious enough to talk with me. Omar had a secretary, two computers, and
a copy machine, which was extraordinary; in Cuba, even a
photocopier was treated like a loaded gun. He kept an air-
conditioner blasting to protect the valuable machines, and his
secretary was the first woman I had seen in Santiago wearing a
sweater.

'Marvellous,' Omar said, when I explained my interest in
reading old newspapers. 'We will help you, of course.' The
library card could be arranged, of course. And why not interview some of the local historians? He rattled off some names,
full of enthusiasm. We agreed, heartily, that the history of
Santiago – the Jerusalem of the Americas! – had never been
properly told. The conquistadors had come here, the great War
of Independence had been fought here, and, obviously, Santiago was the *Capital Moral* of the Revolution. Why, this very
building we were sitting in had been the Colegio La Salle, the
rival school to Dolores. The Castro brothers had attended
school here briefly, under the tutelage of the Christian Brother
monks, before transferring up the hill to Dolores and the Jesuits.

Doubtless the Commander had been in this very room while a boy!

Of course, Omar said after the requisite pause, this would all have to be coordinated through Havana.

And I would have to find the right *responsable* there, not here. Probably at the Casa de Amistad con los Pueblos, the House of Friendship with the Peoples. They ran all bilateral cultural projects of this type. It would only take a few months, he said, until I raised an eyebrow. Then he conceded that getting set up with the House of Friendship could take six months, or more.

And once I had my American university all lined up to sponsor me – what? No university? Then find one! – then the Americans could negotiate on my behalf with the House of Friendship, and produce the exchange of letters, in mutually approved language, in triplicate, in English and Spanish, outlining the precise scope of my project, the questions I would be asking, and the resources I would be entitled to use while reading newspapers in Cuba. That's all he would need to get started organizing the project here in Santiago.

I knew writers and film-makers who had charged eagerly into this process of death by enthusiasm, visiting Cuba repeatedly for years, always convinced that they were about to get the magic cooperation they needed and were promised. Most had gotten no farther than meetings like this, discussing exactly who was going to be the *responsable* for what.

On the way out, Omar said he was sure that it would all work out, but I was already regretting showing my face here, or at the library, and soon enough my fears were realized. I'd left him my phone number, and the same afternoon there was a message from him, urging me to CONTACT ANA MARIA HOUSE OF FRIENDSHIP. The word *urgente* was written on the message, underlined twice. I threw the paper away.

For the next four days there were a string of increasingly desperate phone messages. PATRICIO, CALL HOUSE OF FRIENDSHIP OF THE PEOPLES, with a phone number in Havana.

And then, finally, a hand-delivered note, which caught me in the hotel lobby: URGENT MEETING TO DISCUSS YOUR PROJECT

WITH ANA MARIA OF HOUSE OF FRIENDSHIP FRIDAY MY OFFICE 10 AM.

I don't know why, but I actually went to that one. On Friday I climbed back up the stairs at Omar's office, the stairs that Fidel, Raúl, and Ramón had climbed. The view was just as good as before.

I arrived a few minutes early, and waited for more than an hour with the sweater-wearing secretary. Some impulse of obedience led me there. I still can't imagine why I did that.

But in the event, neither Omar nor the mysterious *Ana Maria Amistad Responsable* showed up. After a long, cold, tense wait, I suddenly sprang up and fled, tumbling back down the stairs, leaping the doorway in my eagerness to get out, and then running into the streets, grinning like Alberto Casas on one of his jail-breaks.

THE WEEKEND WAS STARTING NOW, and the heat and the night-long revels of Carnaval combined to drive the normally quiet daytime streets into utter silence. Nothing moved in Santiago by day, the city caught between breaths. On Saturday afternoon, when I reached the front door at Dolores, I could hear someone screaming inside.

The same porter was inside the door, watching a Kung Fu movie. The TV set was propped on a chair in the middle of the foyer, with two antennae poking up. The black power cord ran across the floor, hooked to a series of extension cords that covered the 40 feet to a plug. Two women were with him. They were so caught up in the chopsocky that they didn't notice me for more than a minute.

'Hello, friend,' the guard said, and went back to watching the movie. Progress.

After a while there was a break, and one of those commercials for cellular phones that had begun appearing on Cuban television. Gorgeous young people strolled in the streets of Havana, pausing to make phone calls to other stunning kids. The advertising could only be aimed at the new class of foreign businessmen who oversaw the tourism economy.

The porter was sympathetic now. He didn't object when I stepped inside and watched the next segment of Kung Fu with him. I introduced myself to his lady friends – neighbours who had just stopped by, in the way that Cubans could spend hours of every day just stopping by. He nodded when I asked if I could examine the small room off the entrance – a narrow, cool space with a high ceiling, which had been converted into a minuscule museum dedicated to His time at the school. Here were a dozen black and white photos from the early 1940s, enlarged almost to a soft-focus incoherence, and clearly showing the cracks and rips of the badly treated original photographs. Mounted around the room in a circle were shots of 1940s Dolores, with the boys in their uniforms or casual clothes.

The photographs showed the boys moving freely through the dining hall, assembling for band practice and studying. It was possible to pick out Him in one because the caption pointed the way: *Fidel Castro, 5th grade. 2nd of Bachillerato 1937–1942*

'Bachillerato' referred to the highest class offered, the baccalaureate course needed to move on to university. Younger brother Raúl was also pointed out ('1939–1945') but, as usual, the oldest brother, Ramón, didn't exist. During the first year of the Revolution, Ramón had criticized Fidel in a newspaper article, and has lived in comfortable isolation on a tobacco farm in a remote part of western Cuba ever since. He is occasionally made available to sympathetic biographers of Fidel, but otherwise lives under the cloak that Fidel has thrown over his entire family life.

The photo captions only mentioned one other boy from Dolores: Renato Guitart, who had died on 26 July 1953, which according to the official chronometer of the Cuban Revolution, was Day One. The whole government and party apparatus took its name ('The Revolutionary 26th of July Movement') from that day.

There were different Castro quotes on the walls, enlarged placards that spoke of the importance of schooling, but only in the vaguest terms. ('It is education that converts a living being

into a human being. It is education that can empty the jails.
I'm an optimist, I believe in that ideals prevail over force.')
Fidel never talked about Dolores; in his millions of recorded
words, there were no genuinely insightful remarks about
himself, his background, or his influences. He acknowledged
no influences. He was apart from history, self-created, without
origins. When the Brazilian theologian Frei Betto pushed
repeatedly, Castro barely conceded that Christian education
had affected him at all.

It took only a minute to survey this room in detail. Then the
guard said again that I could not enter the rest of the school, but
when he stepped off for something I began touring it anyway.
The walls were cracked and the paint dingy, which was normal
for Cuba, even before the Revolution. But I could see slogans
that had not graced Dolores in the old days:
IT IS ALWAYS THE 26TH, one said. And, somewhat defensively,
I'M STAYING HERE. Another was rubbed to incoherence: A RE OLU
ION WITHOU DANG R IS N T A EVO UTION.

Earlier in the year, Fidel had returned to his home town, Birán,
to attend the opening of a photo exhibit in a local sugar mill. The
photos reviewed the Castro family's origins and Fidel's personal
history but, as usual, Fidel missed the opportunity to reflect on his
upbringing. Speaking to an assembly of the students, he said only
that, 'If there's one thing I could reproach myself for, like a pang
of regret, it's not having studied much more than I did throughout my life.'

This was comedy. Even Castro's worst enemies conceded that
he had never, in his whole life, given up his drive to learn, work
and achieve. It was literally impossible to study more than he did.
The young Castro had been a tireless polymath, who exceeded in
virtually every class and activity. He embodied (in the physical
sense) the Jesuit ideal of relentless effort. He had a phenomenal
memory, which was often described as photographic, but which
was really the fruit of disciplined application. As a student, Fidel
wasted no time: he rose early, worked hard all day, converted
even baseball and basketball games into mental training regimens,
and stayed up late reading. His curiosity was all encompassing; he

absorbed arcane material quickly because he was hungry for all forms of mastery and knowledge. Once in power, his work habits – staying up all night reading reports, and then quoting them verbatim at meetings the next day – stood in sharp contrast to the paper shuffling and inertia of the socialist state. Decades of economic disasters have led to many rueful jokes in Cuba. (The national motto is said to be: 'They pretend to pay us, we pretend to work.') The saddest of these comments is the commonplace observation that there is only one man left in Cuba who actually does any work at all. Into his late seventies, Castro gave five-hour speeches that regurgitated columns of figures and even on his hospital bed he was shown reading reports.

By now I had been inside the school for half an hour. The Kung Fu movie was still going, and I asked if I could use the bathroom before leaving. The guard wasn't allowed to let anyone in, he explained.

'I will be quick,' I said.

The bathroom was broken anyway, he said. The toilets didn't work.

'I just need a urinal.'

He couldn't take me to it.

'I can find it,' I said.

And so he gave in. It was up one flight of stairs, in the back. Use the stairs on the left, he said. And forgive him for the condition of the toilets.

I took the stairs up the right, two at a time before he could stop me. Up on the second floor I began to walk as slowly as possible, scouting. All the doors were locked but pressing my eye to the cracks between doors I could see that the classrooms were stripped of the old dark wood cabinets. The walls were devoid of even posters. Rusted and cheap chair-desks, rusty iron contraptions with scarred wooden writing surfaces bolted on, were packed one against the next, more than 40 per room.

The toilets were indescribable. They didn't seem to have worked in years, and were jammed with trash and, improbably, several tall boards. I clambered over trash and used a trench urinal in the back.

I came down again, slowly, using the opposite staircase, walking around the patio, counting off the arches, and noting the basketball hoop, still in the same place as some 60 years before. To my surprise the guard was nowhere in sight, and the two women didn't even look up. I ducked into the courtyard and snapped five frames with a camera, putting myself in the same spot as the Foto Mexicana technician in 1941. I just had time to hide the camera.

'There was another fellow here,' the guard said, coming back. 'About six months ago. A man came, asking the same questions as you do.'

He held out a business card, which he had kept in his desk drawer. It read:

Bernardo Souto
Formica Española

with an address in Spain. The porter said he was someone from 'before', who had returned to see the school. He'd wandered around, looking, and had left the card. I started to copy down the information, but he gave me the card itself, and then urged me to come visit him again, soon.

Across the street, I saw that the same bar was open, and started to head in. It was only five o'clock, and two young couples sat in the bar, occupying opposite ends of the room, each pair completely absorbed in their courtship. The bartender shook his head at me, smiling. He couldn't serve me, he explained. 'It is workers' night.' Once a month the bar was required to open itself only to Cuban workers. The prices were changed, and instead of dollars they accepted only special coupons, earned by workers as rewards at their jobs.

The closer couple broke off the lovemaking. 'I have a ticket,' the young man said. He held it up. Here was a new experience: no Cuban had ever bought me a drink. But I had to decline. I could drink at the Big House, or a dozen other dollar-bars for tourists. But he would not see that ticket again for a month.

He apologized, and the bartender apologized, and then the

woman apologized, but I found it delightful. '*Es justo*,' I kept replying to their apologies. '*Es justo*.'

JORGE SEGURA, same years as the commander, was nervous when I telephoned. He stalled for a while, but I stalled more, and he finally agreed to meet me the next morning, at 10, before it grew too hot. His house was in the low western part of the city, a district of ancient streets and two-storey mudejar houses. By Santiago standards, the architecture was interesting, with a touch of the colonial flavour of Old Havana. But Old Havana had been squared up and repainted with UNESCO money, reborn as Old Havanaland. Segura's neighbourhood hadn't received even a whitewash. On the far side of a gritty avenue from the Parque Céspedes, it was a dusty, neglected, monotone of cracked plaster and paint that had regressed to some painterly mean of off-white diluted with ochre.

Segura's neighbourhood was wrapped around a tiny plaza where a truly ancient tree shaded a swing set and the entrance to Trinity church. The streets were empty at midmorning, except for a group of grimly competitive boys playing stickball using a broom stick cut short and a ball made of three plastic bottle caps wrapped in tape. They were quiet, determined, as if some feud were being settled. Every batter nailed almost every pitch of the *fufa*, but the art was in advancing through the bases (a light post, a building corner and a storm sewer) with complete insouciance. They walked, never ran, moving as slowly as possible, teasing their way to each base, holding up their foot until a fraction of a second before the throw came in. Although they were playing in the intersection of two streets, they were not interrupted by a car more than once an inning.

Up a block, I found one side of the road filled with blackened pieces of a truck engine, all laid out in two parallel lines. Behind them was a grease-blackened Soviet truck, on blocks, with no wheels. The hood was thrown open, a dark mouth without teeth. Lying on the dusty street were both halves of the engine block, six pistons, the manifold and exhaust, the radiator, the starter coil and the ignition module. It looked like a warning to other cars: turn back! A lean mulatto man, stained darker by grease, was patiently wiping the cylinders with a rag.

'It will run again?'

'Of course,' he said.

As I circled blocks, looking for the address, a clutch of women on a stoop called out various proposals. 'Come here, handsome!' the oldest one said. And then a younger one: 'Don't you need a wife back home?' They giggled into their hands.

There was a plaque on one house, marking the spot where a Revolutionary had been killed while fleeing the Moncada attack in 1953. The survivors of the rout that morning had fled into the back streets around lower Santiago, going in all directions, to all fates. Fidel and Raúl had threaded their way to safety on foot. Three of the fugitives had taken shelter in Dolores itself, which was as empty during Carnaval then as it was now. A Jesuit had negotiated their surrender. Others had run to the houses of friends, like this fellow, who had been betrayed in his hideout and murdered during a sudden police raid. Like all frightened bullies, the Batista police were ruthless.

The army, the police, and the notorious SIM secret police were all hunting for Fidel. If captured, he could be tortured or simply gunned down, as many of his followers in the attack already had been. The Castro family was eager to prevent this, of course, and sought a way to mitigate the dangers. Fidel's older brother Ramón was sent to see various connections around town. Not surprisingly, given the social stratification in Oriente, Fidel's time among the elite served him well: Dolores was thick with families connected to the Church, the political power structure, the Masonic Lodges of Santiago, even the police. Ramón enlisted the Padre Rector of Dolores, who hustled through Santiago, urging the authorities to issue specific instructions to take Fidel alive.

There is some evidence this strategy actually worked. Castro was eventually surprised and captured by an army patrol in the hills. The soldiers were typical of the Cuban army Fidel would face years later: overwhelmingly poor, illiterate, and distrustful of the white ruling class. Fidel was not their liberator but part of this ruling class. The patrol that snuck up on him was mostly black, including their officer, Yañes Pelletier. Surprised while still asleep, Castro and the other Moncada survivors surrendered, but the government soldiers weren't inclined to accept it. 'They are whites!' someone shouted. 'Kill them!' But Pelletier ordered his men not to fire. He had heard from someone, who had heard from someone, who had heard from someone powerful in Santiago. Fidel Castro Ruz was wanted alive. There would be no memorial plaques for the Castro brothers.

Segura's house turned out to be a modest little Spanish colonial thing on the street beside Trinity church. It was a single storey, attached on both sides to similar houses. Painted a dull ochre, it had wooden louvres on the tall windows, with an iron security grate welded on. A man in his forties answered the door, waved me inside, and said, 'My father will be right with you.' As soon as I was inside Segura himself appeared, in pajamas. He was 74 years old, small, wizened and slow moving, but with a lively face, his mind and voice both clear. He pointed me to an iron patio chair in the tiny living room. He had glasses, and hair that was a thorny mixture of grey, white and black. He made cautious small talk, smiling insincerely. I mentioned Lundy Aguilar, and a few other names from Dolores and he visibly relaxed.

'Lundy,' Jorge Segura said. 'Let's see.' Just like Miguel Llivina, he twisted back into his armchair, and reaching behind with a slightly trembling hand, plucked a sheaf of loose documents off a bookshelf. He put the yellow papers and soft manila folders on his lap, shifted through them, and plucked out his Dolores yearbook. It was brown with age. He hadn't even needed to stand to reach it.

Lundy and Fidel were at the University of Havana by the time Segura arrived as a freshman. Still, Segura had always been a tracker of Dolores graduates, back then as much as now. He knew Lundy's later career as an academic, his work writing for newspapers, and that he was living in Miami. Segura was up to date on all the old days, slipping me the phone number of Father Dorta Duque, the Jesuit I had already sat with during the reunion in Miami. Pepín Bou had not mentioned Jorge Segura, but Jorge knew all about Pepín. He had worked with Pepín at the Moa Bay mining company for two years. He was in the headquarters building, doing accounting, while Pepín, a chemical engineer, was out on the refinery site. The two years at Moa Bay were the ones leading up to the nationalization of the plant, Segura explained. They had been through so much together. They were friends.

He was only too happy to look back. The student body at Dolores, he recalled, was very intimate, a small and closed society that did not particularly form into groups, bands or cliques. The students imbibed the sober and timeless culture of the Church, and the general rule was one of eager conformism. Not all the families were rich, Segura noted, there were 'normal' people as well. He counted his own family as one of the normals: they owned a small store with 'only a few things for sale'. The 'highest' families in the school were the Bacardís and the Macaderos. 'There were 238 students during the 1940s. All were white. I remember one negro, only. Everyone was Spanish. We went to the beach, to dances sometimes.

'I never liked geography. I studied the history of Cuba. Literature. Social studies. We had a lot of masses. A religious life, with moral and civic instruction. How to act as a citizen in Cuba. We never had contact with the other Jesuit schools. My favourite activity was basketball. You know José Antonio Roca? We played on the same team, he was the forward, our star.'

He free-associated for a while. 'After the harvest, there was three months of poverty, there was no work. I made few visits to the countryside during the 1940s. We went to Banes,' the town near where Fidel Castro grew up. 'There were two sides to that place, one for Americans, one for Cubans. There was a central, shared part also, but the Americans had their own colony. There were differences. That sat badly with people. But before the Revolution, that area was very tranquil. In the 1940s the pressure for revolution was very low. Agriculture was the main business of Oriente. Since the price of sugar was guaranteed in that era, everything was stable. I saw a lot of Americans in the streets, at the weekends. Many came. Sometimes they passed me in the street, but they never said anything.'

As he talked his eyes ran over papers, and then a photograph. 'That's Piñon, who fell recently,' he said, pointing at one in a group of faces. 'Fell' dead.

He put the book away, depressed. He leaned forward and lowered his voice. 'It's all a disaster,' he said. 'Look at this place.'

After the Revolution, Segura the accountant had became Segura the professor of accounting. Although he was mostly retired, he still held a professorship at the University of Oriente. These days he was usually at home, and rarely out of the bathrobe or pajamas. He was typically found right here in this pale green room, with its neatly kept glass table tops. The walls were decorated with an accumulation of middle-class signifiers: a map of Spain, landscape paintings. The small space was filled with a matching set of Danish modern lounge chairs and a love seat. All the pieces were carefully covered in white, to extend their years. On the table, there was an old photograph of a woman, her hair bobbed in a 1950s style. It was a black and white picture, but hand-tinted in the weak pastels that signified dress (green) and flesh (pink). It was in a nice frame. Segura called out for tea, and five minutes later the woman in the picture walked into the room with a tray.

Segura had been at Dolores from 1936 to 1946. He'd spent five years in Fidel's company, but they hadn't been close. Even then, he had had an accountant's temperament. Small, slight, modest, he didn't mix well with the overweening force of Fidel's personality. He remembered sitting near Raúl in classes.

'The only thing I can tell you,' Segura said, 'is the story of how He jumped from the third floor with an umbrella.' It began when Fidel had idly suggested that an umbrella could serve as an emergency parachute. Other boys jeered the notion. Fidel had insisted. Soon there was a dare, and by the end of the school day everyone knew that Fidel was going to jump off the third-floor gallery with only an umbrella.

He had to prove he was right. With everyone watching, he climbed over the third-floor railing and jumped. What happened?

'Nothing,' Segura said. 'He landed fine.' He lowered his voice another notch, to a whisper. 'What a shame he didn't crack his head.'

A lot of people remembered this same story. Sometimes it was a bed sheet, not an umbrella. From hearing it repeatedly, I'd collated a few mitigating details. Fidel had planned his stunt. He scouted the best spot on the uphill side of the building, where the ground floor rose up, ten feet closer to his launch point. And he had lowered himself over the railing first, dangling down into the courtyard from the bottom rung – cutting another five feet off the drop. Then he had jumped with the open umbrella (or was it the sheet?), which could indeed slow the fall of a 12-year-old boy, slightly.

That was how you did the impossible. You dogged the problem, worried it, wore it down at the edges, improvised your tools, cut it into smaller, achievable tasks, and then, having made the odds ten feet shorter on one end and five feet shorter on the other, you took a giant leap. If you landed right – more importantly, if you *acted like you landed right* – then no matter how much it hurt at the time, forever after people would believe that you did it, that you could do the impossible. That you could fly your umbrella down from the third floor *and no that wasn't a crash that was victory*. That you could run your invasion fleet aground in a swamp, lose all but 12 of your men in ambushes, and then announce, '*Having invaded successfully we are now marching on the capital.*'

Segura overlapped with him at the University of Havana, but they weren't friends there either. Fidel's life was changing quickly, as he stepped on to a larger stage. While Segura was studying accounting, Fidel was cutting a big figure on the campus. Partly it was a change in family fortunes. Ángel Castro was getting more and more land of his own, and rented out a larger and larger army of *macheteros* around Banes, and he made sure that while his oldest son learned the business, his boldest son had everything a young tyro could want in Havana. A new American car and an annual allowance of $10,000.

Fidel cared so little about money that he often blew

through even this fortune, using it to fund his allies in campus politics. The University of Havana was seething with ideological conflict in the late 1940s. Campus factions were allied with the country's political parties, and Fidel tried to push his way to the top of this system, joining an offshoot of the Ortodoxo party during a particularly violent period on campus. The Ortodoxo students were little more than a gang: one prominent student leader who opposed them was assassinated at this time, and in retrospect many discontented Cubans have tried to blame Fidel for the murder. There is no evidence, except the certainty that Fidel did carry a pistol during this period, tucked inside the jacket of his fancy suits. José Antonio Roca had recalled running into Fidel then, on the long steps that cascade down from the university on to the streets of Vedado. Standing together, Roca and Fidel had fallen into an old-friends chat. But Castro insisted on moving to put his back against a wall during the conversation, manoeuvring Roca like a shield. As explanation, Castro simply flashed the pistol in his belt. He certainly had to protect himself from armed enemies at the university; whether he participated in shootings himself is speculation. Roca had thought only that Fidel was out of his head. He left quickly, and avoided Castro after that.

As the Jesuits expected, a couple of their students would grow up to lead Cuba, just not in the direction anyone intended. Aside from Fidel and Raúl, virtually no Dolores alumni still held positions of significance in Cuba. One exception – the only exception I could find – was Fernando Vecino Alegret, from the class of 1954. He'd been much too young to know Fidel personally at school, but had served in the Sierra as a guerrilla fighter and, uniquely, still served at Fidel's side. Alegret had become head of secondary education in Cuba, a post he used to ensure that there were never again schools like Dolores. He was recently promoted to education minister.

'He forgot everything he learned at Dolores,' Segura said.

With the louvres closed against the rising heat of the sun, Segura sat in the dark talking of all this in alternating bursts of enthusiasm and hesitance. Although he lowered his voice when talking about 'Him', this was done out of habit. He was old enough, he said, not to worry about any consequences. He hesitated only because he found it depressing to think about how different the world had been back then, how much Cuba and Cubans had changed.

When Segura spoke of change, he made references to 'them', and pointed outside, at the people in the neighbourhood. Black people. After the Revolution people like Segura began to leave the neighbourhood and people like 'them' had moved in. He rubbed two fingers over his wrist, to make sure I understood. He referred to them as 'people down from the hills'.

The novelist Pedro Juan Gutiérrez had one of his white narrators relate this urban alienation among comingled races. 'The neighborhood was no longer what it used to be,' the novel's despicable, dead-end protagonist complained:

> It filled up with common people from the provinces, uncouth blacks, ragged, dirty, rude people. The buildings crumbled since no one took care of them, and little by little, they became dormitories, thousands of people crowded into them like roaches, skinny, underfed, dirty, unemployed people, drinking rum at all hours, smoking marijuana, beating on drums, and multiplying like rabbits, people without perspective, with limited horizons. Everything made them laugh. What were they laughing at – everything. Nobody was sad or wanted to kill themselves or was terrified for fear the ruins would collapse and bury them alive. Not at all. In the middle of the debacle, they laughed, lived their lives, tried to enjoy themselves as best they could . . . Born in the ruins, they just kept trying not to give up or let themselves be beaten so severely that at last they were forced to surrender. Anything was possible, everything allowed, except defeat.

Segura wasn't one of these loathsome characters out of fiction, but a decent man carrying obsolete resentments. The world had changed too fast for people like him.

'They have announced fish for Monday,' he said. He pulled
out his *libreta*. Like most Cubans, he carried it on his person at all
times, even when he was wearing pajamas. The *libreta* was the
ration book. He showed me the ration for one person, for one
month: six pounds of rice, one pound of salt, twenty ounces of
'grains', four pounds of raw sugar, one pound of refined sugar,
and two litres of oil.

Those were the theoretical quotas. There was always something missing, usually several things a month that weren't
delivered, just as there were unexpected supplements from time
to time, especially for the elderly and children. Macaroni, beans
and 'soy protein substitute' might appear, written into the
bottom of a page. But for every extra delivery, there were
two shortages. Few quotas were met, except sugar. Five pounds
a month per person was more than even the Cuban sweet tooth
demanded. But of course the sugar wasn't for eating. Using a
pair of plastic tubs, a little tubing, some yeast, and a couple of
weeks of patience, the sugar could be distilled into *aguardiente*.
There was a monthly ration of genuine rum, only enough to fill
a single beer bottle. (You had to supply the beer bottle
yourself.) The country was brimming with heroic bootleggers,
who kept people laughing, who filled the void of ideas and
hope, who let Cuba not give up.

Meanwhile there was fish for Monday. Dried mullet: small and
oily, salted and dried, the fish reeked. Mullet was a rare source of
protein and the only bounty of the sea that came through
government hands. Cuba caught other fish, which were frozen
and shipped abroad; the lobster harvest was particularly lucrative,
but those also went abroad, or into tourist hotels. The lobsters
were so valuable as hard currency that mere possession of frozen
shellfish was a serious crime, but there was a black market in flash-
frozen crustaceans, and old men whispered *lobster lobster* to buyers
in the best neighbourhoods. The crustacean would be delivered
separately, like a drug shipment.

They didn't announce a thing until they were sure it was
coming, so the little blue mullets on the ration would likely
arrive, eventually. 'In August,' Segura said by way of example,

'we should get the May soap.' Like everyone, he kept an eye on what was available outside the system. He found the food at the few, small farmers' markets to be always too expensive for him, except for the mangoes, which cost a peso apiece, and the occasional egg, at 2 pesos. There were government stores that sold pants for $11 a pair, but he couldn't afford that, and had to wait for his annual ration of clothing – pants, shirt, shoes – even though it really only came every 18 months or so.

Better to shop at the *candongas*, he said. Cuban soldiers who served in Angola in the 1980s had brought the word and the concept home with them. Based on the traditional practice of African market women, who laid out their goods anew each morning, *candongas* were tiny venues for selling your own possessions. They were usually just a row of heavily used personal goods – combs, broken watches, shoes, a radio, maybe a shirt or a pair of pants – and the key was that they had to be laid out on a cot. This was the only way to bypass the rules against having a business. As long as the goods could all fit on a single cot, it was legal to sell them without any licence. This is why Cuban men and women could be found walking into the centre of town in the early mornings, carrying folding cots. They used old army cots, or hospital cots, or even folding lawn chairs at maximum recline. They would set up in shaded doorways, cover the available cot space with a cloth, and then lay out candy, clothing, the carefully cleaned parts of disassembled tools of unknown vintage, and wait all day for a sale. There weren't many *candongas*, because people had few things to sell, and the authorities tolerated them without liking them. It was government policy to have everyone shop in government stores; the *candongas* only existed because of their association with the Angola veterans, who were given a wide berth by the authorities. These men and women had proven their loyalty on the battlefield, fighting the South Africans; they would not be pushed around.

'Fish for Monday,' Segura repeated. 'It's a disaster. If you don't have dollars, you can't have soap, toothpaste, pork.' He continued, muttering a list of ordinary desirables. 'The whole world needs everything here. Laundry soap, bath soap, toothpaste, shoes.'

There were special provisions for senior citizens and the ill, like a supplemental ration of milk, but these did not go far. Jorge got more help from the men he called 'the Miami brothers' – exiled alumni from Dolores who remembered their old comrades in Cuba. They sent small shipments of goods a couple of times a year, through the Catholic Church. As an accountant, Jorge was selected to set up and administer a little system for distributing these precious goods among the remaining alumni. It was a private ration system with its own version of the *libreta*. Segura had taken a blank, hard backed notebook and divided the pages into precisely ruled columns and rows. Names ran down the left side, a dozen men from the scattered decades of the school's existence. The goods were listed across the top: *Bath soap*, it read in Jorge's rotund, Palmer Method cursive, then *laundry soap toothpaste cooking oil pants shoes socks jackets.*

'The brothers there help us,' he explained. They sent the goods down with couriers, usually Catholic laymen who were visiting Church officials. Sometimes the brothers themselves came: Jorge whipped out a couple of photos of some Dolores alumni from Miami who had made a visit to Santiago a few years ago. They had visited their families here, the way Cuban exiles did: quietly. In Miami you could curse and condemn Castro and all his works, and you could listen all day to voices on the radio demanding tougher restrictions on Cuba, less travel and trade. But if you went to the airport in Miami, or Cancún, or Nassau, and boarded a flight to Havana, you would find yourself in the abashed company of Cuban exiles. More than 100,000 Cuban-Americans returned to the island every year, and they knew enough to keep quiet on both sides of the Strait. In Cuba, they kept quiet about their politics. And once back in Miami, they kept quiet about having been on the island. Over the years, some of the loudest advocates of cutting off all travel to Cuba had themselves been caught at Miami International returning from visits with their families.

There was always one explanation for why this was not the

hypocrisy it seemed: there was an emergency. Cubans from the
US were only allowed to return to the island for 'humanitarian
emergencies' involving their families. But in Cuba, where temporary was permanent, life was one long emergency. It was an
emergency when you needed to go to Cárdenas to see your dying
uncle; it was treason when someone else did it.

I told Segura that I would be coming back some day, and drew
up my notebooks, and the photocopies. Jorge was agitated. He
mentioned the surgery he'd had recently, for a urinary problem.
Antibiotics were so rare in Cuba that they were often stolen.
Poorly equipped hospitals would only issue a single pill at a time –
one per patient per day. A man like Jorge, who could have taken
his two-week course of antibiotics at home, was instead forced to
stay in the hospital for fourteen extra days, waiting for the daily
pill.

His recovery was difficult. He spoke haltingly. It was hard, he
said, to get . . . the things people needed in such situations . . .
virtually impossible . . . to get . . . well . . . 'things like————'
he finally said.

Like what?

'————,' he said again, embarrassed. I wrote the word
down. I understand, I told him. I will remember.

'*Y una copia de Baseball Weekly,*' he added before I could put my
pen away. This was his favourite American magazine. He was a
Giants fan, and always had been. He'd been following their ups
and downs in *Baseball Weekly* since he was a kid. He rattled off the
names of a few players. The great _____. The name meant
nothing to me. What about _____? I had never heard of him
either. How could I not know _____? And _____?
They were the greatest Giants players ever!

'And razors,' he said, when I tried to cap my pen.

Later, when I'd left the house, and then Santiago, and Cuba, I
looked the mystery word up. *Pañales*. Diapers. So, he needed
adult diapers to deal with the incontinence that follows urinary
tract surgery. No wonder he was reluctant to discuss it.

I did come back to see Segura, after six months. I stopped by
the house again, chatted some more, and presented him with a

bag of disposable razors, which thrilled him, and an economy-sized bale of 48 'super absorbent' adult incontinence diapers, size medium, which I had bought at a Kmart in New York. I'd carried them through Manhattan, Miami, Nassau, Havana, and then the streets of Santiago. I'd double-bagged them to save myself explanations.

Segura looked confused when I handed them over. I struggled to translate the phrase on the package, *Pañales* de . . . de . . . de adultos.

Diapers? He'd never asked for them. He had no idea what I was talking about. What would he want diapers for? We stared at each other, slackjawed in mutual incomprehension.

Had I misunderstood him, or heard the wrong word? Or not caught the point of a story? Or was it about someone else? Had it been an earlier problem, that had passed? Had he changed his story? Was he too embarrassed to admit he'd needed a diaper?

I left the bale of super-absorbency on the floor of his house, one of those things that fell into the cracks between here and there. Since nothing was wasted in Cuba, the diapers would move, through the ration system in his ledger, or the black market, or to friends of friends, to someone somewhere who needed them.

The magazine was also a flop. *Baseball Weekly* had ceased publication. I had brought Segura a couple of similar magazines, but they were flimsy fanzines, full of steroid-enhanced players whose names he didn't recognize, and cluttered with marketing ploys. Even some of the team names were different.

'Who are the Devil Rays?' he asked me.

BECAUSE IT WAS SO HILLY, Santiago lacked the long, double-humped buses known as *camelos* that were a signature of Cuban life elsewhere. They had been introduced in Santiago in the 1990s but always burned out their transmissions on the steep hills. In Santiago the best transport was the back of a truck, or a three-wheeled delivery van spitting smoke, or even horse carts, which, in the flatter sections of the city, could carry a dozen people. Those with money could catch a yellow plastic *trimoto*, a

motorcycle rickshaw. Only tourists could afford the official taxis
stashed around the city, but anyone could negotiate a black
market cab. There were usually men standing around in the
Plaza Dolores and other parks offering rides.

Looking to kill my Sunday, I hired a fellow to take me to a
beach resort down the coast that had scuba diving. He had a filthy
Lada parked discreetly around the corner from Dolores. He told
me to lie down in the back seat as we drove out of the city
('police' he explained). In 15 minutes he was driving through
farmed fields. There was a checkpoint ahead, and the driver
veered off the asphalt road, cut down a farm track, made a left at a
hut, and drove for half an hour down an increasingly sandy
wagon track, until he realized he was lost. A cowboy gave
directions, and we cut through a field, around trees, into a
riverbed and came out on the asphalt road. A mile later the
engine died. Using a nail file from my hotel toiletries, the driver
filed some grime off points in the distributor and the Lada started
up. We drove on, past 20 miles of black sand beaches, to the
resort. Like all such hotels, it was a joint venture between the
Cuban government (which supplied the labour and cement) and a
foreign, in this case Spanish, hotel company (which supplied
capital and management). It had hundreds of rooms, mostly
empty, and sweeping views of the coast and the mist-fringed
mountains of the Sierra Maestra.

The driver was not allowed to drive into the hotel entrance. I
arranged for him to come back after nightfall, and then ate a
dismal buffet lunch beside the pool with about 80 French people.
In the afternoon I joined a dive on a nearby reef, the boat full of
agreeable young Europeans on package tours. They had seen little
or nothing beyond the resort. One couple had visited Cuba seven
times without setting foot in a major city. At the resorts, drinks
and food were included at modest prices, so going anywhere else
was losing money. By 9 pm I was back in Santiago.

There were no black market cabs at the Hotel Santiago,
because it stood alone in a sea of crabgrass, too far from busy
streets where men, looking for illegal fares, could loiter anony-
mously. Instead the hotel offered a bank of shiny government

Mitsubishis. I climbed into the first and mentioned a *paladar* that I had heard about – The Hen, or something like that – and the driver told me he knew it. It wasn't far from the Cathedral. He hit a button on the taxi meter, turned up the air-conditioning, adjusted the radio, rolled up the windows, inquired after my comfort, and we set off.

In Havana, there were dozens of *paladares* sprinkled through the various neighbourhoods, but you would rarely find the same place twice, because any given restaurant tended to last only a year or 18 months before being shut down. They might be closed for violating the onerous tax regulations, or for seating too many people, or because the owners had used their profits to flee the country, or because they were ratted out by jealous neighbours, infuriated at the sight of someone else getting ahead, buying TVs and clothes, raising fat children, while they themselves lived on the *libreta*. But in the end, no matter how many were shut down, there were always more *paladares* in the capital. Santiago was different: there were only two legal private restaurants in the city. Havana people always cautioned that Santiago was *muy revolucionario*, meaning that the second city took its Communism seriously. Central planning was rigidly enforced, capitalism ruthlessly suppressed, pleasure outlawed. There was no resident population of foreigners to justify the many restaurants of the capital: aside from the spectacle of prosti-tourism at the Big House, Orientales were rarely confronted by the sight of others eating well. *Muy revolucionario* turned out to mean nothing to eat.

To make time, I asked the cab driver a simple question: 'How are things?'

'Well, that depends on where you ask the question from,' he said. 'It's difficult.' He complained about food prices, so I pointed out that there was more meat for sale than a few years ago.

'Yes,' he said, cautiously. 'There is a little more. But it's expensive. The salary for a Cuban . . . well, let's say it's 140 or 150 pesos. You have to buy food at the farmers' markets, because there is not enough on the ration. If you want *macho*,' he said, using Oriente slang for pork, 'you have to buy it at the markets. And a family needs protein. A family can eat a kilo of *macho* in no time. That's not much. But a kilo costs . . . well, it's sold by the pound, but, 2 pounds to the kilo . . . well, it's 2.2 pounds to the kilo, but 2 pounds costs 40 pesos.'

I did maths as best I could. That meant spending about ten days of your total income for 2.2 pounds of pork?

'Yes.'

In the old centre of town, where the streets narrowed, we came up behind a dump truck. It was a big, rotten old beast of a truck, bent, battered and painted red in the places that showed beneath soot or oil. It sat there on bald tyres, impassive, comfortably squatting across the entire lane from kerb to kerb. A dozen men were milling around it, their hands and arms black with grease, their clothes oily. The taxi driver blew his horn, as did the driver behind us. There was a lot of shouting, orders were issued, boys stopped to watch, some of the men got on the truck, and then after several minutes a man came out, carrying in one palm a piece of a machine, no bigger than a box of matches. He put it on the truck, climbed up himself, the remaining men all climbed into the bed with him, the engine fired up, the stove pipe behind the cab emitted a great dragon puff of black smoke, and with a grinding of gears it, and then we, began to move.

'I was working for a couple from Curaçao yesterday,' the driver said. 'You know Curaçao?'

All I knew about Curaçao was that three de Jongh boys at Dolores had been descended from a Curaçao family.

No, I told him, I didn't know Curaçao personally. 'It's an island,' he said. 'Anyway, the man told me how his grandparents used to dream about Cuba. They thought Cuba was rich. And it's true, before 1959 Cuba had the highest per capita income in the Caribbean, if not in Latin America. Well, the guy told me that when he was a kid, Curaçao was so poor that people used to dream about coming to Cuba to cut sugar cane for 50 cents a day. Now, he said, it's the Cubans who dream about going to Curaçao to cut sugar cane for 50 cents a day.' He looked at me in the mirror. 'He was joking, you know. They don't have any sugar cane in Curaçao. But it's true.' He drove on for a block. 'But Fidel Castro' – the driver actually used the name – 'doesn't care about that. Everything has gone wrong. Nothing ever changes. It's like the devil came to this island.'

The fare was $2.25, all of which went to the government, because it was an official taxi. I gave him $3, and he thanked me, profusely. He was well dressed, in his early thirties, and had one of the best jobs around. All he had to do was tell a sob story to a foreigner and he could make 75 cents without cutting any sugar cane at all.

The *paladar* had no sign. There were 32 people packed around five tables. This was a violation of the law against serving more than 12 customers, but at $7 a plate, the margin was irresistible. And if you gave enough meals to the right people, you wouldn't get in trouble. I'd shared a table at a *paladar* once with the local beat cops who were eating themselves silly.

It took an hour to get seated. This time I shared my table with a Danish woman and her Mexican boyfriend. The Mexican was depressed. In Mexico City, he said, when you mentioned Cuba, people began talking about the enormous dignity of the Revolution, about justice, equality and progress. It was the same in Copenhagen, where he owned a Mexican restaurant. But now he'd seen Cuba. 'There is nothing here,' he said, speaking quietly, in a kind of shock. No dignity. No food, justice, equality, or progress. Nothing at all. *No hay nada*, he said over and over, almost whispering. 'I always thought it was the land of progress,' he added. 'But this makes Mexico look like a rich country.'

We were given menus, but then the owner came out of the kitchen and explained that she had neither pork, nor fish, nor beef. Just chicken. With rice. We ordered chicken with rice, and beer, and waited.

When it came, the Mexican couldn't believe the food. The Dane barely touched hers. But I have a stomach like a Bedouin dog, and gnawed it down to the bones.

'MOST OF THOSE PEOPLE WENT TO THE STATES,' Miguel Llivina told me, during a second visit to his wire-reinforced house in Vista Alegre. He was going through the pages of his old yearbook. Photographs kept prompting memories, and he spoke like a medium at a seance, reciting slowly as the visions came. 'Fernando Alvarez,' he said at one point. 'He lives in Virginia. He inspects chickens. To see if they are healthy. His oldest brother worked in the oil refinery. I worked there too. With the Americans. For the Texas Oil Company. They are called Exxon now.'

I reminded him that he had already told me this. By the time you reach your seventies you accumulate too many stories, and only those that are taken out and tended, aired and brushed up from time to time, will survive the erosion of age.

Nothing in recent decades had made the same impression on Miguel as high school, and that is true for most people: adolescence is our life. Miguel had done things since Dolores, of course. He showed me some pictures of trips he'd made, before the Revolution. He'd been to Spain in 1949, had gone to summer school in Mexico, and had made a tour of Washington DC that same year. But since 1959 the only place he had visited was Mexico, a single time. He'd gone to visit a Mexican he'd known, who had made a successful career in the Oaxaca tourism office. A very successful career: somehow the man had a private jet, which he'd used to visit Cuba once (Miguel had pictures of himself with the plane on the Santiago tarmac) and a large and elaborate house in Monterey. He flicked slowly through pictures of a swimming pool, a dining room with a huge banquet table, white sofas and white rugs, a stained-glass window, and a pottery collection. 'Everything is air-conditioned,' Miguel explained. 'There are a lot of rich people there.'

After closing the album he found, under it, an item that struck him from a new angle. He held it and stared, falling a little inside himself. I gently removed it from his hand: it was an airplane ticket, for a flight on Pan-American. The date of the flight was 10 August 1961. The route was from Havana to Miami. The price was $12.50, each way. He had been forced to pay for a round trip ticket, even though he wasn't planning to come back.

His father got out, his sister got out, his uncle got out. But even though he had paid for this ticket, Miguel had never gotten the permissions and paperwork together, and he didn't make this flight, or any other. He still thought about America. 'You could write a book about the problems I had trying to get there,' he said.

There was an arching cry in the street, and Miguel sat up. He went to the door just as a soft knock touched its outside. He opened it to a tall, rail thin man in a straw cowboy hat. His face and hands were dark from constant sun, his beard was grimy, and he held before him two cardboard pallets filled with several dozen eggs each.

'Eggs,' the man said.

Miguel fussed for a while, inspected the eggs, took out his money, and shouted to his wife Lola in the back of the house, without reply. He looked at the eggs again, but couldn't make up his mind.

'Come tomorrow,' he finally said. 'I'm busy. I don't need eggs until tomorrow.'

I didn't stay long myself. On the way out Miguel gave me a letter, which he wanted me to pass to an old friend. A really old friend, someone 'from before' who lived in New York. Or had lived there. They hadn't seen each other in 35 years. Miguel had heard that he'd separated from his wife, and that he'd had a heart attack. 'I'm thinking that maybe he died,' Miguel said. He gave me the letter, and two addresses for the man. Both of the addresses were from the 1970s.

That might have worked in Cuba, but not in America. In New York I would mail off the letter to the first address, get it back, and mail it to the second, to have it returned again.

Miguel offered to drive me to my hotel. He went off to get the car, and I sat on the porch, in the dark, with his wife. Lola said nothing for a while, so I complimented the pretty back yard and the generous house. 'It is a pain to us,' she replied. They were too old to take care of the house, and needed family. But their children were 'lost'. One son, the Miguel Jr that I had met, had moved to Havana. The other to Spain. The former they saw annually, the latter never.

'He left with a *problemita*,' she explained. A little problem. 'Just a bit of paperwork he didn't get. It was just lacking one signature, but because of that, things are not right.' This was a reference to a

Permit for Residence Abroad, the final and crucial document that allowed Cubans to leave. It was very difficult to get one of these permits, unless you were the son or daughter of a prominent official. And if the paperwork was 'not right', the son could not return from Spain, ever. He was one of 200,000 Cubans in Spain now. The Cuban government would use different definitions of *problemita*: he had fled without permission, defected, become a *gusano*, a worm, a traitor. So their boy, now a man, stayed in Spain. He had been married here in Cuba, and had left his wife and a daughter behind when he bolted. This granddaughter, now a teenager, lived in the house with Miguel and Lola.

'He's waiting until the right moment when things are easier and he can come back,' Lola said. 'But of course, it has been 13 years, his wife divorced him, and the girl has no father. It's lamentable.'

The girl would be entitled to a Spanish passport when she turned 18. 'She will leave, because she will have to, because everyone will have to, *lamentablemente*,' Lola concluded. 'It's the only way to survive.'

The car squealed up. It was a 1988 Lada, the final vintage. Somehow these ugly, squared-off Commiecars never made it into the wall calendars about Cuba, where the roads were inhabited only by lacquered Buick 8s and salt-rusted Chevies with Jane Russell curves. Ladas were more common, and were more desirable, since they didn't guzzle fuel and burn through cases of oil like the old American cars. As we started out, Miguel told me that Ladas were becoming popular even in America now. He'd seen it on Cuban television: they were setting up Lada dealerships in New York and 'many other places', because the cars were so fuel efficient, and inexpensive enough for young people.

We reached the big roundabout where Vista Alegre gave way to the lower city. Down to the left was the old centre, Dolores, Enramada, the parade route, and up to the right my hotel, the anonymous, air-conditioned, pimp-riddled Hotel Santiago. I could see my room on the fifteenth floor, but Miguel was 70, and couldn't see across the traffic circle. He took off his glasses, squinted, then put them back on, and squinted again, and then finally took them off. If he had the glasses on, he couldn't see cars approaching from across the circle. And if he took them off, he couldn't read the dials or see the stick shift.

A car shot by. Someone behind us honked. Llivina put the glasses on again, put the car in gear, then took the glasses off. He squinted, looking for anything moving, and then in a swift motion stabbed the glasses on to his face and floored it.

JORGE SEGURA SENT ME to see a man named Balbino Rodríguez Romero, another accountant, and another Dolores alumnus who had remained in Santiago. From the class of 1958, he was one of the last to graduate from the school. Balbino had attended Dolores for nine years. Balbino's address proved to be a small but beautiful 1950s house near the very top of Vista Alegre. Balbino answered the door and it was obvious he was made of different brush strokes, a spry 61, robust and middle-aged compared to Llivina or Segura. He was fit, with plenty of black in his hair, keen of hearing and quick with a response. Even his clothes were more up to date: a polo shirt and nice sneakers. Unlike the older men, he was part of the hard generation that had risen since the Revolution. Physically harder. Even sitting in the chair he had a wiry attentiveness, his focus snapped in, his hands held in front of him, the fingers splayed against each other in an unwavering steeple.

The duplex house, made of cement, had the usual wide louvres to admit the breezes of Vista Alegre, and Balbino served tiny cups of coffee, which we downed in a gulp. I asked him to tell me about Santiago in the 1950s, and his complaints were not of injustice. 'It was a city without much social life,' Balbino said. 'It had some, but not much. It needed changes. There was no nightlife. There was the Rancho Club, and the what was it called, the one by the airport, the . . . the . . . the Club San Pedro. The city was very *costumbrista*,' he said, meaning set in its ways. 'But there was a rebirth going on in the 1950s. There was a big plant by the Texas Oil Company, I think it was called, and a cement factory, and a new wheat mill, and the port was rebuilt. The new airport was opened. There were new urban developments, like this one.'

He still had his history textbook from Dolores. Opening it at random I fell on a lesson about the Platt Amendment, the dagger at the heart of the troubled Cuban-American relationship. In 1903, Cuba was forced to give America the right to control the island's foreign policy, and also to intervene in case of domestic instability, or even sanitary catastrophe. The Jesuit textbook reproduced an exchange of letters between the US governor general of Cuba, and various Cuban independence leaders over the merits or injustices of the Platt Amendment. Both views were spelled out at the same length, with each side speaking for itself. 'Which view is correct?' the textbook asked.

The answer was not in doubt: the Dolores textbook stated flatly that the Cuban view of the Platt Amendment was correct, the American view wrong. The Platt Amendment reduced the Cuban state to 'a fictional government'. But students were required to write an essay analyzing *both* arguments for their strengths and weaknesses.

I asked him what he remembered of Dolores and he laughed. 'Seven thirty am arrival, study hall until 8, 8 to 8.20 mass, Monday through Friday. Then ten minutes to organize ourselves. Class from 8.30 to 11.15. Then home to eat with your family. About 1.30 classes would start again, and at 4.15 you would finish.' The routine was still engraved in his mind.

Dolores itself had been founded in 1913 as a response to 'US influence after the war', Balbino said. The elite – what Balbino evasively called 'the religious community' – wanted to preserve their way of life, their traditions, their values. An exclusive Catholic school administered by Jesuits looked like just the thing.

'In Dolores there was a strong education,' he said. 'The Jesuits had teachers who weren't priests. It was strong, very rigorous. The discipline was severe. They'd hit us with whatever they could find at hand – a ruler, an eraser. They'd grab us by the ear,' he said, pinching his left lobe, 'or by the hair. But they weren't sadists. There was a lot of order. The Jesuits were specialists in forming disciplined minds.' He remembered the morning drill, as

300 boys marched into the chapel in two files, everyone sitting in their seats 'in five minutes flat'.

The Jesuits, I said, were almost like an army –

'It *is* an army,' he countered. 'The Company of Jesus is an army. I think Fidel got so far in this life because of the discipline he learned from the Jesuits,' Balbino said. 'In my opinion – don't write this down – the Jesuits trained him to think with discipline. To think and work. That's what they taught. Some learned it, others didn't. The pre-Revolutionary society owed a lot to the Jesuits.'

While he was in school, the pre-Revolutionary society was increasingly corrupt. 'In 1956 the police were killing Revolutionary youth and non-Revolutionary youth equally. The police were very violent. The army even more so. They assassinated people before asking a question. And not just killing. They were tortured and mutilated. Castrated. Their eyes were cut out. Batista can never be forgiven. Never.'

Balbino became so emotional reciting these crimes that he had to pause for a moment. 'I don't know what to say about him,' he concluded. 'He took power by force, so force was the only way to get rid of him.'

As a result, Oriente was filled with angry, rebellious young people in search of a leader. That the rebellion occurred in Oriente was no coincidence: with the worst inequalities and the most suffering, eastern Cuba was most ready to explode. And it was partly character. Santiago people often described themselves as 'hot' or 'fiery', slow to move but quick to feel.

'The Oriental is effervescent,' Balbino conceded.

Most effervescent of all was the young Dolores graduate Fidel Castro.

'I was in 7th grade when the *Granma* landed,' Balbino said, and it was much discussed at the school. They talked about the peculiarities of his years at Dolores. There were many anecdotes. How Fidel always liked mountain climbing and hiking. There was a story about Raúl who brought a parrot to school, and taught it to shout '*Salgero veinte cuentas!*', the disciplinary mantra of the most severe Jesuit at the school.

Since we were discussing the Revolutionaries, I told him that I had written a book about Che Guevara. I explained that it was a revisionist history that tried to—

'The Che was a great man,' Balbino said. His frame had tensed up. The phrase *historia revisionista* had set off something in him. He leaned forward.

'Do you want to know what a hero is?' he said, staring at me intensely. 'That is a hero, right there.' He was pointing at the black and white picture on a small table. It showed a handsome, fair-haired man in bright sunshine. It was his cousin, Jorge Sotus, Dolores '44. This was the brother of the Juan Sotus who I had met in Puerto Rico. Jorge was the 'James Dean' Sotus, who had been a captain in the anti-Batista underground. To cover for Fidel's invasion down the coast, Jorge had led a diversionary attack in Santiago itself. The timing was all wrong – Fidel and his men were still lost at sea – and most of the Santiago insurgents were gunned down in the streets. Like the Moncada attack, it was a costly failure that succeeded in delivering a psychic shock to the country.

Dolores in 1958 was abuzz with this conflict. There were arguments for and against Castro. There was a strong undercurrent of sympathy. 'Fidel was an old student,' Balbino said. 'They didn't say much, but I think to a certain extent they were proud of him.'

One of the youngest teachers went further than pride. Father Guzmán, known as 'Seven Foot' for his immense height, was one of the few Cuban Jesuits at Dolores, and a favourite among the students. Guzmán, young, passionate, yearned for change in Cuba. He secretly enlisted in the 26th of July Movement, and in the last months of the war began wearing their black and red armband under his robe. In November or December of 1958 he disappeared. He travelled into the Sierra to meet with his heroes. He returned a few weeks later, disillusioned.

But many more were swept up in hero worship. Of Fidel, Balbino said, 'The youth followed him blindly. Men, women, the old and the young.'

A horse went by slowly outside, pulling a wagon full of onions. *Onions onions onions sweet sweet onions*, a man in a straw hat cried, and touched his whip to the horse's back.

Near Balbino's old textbook was an unframed photo. His Dolores class at their First Communion. There were a dozen boys in white tuxedos, sitting stiffly in front of a dark cloth backdrop. Balbino ran his right index finger over the hard paper. 'All the rest left. Practically all.'

When I left, I walked down through Vista Alegre, passing the neighbourhood's Catholic church. I poked my head in here just to confirm what everyone had told me: there, under an archway, was the statue of Ignatius Loyola.

Perform the acts of faith, Loyola said, and faith itself will come. Perform the acts of wisdom, and wisdom will come.

Act, he said. Act and it will.

'PIONEERS OF COMMUNISM!' shouted the voice that answered my knock at Dolores, the last time. Of course, the school isn't called Dolores now. Cuban schools today are named by men like Miguel Llivina Jr, given sobriquets like the Nguyen Van Troi School, or the Solidarity with Chile School, or School #108. Dolores was called the Central School, due to its location. 'PIONEERS OF COMMUNISM!' the voice belted again. Carnaval was over. It was Monday afternoon, the end of the school day. But the streets of Santiago were so safe, so quiet, that no parents came to pick up their children here. Fuel was so tight that no buses waited. I was alone on Clock Street.

The doors were closed, but I could hear hundreds and hundreds of children being called to attention, a hubbub that died down into the squeaky shuffling of rubber sneakers on the patio. The squeaks grew tiny, precise. They were lining up

'TO ARMS, VALIANT ONES,' the voice shouted. A boy's voice, harsh and instructive, and then some shuffling sound, hundreds of children standing to attention, facing the flag.

'PIONEERS OF COMMUNISM,' the boy shouted, and the students roared it out, as they did every day: 'WE WILL BE LIKE CHE!'

All at once, life. A bell, a great crush of body sounds, voices growing into shrieks, laughter and singing. The doors were flung open and a sea of adolescents, boys in red pants and girls in red skirts, came flushing out the door, sweeping all Cuba before them. All the students wore white shirts, with red kerchiefs knotted loosely around the collar. Every one of them wore the kerchief of the Young Pioneers.

I turned sideways and pressed in, through the front door, swimming against the stream of children. The old courtyard was packed with kids in uniform, hordes of them coursing around in circles and clusters, playing hopscotch and patty-cake, skipping rope, shouting and screaming, laughter echoing up the high walls and doubling back down on us, all accompanied by the slap and squeak of cheap rubber sneakers.

There was a chalk board propped in the courtyard, full of tiny, precise handwriting. It was a list of academic titles on the left, each matched with a figure in a column of numbers down the right.

I approached a cluster of three adults and announced that I would like to speak to the person in charge. They pointed to a man under the gallery, whose very nondescriptness – khaki trousers and a short-sleeved permanent-press shirt with pen in pocket – was the usual uniform of power in Cuba. He was the principal, or director. I introduced myself as 'the visitor who contacted you earlier', mentioned the names of all the historians and institutes and libraries that I had recently thought about visiting, explained that I was making my third 'study' here at the school, and asked him to explain the long columns of numbers.

He hesitated, but then began talking, and was soon running on automatic, pointing at the chalk board and giving his briefing. There were 700 students and 50 teachers. The school held only three grades: 10th through 12th.

Had I misheard him? Seven hundred students?

'Yes,' he said. 'Seven hundred. This is a temporary measure.' In 1941 there had been 238 students in the building.

The curriculum, the director explained, was the same as in every school in Cuba. Not just a national set of requirements, like in the old school system, but a completely centralized lesson plan, detailed down to the wording to be written on a blackboard. Everything was designed for maximum efficiency by pedagogical experts like Miguel the Younger. Listed on the blackboard were

medical school, nuclear technology, accounting, journalism, engineering, and a dozen other career paths of questionable utility in
a country beholden to tourism and envelopes from Miami.

Entrance to university was rationed. Students picked three
careers they wanted to pursue, ordering them in priority. There
was no doubt what was most popular: more than 2,000 students
around the province had applied for medical school. But next to
'MEDICINE' the number read '400': the quantity of open spaces.
Busboys in restaurants earned more than doctors, but obviously
some kind of idealism was still strong within these walls.

The selection of those 400 was a model of Cuba's pure intent
and corrupt reality. In theory each senior was rated on a scale of
100 points. The highest scorers were given first choice. When
medicine filled up, the lower scoring students would be given
their second picks; the lowest scoring were sent to their third
picks. A lot of people ended up as agronomists.

I asked where the 100 points came from. 'Fifty points are
awarded for their grade average, and 50 more come from their
exam scores, and so on.'

And so on?

Again, the look. 'There are other points,' he said. 'For extracurricular activities, and so on.'

And so on. Those who scored less well on the meritocratic
measures – grades and exams – could still benefit from other
influences. Politics. *Amiguismo*. The Pioneers. The Young Communists. Volunteer labour. All could change scores, and all
involved subjective avenues of preference and influence, family
and patronage. There was a system, and then there was the
improvised Cuban genius for non-system, for exceptions and
loopholes.

With the school empty I climbed upstairs. From a third-floor
classroom, looking out of a tall, thin window, you could see all of
Santiago, falling down toward the harbour. The twin bell towers
of the Cathedral stood out against the lines of the bay and
mountains.

Two men climbed the bell towers of the Cathedral, silhouettes
moving against the late afternoon. After a moment they pulled on

the ropes, slowly, and the great bells began to swing, and a clapper struck the hour 20 times or so, at an unhurried pace. Everything here was by hand.

In a quiet city like this, with so little traffic, so few distractions and distortions, everyone within range of that warm, human tolling knew where they lived, which particular hand-shaped place this was. The bells embraced all who lived within their reach.

Down in the Plaza Dolores, a pushcart vendor struggled up the far side of the square, heading up Enramada. 'Peanuts,' he cried out, 'peanuts.' And then, in song:

> Coco water to clean out your insides
> milk fresh from the cow,
> Pineapples and garlic too.

4

LA CAPITAL

WAR AND MAYHEM were on the agenda, although we didn't know it. In the last hours of the old year, the gods gathering for their revelations, the rest of us were blissfully ignorant. Up on a rooftop in Havana, the air was cool, the drinks were cool, the party cool, still in its relaxed, early hours. Guests had been arriving since 7 pm, climbing up the four flights of crumbling stairs and huffing on to the cement patio, where our host, Enrique, lived in an improvised cubicle. The acid novelist Pedro Juan Gutiérrez called rooftop living the epitome of Havana life, and Enrique, the brother of a friend, was the epitome of the city: *puro Habanero* for many generations, a sometime roller of cigars, renter of love nests to enamoured foreigners, and professional DJ known around the town for his mix tapes, cobbled artfully from the latest global playlists.

The Cuban guests arrived in their best party clothes, oversized blazers or too-tight frocks. The foreigners stumbled on to the roof in sweaty T-shirts and guilty expressions. By 8 pm some more Cubans arrived in a frenzied state of excitement, throwing air kisses in every direction. But these were Cubans from abroad, prodigal daughters bearing gifts (cash, usually, but clothes and appliances were appreciated). These were the happy middle few, living in America or Europe, able to return annually to families as long as they took no obvious political stance against Cuba. *Gusañeros*, people called them, with a wink: a mash of *gusano*, or worm, and *compañero*, comrade. Half-worm because they had fled; half-comrade because they came back.

Most Cubans dreamed of leaving, and most never would. But among the trapped on this island were a few volunteers,

foreigners who had chosen to take exile in a country that
produced exiles. The American Revolutionaries expected to be
greeted as heroes, but Cuba distrusted them, fearing spies and
provocateurs, and they were sent to hard labour, to prove
themselves through suffering. Outlaw Americans were still
sprinkled around the city. The radical journalist who lingered
in Havana under a pseudonym. A Black Panther, a cop killer
who, broken by years of cutting cane in the fields, had turned
introspective and retailed his story and dime bags of marijuana
to the curious foreign leftists who looked him up. There was
the CIA turncoat, Philip Agee, the fugitive financier Robert
Vesco, and the anonymous con man I met, sunning himself on
a megayacht in the harbour after bolting from minimum
security.

A radical black American climbed up to the roof, still lithe, and
ready to dance. She was a *mulata fina*, tall, gorgeous, her light skin
dappled with freckles. She'd been born in America as Cheri
Laverne Dalton and joined the Black Liberation Army (BLA), a
revolutionary movement calling for a separate black nation in the
American south-east. Despite this racial agenda, Cheri had helped
white militants carry out a bloody robbery in New York in 1981
that left one guard and two police officers dead. She'd fled to
Cuba (for once without hijacking a plane), where she had
changed her name to Nehanda Obiodun. She was still wanted
in America for armed bank robbery, racketeering, obstruction of
justice, and violating the Hobbs Act, but in Cuba she lived in a
small bubble of security. Paid the dismal salary of a Cuban
professional, she sometimes briefed foreign delegations on racial
progress in Cuba, but was best known for her work cleaning up
the Cuban rap scene.

My favourite group, the Free Hole Negro, had been one of her
victims. The band, whose name punned the phrase 'black beans',
had become popular for raw a cappella anthems denouncing
racism and repression in Cuba, but such problems cannot be
spoken into a microphone, and the Free Hole Negro group was
banned from the Havana Rap Festival. After an outcry, the band
was allowed to appear the next year but just seconds into their set

it became obvious they had not taken Cheri's advice to change their lyrics. They launched into an uncensored song about racism. Within seconds someone pulled the plug, dropping the stage into darkness. Blackouts do occur in Cuba, but once the Free Hole Negro group had left the stage, the electricity came back on.

It wasn't easy being one of these fugitive exiles, betwixt and between, neither American nor Cuban. The novelist Carlos Eire recalled the shock of leaving Cuba as a white boy of Irish descent, only to discover in Florida that he was really seen by some as a dirty little spick. Cheri had undergone the reverse, fleeing America as a black nationalist, only to settle in Cuba, the one place where a *mulata fina* like her would never be called black.

Havana was a time machine. I loved the capital, bitterly and deeply. The luminous blue-grey hurricane light. The storm spray that left cars, people and decaying mansions coated with the white dust of salt. The oily harbour, fuming and ringed with Spanish forts. The blue streak of the Gulf Stream itself, visible from the rooftops every day, a world just beyond. Even storm waves broke against the indestructible city. Havana was battered and defeated on the outside, ground to the colour of dead coral. But the facades, the majestic banks and great trading companies along the sea-bound avenues, only looked dead. Inside, the ancient buildings were warrened with unlit, fragmentary stairways that led to roach- and rat-infested labyrinths of *cuartería* apartments. Even the sordid smells on the inside of Havana, the extremes of human defecation, of squalid life, or pigeon coops, were just as grand in their way as the august Havana that could be photographed. Life was in ruins, in this city, and always had been.

One-fifth of Cubans live in Havana. The people here drop their r's, speak more slowly than in Oriente and walk faster, though that isn't saying much in either case. Habaneros say *papaya* where the easterners said *frutabomba*, and people in Santiago can say what they want, but this is the cosmopolis, the hard, intransigent, crumbling life of Cuba all in one package. A global capital of the quixotic, where free market superstars come to denounce capitalism, apostles of asceticism fall off the wagon, and most secrets are vulnerable to a $100 bill. The parks are full of prostitutes, the houses full of liquor and, in this *capital inmoral* of the Revolution, even cocaine. I'd seen colonels eating lobster with teenage girls at 3 am, English rock stars expounding on socialism from the the lawn of the Nacional, Russian real estate mobsters on three-girls-a-day benders, Mexican guerrillas turned Marxtrepreneurs, Chilean assassins making a killing in fruit juice, and the astounding perverts of all nations, wallowing in it.

Despite the 2.2 million who live here, Havana is notable for its emptiness, for the quietness of its avenues by day, their inky darkness at night. The streets are full of spectacular wrecks, black-eyed houses and abandoned hotels, mansions with holed roofs, featureless plains like the Plaza of the Revolution, a gigantic parking lot where legendary rallies had once been held. The novelist Virgilio Piñera described this city – the hungry Havana under the Revolution – as a static place, inherently incomplete, cut off from its own dreams by the sea edge, a theoretical city larded with unerected monuments to unrealized gestures and unpractised virtues. It is the city where the whole world went to be lied to. I found Havana dangerous to body and soul. A high-low environment where you could get arrested for nothing but everyone got away with everything.

By 9 pm on a roof in Chinatown, on New Year's Eve, under the cool canopy of stars, people were starting to sway. Enrique's latest mix tape was pulling people out of their seats: Cuban hip-hop from Paris, New Yorican soul. A few minutes before 10, a single table of food – paid for by the foreigners – appeared and was wiped clean.

Chinatown was a muddy, crowded but ghostly district of just a few streets, where the ideograms on the walls were unread. There had been Chinese in Cuba since 1847, and the *barrio chino* had 10,000 residents at the start of the twentieth century. Cubans had derided them as drug addicts and homosexuals, and successive governments had restricted their rights, lines of work and social standing. The Cuban Chinese had taken that message to heart: they deserted Cuba en masse during the spiral of military coups and gangsterism that comprised the 1930s and 1940s. They decamped for the US, particularly New York, which gave rise to the curiosity of Chino-Latino cuisine – Manhattan diners dishing chop suey with black beans and rice, mushu pork in a garlic-citrus marinade. Today there are only about one hundred Chinese left. Their housing had been filled in, of course, and it was an overwhelmingly black neighbourhood now.

Before coming up to the party, I had been waiting on the dirty, wet street for Enrique to let me in (a process of bellowing at the roof, waiting, conversing in fourth-floor volumes, and then standing by as he pulled gingerly on a very long piece of string, which curled down through four floors of security grates, broken doorways, concrete obstructions, stairs with and without bann-isters, which yanked the bolt). During the wait I asked a very old black man what had happened to the Chinese. He thought a long time. 'They go away,' he finally said, waving a hand. It was a perfect Cuban answer. Passive. Taking no position on past versus present. Admitting no cause. The Chinese had simply gone away.

Click, the bolt popped. Climbing up, it was a different Cuba even one floor above the street. Homes were the only private space, where people could shut out the block committees, the snoops, the police, and let their guard down. The higher you climbed the more freedom you felt. By the time you reached the roof, four flights of narrow and crumbling stairs, the door opened on a little patio, invisible to the world below or even around. Altitude brought out the best in people.

Almost the moment, now. Three men in white set up *batá* drums, one tall, one fat, one square, and began, almost casually, beating a tattoo. Fifty guests quietened down, and the drums rose up, over the taut-faced people, across the brambled skyline of pirated wiring and jury-rigged antennas, omnidirectional toward the dome of the old Capitol, the crumbling towers of the National Theatre, toward Old Havana and also out, beyond the ferries in the harbour, beyond the fortresses, somewhere far away. The rumba built up, faster, louder, and they started singing.

The trickster, the messenger, the familiar Eleggua was the first to appear, as always. The opener of doors burst out of the doorway to Enrique's rooftop bedroom, arms akimbo, thrashing. Eleggua looked a lot like a woman this time. One of the women, in fact, from the dance troupe that had disappeared into the bedroom 20 minutes before.

Eleggua was wearing the customary red and black stripes, the opposition of life and death. He – she – came out smoking a cigar, and howling, greeted by acclamation from the drummers and the crowd, which was now packed tightly around an oval of dance space. Leaping, twisting and prancing around the edge of the crowd, Eleggua pounded her feet, spun, and finally, returning to the start of her circle, the keeper of paths sat down on my lap, breathing hard and sweating, but smiling. She pulled on a bottle of rum and just continued sitting there, not even acknowledging me.

The message, and messenger, had worked: other gods paraded on to the roof now, in their order. Powerful Ogún, the thundering war-maker. The pale, blue-clad Yemayá, mistress of the salt seas. The luscious Oshún in yellow, goddess of fresh waters and carnal love. Lastly, Lázaro the cripple, hobbling on to the dance floor with his crutch. He wore a loincloth, and was covered with symbolic sores, but Cubans love anyone worse off than they are, and Lázaro was always a favourite, cheered and adored for his ability to take away illness. They all danced in turn, and then together, while the drummers beat wildly and chanted praise. Many in the crowd joined in, singing, shouting, drumming on their own chairs or anything within reach, knocking spoons on tables, singing, firing up their own cigars, calling praise. Now Eleggua noticed she was sitting on me; she forced me to drink, and then passed the bottle of rum to others. She then exhaled through her cigar, ritually hosing me down with a charge of blue smoke, cleansing me from head to toe for some unspecified blessing. She was so skinny that I could feel the bones inside her legs as she sat on me. When she rose to dance, she stuck the wet stub of the cigar in my mouth, and expected it to be primed and glowing when she returned.

For the rest of the night, strangers approached, smiling, patting me on the back. I didn't know why at first, but they thought it was funny, really nice, that a foreigner had been chosen.

Chosen for what? I asked. People just laughed. *Hijo de Eleggua,* they said, passing another bottle. Everyone had seen it. *Child of Eleggua.*

Whatever door had opened, whatever crossroads loomed, you wouldn't find out until you got there. Off in the dark somewhere, the *babalaos* rattled their turtle bones. Soon the new year came, and in the darkness the old one went.

JANUARY 1 AGAIN, THE KEYSTONE DATE OF CUBAN HISTORY, the axle to the Revolution's endless wheel of time. When I stumbled out at noon the streets were empty, the winter sun bright and cool. The trees on the Prado twisted in a strong sea wind, their leaves shushing the city. White caps were visible out beyond the end of the Prado walkway. From a kiosk which sold nothing else, I tried to buy a copy of the first newspaper of the year. They were sold out.

The daily newspaper, *Granma*, was named after Castro's famous boat, the *Granma*, which he had used to invade Cuba in 1956. The curious name of the boat meant nothing to the Revolutionaries, who didn't bother to rechristen it after buying the yacht in Mexico from an American dentist. The American had, of course, simply named the boat for his own grandmother: Granma. Now *Granma* the boat was displayed under glass in a Havana park, and the name had spread. It sounded heroic to Cubans, who didn't realize they were saying *abuelita*. Instead of Oriente, there was a province named Granma now. Factories and housing complexes bore the name. But if you said *Granma* everyone knew which *Granma* you meant: the nation's one daily newspaper. I couldn't help calling it *Grandmother*, but there was nothing funny to Cubans about the paper. The headlines ('Fidel Castro Celebrates with French People') were the only headlines they knew. If *Grandmother* reported that Castro would live to be 120, just months before his 2006 collapse, then who was to say different? I was a loyal reader, when I could find one.

Like a Jacobin, Fidel had not merely redrawn the map of Cuba, he had recalculated the calendar as well. Christmas had been eliminated, 26 July turned into the highlight of the year, 1 January made into a solemn day of reflection, and the decades themselves altered with a new chronology. Instead of 1959 there was the 'Year of the Liberation'. 1960 was renamed the 'The Year of the Agrarian Reform'. In 1962, the 'Year of Planification', there were planning problems. The next year was 'Of Organization', followed by 'Of Economy', and then 'Of Agriculture'. Naming styles changed: the internationalist era of the late sixties and seventies had produced the years of Solidarity, Heroic Viet-Nam, Decisive Force, Productivity, and Socialist Emulation.

The 1980s were mostly dedicated to the twentieth or twenty-fifth anniversaries of events in Castro's life. 1985 was the Year of the Third Congress of the Communist Party of Cuba, but the exemplary names vanished during the chaotic years of the late 1980s and early 1990s, the clock set back by the collapse of the Soviet system. By the late 1990s Cuba had switched to a tourism economy, and the slogan years reappeared as a recitation of long dead heroes. José Martí and Antonio Maceo, while the year known outside of Cuba as 1997 was internally known as 'The Year of the Thirtieth Anniversary of the Death in Combat of the Heroic Guerrilla and his Companions'. This invented count of years was carried on the front page of *Grandmother* every day, reprinted in documents, recited ritually by loyal functionaries and shouted about by students.

Temporal confusion was reinforced by the stopwatch system, which dated events from the Moncada attack of 1953, Day One of Year Zero. So that meant that 1997 was also known officially as 'Year 33', a Khmer Rouge title. For my money the lamest year had been 2001, known as the 'Year of the Victorious Revolution in the New Millennium' because Castro, alone in the world, had refused to celebrate the millennium in 2000. And according to today's newspaper, I was no longer living in any 2004 *anno dominum* at all, but had embarked on something called the 'Year of Glorious Anniversaries of Martí and Moncada'. Nothing epic, nor even actionable. Instead of achievements, anniversaries of achievements.

In 1952, the alumni guide for Dolores had listed Fidel Castro Ruiz (sic) as 'Lawyer, Havana', and half a century later that was still true, although he had a bigger house and they spelled his name right in publications. Castro's life had been transformed

Colegio de Dolores, 1941. Above the railing: 'We are more than him', said Daniel Gonzales, holding the starred Cuban flag, just left of centre. José Antonio Roca, centre, carries the large standard of Dolores to the right of Roca. The pale boy, fourth in from the right edge, is Pepín Bou. Below the railing: José Antonio Cubeñas is directly beneath Roca. Also with his back to the railing, fifth from right, his shoulder touching a white flag, is Fidel Castro. Fidel's younger brother Raúl is one row below Fidel, third from right

Fidel Castro (bottom, left) and friends at the scene of his fist fight with José Antonio Cubeñas. Fidel, star pitcher on the Dolores baseball team, was called 'ball of filth' for his rough manners, dirty clothes and country speech

The Jesuits gathered in the school's upper patio

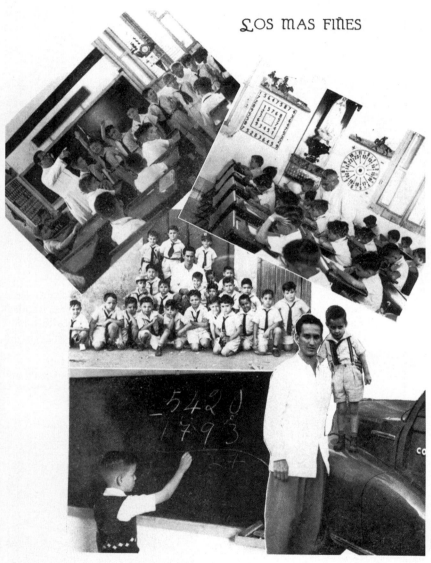

LOS MAS FIÑES

- con certámenes de cetecismo
- y preocupados con los números
- se preparan para ser grandes como su profesor Pila

A page taken from the 1954 Dolores yearbook. The boys are working out maths formulas and learning the Catholic catechism

Seeking commercial sponsors for a volleyball team, (from left to right) José Antonio Cubeñas, Ceferino Catá, Sócrates Pinto, Guillermo Martinez, Alcides Nuñez and Fidel Castro (kneeling right) pose with a locally made health tonic. The publicity shot failed

José Antonio Cubeñas holding the school portrait taken in 1941

José Antonio Roca, star of the Dolores basketball team, Virginia, 2006

Brothers in the field. Fidel (far left) eats whilst standing with his brother Raúl, Sierra Maestra, Cuba, 1958

Brothers in office, 2003

The Padre Pico Steps, Santiago de Cuba, 2006

Kiki de Jongh, an architect,
Havana, 2004

David de Jongh, a doctor, Hialeah,
2005

Alberto Casas, cattle baron and provocateur, in 2005. He died in Puerto Rico shortly after updating his list of boys in the school photograph

The prophet, Lundy Aguilar, taken in Florida, 2004. By 2006 Alzheimer's had robbed him of his foresight

Little Havana, Miami: capital of an imaginary country of a million Cuban exiles. Today more Dolores alumni live in Florida than in Cuba

Elizardo Sánchez, Havana, 2004.
A leading dissident, he grew up
outside the walls of Dolores

Fidel's mysterious illness in 2006
was described as gastrointestinal.
The illness silenced him for the first
time in half a century and forced a
de facto transition to his younger
brother Raúl

Dolores is still a school today. It has three times as many students as in 1941
but its future is uncertain

here, in the capital, but he still seemed to dislike the city, pushing resources to any other part of the country at the expense of the metropolis. This was justified as support for the overlooked regions, but the city had never been drawn to the puritanical side of the Revolution, had never been as desperate to sacrifice, and Castro knew it.

Everyone in Havana knew him, too. Knew him *personally*. Even me. I'd seen him in the flesh at a small rally, where I crawled in among the cameras to stand close, scrutinizing the lines in his face and the tremble in his hand. Castro was always known by his familiar grey beard, which had thinned out, allowing his Celtic skin to gleam through. The beard was surprisingly wide at the bottom, untrimmed bits bristling out past the mortar boards and gold braid of his twill dress uniform. I'd seen him across a huge field another time, a tiny figure in green, giving the same speech as always. I'd also bumped into him in Havana a couple of times, as he marched out of a building to shouts of 'Viva!', or swept past the Hotel Inglaterra in the back of a Soviet limousine (just the one car, just the one military attendant in the back with him). I'd learned to watch for him around 11.30 in the morning, when the broad Fifth Avenue was cleared by police for Castro's morning commute. For these regular runs, Castro rode in one of three identical black Mercedes-Benz 560s, in a convoy of jeeps and Ladas, tailed by an ambulance, about a dozen vehicles. In all, the Castro brothers, their families, and their bodyguards have a fleet of about 300 cars.

The convoy usually took him to his offices tucked within the huge, unlabelled military headquarters on Independence Avenue. There Castro has stood at the centre of all flow charts, surrounded by triumphant statistics, pulling levers on imaginary controls, making lights blink on wall maps. His personal bureaucracy, the obscure Council of State, translated his whims to the larger group of about 300 people who actually ran the country – ministers, deputies, vice-anythings, favourite aides, leading military officers, cabinet secretaries, Party bureaucrats, key players of various kinds, whoever could hold Fidel's fancy. They in turn controlled the larger apparatus of power – the armed forces, the ministry of interior, the few revenue-producing businesses, and the administrative cadre, especially the 780,000-strong Communist Party. The one thing these 300 top people all shared – on an evolutionary model, this was a survival adaptation – was an unwavering and explicit personal loyalty to the one man, to Cyclops himself. Castro always had the final say on any issue he cared to speak about, which allowed him to maintain a messianic tone of constant crisis, where a standard feature of daily life was his prediction of imminent destruction by powerful enemies.

By his own count, Castro had stood at the head of the Cuban Revolution for more than half a century. Through 2006 he still appeared at rallies, commemorations and memorials, at openings and closings, at graduations and inductions, welcoming ceremonies and farewell events, banquets and baseball games, TV shows and hurricanes, a well-worn path that eventually put him in the orbit of every person on an island of 11 million. Especially in Havana, it was easy to feel him close, to absorb by osmosis the core value of the system: the Revolution was the man, and vice versa. At night the evening news would recap his movements, and later he would be on one channel, or both, featuring in the documentaries, in special reports, in taped summaries, or in the stupendous speeches that ran live, sometimes until 2 or 3 in the morning when he would command hours of everyone's life on a daily basis. This was taxing for the rest of us, but for Cyclops it was life.

He repeated himself, deliberately. The speeches, the observations, ideas, even gestures, were echoes of previous rallies, events and speeches. Slogans forced form on to the mind:

The New Man. The Ten Million Ton Harvest. Fatherland or Death. Socialism or Death. Not One Step Back. Special Period in a Time of Peace. The Heroes of Moncada. The Heroes of Yará. The Martyrs of Imperialism. The Freest People in History. The Sacred Principles of José Martí. Be Like Che. Not One Step Back. I'm Staying Here. It's Always the 26th. Until the Final Victory. Heroes of the Triumph. First Free Territory of the Americas. A Revolution Without Danger is Not a Revolution. Cuba, Land of Men of Stature.

The public was enjoined to speak in one voice, not just the same words but the same accent, the same rhythm. Roberto Robaina, a Castro favourite, had actually been disgraced and sidelined in 1999 for failing to chant 'Socialism or Death' with sufficient vigour at a rally.

With the people numbed by slogans, hunger, preoccupation and prophecies of disaster, the static society was ruled by that impossible creature, the 'revolutionary state'. In practice this meant secretive, topdown rule. People were told where to stand, and then stayed there, cowed by the mere possibility of surveillance. Occasional show trials, with their theatre of power and powerlessness, set the tone. Democratic socialism, Cuba's official ideology, was neither democratic nor socialist. Castroism, the cult of the man himself, was the ideology of Cuba. The Revolution hadn't withered, or failed, or been abandoned. It had been assassinated by the man who invoked it most. As Castro lay on his hospital bed in 2006, unable to speak for himself, his true nature lay revealed. There is no Fidelism without Fidel. He had an official heir (Raúl) with unofficial rivals (the disgraced Robaina, foreign minister Ramón Felipe Pérez Roque, culture minister Armando Hart, and either of the Leal brothers, who ran favoured projects for Castro). Fidel himself once suggested that Elián González would replace him. But Raúl and whoever came after him was to be pitied.

As a Cuban dissident once said to me, 'You can't make an elephant out of a hundred rabbits.'

THE NEW YEAR started off badly. People woke up hungry that first morning – the ration was down – and found the Revolution stumbling into its second half century. And then at noon, with our headaches finally clearing, the gods delivered their stunner. Even though I'd had Eleggua on my lap, I didn't get the news until I finally found a bookstore selling the newspaper on Obispo Street.

Obispo was the most handsome street in Cuba, a narrow path through the centre of Old Havana. It began near the royal palms of the Parque Central, ran past the Floridita, where

Hemingway quaffed his double daiquiris without sugar, and terminated at the Plaza de Armas and the old forts guarding the harbour. It was a pedestrian street, although people drive down it anyway. This was the old way of life, narrow sidewalks and stucco houses, crumbling facades propped up with heavy beams that angled into the street. Antennae and brambles of improvised wires were strung overhead; laundry dried on balconies. Tourists plied slowly up and down Obispo, looking for the doorway drunks in Hemingway stories, or for the shadows in Walker Evans photographs. Although *Meester 'way* made a habit of warming his seat at the Floridita by 10 am, I thought noon was still too early, and stepped right past. Up the block two bookstores faced each other.

On the right was Moderna Poesía, the most important bookstore and publishing house in the old Cuba, in a rounded, art deco building. In Miami the former owners of this store had reopened a clone, also called Moderna Poesía, but the Havana original, with the name still carved in marble, was long shuttered, the empty rooms concealed behind travel agency posters. But across the street was a small government bookstore, where I had finally found *Grandmother*. The store also was doing a brisk trade in postcards, sold for a dollar apiece to the tourists walking Obispo. But few people even looked at the books, and no one was buying. Half the shelves were covered with murder mysteries, pirated Cuban translations of Agatha Christie and John Grisham. The other half were books about the Revolution. There were four score about Fidel Castro, and an equally large selection that were by him – reprints of his speeches, laborious political texts, transcriptions of interviews in 1966, 1976, 1986 and 1996.

Fidel on Religion. Fidel on Socialism. Fidel on Human Development. Fidel on the Crisis of International Relations. Fidel on the Heroic Events of Moncada.

Then Che. There were just as many by, or about Che Guevara, with an especially large contingent of photo books, most about him, but some actually by him (he was a shutter bug). If there was an atlas in the store, it was an atlas of Che's travels, or military campaigns, or of revolutionary movements in Latin America.

There were, in addition, a few Russian novels and several tracts on Socialist Economics.

Despite the careful exclusion of so many schools of thought, it wasn't really the missing political books that the government feared. Explicitly political books, like Orwell's *Animal Farm* or García Márquez' *The Autumn of the Patriarch*, were effectively banned, their arguments mocked and countered with propaganda barrages. It was literature *without* politics that frightened dictators. In a revolution, the personal was always supposed to be political. In Iran, the Islamists criticized Jane Austen for creating a world where men and women chose among dictates of love and conscience, and only love and conscience. The very idea that huge zones of human thought, areas of feeling, and fields of endeavour could lie beyond politics was a threat. Literature could puncture the universe of authority. One of the few idealists in the *Dirty Havana Trilogy* by Pedro Juan Gutiérrez explains why there are no good novels in Cuba: 'It terrifies the Old Man to think that any small space set aside for personal freedom might become a space where free ideas were exchanged.'

No good novels. No good newspapers or magazines. Just police procedurals and propaganda. Along with my copy of *Grandmother* I bought one piece of hackwork here, an encyclopaedia of Cuban exile leaders where they were identified by their criminal records and participation in various violent schemes (admittedly, the book was accurate). A first glance at the newspaper showed there was an item about a new book, *Cuban Business in 1958: a Documented Analysis of the Bourgeoisie*, which was now in Cuban bookstores. It was a guide to the 1,374 wealthiest business clans of the pre-Revolutionary era, 'an overall analysis of the Cuban bourgeoisie . . . their habits and way of life, where and how they lived, how they dressed and how they ate'. The distinguishing characteristics of this 'traitor' class were 're-linquishing its nationality and its principles to embrace extreme right-wing sectors of finance capital'.

I held up the newspaper, with its picture of the book party, but the clerk had never heard of the book. There were no copies in this or any other store I visited.

And then, standing out on Obispo, I finally looked through *Grandmother* systematically and saw why it had been sold out. This issue contained real news: the Letter of the Year, the Santería prophecy for the year ahead. The Letter was the result of a crucial divination on New Year's Eve. Some 800 Santería priests, the leading *babalaos* of Cuba, had gathered in Havana to spend hours in their arcane rituals and devices. After some form of interpretation, and probably a little negotiation and editing, the Letter of the Year was proclaimed to the public. A committee of the highest *babalaos* would emerge amid chants and drumming, and their supreme leader, a wrinkled priest named Victor Betancourt, would step forward to read it.

The most important thing about the Letter was a single phrase that had emerged during divination. Cubans, even those who do not follow Santería, were paying close attention to this key phrase, knowing that the Letter of the Year would influence the country greatly, one way or another.

'*The King will turn in his crown before dying*,' Betancourt had announced. That was the slogan.

A king. A fallen crown. Death. This was dangerous stuff, so before anyone had a chance to even ask, Betancourt volunteered to journalists that the most obvious reading of the divination was wrong. No, he said, it did not refer to Cuba. Nor did it refer to Fidel Castro himself still skipping around the island. Nor did it mean that Castro's life or presidency would come to an end in the next 365 days. The phrase had no connection to Castro at all, Betancourt insisted. The Letter of the Year and the slogan within it both described events far beyond Cuba. It could be any king, anywhere. Any ruler. Any country. 'This letter is for all humanity,' Betancourt said.

The news was electric, literally. Betancourt released the Letter of the Year to the press, and within hours the incredible prediction – The King will turn in his crown! – had circulated by email to Miami, and from there worldwide, wherever devout followers of Santería had settled. The Letter of the Year was already being discussed on the AM dial in Miami as I sat reading it in Cuba. In that airy sphere of debate, there was no doubt about the meaning. The King will turn in his crown. Whatever Betancourt said, it meant Castro was finally on the way out.

But Betancourt continued reading, beyond the sensational slogan. The rest of the Letter was full of terrible imagery. The future of 'all of humanity', included 'war, government collapse, the deaths of prominent personalities and marital infidelity'. With American troops forming in the desert for a race to Baghdad, the Letter went on to describe 'the collapse of a government somewhere in the world' and the 'enslavement' of a people after a war. The economic news was also bad. The Letter warned of the 'rupture' of global commercial relations, an increase in corruption, and trouble in economic markets.

Also, there would be plagues of 'grave neurological and psychiatric illnesses, infectious disease and liver ailments, as well as food poisoning and other sicknesses'. And environmental problems, hurricanes, flooding, droughts and numerous earthquakes.

So that pretty much covered it. The Year of Glorious Anniversaries was going to suck.

THE TOILET PAPER AT ELIZARDO'S HOUSE was made from *Grandmother*, the newspaper, which he cut up into small squares and stacked by the commode. I recalled this while waiting out front in the shade of an unruly gum tree for Elizardo Sánchez to come out.

As usual, I'd had the cabbie leave me at the end of the block, and scuttled up to the gate, looking over my shoulder to see if anyone was watching. At this house, out of all the houses in Havana, it was a good bet someone *was* watching. A rooster crowed next door, which made me check the time: 3 in the afternoon. The rooster crowed again, and then Elizardo came out.

He was the most relentless human rights campaigner in Cuba, the most persistent dissident still at large, and the most rebellious pacifist on the island, but he moved like a Cuban, as though he had 20 years to get from the front door to the gate. He came trundling out of the house, nodded, paused, looked around, stepped off the porch heavily and swung his legs stiffly. He was clean-shaven, tall, big-boned, top-heavy, his skin a kind of translucent parchment. Another pale *gallego*, poured from the same mould as Fidel himself. And Elizardo was from Oriente to boot. I always thought he would be president of Cuba some day, if only because he looked the part.

Elizardo led me inside the chain link fence, padlocked the gate, and then he went to the front door, unlocked that, led us inside, and closed and locked it again. Now I noticed that his hair, an upright shock, had turned completely grey. I'd been to this house in the Miramar suburb two dozen times, and this was the only change I could notice in him.

In 1991, after Sánchez had returned to his home from 11 years in jail, the local block committee had been ordered to screw up a mob and denounce him. This kind of demonstration – called an 'act of repudiation' – was a ritual in Cuba. His neighbours marched in front of the house, denouncing him as a worm, traitor, enemy of the people, servant of imperialism and criminal scum. The slogans were pro forma, nothing more inspired than 'CASTRO SI, YANQUIS NO.' The demonstration was led from in front, and watched from behind, by men in boots with civilian clothes, and carrying walkie-talkies. 'Worm,' these leaders shouted. Eventually the mob was encouraged to throw bricks and rocks at the windows, and someone – a someone wearing combat boots – had tried to kick the front door down. The first time I had visited Elizardo Sánchez I had traced a finger over the black smudge of that boot sole, which had cracked but not broken the door. 'They have to do it,' Sánchez explained of his neighbours. Those who participated were favoured in various small ways, but they also avoided disfavour.

Elizardo had repaired the door. Later he added metal *rejas*, or grilles, over the windows. A few years after that he put up a chain link fence, high enough to stop most bricks, with a gate that he kept padlocked. He pointed out the latest addition: broken glass had been cemented into the top of the garden walls and along the roof edge of the house. But this latest measure wasn't to keep mobs, bricks, or the police out. 'Crime is up,' he explained.

We settled on to opposed sofas in the front room of the house. There was a photo on the wall of Sánchez shaking hands with Ted Kennedy. Another with José Aznar, then the Spanish prime minister.

Sánchez had gone to jail repeatedly on technicalities like buying black market gasoline, which everyone in Cuba does. His real offence was leading the grandly named Human Rights Concordance, which was a loose association of like-minded opposition groups within Cuba. Sánchez and a few hundred people like him around the island were internal dissidents, who refused to go into exile. Cuba had repeatedly allowed Elizardo to leave, in hopes he would not return, but he just went abroad to collect European human rights awards and confer with politicos in America, and always came home.

Because of this he was condemned by some exile politicians in Miami as a 'collaborator'.

'They found your business card,' was the first thing Elizardo told me. I'd left it with him years before, and the police had raided his house, pawed through his files, found the card, and asked him about it. I was one of many journalists who talked to Elizardo, and as a foreigner had de facto immunity. I asked him who 'they' were but it was always the same: 'MinInt,' he said.

The ministry of the interior. The domestic security apparatus of Cuba, charged with protecting the country from internal enemies, set up and run by Raúl Castro, MinInt was huge. Cuba's 100,000 police officers reported to MinInt, but the organization also controlled a genuine field army of its own, with armoured units and infantry, that was designed to discourage any coup attempts by the regular army. MinInt also had elaborate facilities for secret work, for clandestine operations, counter-intelligence and eavesdropping. MinInt was responsible for surveillance and ran the 'Special Brigades', the plainclothes thugs who did much of Cuba's dirty work in the middle of the night.

MinInt had spent about five hours copying his hard drive and searching his files, making careful notes, and then leaving everything with him, almost as neat as they'd found it. Like a foreigner, Sánchez had ties outside Cuba, and therefore a level of immunity.

In his living room, Sánchez now detailed for me the latest ways that Cuba was falling apart. The economy was completely dependent on tourism now, which brought in far more money than sugar. Tourism had evaporated after the terrorist attacks on September 11, 2001, then rebounded, but was still vulnerable to hurricanes, politics and the mood swings of European vacationers. The only bigger money than tourism came from the enemy: Cuban exiles sent about a billion dollars a year back to the island in small remittances to friends and family – far and away the single biggest source of income to Cuba. Although Washington tried to stifle this transfusion of cash in 2003, the new rules were so easily evaded that the total remittances were exactly the same a year later. American government restrictions had no effect at all. The unemployment rate in Florida, by contrast, determined (almost exactly) Cuba's economic fate. When Cubans in Miami sneezed, Havana caught cold.

The regime was getting squeezed from the other side, too, Elizardo said. The costs of running a police state with a centralized, astonishingly inefficient economy were high. Police officers in Cuba were, about 1 per cent of the population. Like army draftees, these policemen needed to be fed, clothed, trained and kept somewhat happy, lest they become a threat to, rather than a support for, the government. The number of prisoners was also very high, about another 1 per cent of the population. This was a level of per-capita incarceration that only a few countries – South Africa, Russia and the US – could match. There were about 90,000 prisoners spread through a chain of remote jails up and down the length of the island, an archipelago of punishment that Cubans called the *cordillera*, or mountain range.

Cuban prisons were filthy and cramped, though not as bad as most others in Latin America. What separated the Cuban justice system from others was its arbitrariness. By law, anyone could be arrested, at any time, and held incommunicado, on any charge or no charge at all. The government was required to charge a suspect within a week, but some people sat in jail for a year before learning what crime they were accused of. Trials were ceremonies, conducted without evidence, or the right to choose a lawyer (again, both were guaranteed in law but ignored). The judges, who sat in panels, were a mixture of professionals, who had studied law, and (a Soviet invention) amateurs who were qualified only by their loyalty to the system. Putting two 'model workers' and party stalwarts on the bench kept the professional judges subservient. The system was *designed* to be unjust, as Human Rights Watch spelled out:

> Cuba has developed a highly effective machinery of repression. Cuban laws actually guarantee the denial of civil and political rights. Cuba severely restricts free expression, association, and assembly, silencing dissent with heavy prison terms, harassment, or exile. Human rights advocates, journalists, and other independent activists face steady government repression. Cuba refuses to legalize independent labor unions and restricts workers' rights in the international investment sector. The conditions in Cuba's prisons are inhumane. Cuba's courts fail to ensure fair trials. Nevertheless, Cuba retains the death penalty.

Ordinary criminals were often charged with vague, politically tinged crimes like 'dangerousness', or 'antisocial activities'. Meanwhile, genuine political dissidents were charged with petty criminal acts. In the legal code there was no distinction between political and other crimes. Both populations were mixed together, murderers and pacifists put into one cell. The length of sentences could never be certain: some people were released unexpectedly, after serving half their time; others were held in jail without explanation after their designated time was up. Oscar Elías Biscet, for example, was a follower of Gandhi and Martin Luther King, who had been arrested for advocating civil disobedience. After Amnesty International started a letter-writing campaign on his behalf, Biscet was released early. Thirty-seven days later he was rearrested.

The dissident groups were routinely penetrated by MinInt officers from Section Four, the bureaucracy that specialized in counter-intelligence against internal enemies. Section Four would put sleeper agents into dissident meetings, men and women who hung back for years, even a decade, quietly listening, until they were trusted and promoted. After a wave of arrests of real dissidents, several of these fake dissidents would then appear at a press conference in Havana, announcing that they were loyal revolutionaries, and that those arrested had been traitors and mercenaries in the pay of foreign agents.

So trusting people was not wise: the first time I sat down with Elizardo Sánchez, more than ten years before, he had announced that everything we said was being recorded. This was no surprise to me: my tape recorder was sitting in the middle of the table. But he pointed overhead, to the light fixture. 'Assume they are listening,' he said. 'Assume that every thing you say will be repeated back to you by an official some day. They bug our phones. They can listen whenever they want. I myself have found five microphones in this house. I don't think there are any now. But you never know. They cannot listen to everyone all the time, but if they want, they will find a way. Anyone can be working for them, even you or I.' He pointed at the ceiling one more time. 'We will never advocate violence,' he said, 'or anything illegal. We have to comply with the laws. But at the same time the law is an *absurdo*.'

The surveillance was often remarkably crude. The phone taps were so bad you could hear the MinInt woman breathing in the background – they 'eavesdropped' by listening to the conversation on ordinary office telephones. Some dissidents would even get in arguments with the MinInt clerks eavesdropping on them. The state did not try to hide what it was doing, not from the dissidents: it was better that they felt the breath of the state once in a while. Just the possibility of surveillance did most of the government's work.

Sánchez himself was the subject of a curious attempt at 'exposing' him as a MinInt agent. The government had politically claimed him as one of its sleeper spies, announcing that Sánchez had been cooperating secretly for five years, betraying his fellow dissidents. There were even two photographs of Sánchez in compromising situations: in one, he was warmly greeting a three-star official of MinInt; the other showed him sitting on a park bench with a uniformed intelligence agent.

Sánchez laughed when I asked him about the incident. He called it a crude attempt at sowing distrust. The photographs were genuine, he admitted. He had met with both men after they initiated contact, hinting that they were sympathetic to the dissident cause. As an advocate of a 'national dialogue', he had a policy of meeting with anyone in the government who wanted to talk to him, even a MinInt man who smelled like a rat. But Sánchez had insisted on having the meetings in public places. Broad daylight was an unlikely place to hide; it seemed only to suit the photographer, who had used a long telephoto lens. What secret agent would meet with his uniformed handler, on a busy street, right near his house, at noon?

To me, the MinInt photographs smelled bad, like a ham-fisted effort at spy vs. spy. I stayed with the same policy Sánchez had urged on me long ago: I assumed he was telling the truth, without forgetting that it could all be a lie. Cuba in a nutshell.

The Romanian poet Norman Manea described the debilitating effect of living within such a closed all-encompassing system:

> the mixture of paranoia and disorientation . . . the ways in which discouragement turns into resignation, then submission . . . Life as a series of postponements, a tumorlike growth of mistrust and fear, an all-encompassing schizophrenia. A step-by-step reduction of private life, and finally its abolition, as time itself becomes subject to ever increasing taxation and eventually total expropriation by the state: the hours sacrificed to standing in lines, to ritual political meetings and to rallies, on top of the hours of work and the hours of helpless exposure to the inferno of public transportation . . . and when you were finally home in your birdcage, you found yourself lost, mute, staring into an emptiness that could be defined as infinite despair.

In Cuba, the survival adaptation for this inferno was the usual *doble cara*. You complained on Saturday night about the government; on Sunday morning you went to the plaza and shouted *Viva!* Both statements were sincere, because only the insane remained sane. Faulkner called it 'furious unreality', the hot embrace of the impossible.

'*DIOS MIO*,' Elizardo Sánchez said when I showed him the 1941 photograph, with its 238 faces. 'This is the key to Cuba before the Revolution.'

As was proving the case across Cuba, I didn't need to introduce the photograph, or explain it. He knew it was the Colegio de Dolores immediately. Sánchez himself was *puro Oriental*. He'd grown up in Santiago, and in the 1940s and 1950s had walked by Dolores 'a million times', he said. He'd never set foot in the school, but everyone knew this image because events at Dolores were routinely in the newspaper.

'For me it was impossible to dream of going inside those high walls. My father was a telegrapher. You know,' he said, tapping a code on to the table top, 'he sent letters. So I went to a government school, a public school.' The dominant reality for Dolores students, Sánchez said, was their class. They lived within the bubble of privilege. 'They had little contact with the ordinary people,' Sánchez said.

'They had a special bus, a really nice bus, painted up to read COLEGIO DE DOLORES, that took them home. I remember seeing the bus going through the streets, headed to the big houses in Vista Alegre.'

Although I had found some in Santiago, and would now look for them in Havana, Sánchez assured me that most of the Dolores boys had gone into exile. He was in the unusual position, for a Cuban, of actually knowing what life was like for the exiles, since he'd met many while visiting America. He'd known Lundy Aguilar slightly; although they had grown up on opposite sides of the Dolores walls, they had met in the US and shared ideas about non-violence and the importance of dialogue.

Going into exile only substituted new problems for old ones, Sánchez said. In America, the Cubans were still 'strangers', lost to their own roots. They didn't know Cuba as it was now, and lived without fully participating in the life of America, Spain, Mexico, or wherever they ended up. 'There's a double isolation,' Sánchez said. 'Lundy has said that his clock stopped in 1959. His view of Cuba is of the society before.'

But even those boys from Dolores who had never left Cuba were still in a kind of isolation, Sánchez suggested. Their privileges, their fortunes, lives, homes and country had all changed around them, while the culture and values they grew up with were locked in amber. They were, like many Cubans, internal exiles.

'*Inxilio*' was the word Sánchez used. Inxile. Another coinage to paper over the cracks in reality. '*Inxilio*,' he repeated, rolling the word slowly.

Pointing to the photo again, Sánchez said, 'That saved his life.' He told me the story again of the way Castro had been hunted after the Moncada attack, while his brother and the Padre Rector at Dolores had intervened with powerful people to spare Fidel's life. Dolores served 'to protect El Jefe when they were looking to catch him', Sánchez said.

From fugitive to hunter of fugitives, from rebel to scourge of rebels. Castro spent much of his time obsessing over domestic enemies, and Sánchez had indeed assembled a long list of the opposition groups throughout Cuba. The best known of these was the Varela Project. Under the guidance of Oswaldo Payá, a long-faced Christian activist who I'd met in Sánchez' house years before, activists had gathered more than 14,000 signatures requesting an open national debate about economic and political changes. Under Cuban law, they were allowed to submit their petition to the National Assembly, but the legislature ignored them, and a year later Castro retaliated by staging a 'referendum' in which 9 million of Cuba's 11 million citizens – that is, everyone but children – signed a statement that the Socialist Revolution was 'untouchable'. Castro stated afterward that he had won 99 per cent of the vote.

Payá and Sánchez worked together, but it was risky for dissidents to meet, and they had separate agendas. Payá was convinced that a Christian orientation and legal reforms within

Cuba could work; Sánchez thought the regime could be moved by outside forces, like a moderation in US policy and a strengthening of European arm-twisting. He was interested in the construction of civil society, of organizations that could serve as an alternative to the Revolution, building a kind of shadow society within the confines of Cuba. He'd introduced me to a team of economists who, working privately in Havana, put out reports on the Cuban economy that used more reliable statistics than those in government reports. There was an association of independent journalists who tapped out dispatches on manual typewriters for internal distribution and publication abroad. There were private librarians, building a network of lending collections where banned, sensitive, or rare volumes were accessible to the public. There were independent lawyers, the Agramontistas, who tried to make Cuban courts uphold their own laws.

By cross-indexing their locations throughout Cuba against their leaders' names, and their particular focus, Sánchez had made a computer database of the dissident network, a constellation of dissent:

The Escambray Association of Human Rights
The Humanitarian Association of Followers of Christ the King
   in Havana
The National Association of Rafters
The Association for Free Arts
The Association of Political Prisoners and ex-Prisoners in
   Güines.
The Frank País Independent Library in Santiago.

Franz Kafka, Gandhi, Martin Luther King Jr, José Martí, Vaclav Havel, Abraham Lincoln and dozens of minor Cuban nationalists were commemorated in the names on the list. There were Christian groups, women's groups, parallel professional organizations for doctors, youth groups, eco-pacifists, and people in favour of Civil, Human, Political, National, Liberal and Workers rights, alongside the devotees of Peace, Love, Freedom, Democracy, Christianity and Transition. Far and away the biggest constituency, however, were private libraries. There were 79 of them on Sánchez' list. Tens of thousands of Cubans had used the private libraries.

A staff member at the New York Public Library, named Robert Kent, had been in touch with a few of the librarians, and had even come down to Cuba bringing gifts of books. Fascinated by their movement, he'd returned again and again, and soon came to the notice of MinInt. Bringing books into Cuba was not illegal, of course. Banning books, or shuttering libraries, was something even the Cuban government could not easily justify. But the American librarian was soon outed in *Grandmother*, not as a mild-mannered book-lover from New York City, but as a mysterious CIA agent named 'Roberto X'. He was labouring to split and divide the Cuban people, the newspaper reported, and was also plotting to assassinate a high-ranking Cuban official.

'Roberto X' was in the stacks of the New York Public Library when this sham occurred. Unable to return to Cuba, he had passed me the address of Hectór Palácios who ran the best private library in Havana. I flagged down a 1954 Pontiac in the street, and the owner, who was running errands, agreed to taxi me to the address for $2. It was just on the other side of Vedado, in a crowded, humid apartment in the back of a 1940s building. Palácios greeted me, unsurprised by the sudden appearance of a journalist: I was the forty-sixth in the last year, he said.

He gave me a glass of tap water and showed me the offending library: a small room lined with bookshelves, packed with an assortment of old and new, mouldering copies of *Don Quixote* beside Russian editions of *The Gulag Archipelago*, technical manuals, Cuban histories, textbooks, and reams of uncountable junk. I donated a Spanish copy of *The Autumn of the Patriarch* by García Márquez, which describes the last days of a green-clad dictator, somnolent inside his palace, who has ruled over a tropical island for a full 200 years of remorseless decay, until even the harbours have silted up.

No wonder the Cuban government felt threatened by books. Within months of my visit to the library in Vedado, Cuba suffered its worst round of political arrests in decades. With the attention of Europeans focused on the American invasion of Iraq, Castro ordered an island-wide round-up of 75 human rights campaigners, democratic activists, and the leaders of the various independent associations, including ten librarians. Palácios was one of them. After being held incommunicado, and then presented with government lawyers one day before trial, all 75 were convicted of being 'mercenaries in the pay of the United States', and given sentences ranging up to 28 years. Palácios got five years.

The government provided expert advice at the trials, in the form of Eliades Acosta Matos, director of Cuba's National Library. The private libraries were an 'aggression' against Cuba, Acosta Matos said. In a subsequent article in *Grandmother*, he denounced 'lies and subversion, such as the "independent libraries" ', employing the extra quotation marks to imply that they were not private, but foreign-sponsored, because Robert Kent and others had received travel funds from the US government's National Endowment for Democracy.

If that wasn't enough expert advice, Castro himself spoke up, complaining that the librarians had circulated several copies of the United Nations Universal Declaration of Human Rights. Castro specifically labelled this document 'counter-revolutionary', and demanded an investigation of how it had been smuggled into Cuba. For good measure, he labelled them 'mercenary scum' with no support in Cuba.

European governments protested the arrests, and froze diplomatic contacts with Cuba. Castro promptly announced that it was Cuba that was breaking off relations, because Europe was meddling in the sovereignty and dignity of Cuba. But the tiff lasted only 18 months. At that point Castro transferred a few of the 75 out of the remote *cordillera* to the central jail in Havana, Combinado del Este, a model prison where the meals were square and prisoners were allowed to use a pay phone once a month. A dozen of the dissidents were now discovered to have medical problems, and one by one, over the course of months, that dozen were released. Cuba, which had touted the arrests and trials to its people, barely acknowledged the releases at home, but demanded and received credit for a humanitarian gesture in Europe. Diplomatic contacts were restored by eight European nations, including Britain, Germany and France, all of whom made an explicit pledge to the Cuban government that they would no longer invite any Cuban dissidents to embassy cocktail parties.

The 75 were down to about 60 then and most are still in jail as I write. Many of them are senior citizens, with health problems exacerbated by the conditions, the poor food and mistreatment. Palácios, 'physically destroyed' in his own account, was released from jail after three years.

The books from their libraries had been confiscated as evidence, of course, probably including *The Autumn of the Patriarch*. After the trial, the presiding judge declared that the books were 'lacking in usefulness', and ordered them 'incinerated'. More than a hundred copies of the Universal Declaration of Human Rights, along with biographies of Martin Luther King Jr, Vaclav Havel, José Martí and Aung San Suu Kyi, and the novels of George Orwell and Guillermo Cabrera Infante, were all taken out and burned like trash.

EVERY CUBAN HOUSEHOLD has a *libreta*, the ration book Jorge Segura had shown me. During the early 1990s, during what Castro called in his speeches 'The Special Period in Time of Peace', the ration fell to starvation levels, and I myself knew people who had eaten cats. Over the course of the late 1990s the ration edged upward only slowly. In 1999 Cubans were still getting 31 per cent fewer calories than they had eaten in 1985. By 2002, the *libreta* delivered only enough rice, beans, pasta and protein substitutes to meet 65 per cent of nutritional needs. (Even this figure, produced by the Cubans themselves, was called 'very optimistic' by a specialist based in Cuba, Miren Uriarte of the University of Massachusetts.) Despite the booming tourism economy, and the rapid spread of dollar stores stocked high with food, the *libreta* ration actually declined during 2003. Most Cubans ran out of this 'monthly' food by the 17th or 19th of the month, leading to the observation that Fidel was phasing in reforms slowly – Cuba was socialist until the 19th or 20th, and capitalist after that.

If you started feeling hungry on the 21st, it was no joke. Putting food on the table meant a trip to a farmers' market or one of the hard-currency shops. That required real money, the kind that could not be won in dutiful service to the Revolution. Most people earned between 200 and 300 pesos a month – $8 or $12 at the market exchange rate. That exchange rate was partly irrelevant: in a heavily subsidized economy, a month's rent often added up to only a single US dollar, and a kilo of the very lowest-quality rice from Vietnam was usually available for just pennies. Nonetheless, a Cuban paycheck was too thin to put food on the table. Only half of Cubans had regular access to dollars, from a relative abroad or a tip-producing job at a hotel. To survive, people sold bootleg rum or siphoned gasoline, repaired tyres or televisions, bartered with farmers, drove unregistered taxis, cooked unlicensed meals with lobsters stolen from hotel freezers, rolled cigars and, of course, accepted gifts of cash and clothing from foreign boyfriends.

Food wasn't the only thing that stumbled along. Production of pharmaceuticals dropped even as Castro bragged about his biotech industry. The importation of vital drugs was declining. Printing of books had ceased completely for a while, and was still tightly restricted. The education system, the pride of the Revolution, had declining enrolment, particularly in the universities and technical schools. Even the sugar industry was in virtual collapse.

This wasn't the plan. Almost as soon as the Revolution came to power, Castro had committed the country to a staggering increase in sugar production, a kind of granulated Great Leap Forward. In 1963, with President Kennedy calling for a man on the moon before the end of the decade, Castro declared his own goal for 1970: a 10 million ton harvest. It would mean doubling the average harvest. Even in the very best years Cuba had produced only 8 million tons. The 10 million tons (the total of refined sugar created by the end of the harvest) would bring in vast revenues, and save the Revolution from a shrinking economy. The new slogan ('Ten Million Tons!') appeared on posters, on the radio, and in the pages of *Grandmother*, year after year. Even though the sixties saw little progress in sugar, when the 1970 *zafra* (cane harvest) commenced, in the last months of 1969, the government insisted that a massive outpouring of Revolutionary fervour would create success. Eleven thousand workers from Havana, and thousands more from other parts of western Cuba, were trucked eastward into the sugar heartland of Oriente. During January and February of 1970 *Grandmother* kept reporting good news. But months went by – too many months. It was taking a long time to gather all that sugar. Eventually, the government announced a date – 15 July 1970 – when the last of the 10 million tons would be processed. To mark the event, there would be a national ten-day celebration, ending with a huge rally.

In the second week of May 1970, the sugar propaganda stopped. In the third week, billboards around the country were suddenly repainted, the words 'Ten Million Tons', in use since 1963, erased, the space whitewashed in preparation for something new.

The missing words hinted at what was coming. Speaking on 20 May, Castro loudly debuted a new slogan:

FIDEL CASTRO Says:
We will turn the set-back into a VICTORY!

Havana (PL) – I am completely certain that we will turn the set-back into a victory, Major Fidel Castro said on Wednesday, May 20, in making a detailed report to the Cuban people on the difficulties which make it impossible to reach the goal of ten million tons of sugar, which had been set for 1970.

The Cuban leader underscored that while it is true that we will not reach the ten million ton goal, the people have made a gigantic effort and have achieved a great victory.

A great victory. That was the first notice of the most iconic of all the Revolution's failures. After seven years of build up, the Ten Million Ton harvest was never mentioned again. Castro announced only that miraculous numbers had been made in other harvests. (Rice production was 'several times' that of two years ago; the catch of fish had increased eight-fold.) Without saying what had gone wrong, Castro heaped blame on 'the imperialist beast' that was trying to swallow Cuba, attacking Americans for a 'habitual lack of honesty, their criminality and cowardice'. Any claims that the mass mobilization of labour for the harvest had been less than a total success were 'perfidious' lies spread by 'counter-revolutionary bandits at the service of US imperialism'.

The final figure for the 1970 harvest was 8.54 million metric tons. That was a good harvest, but not good enough. Even Batista had been able to gather in 7.3 million tons a full 20 years before. And the Ten Million Ton effort came at the cost of an economic catastrophe. As with Chairman Mao's programmes for rapid industrialization at any cost, the giant sugar programme had undermined the rest of Cuba. Food production fell as land was sucked up for cane plantings, often in marginal areas, or hills; with workers pulled from the cities, other activity ground to a halt; with fuel committed to the harvest, electricity production sputtered and civilian transport vanished; with machinery from tractors to mills pushed beyond the limits of endurance, break-downs and irretrievable destruction followed. Workers returning from the *zafra* (cane harvest) reported a wasteland of rotting cane, broken machinery and abandoned efforts. The sugar was so badly milled that it was rated at the lowest commercial grade in six years. And it was the slowest sugar harvest in Cuban history. A plague of rats arose on the island, feeding on the mountains of sugar cane rotting everywhere.

THE 'SETBACK' OF 1970 inadvertently helped launch what many Cubans recall as a kind of Golden Era. Broke and desperate, Castro turned after 1970 to ever greater imports of Soviet equipment and personnel. Russian technicians and boxy Lada automobiles began to flood into the country, along with ever-increasing Soviet subsidies of cash and oil. The Soviets acted as a brake on Castro's wilder schemes, and invested themselves heavily in rebuilding the Cuban economy and creating work for Cubans. They opened their universities across eastern Europe to a flood of Cuban students, creating a professional class with high aspirations. With subsidies, life in Cuba in the 1970s began to ease. People remembered it well: travel, if only to Moscow; work, if poorly paid; more food, even if it was lousy. Life seemed almost normal, even if the new air-conditioners all had their knobs labelled in Cyrillic, even if the new Soviet embassy towered over Miramar like a wizard's dark tower. The setback was thus converted into victory, just as Castro predicted.

But the new problem was credibility. The failure of the Ten Million Tons put an end to the heroic image of the Revolution. Foreigners once again dictated Cuban affairs, albeit Russians. At home, cynicism replaced solidarity, and careerism supplanted volunteer labour. The 'system' in Cuba became split in two – a lower level, street reality of compromise, black markets, and the gossip known as Radio Bemba, and then above it a superstructure of loyalty oaths, slogans and timeserving. Before the Ten Million, people actually believed that Cuba could change everything, even the world. After, they accepted that Cubans would just make do.

Sugar harvests continued after 1970, of course. Along with nickel, sugar was one of the only things the Soviets actually needed from Cuba. But when their subsidies ended in 1992, and the harvest spiralled into terminal decline, eclipsed by a new harvest with its own propaganda language, 1998 was declared 'The Year of One Million Tourists'.

The sun and the beaches could not be ruined, especially with foreigners running the hotels, and Cuban prostitutes desperate to fill the beds. Soon the rising tourism harvest surpassed the sugar as the number one source of retained earnings for Cuba. By 2002, holiday-makers brought in some $2 billion in revenue, compared to just $440 million for the sugar cane harvest. After 2000, government officials closed some 70 mills, more than half of those on the island. Elaborate plans were announced to retool the mills, modernize them, and then restart sugar production with renewed vigour. But several of the older mills were converted into museums. About 100,000 workers in the sugar industry were reassigned. All got to keep their paychecks; a few got retraining. But even more were put to work replanting the fields with vegetables.

Actually, it wasn't the fields they replanted. Although the cane fields, some of the best agricultural land in the world, were lying abandoned and fallow, the government needed to show that the sugar facilities themselves were being returned to production. Despite the fact that the mills were surrounded by fallow agricultural land, workers were ordered to dig up the railway tracks, to bury manufacturing sites in truckloads of new soil, and then plant vegetables. The sugar harvest in 2003 was 2.2 million tons, the lowest figure in 70 years.

I KNEW A COUPLE OF *JINETEROS*, Victor and Jorge, who sold fake cigars of the lowest quality in the street. They were always hungry for my sandwiches and old T-shirts, and would wait for me at my hotel, sometimes following me around while prattling about how difficult life was in Cuba. They were particularly outraged by the appearance of slums in Havana, a new phenomenon. These were called the *lleu ipon*, a corruption of the phrase *llegó y pongo*, or, roughly, Come and Stay. Victor and Jorge talked so much about the awful shanty towns rising up on the outskirts of the city, hidden away from the sight of tourists, that I impulsively challenged them to show me the worst slum in Havana. They fetched a black market cab, an old grey rumbler which reeked of gasoline. Through a cracked windshield, I watched our progress down to and around the harbour, through Regla, and then up the hills on the far side. Hemingway's house was somewhere out in these hills but I'd never been. We turned left, and rolled slowly past ranks of standardized apartment blocks, the precast concrete that the Revolution had scattered all over the island. The cab driver wouldn't descend down a muddy track; we got out, crossed a field of soy beans on foot, and came over a ridge to where hundreds of small cement houses were spread out below us. This was it: the worst slum in Havana. The homes were lined up in perfect rows along wide streets of mud, everything squared away. Each house was painted a different colour. Each had a small front yard. We peered inside: two rooms. This wasn't luxury – bare bulbs hung from the ceilings, and only a few of the houses had running water – but they had solid roofing and sanitary conditions. Blocks without plumbing had their own well with a hand pump. I couldn't help it – I started shaking my head and then couldn't control myself. I smiled and finally laughed.

Victor and Jorge looked confused, wondering why I was laughing. 'Look at how these people have to live,' Victor said, fuming. He thought this was squalor.

I wasn't impressed. I'd spent a month in the *pueblos jóvenes* of Lima, where hundreds of thousands of people threw together improvised slums, building their own crude shacks, often of cardboard. Electricity was a dream, and they had to walk a mile to find a water pump, and then wait in a line of 200 people to get a gallon. Even thatched roofing was considered a luxury. But Victor and Jorge had never seen Lima, or Bogotá, where the dense slums were filled with desperate war refugees in rags and gasoline-sniffing children begged through the streets. They'd never seen the steep *favelas* above Rio de Janeiro, crumbling, muddy slums where hovels slid down the hillsides in the rain, and teenage gunmen roamed at will. I'd spent two days amid the million squatters on the flats outside São Paulo, moving from crime scene to crime scene amid true, hungry poverty. In Cambodia, the young men like Victor and Jorge went barefoot, living four to a woven mat. This *lleu ipon*, the worst in Havana, would be taken for paradise in such places. Every single resident had a roof, clean water, education and access to a doctor. If Peruvians knew about this slum they would move to Cuba immediately.

It is impossible to reconcile the tradeoffs Cuba offers. Who would choose one life over another? Thanks to the socialist school system, everyone, even the slum children, could read. Thanks to the socialist political system, they weren't allowed to. Books and magazines were banned, the internet filtered, and the government monopoly on newspapers was enforced by censors who measured every idea against the words of the Leader.

Even as this machinery of repression ground out a frightened, yet pacified Cuba, right across the water the Dominican Republic was torn with gang wars, its health, law enforcement and education systems collapsing, the country bankrupted by a colossal financial fraud engineered by corrupt politicians and wealthy executives. More and more Dominicans took to boats in a desperate bid to reach Puerto Rico and then the US mainland. Which was better? Repression and control, or freedom and chaos? An island with a way out, or one with no exit? A place where no one starved but everyone was hungry, or one where the hungry could hope to some day become fat?

Cuba, for all its crippling chaos, management whims, bizarre programmes and wasted efforts, had still managed to lift itself up into a world player in surprising fields: Olympic sports were a well known example, but Cubans never tired of pointing out that they had put a man in space (albeit on a Soviet mission). The strength of Cuba's technical university system allowed it to develop a business in drug production and biotechnology research – the country had exported 80 million doses of hepatitis B vaccine, developed a potent blood pressure medicine, PGP, that was sold worldwide, and had even put potential HIV vaccines into trials. Castro always talked up the statistics on infant mortality, which had dropped from 100 deaths per 100,000 births before the Revolution to just 5.9 today, a figure that puts many American cities to shame.

When he wasn't taking credit, Fidel apportioned blame. Before falling silent in 2006, Castro sustained his legendary eloquence deep into old age, and indulged himself in unstoppable diatribes on what he called *el bloqueo*, the blockade, as if Cuba were ringed by American warships. The American government referred to the same phenomenon as a trade embargo, but in either case it was a net of more loopholes than thread, a phantasm of exceptions, evasions and emergency measures which fooled only the naive. Whatever the politicians said in either capital, the US trade embargo had never been systematically enforced. And the loopholes filled pages. Americans could visit Cuba to attend scientific conferences, or even the Havana film festival. In Baracoa I had stumbled on a bus full of inebriated Americans who were 'studying Afro-Cuban rhythms', they said. There were always workarounds. When one loophole closed (no more cultural tours!), another one promptly pulled wide open (hello religious tours!).

There was a mutual dependency between Castro and his worst

enemies, the Cuban-Americans. The exile leadership in Miami loved the embargo, as long as it didn't apply to them. They protested successfully when threatened by the Bush administration to actually enforce rules limiting them to one visit a year. Financial restrictions on how much money one could send to Cuba, and how often, were also fine, as long as they weren't enforced. Miami was full of businesses that specialized in evading the embargo, using Cuban-American couriers (the *gusañeros*) who travelled back and forth every month with clothes, computers, air-conditioners and even tyres, as I'd once seen in the Cancún transit lounge.

The Bush administration only increased the scale of American hypocrisy: while attacking Cuba verbally, Bush actually expanded trade. Bush held a Rose Garden ceremony where he vowed to crack down on Cuba, yet it was Bush who ripped open a vast new loophole in the trade embargo. There had always been a special exemption for shipping food aid to Cuba after hurricanes, on the theory that humanitarian relief efforts were good for US diplomacy. But Archer-Daniels Midland, ConAgra, and American congressmen from farm states lobbied hard for the right to ship food year round. Soon a hundred cargo ships a year were arriving direct from the US with loads of Louisiana rice, Arkansas chicken and Kansas wheat. During Bush's first three years in office, he authorized $780 million in sales to Cuba; another billion soon followed, virtually unnoticed as the same administration fined two American yachtsmen for organizing a race to Cuba, prosecuted a handful of professional cigar smugglers, and withdrew permission for scores of cultural tours by Americans.

I sometimes had trouble believing that a trade embargo even existed. Cuba was full of American products from computers to Coca-Cola. More than 140,000 Cuban-Americans returned to the island each year, flooding Cuba with US dollars and American goods. In most years I was one of the 30 or 40,000 non-Cuban-Americans who visited. In one year I was even four of them, flitting in and out of Cuba without hindrance from immigration officers on either side in spring, summer, fall and winter. It was enough to tell the Cubans that I was a tourist, and the Americans that I hadn't been in Cuba at all.

As a gesture of puny defiance against all these guardians, I tried to do everything I could find that was illegal in Cuba. I encouraged the overthrow of the government, gave out subversive books, handed pens, notebooks and typewriter ribbons to Castro's critics, drank only moonshine, and smoked only tobacco stolen from state warehouses. Whenever possible I ate in people's living rooms for a few dollars. I tried to hire gypsy cabs out of back alleys, even though the ancient American cars were death traps, with broken windshields, suicide doors, seats that sprang springs, and fumes of oil and gasoline that could overwhelm you. If we needed gasoline the driver would get it from a tin can behind someone's house. I had to lie down sometimes in these cars, to hide from police in the street, but with private taxis the money went straight into a Cuban's pocket.

And so with lodging. In Havana I had taken a room at a private house near the University of Havana. The building was beautiful, with a little patio in back, and you could walk everywhere from this central location. The owner, who I will call F, spent his earnings on a definitive collection of 1970s rock, almost a thousand CDs lining the walls of his house. F was also one of the better (and better supplied) cooks in Havana, turning out huge meals of fried fish, yucca and plantains. F's house had the disadvantage of being both legal and illegal. He was allowed to rent a room to foreigners – but rented four rooms. Three Air France stewards and an Israeli girl were distributed in the other rooms. Once, when a tax inspector appeared, to verify that F was renting only the one room, I'd been thrown to the street with three minutes' notice. But the food was good, and the money didn't go to the state, at least not mine.

F had skills beyond cooking. My first four days in Havana had been consumed with trying to find Kiki de Jongh, the Dolores boy whom Alberto Casas had listed as 'architect, Havana'. Phone books, computer searches and telephone inquiries had produced nothing, but on the fourth night F, seeing my frustration, asked who I was looking for. When I told him, he sat silent for a moment, and then went to the phone. He called a neighbour who was an architect. That man knew nothing but passed F to a colleague in the architects' association. That man wasn't at home but F soon had another phone number, and within five minutes the man was on the line. Yes, he'd heard of a de Jongh who was a prominent architect from the old days. I watched F jot down another number and make one more call to a friend of the friend of his friend's friend. That person needed only a few minutes of searching to come back with an address on the Avenue of Presidents, and yet another phone number. I took the paper from F's hand and dialled the digits myself. Kiki de Jongh answered.

Cubans like to say that every person in Havana knows every other person in Havana. I'd never understood the claim, but F needed just 15 minutes to prove it true.

THE OLD HILTON is the tallest structure in Central Havana. At the heart of Vedado, it is a modernist slab that leaps 27 storeys out of a block-sized plinth. On one side was La Rampa, the wide, sloping boulevard down to the sea, lined with a couple of movie theatres, Chinese restaurants, several hotels and banks of airline offices. There had been nightclubs and bars once, but the street was quieter now; many of the restaurants were closed. One or the other of the movie theatres had a show, but not both. At night, the few tourists and *jineteras* on La Rampa didn't linger, preferring darker corners of Havana.

The severe minimalism of the Hilton was softened by a white and blue colour scheme, and the swooping lines of the side pavilions, in trapezoids and domes, with a curving pool and round porte-cochère full of sputtering taxis to break up the boxy main tower. Built at enormous cost in 1957 it had 630 rooms, five restaurants, and was a spectacularly bad investment. In January of 1959 Castro moved into the presidential suite. His large troop of bodyguards slept in the lobby, in dirty fatigues, draped in ammunition. Instead of paying their bills, they nationalized the hotel, renamed it Habana Libre, and the government has maintained it as a living museum ever since. In the 1960s and 1970s it was the only place in Cuba with open international phone lines and daily newspapers from abroad. Tourism had diversified Cuba's points of contact with the world, but the Hilton – the Libre – was still a bit glamorous.

In the lobby, almost nothing had changed. Palm trees reached up into the three-storey atrium, topped with round skylights. The Trader Vic's restaurant in the basement had been kept literally untouched: photos on the walls showed that not even a tiki lamp had been moved since 1959. They served the same faux-Polynesian menu, just more slowly.

I sat in the lobby, for an hour, waiting for Kiki de Jongh, the youngest of the three brothers. When I had first called Kiki, and mentioned the school, he had been suspicious. He refused categorically to see me, explaining that he was too busy, and that I should have arranged an interview through 'the government'. But I kept him on the telephone, and mentioned the names of various of his old schoolmates. I finished up by agreeing that he should not meet me at all, that it was completely inappropriate, and that we would not speak again until I had arranged everything formally. And then, in passing, I mentioned that I should send him a book I had written about Che Guevara. He agreed to let me drop it off at his office; finally, in the midst of a confused discussion about the address, he said it would be easier to come and get the book himself. I couldn't bring him to F's house, so I named the Habana Libre, and a time. Just before hanging up, his good manners kicked in. He agreed we could talk for 'a few minutes' when we met.

Kiki had described himself on the phone as 'short, though not by the standards of a Cuban, and fat, though not fat like an American'. So I sat and watched, looking for someone who would fit that description. It was easy to wait. I had a drink, and a strong breeze whipped the lush tropical plantings outside the Hilton. All foot traffic into the hotel had to flow through a single doorway, which was guarded. The doormen were like those at all Cuban hotels: uniformed, and severe more than friendly, correct more than warm. Their job wasn't to open doors, but to close them – to close them against ordinary Cubans who tried to enter the hotel. Keeping foreigners and Cubans separate was an essential task, complicated and subtle.

The Cubans rightly said that their doormen were simply engaging in security, keeping prostitutes and other criminals away from their prey. There had been a wave of small bombs at Cuban hotels in 1997, small pipe bombs designed to scare off foreign visitors. The attacks had been carried out by Salvadorean mercenaries, posing as tourists, who took their money and marching orders from a shadowy group of Cuban exiles based in Central America.

The bombs were supposed to be tiny, symbolic explosions that would merely frighten away tourists, knocking the legs out from under the Revolution's economy. But the bomb placed in front of the Copacabana Hotel, a few blocks from here, killed Fabio di Celmo, a 32-year-old Italian tourist. Despite this, tourism had survived and continued to grow.

In Cuba, however, security always meant more than physical security. In hotels, it meant keeping out the Cubans who entered hotels for reasons the state did not like. Prostitution was one of those reasons: the state condemned it, and excluded it, but it flourished anyway, through the back door and the side door, and in the cheaper hotels. The policy was bipolar. Castro would rant against prostitution on television, but then actually bragged that Cuba had 'the best educated prostitutes in the world'. There were other kinds of Cubans doing other kinds of things that had to be stopped, like meeting foreign journalists and activists, so it was safer to have a blanket policy of keeping all Cubans out.

This the doormen did to one Cuban after another. I saw them split apart a couple, turning away the Cuban man while admitting the foreign woman. The couple had been holding hands as they walked through the door, but were separated, amid vehement objections. She continued in, and the man waited outside. Then Kiki walked right in.

What was it? What did the doorman understand about Kiki, immediately? Cubans lived within a sphere of secrets, speaking an idiom of silent signifiers, subtle gestures, and ambiguous euphemisms. Kiki walked past the doorman without hesitation, knowing that he would be admitted; the doorman looked but did nothing, also knowing that he would be admitted. It took no speech to come to this mutual comprehension: in Cuba, the less said the more spoken. Power was inversely proportional to volubility: those who talked most had the least, while the highest ranking person in any situation was the one who stood silent.

Was it his age? Kiki was 72, his skin touched with liver spots. Maybe the doorman sensed this venerable man as no possible problem. Or maybe it was another quality of Kiki's skin: the pale, even, pink tone. Cubans were infinitely sensitive to skin tone, to the gradations of class expressed in bloodlines.

Maybe it was his clothes? They looked ordinary to me: a wool driving cap, a simple jacket. Perhaps there was something encoded in the crease of his pants, or the cap, that was beyond my sight.

Or maybe it was simply presumption. A Cuban could bluff his way through these doors, if he had the rare qualities to pull it off: the right skin, the 'foreign' clothes, the well-fed look of money or opportunity, and above all, the *huevos*, the balls, to walk in the door like he owned the place. Whatever Kiki was, it was enough. He shuffled inside without objection. One in a hundred.

He walked steadily, but slowly, with the help of an unadorned cane. His hands and wrists showed a few of the bulging veins of the aged, but Kiki had a smooth, untroubled face, and very few wrinkles for a septuagenarian. He wore a yellow, short-sleeved shirt, a grey cap, and laid the walking stick across his lap as he sat down. He was an architect by profession, precise in his gestures and almost unique in his open admiration for the Revolution and its works – a revolutionary from Dolores.

He fell silent when I produced the photograph. He looked at it for a moment, and then in the familiar gesture of the aged, took off, cleaned, and put back on his glasses. With night falling, the ambient light in the huge atrium was barely enough.

'I started in '38,' he said as he stared at the image, 'and was there ten years.' He had grown up in a home that was intellectual, cross-cultured, and outward looking. His ancestors, he explained, were Sephardic Jews, exiled from Spain in the very year that the great Admiral of the Ocean Sea first landed in Cuba. Kiki's people had gone to Holland, acquired a Dutch name, and centuries ago had made the jump to the Caribbean, and eventually Cuba, picking up a Spanish 'de' along the way. They were Catholics now, but only by background. Despite going to mass at Dolores every day for ten years, Kiki was not what the Revolution called 'a believer'. He had the new faith.

His father had been born in Cuba, but raised in the US, and was 'one hundred per cent American', Kiki said, without pride. The most lasting cultural legacy of this 'Americanness' was a 29-volume encyclopaedia, in English, that his father had brought back to the island. It was the famous 1911 edition of the *Encyclopaedia Britannica*. Never mind that the book was British, not American: it was his introduction to the English language, to American science, and to global history and culture. Kiki claimed to have read it from A to Z in his youth, all 40,000 entries, absorbing the language that way. (He still understood English, but declined to try and speak it.)

The 1911 *Britannica* was probably the greatest encyclopaedia ever compiled. The articles in it were often by the world's greatest experts in each field, and frequently ran five or ten times larger than those in modern encyclopaedias, a comprehensive wealth of detail embodying the principle that all knowledge could be made available to all people. Connoisseurs practise the art of distinguishing between like things. Kiki argued that the 1911 edition, the *Britannica*'s eleventh, was the 'last really good' encyclopaedia in the world. Before then, the state of knowledge was not advanced enough for the books to be comprehensive, he explained; after that, knowledge became highly specialized, and the age of the generalist declined, as did the *Britannica* series. It was the last moment when the world's learning fitted into one set of covers.

The boys at Dolores were 'aristocratic', Kiki agreed, when I used that word. They were 'an economic, social, and power elite', he said. But still making fine distinctions, he said they were not right wing. 'Those who left?' he asked himself. 'They weren't reactionary.' They were just ordinary exemplars of their class. The boys from Dolores grew into men who were educated, culturally advanced and scientifically minded, he said, and accomplished in their fields. They were not the true ruling class of Cuba – not the old-guard plutocrats, nor the conservative social elite, nor the hard-line reactionaries. For people in those true ruling groups, it was plain that their lives were incompatible with any revolution at all. By contrast the young men from the photograph were *personally* conservative, but modern and even progressive in their outlook. They believed in the Jesuit tradition of merit, in a society open to talent, where all were equal before God. They accepted that Cuba was broken, Kiki said, and needed fixing. The Batista dictatorship was crushing society. The liberal aspirations of the 1940 constitution had been smashed. Torture and caprice ruled the island. Exploitation, corruption, and violence were holding the nation back. 'Logically,' Kiki said, 'the people of Cuba wanted change, including them.' Here he tapped the photo. 'The problem of Cuba had no solution except the Revolution,' Kiki said with great satisfaction. 'It was the only possible solution.'

So even the prosperous Dolores alumni initially supported the Revolution, led by their old schoolmate. They supported literacy campaigns and land grants and sending doctors into the countryside. But there was, soon enough, one simple aspect of the Revolution that they could not accept. 'It affected their economy,' Kiki said.

Money. It came down to the laws of economics. His Dolores comrades had been comfortable in pre-Revolutionary Cuba. They were 'fundamentally accommodated to their position', as Kiki put it. And once Castro's reforms began to hit their pocket books – their businesses nationalized, their lands redistributed, their wages put under state control, their country houses turned into dormitories for the masses – they reacted. They became, Kiki now said, 'fundamentally reactionary'.

'They had to be,' he explained. The complacency and sterile thinking of their class left them unable to cope with the changes. They lacked the imagination, the vision, to see the larger necessities of the Revolution. 'The only thing they were told was to defend this, the thing they had,' Kiki said. 'If you are taught every day to repeat something, you repeat it.'

His reasoning was problematic. He himself said the Dolores boys were mostly from families that were, in the context of 1940s Cuba, liberal and progressive. He was arguing that the Dolores boys weren't reactionary, but then suddenly became reactionary? That Dolores taught them to think critically, but then they just repeated the mindless verities of their class interest? Was it really just a matter of the pocket book?

His view of history leapt right over the conflicting loyalties of men who supported the Revolution and then opposed it. It could not account for the exceptions, men who thought, felt and acted outside their own class interests, men like Fidel, or Kiki himself. It bypassed politics entirely, discounting all objections to the new system. The turn from democratic promises to absolute rule. The construction of an all-encompassing surveillance society. The seizures, the shortages, the arrests.

When I cited these objections, Kiki said, 'It's true the Revolution was very hard. But no Revolution can be weak.' Our few minutes had turned into an hour and he had reached his bottom line. 'They *have to be* hard,' he said with enormous emphasis. 'Changing a country is a very difficult task.'

He shook his head, the tutor frustrated with a dim student. 'What did you expect, Patricio?' he said, as he rose to leave. 'What did you expect?'

5

THE HEROIC YEAR

THEY HAD TO LAUGH the first time they saw the boat. Nervous laughter, the kind that follows a shock to the senses. It was colder out there on the end of the dock than they had expected, with a stiff breeze coming off the Florida Strait. January in Key West, and you remembered you were on an outlying island, a distant outpost amid deep water. The wind was bad enough. A huge storm cycle was just starting to lick its way up the Caribbean, to Florida, then up the East Coast of the US, all the way to New England. Even on the end of a dock, still attached to an island, you could feel it rattle the old navy boards.

And the boat! Somebody made an appreciative whistle. And somebody else, quietly: '*Mira; carajo coño!*'

And another, saying what all were thinking: 'Whose idea was this?'

And, following up: 'What did you get us into, Admiral?'

'Me? It wasn't me!'

So it was nobody's idea. It had just happened. Lundy and a dozen men like him had started out with a simple assumption. They would need a boat. And now they remembered that you must be careful what you wish for.

There was nothing unusual about this impulse, the desire for a boat. Nothing unusual in a few Cuban men needing a way to go to sea. Or about Cuban men gathering for a journey into the Gulf Stream, even in January. Cubans have always gone back and forth over treacherous depths in the most unseaworthy of small craft. In the 1800s, the same Straits had been full of Cubans and Americans in small boats, fleeing one revolution or another, sometimes sneaking a family member out, or sending a load of weapons in. There were 'filibuster' gangs of Americans trying to invade Cuba, and exiles and failed coup plotters getting out, decade after decade. The conspirators of 1930s revolutions snuck in and out of Cuba by boat, and in Hemingway's worst book, *To Have and Have Not*, it is Cuban Revolutionaries who commandeer a small boat for the trip. And of course, like his hero, José Martí, Castro himself had done it, crashing ashore (from Mexico) in 1956, aboard the overloaded *Granma*.

On the water all were equal. Exiles, invaders, American adventurers, gunrunners. Whatever the politics or century, they were sooner or later subject to the mercy of the sea. And in January, the Straits were returning to their natural condition: stormy and unpredictable. The Gulf Stream currents were slowed by the prevailing winds of winter but also broken up, cross-hatched with different impulses. And they were already busy with Cubans, moving north and south, in more small boats.

Lundy and the others had assumed, from the beginning, before they even knew what they were doing, that the first thing they needed was a boat to do it in. Maybe a fishing boat. Or a yacht. Or a launch. Any old thing. Cubans would go back and forth in whatever floated – inner tubes, surf boards, waterproofed cars and $25 plastic boats purchased in Florida drug stores. If the weather was right, and if you took the shortest route, the famous 90 miles between Key West and the northern beaches near Havana – and both of those were big ifs – then in such perfect conditions you could do it in a bathtub. And of course, people have done it in bathtubs. So Lundy and his friends thought first of all that they would need a boat.

But this thing, Lundy scoffed. The Americans had offered them 'a boat', but this wasn't a *boat*. It was a goddamn warship! It was a PT, the same kind of ultra-fast torpedo boat that the incoming American president, John F. Kennedy, had commanded during World War Two. And it wasn't some mouldy relic, either. At 80 feet long and 20 feet wide it was bigger and faster than anything Lundy and the other men had ever ridden. Though made of wood, it still displaced 56 tons. They climbed down inside, and found that their whole group of volunteers – a dozen like-minded

fellows, unsure of what exactly they were volunteering for —
could fit inside the bridge.

The PT had been stripped of its original equipment — four
heavy torpedo launchers and braces of 40 mm cannons for
fighting aircraft — and the hull emptied out, so that it could
carry cargo. There were three engines, each a powerful 12-
cylinder Packard that could drive the boat into a planing sprint of
41 knots.

So maybe, in a time when no decisions were made, when
everything simply occurred, then maybe it was this moment on
the dock, out of all the stumbling, sleepwalking steps of this
dance, that they themselves really felt most what they were in for.
Each man had his reasons, his route to the dock, but now they
were here. A crew, and now a boat. An 80-foot-long monstrosity, a brawling, roaring torpedo boat, designed for suicide
charges against the Japanese fleet.

Up on top of it, on the roof of the bridge, were two long and
heavy shapes, concealed beneath canvas. The cloth spray skirts
were fixed tight with neat sailor knots, but there was no hiding
what was up there, nodding slightly to each wave that penetrated
from the choppy Caribbean. Fifty calibre machine guns. Just
enough firepower to prick the crocodile's tail.

IN CUBA, 1961 was supposed to be called The Year of
Education, but that name didn't really stick. In the street and
in memory, it was something else. Action engraved itself into the
Cuban consciousness, and what happened that year was that
everyone learned to read. So people said that if something had
happened then, in 1961, it had happened during the Year of
Literacy. If someone had left Cuba during '61, then it was during
the *año de alfabetización*. For Cubans on the island, that was it, the
landmark of temporal navigation. Everything about the Revolution was before, or after, 1961, the Year of Literacy.

Cubans breathe hyperbole. A third cousin twice removed is
your brother. Your actual brother is your twin. Strangers are
esteemed comrades. Anyone who ever got a university degree is
addressed as *ingeniero* or doctor. Flowers of speech denote the

greatness of passion, or event. Cuba is not merely an island but 'the Pearl of the Antilles'. Cuba is not merely beautiful, but, as Columbus said, 'the most beautiful land ever seen by human eyes'. The Revolution is not merely good, or great, or even perfect, but is *the most perfect, the most just form of government ever devised by man in history*.

Even the calendar had to brag. Titles were lathered on like lipstick on an old woman. Because 1958 was a time of of war, fear, hope and rebirth, the novelist Guillermo Cabrera Infante had called it the 'Year of Grace'. Everyone called 1959 'The Triumph'. And 1960 was 'The Reform', for the massive land redistributions. The decades went on, the Cuban government spilling out the official names, but only these first, popular names and first, shattering years were engraved with a collective title: everyone called that era 'The Heroic Years', a name that covered the searing black and white Revolution of '59 through the cascading confrontations that ended at the humiliating Cuban missile crisis of 1962.

But there was only one year that was *the* Heroic Year: 1961. The year of education, and of the first re-education camps. Beginning with a break in Cuban-American relations, and ending with Cuba's tumble into the deep folds of the Soviet cloak. The year of confrontation. The Bay of Pigs, cleaving the country into supporters and opponents, unity or exile, with us or against us, the year of stagnation.

Like all Cubans, the boys from Dolores began 1961 in one country and, whether still at home or suddenly abroad, they ended it in an entirely different place. People had fled the Revolution before, and would do so after, but 1961 was the year that created the Cuban Exile as an institution. It was the year of the great exodus under Castro, a flood tthat would not be surpassed until the Mariel boatlift of 1980, when more than 100,000 Cubans fled.

Mariel was a bookend, the flight of the poor and hopeless of Cuba, the fed up and forgotten. But the earlier, 1961 exodus was a very different wave of emigration, a flight of those who could afford to leave. In 1961, the exodus was by airplane, or passenger ship, not inner tube. It was an uprooting of those who, even as their world collapsed around them, still had the ability to slip through the narrowing loopholes of the Revolution, to gather the money for an airplane ticket, and to manipulate not one but two chaotic governments (their own, and that of their targeted exile) in a rapidly changing situation.

About two-thirds of the boys from Dolores cut a path through this wilderness and into foreign exile. The rest found that they, too, had left, even without leaving their homes.

THE YEAR OF LITERACY was probably the most selfless and successful act that Fidel Castro ever undertook, with the largest moral component, the widest support, and most profound impact on Cuba and the world. Starting on 1 January 1961, some 200,000 Cuban volunteers, mostly very young, were given uniforms, an allowance for food, and an assignment: go into the most backward slums, the most remote corners of the countryside, climb the steepest mountains, and teach a million peasants to read in just 12 months.

That first day of January the initial brigades were photographed climbing into cattle cars for the train ride out of Havana, to the Escambray mountains in central Cuba and points east. Movie cameras followed them every step of the way: for those who didn't care to read about it, the literacy campaign was being memorialized for a film called *El Brigadista*.

These volunteer teachers also carried tin hurricane lanterns, donated by Maoist China. Farm workers had time for school only at night, and most of the illiterate also lacked electricity. The Chinese lanterns substituted for light bulbs, and became the symbol of the campaign, the light of knowledge. East Germany, Czechoslovakia and the USSR also donated tens of thousands of pairs of eyeglasses, a literal opening of vistas for Cuba's poor.

The students were adults, but began like any child, learning the alphabet, and filling their new notebooks with the first shaping of letters, trembling curves and hesitant capitals. By instruction, the first words they would ever write were:

CUBA
FIDEL
RAÚL

Later they would learn to compose their first sentences:
The Agrarian Reform Advances.
The campaign is strengthening.
The organizations of the masses are being integrated at the national level.

Classes ran on a continuous basis, more and more of them as the Year of Literacy went on. As a kind of final exam, every student had to compose a letter to Him. The basic text was dictated by the teachers. The newly literate simply added the sentiment and demonstrated their penmanship and conformity.

Fidel,
I am very proud to know how to read.
Thanks to you, I can write you this letter to tell you: Fidel, how great you are.
Thank you,
Irma Moquera Barrea
Piñar del Rio

On 5 January – just the fifth day of the campaign – a young volunteer teacher named Conrado Benítez reached his post, high in the Escambray mountains. He wore the uniform of the campaign, a set of military-style green fatigues, with a particularly broad beret, and a black and red armband. Black and red: the revolutionary colours. He carried a lantern, not a gun, but there were reactionaries in the hills who saw him as an invader, a Communist, a traitor, and they shot him dead.

The government reacted swiftly. Troops pushed through every hamlet of the Escambray, hunting down what were called 'bandits'. After Benítez was lionized in the newspapers and on radio, there was a flood of new volunteers. The literacy campaign was accelerated, rather than slowed by the murder. The very next group of teachers to go into the field was named the 'Conrado Benítez Brigade'.

Just 5 January, and the war – anticipated and feared, predicted and denied, talked about and plotted – was under way.

THERE HAD BEEN A LOT OF TALK IN MIAMI. It had started with a whisper in 1959, built to a rumbling in 1960, and was deafening as 1961 started. Every Cuban from Miami to New York seemed to have a gripe about Castro, his draconian Revolution, and the need for Cubans to finally do something. People had convened a lot of meetings. There was one going on in Miami in January, with 60 different groups arguing about what to do. The conference was so big that it had to be organized like a trade convention, with booths for each individual group, and bitter enemies and former betrayals filled the hallways. Some of the talkers were right-wing politicians from the old Cuban parties, and some were Batista cronies, seeking their old fortunes. Others were ex-guerrillas and 'true' Revolutionaries recently purged by Che Guevara. There was even a contingent from the Cuban-Hebrew Congregation. As would prove usual for *El Exílio*, all that these Cubans could agree upon was what they were against: Fidel Castro. They took a dramatic but empty name – the National Revolutionary Council – and went on protesting, fulminating, releasing declarations and announcing imminent victories, a cathartic but impotent strategy that would continue for decades without putting a scratch in Castro's Chevrolet.

But as these talkers and shouters, pamphleteers and archivists, demagogues and democrats, demanders and the glad-handers mouthed their great chorus of 1961, there were those whose silence spoke for them. Those who were done talking. The same year would now shed off a splinter group, the doers. There were all kinds of men who vanished into the dark violence of 1961, but perhaps none more surprising than the great democratic theorist, Lundy Aguilar. He was one of hundreds of Cuban men who evaporated from the streets of South Florida as the winter of discontent gave way to a CIA spring.

In January of 1961 every Cuban already in exile, and many still on the island, knew one thing: some sort of anti-Castro military force was coming together. A big effort, taking shape somewhere. Men kept disappearing with their duffel bags. Everyone knew someone who knew a young man who had gone off to somewhere to do something that couldn't be discussed. War was coming.

The number of Cuban families arriving in exile was also rising fast. These people were freshly, radically converted to the anti-Castro cause, and in January of 1961 they brought more than enough young men into Miami to replace, and then follow, those who had recently gone off to join secret military programmes. It wasn't hard to see what was happening. Batista himself could be found sitting in the back of a bar in Hialeah, meeting with wealthy men, recruiting, organizing. And as far away as New Orleans and Venezuela, plotters, frauds, men of action, mercenaries, smugglers and agents were weaving their nets.

In Miami, lots of new American faces were beginning to turn up. Some of them were just freelance tough guys, or wealthy Commie haters with crazy schemes, or new age filibusters looking for personal glory. Some crackpots from New Orleans – not a Cuban among them – had already run down to the island in an old boat, shot up some buildings on a beach, and got themselves arrested. But there were other Americans too, men with suits, sober faces and US government credentials. They rented offices, and settled in to stay. Kennedy would be installed in Washington before the end of the month. New blood. New money. By spring, Miami had the second largest CIA station in the world.

Which is how mission creep took over. Lundy and his friends had begun by talking about innocent things – the fight for democracy in Cuba, propaganda campaigns about their rights and losses. When the talk eventually turned to action, they had discussed getting a boat and going down to Cuba to rescue loved ones. They enlisted in the MRR – the Movimiento Recuperación Revolucionario, founded by Jorge Segura of Dolores. But their vague ideas were now being fed with American money, and equipment, encouragement, and even incitement. In Miami as a whole, the talk quickly turned military, with the Americans urging strikes on Cuba's Revolutionary armed forces. And since the Revolution had taken over everything in Cuba, almost everything was a legitimate target, especially sabotage, like the burning of crops and the destruction of Cuban industry. Then, with increasing regularity, there were frankly criminal schemes put forward, plans for assassinations, some promoted by the Americans, others generated entirely by groups of Cubans. The American military branches began seconding men and resources to the effort, more and more, faster and faster. So if some Cuban friends got together in the fall of '60, and started training with a few old rifles and a 22-foot fishing boat, by January a group of short-haired American men would show up with cash, crates of machine guns, and the keys to *goddamn warships*.

You couldn't expect young men to turn back from a surprise, from a vision at the end of a dock. You couldn't expect them to stop and think, or to say the weather was too bad, or the implications of the mission too abrupt, or, simply, this wasn't what we wanted. Momentum took over, the automatic flow of events.

Whatever they felt, Lundy and his new crew mates stowed their gear, started the engines for the first time, unhitched the hawsers, and motored slowly out of the Key West harbour, past low mangrove islands, and almost immediately they were into the choppy, miserably cold blue of the Gulf Stream.

The waves were terrible at first, but once the motors were unleashed they couldn't believe what happened. As the boat roared into a deafening, full-throated scream of power, it lifted into a plane and the ocean smoothed out. Lundy's position was manning a .50 calibre machine gun, right up on top of the bridge. As he stood with a friend, their hair whipping in the wind, they had to hold on tight, and take a certain amount of slamming up and down, but their elation was evident enough. The PT's shape allowed it to plane over the rough parts, and its weight and size allowed it to cut the winter waves right in half with little fuss. It filled them with confidence.

For a few hours, they simply enjoyed it, learning how the boat could twist into the tightest of turns, and even accelerate as it came out of them. How one moment they could flutter along quietly, barely moving, and then burst over the waves like a cavalry charge. There was not a boat in the Caribbean that could outrun or outmanoeuvre theirs.

But it drank a lot of gasoline. An Achilles heel. The Packard engines were powerful, but thirsty. Almost all travel had to be low and slow, and when the boat did plane up and fast, it had to be on a short leash. After just a few hours of sprinting around, showing off, learning the handling and the feel of their future, shaking the cold sea stomachs out of themselves, getting used to the idea that they were going somewhere on this boat someday, then already they had to turn back for fuel.

So that was the first lesson. Resupply. Amateurs talk strategy, professionals talk logistics. January, and everyone was learning new arts.

ON JUST THE SECOND DAY OF THE YEAR, at the United Nations in New York, the nation of Cuba had formally charged that a neighbour was preparing to invade the sovereign island, using an army of mercenaries, which was now training in Guatemala. This allegation had the benefit of being true: as far back as March of the previous year, President Eisenhower had ordered the CIA to prepare an invasion army of Cuban exiles to overthrow the Revolution, and they really were in Guatemala, training.

So the American goal was just what the Cubans alleged. Yet they were wrong about one thing. Instead of a masterful and carefully coordinated plot by the most powerful country in the world, they were facing a chaotic and disorganized array of schemes, often by bumbling amateurs. The professionals weren't so good either: the CIA was working at cross-purposes with itself, in a confusion of overlapping, simultaneous projects to under-mine Castro, schemes that involved all sorts of people in and out of American government, the military, the intelligence services, freelance crusaders, NASA and mafia hit men. The most extreme

CIA measures were eventually lumped together under the title Operation Mongoose, a mishmash of sabotage, raids, assassination attempts, coup plotting and competing invasion schemes.

The outgoing president, Eisenhower, handed on this jury-rigged and bum-rushed contraption to the incoming John F. Kennedy on inauguration day that January. The young president took up the project without much debate or trepidation: the entire Washington establishment shared the same desire to knock over Castro. But in Washington and New York the first element of this plan was denial: shedding lies in all directions, American diplomacy feigned outrage at Cuba's allegation to the UN. A day later the American government withdrew its ambassador to Cuba, closed the embassy, and broke off all formal diplomatic contact.

Lundy's boat in Key West was a sideshow. The real American plan for Cuba was built on the CIA's experience overthrowing the governments of Iran (1953) and Guatemala (1954). In both cases, they had relied on an indigenous elite to do the dirty work, whether army officers staging a coup (Iran) or an invasion by a token force of 'patriots' (Guatemala). The CIA believed that Castro could be overthrown in a coup, or killed, with the invasion being merely a backup plan. The idea was to send about 3,000 Cuban exiles ashore at Trinidad, in south-eastern Cuba. Once in possession of the town and its airstrip, these men would declare themselves the provisional government of a new, free Cuba.

Invading a sovereign country like this raised no eyebrows in Washington. Cuba was fair game. No one blinked at assassination schemes either. In February 1961, the CIA was directly involved in an attempt to poison Castro through a box of cigars. Another plot soon followed, this one to coat his wet suit with a poison. Before the year was out, there would be an attempt to poison Castro's milkshake at a Havana lunch counter. This one failed when the soda-jerk lost his nerve.

The core assumption underlying all the American efforts – sabotage, assassination, invasion – was that by 1961 Cubans were deeply divided. This was partly true. Across the island, in Havana, in Santiago, and even in the Colegio de Dolores, there were new and bitter divisions. The unity and joy of the early, heady days of the Revolution were expiring. But these divisions, however real, were not proportioned out the way Americans assumed. The majority of Cubans were still pleased with the direction of their country, and saw Castro as the guarantor of literacy, land for farmers, and the punishment of the guilty. But theirs was not the voice that carried farthest. It was the objections and fears of the Cuban elite that reached Washington, echoed in New York, and dominated in Miami. America was listening to the cries of those who had lost land in the redistributions, not gained it.

Castro was slowly spreading his hand over Cuba, touching more and more aspects of life on the island. But at this point the big corporations and wealthy foreigners had lost out, while Castro had not yet alienated many Cubans by seizing even small businesses. Life ticked along for most people, more or less the same as before. Castro's own personal popularity was very high. Most people liked the new order, and the urgent summons to rebuild Cuba, to reshape the society, to bring justice to the poor and bread to the hungry. Castro still denied he was a Communist, or even a socialist. Those words were not popular, not part of the mass movement of ordinary, middle-class people that had risen up to oppose Batista. So the words were never used.

What wasn't said mattered. It was in the things forgotten that Cuba's Revolution was revealing itself. Since long before coming into power, even before taking to the hills of Oriente in '56, Castro has offered two central tenets for his revolution: the restoration of Cuba's beloved New Constitution, from 1940, and then free and fair elections within one year. Constitution; elections. This two-part promise was central to Castro's appeal as a student leader at the University of Havana; he spoke of it on Rebel Radio, the guerrillas' clandestine station; it was written into the platform of his 26th of July Movement. The 1940 constitution, and then elections.

The twin planks of the rebellion couldn't have been clearer, or more carefully repeated, or more widely agreed upon. Because of this moderate agenda, even the head of the Bacardí company, Pepín Bosch, had supported Castro and the guerrillas financially.

Other wealthy men helped with money, or put their farms at the disposal of the guerrillas. Cuban exiles in New York and Florida had poured money and rifles south to Castro, the great democrat, the principled lawyer who would restore the country to the people. On the island, the middle class responded to these ideas in huge numbers, contributing to fundraising drives for the guerrillas by buying their clandestine 'treasury bonds'.

Even many Americans in Cuba, including some in the US embassy, expected that Castro – a middle-class *blanco* lawyer talking about democracy and constitutions – would make a fine replacement for Batista. A dozen American volunteers found their way into the Sierra Maestre and became guerrilla fighters. The CIA even went as far as sending Castro a token shipment of arms, in an effort to court him. Several American corporations, like the national Telephone Company, held back taxes due to the Batista government and gave the money to the rebels instead. Who wouldn't support a man with a platform like that?

Like the exile, the Revolution itself had been founded on the shoulders of people like Castro: middle-class whites seeking to reclaim their voice, their votes and their destiny. With the overwhelming support of that middle class, a smattering of the rich, and the acquiescence of the poor, Castro became not merely a liberator, but a ruler.

Within three months of coming to power Castro began to backpedal on his claim of elections within one year. The country had to be put in order first, he said. There was a crisis situation, which demanded delays. Appearing on *Meet the Press* in April 1959, Castro said it would be 18 months until the elections. By early 1960 the vote was said to be two years away. And in early 1961 the government suggested that it would take at least four more years to create the right conditions for a national vote. Nobody talked about the 1940 constitution any more.

IT ISN'T NECESSARY TO SPECULATE about what Havana looked like in those January days. Two years into the Revolution, the social interactions and the ordinary street life of the city were all recorded on film by a teenager named Orlando Jiménez-Leal.

Just 19, he was a precocious cameraman who had taught himself to master the new generation of small, light cinema cameras that were starting to change documentary film-making in America. With integrated sound, fingertip focus, and magazines that held 400 feet of film, the cameras allowed someone like Leal to turn ordinary observation into an act of self-creation, the film-maker suddenly as central as his subject. This potential had excited Cuba's most powerful film critic, Guillermo Cabrera Infante, who urged his friends in Cuban television to lend the 19-year-old *wunderkind* a camera, and to give him the tag-ends of film rolls left over from official projects. Leal cobbled together these scraps of film stock and set off into the streets of the city, his finger on the trigger, looking for the ordinary realities of this transitory Havana, a city pinned between worlds coming and worlds going, where the high and low were in new and uncertain relation.

Foreign tourists had deserted Cuba by 1961, scared off by the appearance of barbed wire around government buildings, and by new checkpoints on the roads, manned by militiamen exploring their first taste of power. Castro had welcomed the departure of the tourists. He'd closed all the casinos, and made a great show of opening the beaches at Varadero and other resorts, which had been restricted to hotel guests under the previous regime. He cancelled the 1961 convention of ASTRA, the association of travel agents, announcing that Cuba no longer needed tourism, a parasitical industry that reduced the citizenry to servants and prostitutes. Since the hotels of Havana were empty, the Revolution moved hundreds of poor people down from the mountains and into their empty rooms. The main salon of the Nacional, where Errol Flynn and Winston Churchill had relaxed with drinks and cigars, was converted into a school for tailoring, the high ceiling echoing to the curses of pricked thumbs.

Shooting at night in January, Leal filmed the people of Havana commuting through the darkened port, their faces weary from work. His lens caught the rough water at the Regla ferry docks, the same storm surge that was shaking the old navy dock up in Key West, the same waves that were bobbing Lundy's machine gun up and down. Leal caught the out-of-focus forms of men ashore, and some of the idlers standing around in bars, drinking and dancing. On the surface, little seemed to have changed in this Havana. People still crowded into little spaces to celebrate, even if the foreigners were gone and it was mostly just Cubans now. They still played music, and sang, and danced, and got drunk. They still dressed within the social conventions of the pre-Revolutionary era, so that even poor men wore skinny neckties and porkpie hats. Black, white, mulatto, they tumbled into bars, drank from dirty glasses, and twirled on the tiny dance floor as musicians scraped at *guiros*. The bars were sweaty, dirty, cheap. Old women lifted their wrinkled arms over their heads to dance rumba, gallants showed off by dancing the funky chicken, and people ordered drinks or food.

Shot entirely in black and white under the artificial lights of street lamps and inside brightly lit bars, the film had no dialogue, only the ambient noise of Havana on an evening in January of 1961. Absolutely nothing happened. But the 19-year-old Leal had unwittingly pulled the trigger on the old culture of Cuba, assassinating it even as he preserved it on silver nitrate. His scraps of film, coiled up inside the camera magazine, needed only half a year to become deadly weapons.

IT WAS HISTORY THAT SENT LUNDY back to the boat in February. At some point, the slow growth of intellectual truth had bound him to this fate. He had asked to join the MRR group first of all, because his friends were in it, and he felt envious that they were doing something. And there was a 'metaphysical' reason. For years now, in print and in speech, he had warned that Castro could become an absolute tyrant. He had to live up to his own beliefs. There wasn't any firm decision, or moment of revelation, or sudden insight. He just followed logic to its consequence. 'Why not?' he asked himself. 'I'm a coward, but I have to do something.'

Everything was growing: the MRR now had 66 men in covert operations, and the CIA had supplied them with a second and now third PT boat, a little squadron berthed in Key West. They had started out very green in January, but they weren't fools, and learned to run the boat well, and to be good soldiers, even if the CIA gave them crappy used boots and only vague information about the future. For Lundy, it was perhaps a Jesuit leftover to believe that everything that could be done, could be done well, even raiding, and he earned the coveted job of machine gunner on their second mission. They went down in February, approaching the north-east coast in the dark, and started probing for the mouth of the Bay of Nipe. The professor, the student of Cervantes and Shakespeare, was on top, clutching the machine gun, and he spent hours peering into the murky night. Even with his crew mates around him, war was a lonely place. Downstairs, amid the regular crew, was one passenger. An MRR operative, a messenger was supposed to go ashore inside the bay, but they couldn't, for love nor money, pierce the darkness and learn where that was. Every shade of blackness in the night promised some wreck and ruin. A lookout could spend the whole night this way, miserable, nervous, simply afraid.

Lundy was by nature dispassionate, an agile dissector of doctrines, seldom angry, proud of his Jesuit self-control. He didn't *hate* the Revolution, because hate clouded the truth. And the literacy campaign and other social programmes were fine by him. Class meant nothing to him: like Castro, Lundy was only an ephemeral member of any elite. His father was a judge. They had lost no broad ranches to the agrarian reforms, nor seen any empires of wealth. Instead it was the love of history, of Greek arguments and valiant citizen-soldiers in Athens and Paris and Philadelphia that had led him, like a catechism, through the same questions, again and again, each one leading to the next.

Does absolute power corrupt, he asked himself, standing on the roof of the boat, *absolutely?*

It must.

Is violence against a tyrant justified?

It was, in the case of Batista. And so it must be once again, in the case of Castro.

And then the old questions, the same ones come around again. *Will you choose? Whose side will you be on? Which standard?*

Last of all, and fraught with the most implications: *Will you act?*

The decision could not be evaded. You had to choose, and act.

But in the dark night off Nipe, what action was there? There was nothing to see or do. And more nothing. Shapeless night. An hour went by in silence.

They weren't supposed to talk on the guns, but the waters of Nipe were famous for their quantity of sharks, which led someone to joke that 'they' should have eaten 'him'. This was a reference any Cuban could understand: one of the famous incidents in Castro's life was a long swim through these shark-infested waters.

Everyone knew the story, because the Revolution's propaganda apparatus had already begun mythologizing the events of Castro's life, finding prefiguration in the leader's youth, and omen in his feats of superhuman strength. Nipe Bay was one of these moments, and Lundy had heard the story from Castro's own mouth. He had seen Castro twice after the Revolution. The first time was just a brief visit to the presidential suite of the Havana Hilton in the earliest days. Castro had a lot of new friends, but few old ones, and Lundy was gradually able to penetrate the rings of security and hangers-on, the guerrillas with M1 rifles who lounged in armchairs down in the lobby, the crowds of journalists, politicians, beautiful women and high-ranking *barbudos* in the dark hallway of the top floor. Lundy was finally admitted to Castro's suite, which had a sweeping view over Nuevo Vedado, the heart of modern Havana. Directly below was La Rampa, pointing toward the ocean like Cuba's national driveway.

They exchanged best wishes and laughed. From Dolores to Havana and the presidential suite of the Hilton. Lundy spied the books on Castro's night table: a volume on Marx that looked, from its smooth spine, like it had never been opened, and a well-thumbed copy of the speeches of Perón. An autocratic populist, Perón had thrilled 1940s Argentina with his rhetoric on behalf of the poor, and his wife bedecked in diamonds. Perón talked about progressive themes like universal jobs, health care for all and pensions for the old, and his supporters had lapped it up, but gave increasingly deranged speeches about his secret plans for atomic bombs, and even a space programme. Perón's flights of fancy were a reminder of how far nationalism, calls to glory, and the total escape from reality could take a politician.

Nipe Bay was Fidel's debut as a man of action. Chatting with Lundy in the Hilton, Fidel quickly turned the conversation to the story of that first failed attempt in 1947 at overthrowing a dictator. The dictator was Rafael Trujillo, the country was the Dominican Republic, and Fidel described the events 'as if it was the battle of Waterloo', Lundy recalled.

Trujillo was a monster who deserved the bullet he eventually got. Another self-styled President-for-Life, he spoke of freedom while crushing dissent, gave nationalist speeches while doing whatever the United States wanted, and declared himself the saviour of the Republic while looting the treasury. Trujillo always wanted to be called by the same intimate street term that Castro liked: *jefe*, or boss. It was a kind of fake intimacy with ordinary people, an assurance that absolute power did not mean what it seemed.

In 1947, Trujillo had just committed the latest of many outrages, sending his police to massacre a huge number of Haitian immigrants working illegally in his country. It was an act of genocide, immediately infamous worldwide, and in Cuba Castro joined a badly concealed plot to overthrow Trujillo. About 1,200 men boarded four boats and set sail from Nipe Bay, heading out into the ocean and making a right toward the Dominican Republic. On board the main boat, the *Caridad*, were hundreds of Cuban toughs, many of them, like Fidel, members of the 'Happy Trigger' political gangs in Havana. Some of Castro's biggest rivals were on the *Caridad* with him, and the disorganized plot lacked clear leadership or even a battle plan.

The one thing they did have on board was ego: everyone had been talking, loudly, about their would-be Revolution. The Cuban government knew exactly what they were up to, and an hour or so after the *Caridad* and the other three boats turned out of Nipe Bay, they were intercepted by the Coast Guard. The *Caridad* was ordered back to port, and the invasion now became a humiliating embarrassment. In a panic, men started throwing their guns overboard. Castro, rather than face arrest, jumped into the shark-infested waters and swam for it.

By his own account, Castro had swum through the night, covering about eight or nine miles, before dragging himself ashore. Most people would drown attempting such a long swim in ocean conditions. Some of Castro's enemies on the *Caridad* later claimed that he had actually left the freighter in a small boat, and rowed ashore, but he was a good athlete, fit, and disciplined in a crisis, so he could have swum it.

Lundy himself had already heard a different version – that Castro had indeed swum away from the *Caridad*, but had been rescued by fishermen at some point. And Castro hadn't fled the boat to avoid arrest. He'd fled to avoid being murdered by his rivals, who blamed the talkative Castro for advertising their plot in advance. Castro did have trouble keeping his mouth shut. Just two days after coming ashore, he was back at the University of Havana, giving speeches where he bragged about leading the coup attempt. He even named many of the other participants, who were at that moment under arrest, busily denying their participation.

Whether or not Castro really swam eight or nine miles, at night, through shark-infested waters, was irrelevant. By 1960 it was already the official story that he had.

In April 1948, Fidel participated in the infamous *bogotazo*, a civil war that erupted among political parties in Colombia. (He also spent part of the year honeymooning on Manhattan's Upper West Side.) This was followed by the Moncada attack of 1953 and then the *Granma* invasion in 1956. Lundy saw now the connection: Nipe Bay had started as a principled gesture of violence against a corrupt dictator, and now, in Castro's telling had become a kind of miracle, a moment that Fidel saw as separating himself from other men. Just weeks in to his rule, the escape, the swim, and the sharks of Nipe Bay were taking shape as the miraculous evidence of his own power. 'The appetite was there,' Lundy recalled of the encounter in the Hilton. 'He knew he had to control it. But it was there.' Lundy whispered all this out during the long night watch atop the boat, circling back and forth in search of Nipe Bay. It had happened right there, wherever that was.

They simply could not find the mouth of the bay. Nipe had a narrow entrance, hidden by sand bars. And it went like that all night, darkness and false visions as the boat growled quietly, and turned this way and that.

The *zurdo* (the klutz) wasted a lot of effort trying to look martial that night. He stood at the gun, gripping it, ready to fight. But the gun felt useless, a toy. The only time they ever fired it was at the start of each mission, as soon as they cleared into international waters. That was just a short burst to check that everything worked. When Lundy looked over at Jorge de Moya, who manned the other gun, he saw him equally poised, ready, clutching his .50 calibre, but looking ill.

'How are you doing?' Lundy finally asked.

'I'm fine,' De Moya said. 'Except I can't move my hands.' The blood had drained right out of them.

'Are you afraid?' De Moya asked.

'I think so,' Lundy said.

They probed along the coast like that all night, finding only the wrong places. Then, when the first crack of indigo appeared in the black sky to the east, they knew how quickly dawn would come. The courier mission was aborted. They turned the boat north and ran for Key West.

OSWALD WAS IN MINSK and Kennedy was still in Georgetown when Pepín Bou found himself right back where he had started. In January of 1961, twenty years after bouncing through the hallways of Dolores with Fidel, and long after leaving the city and the country, he was back in Santiago de Cuba.

After Dolores he had left not just Santiago, but Oriente and Cuba, heading to college in America. He had spent the 1940s earning a degree in chemical engineering. In 1955 he and his wife, Celia, moved to New Orleans. Pepín found work with a big American mining firm, the Freeport Sulfur Company. A daughter was born to the couple there, third of an eventual four, but the Bou family did not stay long in America, or put down roots.

Within two years they had returned to Cuba. Freeport wanted to open a state-of-the-art nickel-processing plant in Cuba. The plant would employ a new sulphuric acid refinement process, a complicated innovation that extracted much more profit from a given ton of laterite ore, but which required a big investment up front, with new machinery and a skilled staff. Cuban engineers were in demand, and Pepín jumped at the chance.

In 1957, Pepín deposited his family in Santiago and then pushed on to the new site at Moa Bay. It was an area rich in minerals but one of the most isolated places in Cuba. It had a good anchorage, which was perfect for shipping in an entire American-built refining plant, assembling it, and then shipping out Cuban nickel, all with hardly any connection to Cuba itself.

Moa Bay was a bad place to work, and a worse place to live. The mine itself sat halfway between Birán, the backwater where the Castros had grown up, and Baracoa, a legendarily remote town that claimed to be the first spot Columbus came ashore in Cuba. That is to say, it was halfway between nowhere and nowhere else. There was no road to Moa Bay, just a cart track, poorly carved, which expired in mud during the rainy season. Only the best trucks could get across that way at all. Most of the mine equipment was brought in by ocean barge, straight from the US, and the ordinary crews were brought in from Santiago by boat, or via miserable day-long treks in the back of a jolting truck.

The supervising engineers, like Bou, were in a privileged position. If the weather was good they were flown from Santiago on a DC3 for an 11-day shift. Then they were flown out for four days at home, followed by another 11 days on site. Assembling an industrial facility in a wilderness was aggravating, and the long shifts isolating. The men lived in dormitories, and there was no telephone. The only entertainment was listening to the radio. The nearest people were in a puny village along the coast, with mud streets, one bar that had hitching posts in front, and no whorehouse. Everybody just worked, and steadily during 1958 the Freeport equipment was barged in, assembled, and by the fall three out of four refining lines were in operation.

Like the Havana Hilton, the mine was a badly timed

investment. By November of 1958, more and more towns in Oriente were falling under rebel control, and in early December, a column of guerrillas under Che Guevara broke out of Oriente, storming west into central Cuba and toppling garrisons left and right. At Moa Bay, everyone listened to the radio at night, helpless, disbelieving. The whole east of the country was grinding to a halt, all commercial activity and even daily routines suspended, with strikes breaking out, and underground militias rising up. The replacement crews in Santiago could not be rounded up, and the barges stopped coming. As the guerrilla offensive spread, every American corporation in Cuba suddenly lost its appetite for business. Freeport abruptly ordered the mine shut down and the crews sent home.

Pepín thought it would be a matter of waiting things out. A few months, perhaps. After 1 January 1959, the chaos began to resolve itself into a semblance of normality. The mine didn't reopen in 1959, but the equipment still needed upkeep, and Freeport kept one engineer on duty at Moa Bay throughout the entire year, serving out the same 11-day shifts. Pepín only had to stand that lonely sentry duty a few times, but those days were the worst. History was being made in Havana, the country slowly beginning to wake up to the repercussions of a new era, but Pepín would be sitting in the middle of nowhere, cleaning the equipment and waiting, cleaning and waiting.

In July 1960, still marking time, he served what turned out to be his last shift for Freeport. Without warning, Castro announced in a speech that the government was nationalizing a whole host of foreign companies. Suddenly Moa Bay belonged to the people.

THE BOYS FROM DOLORES were seldom without resources. Pepín found a new job easily enough. His father was head of sales at Bacardí, the most famous rum distillery in the Caribbean. Pepín landed a desk job in the company's red brick headquarters edging the Santiago harbour. Pepín's job was connected with a beer brewery in Santiago that produced Hatuey, the island's favourite beer.

Pepín had supported the Revolution, but that was no distinction: even top Bacardí executives had supported the guerrillas, and during 1959 had welcomed fatigue-wearing Revolutionaries into the executive offices to help coordinate production. By some estimates 90 per cent of Cubans had sided with the *barbudos* in the hills. Pepín had done nothing to actively support the Revolution – during the fighting, he'd given some money, like many people – but he considered himself a sympathizer.

Sitting on the fence was no longer enough. In early 1961, after he'd been at the brewery just six months, four men in the new uniforms of the Revolutionary Militia appeared at his office door. They were armed, but led by a civilian in a tie and jacket, who was carrying a telegram addressed to 'Engineer Bou'.

'Can you read?' the man asked. He was offering to read the telegram out loud, if Pepín needed that. Bou wanted to snort – could anyone called 'engineer' *not* read? – but he restrained himself. It was the Year of Literacy, and the rights of the uneducated were much on everyone's mind.

Engineer Bou took the telegram, and so became the last person to find out the news. The message had come straight from the office of the President of the Republic, in Havana. Pepín was to report to the capital in three days. His air ticket, and a room at the Hotel Nacional, were already reserved.

This was not an invitation to decline. He flew to the capital on the second day, and while checking into the Nacional he ran into another engineer he knew. José Batlle had been a student at Dolores, though not in the same years at Pepín. Still, they knew each other in the way Cubans do: they were Oriental, they had mutual friends through Dolores, and Batlle had also worked for Freeport Sulfur at Moa Bay. They called to each other by their nicknames, Pepín for the older man and Pepito for the younger.

Soon they realized that the soaring, half-timbered lobby of the Nacional was full of engineers. Mining engineers. *Nickel* mining engineers especially. Most were Moa Bay people. That meant an initiative to restart the plant.

The next morning Pepín and Batlle were picked up in the curving driveway of the Nacional by a government car, with Che

Guevara's personal driver, a Cuban navy sailor, at the helm. They were taken to the Banco Nacional, where Che had set up his economic ministry. In the big conference room there, they joined a much larger group of mining engineers, making three dozen people, total. This was a group that Batlle called 'the whole world' of Cuban mining. Now they realized that only a small minority of them were from Moa Bay so it had to be a nationwide initiative.

Although they had been told that Fidel Castro himself would attend the meeting, in the end, after a long wait, it was Che who came. He had a big entourage that included some *barbudos*, some bureaucrats, and Pepín's old schoolmate, Raúl Castro. More importantly, Raúl's wife was there: Vilma Espin, one of the most influential of all Revolutionaries. She was an old friend of Pepín's and greeted him warmly, but when Bou nodded at Raúl, smiling, the number two man in Cuba did not acknowledge him. Like Fidel, Raúl was suddenly shedding old versions of himself, along with those who had known him before the fatigues.

Che stood, and laid out a new mission in soaring terms. The Revolution was going to restart production of nickel at Moa Bay and increase it at all the older plants, starting immediately. The Revolution needed nickel to barter with the Soviets, who used it to harden the metal in aerospace components, including missiles. In exchange, the Soviets would give their help in other matters.

'Who is disposed to volunteer?' Guevara asked. Only two or three people raised their hands.

Che protested, and complained about their lack of patriotism, and then revealed that it didn't really matter whether they wanted to do it. 'If you want to work in Cuba,' he told the engineers, 'then you have to go to the nickel plants.'

When Pepín got back to Santiago, he found it was true. A telegram from Havana had beaten him to the Bacardí building. Pepín was stopped as he walked in; 'Engineer Bou' had been banned from the premises.

So it really was nickel or nothing.

AT DOLORES THE BUBBLE OF PRIVILEGE was trembling without yet bursting. Entering the third full year of the Revolution, the school carried on as much the same as possible, but it was obvious something had to change. In late January, Belén, the Jesuit sister school in Havana, had been closed by the authorities. Eighty militiamen had taken over the 60-acre campus, shutting it down and transferring 1,200 students to public schools. Although the government cited educational reform as the reason for shutting Belén, everyone knew that the school was a nexus of Havana's most recalcitrant families, a rallying point for the Catholic, the wealthy, the stubborn, the rich.

Dolores remained open, nervous and expectant, hopeful that off in Santiago, the *ciudad revolucionaria*, there would be less pressure. Each day the students went through the motions as before, the morning mass, the same curriculum, the students cycling in and out of the classrooms as if nothing was going to happen.

The education was as rigorous as ever, but something had changed. A reactionary atmosphere had crept into the building, an increasing stance of hostility toward the changing world outside. Reflecting the views of their parents, most students had now turned fervently anti-Castro. In mid-January Padre Seven Foot, the teacher who had worn a 26th of July armband in 1958, and briefly travelled with the guerrillas, became the centre of a dispute. Even though he had turned against Castro, students taunted him, and parents complained about the presence of a 'Communist' at the school. Finally the school asked him to take a leave of absence until things had calmed down.

What didn't change was just as important. One of the boys, Bernardo Souto, thought the school was still wonderful, still rigorous, but out of step with the times, with the social changes occurring worldwide as the 1960s swept in. The Revolution outside Dolores merely highlighted what was different within the walls. The school was elite and expensive in a country now ruled by the poor majority. Most noticeably, at a moment when Cuba was abandoning all forms of social and racial discrimination, the once progressive Dolores was becoming hidebound with social views that only seemed to retreat as the world outside advanced. The school was, Souto recalled, 'a little segregationist, a little misogynist'.

In late February, in the middle of the morning session, it finally happened. There was a commotion out in the halls. The Jesuits were called together, the teachers brought out of the classes to hear something. Various adults were seen whispering. And then the school bell began to ring out, fast and hard. It wasn't Lundy's old bell ringing the new hour; it was the last bell, ever. The students were told to assemble in the courtyard. They went through the drill once more, all the boys ranging down the stairs in open order, swirling into the patio, forming their neat lines.

Go home, the Padre Prefect said. He stood facing the student body, standing behind the high black railing. The message was simple: go home at once, and for good. The militia was on its way, and the Colegio de Dolores would be closed, permanently.

The boys gathered their things and went out into the street, standing about as if this was any other day. The militia arrived, searched the building, and posted a guard who locked the door. The Jesuits, who lived in the school, were allowed to stay, but even boarding students were forced to leave, with all their things, immediately.

The Jesuit mission in Santiago was over. There was no place for an elite in the new Cuba, even an elite of merit, of talent. There would be only one kind of school, the Revolutionary school.

Like other members of the class of 1961, Souto no longer had a school to graduate from, but that spring the Jesuits gave him and the other seniors diplomas, so that they could qualify for higher education. Souto's grandfather had come from Spain penniless, and settled in Santiago impulsively, based on the fine appearance of the city from the ship deck. He had built a corner store into a big business with coffee-roasters and warehouse. His grandson took his psuedo-diploma, the last ever granted by Dolores, and reversed the journey, returning to Spain with nothing. Bernardo Souto settled in Bilbao, the Basque capital, where he was a salesman of formica counters and other kitchen equipment. He had been back to Cuba just once, in 2003, to see Santiago one last time. He had stopped by Dolores; it was his business card that the guard at the school had kept.

WHEN DID THEY KNOW? The very first day, that day of Revolution? Or on the tenth? The four hundredth? When did they sense that something had gone wrong? Or was everything still in play, all results still possible? Do dreams become true slowly, in gradual revelations, or all at once, on a deadline?

Memory was writing Cuban history now, and the curious Cuban art of retrospective prediction ordered all understanding, even as the events occurred. The human need for agency, for patterns, gave purpose to the chain of events. People needed a guide, augury in a voice that crystallized the new truths, explaining that things had gone bad, permanently wrong, at a particular moment. And that moment was usually the one in which each recollecter decided. It was the decision to leave that brought with it the knowledge that all was done, every hope over. Hindsight is 20 Cubans talking about the Revolution.

For Guillermo Cabrera Infante, novelist, film reviewer, and bad-boy intellectual of Havana, the prophet was a writer he called 'the Turk'. In 1961, Cabrera Infante was the editor of *Lunes*, or 'Mondays', the Revolution's own cultural magazine. *Lunes* had a circulation of 200,000, and a mandate from the government itself to create and chronicle the rise of the new society.

That was the point of interviewing the Turk. (His real name was Nazim Hikhmet.) He was a celebrated Third World writer, and he came to visit Cuba because the island was suddenly at the centre of history, a standard-bearer in an age of decolonization and independence movements. Writers were pouring into Havana, global intellectuals rallying to the combination of social justice and tropical splendour. The Colombian Gabriel García Márquez took a job as a staff correspondent for the new Revolutionary press agency. Alejo Carpentier quit a comfortable job in Venezuela to move back to Havana. Carlos Fuentes, Mexican novelist, was waiting in Havana to cheer Castro's arrival. Mario Vargas Llosa, a Peruvian, rushed to Cuba to offer his solidarity to the new government, and returned frequently, as did Julio

Cortazar and Jorge Amado. The hemispheric boom in Latin literature became intimately tied to Cuba's ambitious Revolution. and *Lunes* was taking the measure of these foreign intellectuals, chronicling their enthusiasm for the Revolution, and its many projects.

But when the editorial board of *Lunes* invited the Turk to sit down for a formal interview, to chronicle his conclusions about Cuba, they did not get the quotes they were expecting. Although he had come to Cuba in hopes of finding a new thing, a previously unknown iteration of freedom, Hikhmet found in the spring of 1961 something old and familiar: a military regime eerily reminiscent of the 'revolutionary' Turkish governments that had repressed his freedom in the name of their own power.

'Leave,' Hikhmet said. A poet, he needed only one word.

Cabrera Infante was shocked. So were his colleagues. *Leave Cuba?* Join the crazed exiles, with their war on literacy campaigners and their American paymasters? Why would progressive intellectuals leave Cuba? There were problems, but surely this was no time to run away! Cabrera Infante had been a staunch supporter of the Revolution. The agrarian reforms were long overdue. And why should foreign companies, with corrupt ties to the old dictatorship, get to control the sugar, the telephones, the banking, and every other business of importance in Cuba? Anyone could see that the Revolution's new literacy campaign was a wonder. Only a fascist could be against it.

But this was indeed the very *last* time they would be able to run away, Hikhmet warned. He had spent 17 years in Turkish jails, imprisoned by a 'revolutionary' regime that had begun with peace and justice, and then degenerated into a dictatorship. He was sure that Cuba would go down this road as well. It had to.

The Turk spoke in the bleakest, most urgent terms. 'Travel,' he ordered the assembled writers and editors. He urged them to 'invent' trips abroad, immediately, on any excuse, and then stay there. As a last resort, those who couldn't get abroad might be able to protect themselves somewhat by becoming famous, by drawing international attention. 'Make yourself seen outside,' he counselled them.

But even literary prizes or international friends would not be enough. Sooner or later, they would have to run for it. The time to start planning was now. 'Above all,' he told the disbelieving table, 'start to choose your lucky star!'

He meant, your north star. Your escape route. Your destination in exile.

SANTIAGO'S CATHEDRAL, A BEHEMOTH OF OCHRE PLASTER with two bell towers, sits right on the Parque Céspedes. In March one weekend, at the end of the main Sunday mass, the families who came out of the church were confronted by an angry crowd. Most of those attending services here – the most important church in eastern Cuba – were white. Most of those in the crowd were black or brown. Most of those leaving church were well-to-do, nicely dressed, keepers of social traditions, the establishment, the included. Most of those in the crowd were humble, the poor, the outsiders and the excluded.

Watching the rich and prominent stroll out of mass on Sunday into the city's main square had been a form of entertainment for centuries. But now the mood was different. The wealthy and the well known were greeted with insults. Arguments started. Threats flew. Then someone slapped a wealthy woman, and the parishioners were suddenly confronted by a rain of blows. As they fled, people were thrown down, the expensive dresses of the women torn by a taunting crowd, the men punched until blood stained their mouths. It was a scuffle, not a massacre, but the dynamic of who was excluded from what had changed. So had the position of the Church.

Those rich had never been more than a tiny minority in Cuba, and their traditional power and influence – a system built over centuries – were abruptly gone. The ancient social dynamic of Cuban life – the way people related to each other, the customs, speech, habits, and gestures of daily existence, the divisions among whites and blacks and browns, the role of money, ownership and labour, the moral force of the Jesuit and the Santero – all of it was abruptly inverted. Lifetimes of resentment found sudden outlet in symbolic attacks on the aristocracy of Cuba.

Just as Dolores had been closed, in the first days of April it was the turn of Santiago's tennis club and yacht clubs. These symbols of exclusivity were seized and shuttered by the government. The island was now caught in a self-reinforcing downward spiral: the more the elite and the exiles abroad attacked Castro, the more tightly he gripped their throats at home. The more they lost, the more they renewed their attacks. The more they resisted, the more justification Castro and his supporters had for their growing paranoia.

Right from day one, some people had begun fleeing the new Cuba. At first, it was those directly implicated in the previous government. Batista himself flew out of Cuba just four hours into 1959, carrying a million dollars in his suitcase, and taking a hundred of his closest friends for company. When the new government threw open the filing cabinets, exposing the particulars of corruption, the atrocities committed by the police, and the rake-offs that allowed great families to enrich themselves, there was a trickle of departures – the panicked flight of a few millionaires, of some notorious torturers, and of informers who had blood on their hands. But the air was rendered fresh and pure, and only a few instinctive creatures – the rebellious Alberto Casas, with his hands toughened from milking cows – fled simply because they could. Few people sensed anything wrong. On the contrary, Hugh Thomas, the greatest foreign historian of Cuba, said that a 'lyric spirit' had descended on Havana in that year, while few people could avoid being 'entranced by the nobility, the vigour and the charm of the revolutionaries'. The year 1959 'was a unique moment of history, golden in promise, the dawn of a new age'. But it was also, Thomas noted, the end of one world. And when one world dies, another must be born, a process that cannot be painless. It was sunset, not dawn, that gilded the light over Cuba.

During 1960 the number of people fleeing increased, with members of the political class and the wealthy beginning to feel some inchoate threat. In that year, those who fled were usually the few who were comfortable enough to do so without losing much. But a few ordinary people who were particularly sensitive to their precarious status – a substantial portion of Cuba's Jewish and Chinese communities – headed quietly for the door.

Lundy Aguilar had fled that year, the rare philosopher to take his own advice on history. He had warned in a newspaper column that 'the vital thing in Cuba is to avoid a situation in which violence triumphs, and where the heroes of today are converted into the oppressors of tomorrow'. These premonitions did not mean Lundy was against the new government. As a noted thinker with personal ties to Castro, he volunteered at the new Institute of Culture, trying to help consolidate the social transformations enacted by the new government, like the lifting of all race-based distinctions, and an early programme to send 'mountain teachers' out to remote villages.

It wasn't hard, as Thomas noted, to see good in what was happening. Castro had started by sharing power, appointing a moderate, traditional politician to serve as president of Cuba. Despite the talk of a new era, much remained the same at first, and Castro courted a moderate image in the United States by appearing in New York and Washington, talking (in English) on television, and assuring everyone that he would reinstate the New Constitution and set up elections.

But after seven months at the Institute of Revolutionary Culture, Lundy was convinced that the self-aggrandizement he had glimpsed in the Hilton was emerging. Castro dismissed his puppet president, and began consolidating his own power. Lundy resigned from the ministry and went back to his law practice.

In May of 1960 he had been provoked to take up his pen by the shutting of a right-wing newspaper. This was *Diario de la Marina*, a Havana daily that had grown increasingly strident in criticizing Castro. In May, the government – via an outraged 'workers committee' – had stormed the *Diario de la Marina* offices, tossing out the staff and locking the doors. When the Revolutionary government refused to allow the paper to reopen, Lundy wrote, for the rival newspaper *Prensa Libre*, his last column:

THE HOUR OF UNANIMITY

Liberty of expression, if it is to be genuine, must be shared by everyone and not the prerogative of any one person. That is the issue here. There is no need to defend the ideas of *Diario de la Marina*; what must be defended is the right of *Diario de la Marina* to express its ideas. And the right of thousands of Cubans to read what they consider worthy of reading . . . if they begin by persecuting a newspaper for having an idea, they will end by persecuting all ideas . . . the silencing of an organ of public expression, or its unconditional absorption into the government line, means nothing less than the subjection of all real criticism. And since they won't, or can't, refute the argument, they silence the voice. The method is old, the results well known.

And so to Cuba comes the hour of unanimity: the solid and impenetrable totalitarian unanimity. The same fate will now be repeated for all publicity organs. There will be no divergent voices, no possibility of criticism, no public refutations. The control of all methods of expression will speed the labor of persuasion: fear will do the rest. And, beneath the vociferous propaganda, silence will remain. The silence of those who cannot speak. The complicitous silence of those who, being able, do not speak.

Instead of a multiplicity of voices, they prefer the formula of one guide only, one route, and total obedience. So comes the totalitarian unanimity. Because totalitarian unanimity is even worse than censorship. Censorship obliges us to silence our own truth: unanimity forces us to repeat the lies of others.

This was the last defence of free speech ever published in Cuba. Aguilar was denounced on the radio and even by a worker's declaration from inside *Prensa Libre*, which called for the paper to repent, and for the author of this offending editorial to be sent 'to the wall', meaning, taken out and shot, like one of the Batista assassins. *Prensa Libre* was shut down on the third day. A friend with connections in the government stopped by Lundy's house to suggest that he would be wise to leave Cuba immediately. He departed within days.

All such departures in 1959 and 1960 were incidents, individual acts, when compared with what would come. In January of 1961 the rupture of diplomatic relations with the US, and the quick tit-for-tat of accusations and confrontations that followed, opened a set of flood-gates. By the end of that January flights out of Cuba were packed solid. By March of the Heroic Year, three-fourths of the faculty of the University of Havana were living in South Florida.

This diaspora, the Exile, took its shape from this flood of middle-class Cubans. Unlike earlier waves, these people were not directly affected by the nationalizations, by the confiscation of huge ranches, by the threats that had been made in 1960, or by the crimes of '59. But the indirect effects were adding up. Companies closed down, business atrophied, commercial affairs of every kind withered. Dolores graduates fled in great numbers that year, but so did ordinary people and even dedicated revolutionaries. Eloy Gutiérrez Menoyo, one of Castro's top commanders during the Revolution, bolted in mid-1961 with a dozen supporters, denouncing Castro for betraying his promises of a 'revolution as Cuban as the palm trees' and 'bread without terror'. Their way out was smoothed by new American legislation. The US Congress authorized the Cuban Refugee Assistance Program, which allotted $100 a month to each Cuban exile arriving in America, paid for health care, and arranged college loans.

The shuttering of private schools and the creation of a new Revolutionary curriculum were guaranteed to alienate the well-to-do families who had been running Cuba up to this point. Opponents of Castro, whether in the State Department, the Catholic Church, or on the streets, spread rumours that children would be the next victims of Castro's agenda. Godless Communists were taking over, according to the gossip of Radio Bemba, and Cuban children would henceforth be subject to brainwashing lessons on the glories of Marxism. The new public school curriculum would supposedly create not educated children, but robotic cogs for a totalitarian machine. Catholic officials fanned these fears, reminding anyone who would listen that during the Spanish Civil War, churchmen had been shot by the anarchists and the Communists, and children had supposedly been sent to re-education camps. Whether it was true, or merely CIA propaganda, the rumours spread like a wildfire. As Carlos Eire put it: 'Everyone knew someone who had known someone who had known someone whose kid had been sent to Russia.' That was enough.

The first to go were a few students from wealthy and deeply Catholic families in Havana, but as word of this spread it initiated a cascading disaster. When the Catholic schools of Havana were closed in January the Church organized an evacuation of about 200 students, who were flown to Miami and enrolled in Catholic boarding schools there. The Church called this Operation Peter Pan, but there was no magic at work. In February, with Dolores shuttered, Santiago families began exporting their children as well. Hundreds, and then thousands of families signed up to have the Church take away their children. Overwhelmed, the Miami diocese flooded its schools with new children, and then had to set up five camps across Southern Florida to accommodate thousands of Cuban children who were suddenly appearing. When the camps were full, the Church began to disperse the Cubans to foster homes in Florida, and eventually across the US.

Here was the Cuban gift for mutually reinforcing self-destruction. With more children leaving, the Revolution reacted defensively. Castro saw a resource vanishing: boys of military age. First the government banned boys of draftable age from leaving the country. Then it was boys *approaching* military age who were banned. This in turn fed the fears of parents: why did Castro need their sons, if not to re-educate them, to turn them into his rifle-toting New Men? So families began to fake the ages of their male offspring, slipping their 16-year-olds out as 15-year-olds.

Everyone assumed that this Children's Crusade was merely temporary. The outgoing children were assured they would be gone only a matter of months, a semester perhaps. There was a universal expectation that some looming conflict would straighten things out. Castro would get his. The government would be undone. But they were, as always, underestimating the Revolution.

All year the flights kept going, a thousand children a month in the spring, and growing fast. One of these Lost Boys – a successful radio executive in Washington DC when he told me this – described his abrupt transportation from tropical Cuba to a snowbound Kansas, placed with a family who, though kind, spoke no Spanish. He never saw his parents again. Decades later he still had never seen Cuba or his family there. The wry novelist Carlos Eire had himself been a Peter Pan child, exported from that palm-frond world of Cuban youth to a dingy foster home in Miami crawling with cockroaches. There they ate gruel and lived under strict regulation, more like inmates in a reform school.

By the end of 1961, Peter Pan had swept up 14,048 boys and girls (only a very few of the latter). The Revolution was not 'straightened out'. Carlos Eire did not see his mother again for years. Many Peter Pan children became accidental orphans, separated from family permanently. Almost none would ever set foot in Cuba for the rest of their lives.

BECOMING AN EXILE WAS STILL POSSIBLE, legally speaking, and not just for children. For any family seeking to leave the island the first step was to stand in line at the nonexistent American embassy in Havana; diplomats from Britain (and later Switzerland) processed American paperwork. Children could get a visa waiver automatically, but adults had to apply, demonstrating that they had financial sponsorship in the US, meaning family, a friend, an employer, or some connection. Adults could also apply for a special new Cuban refugee quota set up by Congress. Just getting the right paper to apply for the right combination of waivers, applications, visas and supporting affidavits could take months.

Then came the need for a passport. The Cuban government would not accept the old, pre-Revolutionary ones. Everybody had to apply for a new passport, and since this was an obvious prelude to leaving the country, asking for a new Cuban passport became the decisive step in the whole process. Once the government in Cuba received your passport application you had effectively declared your opposition to the Revolution, and there was an immediate response. Inspectors from the government often arrived the same day to confiscate everything in the house. This was done by making a detailed inventory: the number and type of books, the utensils in the kitchen, the nature of each picture or painting on the walls, the types and models of appliances and the size and style of the furniture, the lamps, the clothing in the bureaus, even the toys. All this now belonged to the state. Those leaving Cuba would take none of this with them.

The audit, as this inspection is known, immediately generated its own counter-industry. Cubans learned to sell or give away their possessions before applying for the exit permit. By the time the inspectors arrived, the house would be emptied. The giving-away-of-the-goods became a sad ceremony in Cuban life. Cherished books were handed out ritualistically to old friends, dresses and their particular memories were distributed amid weeping, chairs were hauled off by cousins.

Once the auditors had made their inventory of the house, it was too late. They would return on the day before your departure, whether a month or a year later, and verify that every single item on the list was still in place. It belonged to Cuba now.

WHAT BELONGED TO CUBANS THEMSELVES was an increasingly short list, especially those leaving. The about-to-be-exiles were allowed a few items. Two each of shirts and pants. Three each of socks and underwear. One sweater, one hat, one set of pajamas and one book. Not counting what you were wearing, of course, which led people to put on three shirts. The militia, in turn, began to enforce a new rule against wearing multiples of anything. With each month the rules became tighter: the definition of jewellery was extended to include watch bands, the maximum weight of all possessions was detailed, and the dimensions of suitcases specified. The allowances in turn gave rise to a new economy. There was a boom for seamstresses all through 1961, since they could help beat weight restrictions by sewing up special bags, which were sized the absolute maximum permitted, but made of the lightest canvas, so that more of the weight allowance went to clothing. It did not matter if this gossamer luggage tore or wore out: it would be used only once.

Those who, after months of such manoeuvring, finally made it to Havana airport, found that family separations were made more wrenching by the long process of examining paperwork, which was conducted after the departing Cubans had been separated into a special lounge. This had been walled off from the rest of the airport with glass, and was called *la pecera*, the fishbowl. On the outside, families waited and watched for the four or five hours it took as those departing were searched by Cuban militiamen, who confiscated anything on a checklist of contraband items, weighed the luggage, and counted items of clothing. Guards took children aside and made them drop their pants, peering into their underwear to make sure that no prohibited items – jewellery, money, etcetera – were being hidden down there. For Carlos Eire, the snap of elastic on his belly that afternoon in the fishbowl, the casual way he had been scrutinized down to his prepubescent *cojones*, was the most embarrassing moment of his life, a stinging symbol of the state's intrusion. Decades later, he admitted that just the sight of a glass coffee table could send him spiralling back to those final hours in Cuba, standing in the *pecera*, looking back through the distorting lens at his father for the last time. Exile started right there.

MIGUEL LLIVINA TALKED of the same thing as everyone else. His friends and former classmates around Santiago were all applying for visas to America, or any other country that would have them. They were arranging business abroad, trips to see family, tourism, whatever they could. The world he knew – professional middle-class Santiago – was dissolving. Some were still siding with the Revolution, more were turning against it, but almost regardless of what they believed, his friends were talking about leaving the country, at least for a little while. After many anxious discussions with his wife, conducted in the hushed tones that seemed appropriate, Miguel decided to follow suit.

Like Pepín Bou and José Batlle, Llivina had gone to work at Moa Bay for a while. When the American owners had halted production in 1958 there was no need for an accountant and Llivina returned to Santiago and moved back into his father's house. During the first year of the Revolution he found work. His new employer was the Texas Oil Company West Indies Ltd; as the name indicated, it was the Caribbean subsidiary of an American oil company. The Texas Oil Company owned the only refinery in eastern Cuba, which sat on the far side of Santiago's harbour. Built in 1957, the state-of-the-art plant attracted American and Cuban engineers, technicians and professionals to Santiago.

The Texas Oil Company plant refined 20,000 gallons of crude oil daily. As part of its contract with the Cuban government, the company was required to refine 'national oil' – that produced in Cuba. But Cuba produced very little of its own oil. In 1960, the Revolution began sending sugar to the Soviet Union, receiving in return regular shipments of Soviet oil, and also of weapons – both heavy and light arms. The Soviet ships, bearing Black Sea crude, began entering Santiago harbour, passing the recently confiscated Smith Island where Desi Arnaz had swum, which was now called Granma Island.

The Texas Oil Company was, like other American-owned refineries in Cuba, willing to process this Black Sea oil like any other oil. Despite the tension between Cuba and the US, this was simply good business sense, another day at the job for oil men who were eager to avoid conflicts with their host government. But the US State Department was looking for ways to pressure the Cuban government to return 'American' properties. So it urged the American-run refineries in Cuba to reject the Soviet oil. Reluctantly, they agreed. The Cubans countered by declaring that since the Black Sea crude was the property of all Cubans, it was therefore the 'national oil', covered by the contracts, just as if it had come out of the Cuban ground. When Texas Oil refused, the Cuban government declared the company had broken its contract. A barge appeared at the refinery dock one morning, and a group of Cuban administrators stepped on to the docks. There

were no guns present: just clipboards and lawyers. They announced that the plant had been nationalized.

The American manager simply got in his car and drove home,
never to return. But Miguel Llivina, like other Cubans at the
plant, and indeed most of the Americans as well, stayed put. He
didn't know what else to do, so he kept going to work. History is
transcribed from grand gestures and decisive instants, but the force
of events was just as often a liquid accumulation of conflicted
and unsteady hearts, millions of non-decisions, passive re-
actions and timid gestures. Survivors are not troublemakers.
Invisibility and compliance are the keys to riding out such storms,
not heroism. Most Cubans just waited. They thought they were
already masters at that.

SUCCESS, WHEN IT CAME, was nearly the end of them.
Lundy made his third run with the PT in March. As they prepped
the boat at the dock in Key West, looking over the guns and
motors, 22 Cuban men in uniforms arrived. They climbed aboard
and went down into the hold, clattering with a wide array of
personal weapons, and heavy packs of ammo. There was supposed to be secrecy about the mission, even at this point, but from
their fatigues and guns it was obvious they were commandos, and
it was inevitable that, in the tight-knit world of Cuban exiles,
some of the crew knew some of the men coming on board. So the
name of the target came out soon enough: the oil refinery in
Santiago. First they would sabotage the big refinery, and then the
men would fall back on the Sierra Maestra, where they would
link up with local partisans who were fighting Castro.

They left at night, of course. But it wasn't possible to conceal
everything – their 'secret' base in Key West was right next to a
brightly lit marina, so that fishermen and even tourists driving by
could see the boat slip out. The trip down was fine, including a
refuelling stop at a new dock in the Bahamas, and the weather
cooperated – bad enough to conceal a small boat on the big sea,
but not too nasty. The PT slid in toward the shore of Cuba,
north-east of Santiago Bay, in the dark of another night. They
dropped off the men, leaving them on a beach in the small hours

without incident. The commandos set off to meet a contact, and then work their way around toward the city.

At first light, well off Santiago and running back toward the Bahamas, the squalls on the ocean parted, and Lundy saw a black shape far out ahead of them. In a glance they could all see what ship it was. An American frigate. But it wasn't under American colours. Like the PT boat they were riding, it was one of the surplus ships from World War Two that the US had been handing out. Only this one had been sold to the Cuban navy of Batista. Now it was under Revolutionary officers and the 26th of July flag. It could run at 32 knots, for days. It had 4-inch deck guns, which could lob shells about eight miles.

Lundy felt the PT turning under him, and then the deck rising as the boat planed into a sprint at 40 knots. The frigate turned to intercept and accelerated, throwing up a bow wave.

Lundy saw a spout of water rising up behind him, an exclamation point lifting out of the PT's wake. And then, as if in reply, the distant crack of the frigate's gun.

The gap between the ships opened. And then again: a splash, followed by the report of the gun trailing over the water. Clutching the machine gun for stability, he knew there was no point firing back. Even at close range the .50 calibres would be useless against a steel frigate.

But the distance kept opening. They didn't dodge, but they didn't run exactly straight either, moving in long and fast lines, just weaving away from the frigate, their thoughts flying out ahead of them toward the Bahamian Keys. But the frigate kept charging. The CIA man had told them they could only call for help once they reached international waters. When they thought they were far enough out, but still being pursued, they called the given frequency, again and again, without reply.

Was it getting smaller? It had to be. There were no more shots. In slowed-down time, the frigate shrank, and went hull down over the horizon, until finally Lundy, still holding the .50 calibre atop the bridge, thinking about his children, still thinking that he was going down, saw it vanish.

Eventually, after the long trip home to Key West, they were

told the commando mission had been a success. But there were
no details. Nor any howls of protest from Cuba.

WHAT WAS TRUE AT THIS POINT, the last moment of the
original Revolution, and the first birth pang of the Exile? Who to
believe? The gossip they called Radio Bemba was whatever truth
Cubans themselves broadcast, in fear and expectation, in Santiago
or Hialeah. Fantasy. Rumour. Third-hand facts. In Miami the
story spread that a force of exiles was massing in Central America.
The couriers that went back to the island, carrying plans and
messages, only added to the confusion. Some disappeared, or
were arrested. Others had been double agents all along. Some
succeeded all too well, sending back reports of tremendous
successes, new breakthroughs, garrisons ready to mutiny, secret
armies, the imminent overthrow of Castro and all his works.
Within Cuba, the reports were equally wild: mysterious airplanes
overhead, secret purges, midnight arrests, parachutes drifting
down over the Escambray mountains, speedboats moving in
and off shore as the nights of winter gave way to spring.

A turn of the real radio dial was head spinning. On one
frequency, the Revolution had never been stronger. On another,
Castro was doomed, in his final hours. A powerful new station,
Radio Swan, started up on the AM dial, declaring in Cuban
accents that a new order was coming, that Castro's days were
numbered. The only reliable source of news was found amid the
denials. No, the president of Guatemala announced one day,
there was no truth to the rumour that groups of armed Cuban
exiles were on Guatemalan territory, training. No, America didn't
have any connection to the clandestine radio stations. After
Castro almost bragged that acts of sabotage had increased, and
that millions of dollars worth of sugar cane had been torched in
March and April, the United States said it had not been involved,
and had no intention of attacking Cuba.

But in the end, there was a set of facts, a bitter truth. Despite all
the sabotage and shoot-em-ups, the couriers and commandos, in
the end these exile successes were either imaginary, or irrelevant.
The resistance groups were either fraudulent, or genuine but

heavily penetrated by spies who betrayed every plan. The arms shipments, all the tonnage moved by sea, all the parachutes flung down in the night, added up to nothing. Different groups of raiders were led into traps, or arrested as they slept, or wiped out in ambushes, or simply scattered and disbanded in the mountains.

For Lundy it could not be said to have been a waste. There had been a reason to fight, or to try. But it didn't add up to anything. Out at the refinery in Santiago, Black Sea crude went in, and gasoline, heating oil, and aviation fuel came out.

Miguel Llivina never heard about any acts of sabotage, at least not at the refinery, and there wasn't any spectacular commando attack. Under the new management things went on more or less the same. Even in April.

JUST BECAUSE EVERYONE REALLY IS AGAINST YOU doesn't mean you aren't paranoid. In Cuba, there really were strange airplanes overhead, but Castro was never satisfied with reality. Parachutes did indeed drift down over the Escambray mountains, but he did not limit himself to that. Arms caches were indeed discovered, but that was no reason not to invent allegations. Anti-Castro guerrillas did try to fight in the Sierra Maestra and central Cuba and the CIA really was massing an army to attack. But reality was no longer enough.

So, with the hour of fate approaching, Castro mobilized his police and army to confront the enemy. But he didn't send them to the beaches to build defences, or to the mountains to dig bunkers. In the last days before what would actually turn out to be, for once, the real invasion that Castro was always talking about, Cuba's leader mobilized his resources to defeat the enemy inside Cuba – that is, his own citizens. The police and militia were sent out in mid-April to engage in mass round-ups of the usual suspects. Anyone who was associated with disloyal 'elements' in Cuban society was put under suspicion. This began with the known critics of Castro, among them the hierarchy of the Catholic Church. All the bishops in Cuba were confined to their residences, or held by the Department of State Security. Church properties were occupied by the new block committees.

But it spread rapidly, a vast net, thrown in haste, which swept up people almost at random. Local authorities, acting on gut instinct, locked up people all over Cuba. The wealthy. The religious. Students and businessmen. Active dissenters and the merely suspicious. The old families and the young toughs. By some accounts, 100,000 Cubans were either arrested, informally detained, or ordered not to leave their houses in the days just before the Bay of Pigs.

But even a broad net, if poorly aimed, will miss some fish. In Santiago, Dr David de Jongh, the oldest of the de Jonghs, spent the days before the invasion at his medical laboratory, wearing his medical coat, carrying out his duties. But he'd been talking with friends, and was one of those who actually was getting ready. He didn't know what he was getting ready for, but he despised the new government, and remembered Fidel from Dolores all too well.

Radio Bemba said an invasion was coming. David's family was wealthy, with resources and lands and hobbies, especially the Cuban love of bird-shooting. He gathered together a handful of weapons from their various properties – rifles, shotguns, pistols – and took them to the lab. There, in a kind of secret shelf inside each of the long lab tables, he stored the guns. An amateur searcher would never notice the hidden storage space, which was surrounded by medical equipment. Whatever happened, whoever came down on which side, he would have some guns ready.

But nobody came to the house to detain him, and nobody came to the lab to search it. He was a respected medical figure, the owner of a blood bank, a clinician. Of the 100,000 names on a list of enemies, he, even with his guns, was missed.

THEY WENT OUT ONE LAST TIME, IN APRIL. Instead of the quick overnight dash toward Nipe Bay in the north, it was now a four-, five-, or six-day mission. Refuelling in the Bahamas took time, and by April the only infiltration teams that could still be located were operating on Cuba's far southern coast, requiring a longer journey around the crocodile's tail. And the boats themselves were slower, because they weren't carrying humans any more but something much heavier.

The American way of war is to do more, to count tons, to total up firepower, to win victory through ammunition. The CIA men in Key West assumed that the victory in Cuba depended on equipment. They put increasing pressure on Lundy and the other men for more deliveries, faster. The Americans had grown so frustrated with weather cancellations, and missed drop-offs by the many ghost ships, that they had tried to switch the supply effort to airplanes. But that was an expensive plan, requiring an air fleet and Cuban pilots trained in the art of precision air drops, which required perfect communications, navigation, timing and flying. The resulting air missions that spring were a disaster: only three out of 68 air drops actually succeeded in delivering weapons on time in the right place. In early April there was a renewed effort with the boats.

They went out again, two boats together this time, both of them wallowing under the weight of their cargoes. Down in the hold of each boat was what the American CIA officer accompanying them called a small pack: arms, ammunition and radios for one hundred men, along with 57 mm recoilless rifles, light machine guns, and medical and food supplies. These two small packs, supplemented with some heavy weapons, would serve 200 anti-Castro insurgents. With a couple more runs they could equip 500 men. And the goal was even larger: five of these 'full packs' added up to 2,500 men. You could do this kind of maths forever: the more missions the more weapons the more attacks on Castro. The logistical tail was wagging the dog.

They went from Key West to the Bahamas, refuelled, and then probed toward the south coast of Cuba. There was no frigate this time, and they managed to get both boats into the beach in the middle of the night. Lundy waded ashore with the CIA man and waited on the sand for his contact.

And waited. Lundy had driven the boat himself, so he was pretty sure this was the right beach. But nobody came. More than an hour went by, but there was no sign of the contact, or his phantom resistance army, eager to take possession of 200 rifles.

Another screw-up. When they had already stayed too long, they heard a speedboat motor running in the distance, and even the CIA man agreed it was time to leave. Getting the boats off the beach took time, and at first they motored very quietly to avoid discovery. The PTs were still rolling heavily in the sea, and could not make time. They would still be in Cuban waters at first light. Having risked so much, so many times, for so little, they were in no mood to run more unnecessary risks.

During his own invasion of Cuba, Castro had also been late, lost, and facing daylight in a small boat. He had thrown his heavy weapons overboard in order to lighten and speed the *Granma* to safety; Lundy's crew decided to do the same, and without further ado began tossing firearms and ammunition for a hundred men into the sea.

The CIA man exploded when he saw what they were doing. 'Those weapons belong to the American people,' he shouted. When he tried to stop them, another crew member threatened the American, asking Lundy to translate something into English. 'Tell him that I will kill him,' the crewman said, and went back to throwing things overboard.

Everything they threw overboard freed the boat, and they sprang out of Cuban waters and toward home. Plans were drawn up for another mission, but time had just run out on their little sideshow.

THE FIRST ATTACK OCCURRED ON 15 APRIL. There had been reports of individual and mysterious airplanes earlier, dropping parachutes or shooting at things, but on the 15th the secret planes came out of hiding, bursting over the island at dawn and striking a couple of Cuban air force bases, strafing and dropping bombs.

The planes were B-26 bombers, a kind of small, light and fast strike aircraft developed by the US for close ground support during the Korean War. They carried just two men, and were swollen with weapons – eight .50-calibre machine guns, a bed of eight rockets to hit ships and armour, and a belly rack for small bombs, or even napalm. They were designed to fly low, to dodge and shred. On the morning of the 15th they were making 'prep' strikes, an attempt to eliminate Cuba's small air force on the ground, before it could join the battle that was about to take place.

At first, there was some confusion. Cuba itself had a squadron of B-26s, which Castro had inherited from the 1950s air force. That was the point: the incoming American B-26s that attacked that morning would look like the B-26s already on the ground. Even the paint job was the same. It was supposed to look as if Cuba was being attacked by its own air force, as part of a military mutiny. The planes were flown out of American-built bases in Central America, where American pilots had trained Cuban exiles to fly them. Americans had paid for, fuelled, and armed the planes, and then helped draw up the strike missions. Americans had provided the bombs and bullets. Americans had given the orders. Yet what killed the Bay of Pigs invasion, above all, was the obsession of the Kennedy brothers in Washington to conceal all this, to hide the obvious American role. President Kennedy himself had intervened at the last minute to cut in half the number of air strikes the exile B-26 pilots could make, hoping to reduce the visibility of the American hand. There was never the slightest doubt in Washington about the wisdom of over-throwing a government in Cuba; the only real issue was how to avoid getting caught.

The two pre-emptive bombing strikes on 15 April were supposed to mangle Cuba's little air force of propeller planes, clearing the way for the invasion. With control of the air, the exile pilots could roam over every land battle, smashing Castro's troops whenever they massed to counter-attack. But the prep raids were flawed in execution (the attacks did little damage) and disastrous in their fundamental misconception. They simply gave Cuba a warning of what was coming.

CUBA IMMEDIATELY DENOUNCED THE AIR RAIDS at the UN. The attacks, a Cuban diplomat told the tense General Assembly in New York that very day, were American aggression. Although the CIA had painted the bombers with Cuban flags, it only took the Cuban diplomats a few hours to produce photographs that showed the attacking airplanes were clearly a different model to the ones in the Cuban air force. So much for the theory of deniability. The air raids, the Cubans announced, were an obvious 'prologue to a large-scale invasion'.

The US ambassador to the UN, Adlai Stevenson, vehemently denied any American involvement in attacks on Cuba. He later said that he had not known the truth, but ignorance on that scale is hard to credit. Miami, Washington, Havana and New York were all crawling with rumours about US involvement. Newspapers in Central America and Florida had reported on parts of the Bay of Pigs plan. The *New York Times* had published a report about an army of Cuban exiles massing in Central America, and the newspaper pointed out that America was certainly involved, somehow. Half the Cubans in Miami seemed to know someone involved in the invasion or related missions, like Lundy's boat raids.

Castro had been preparing his people for months, warning in speeches that a Yankee invasion was imminent, carried out by a combined force of Cuban exiles and American spies. The signs of the coming battle were everywhere. On 15 April, everyone who wanted to know already knew.

THE 15 APRIL AIR RAIDS did not destroy the Cuban air force, and only killed seven people, but they had another huge effect: they led Castro to pronounce out loud a word he had been carefully avoiding for years.

As soon as the bomb debris was cleared away, Castro called for a public funeral for the seven dead, to be held the very next day, the 16th. It took place at one of Havana's major intersections, the meeting of two avenues in Nuevo Vedado, a spot overseen by the Charlie Chaplin Theatre on one side and the city's most famous graveyard on the other.

It was not a funeral, but a rally. A large crowd of enthusiastic civilians filled the avenues, but a group of armed militiamen was placed between Castro and the television cameras, so that lifted rifles accompanied his cheer lines. Castro spoke for hours, extolling the victims, and building up the emotions of the crowd with his rhetorical questions and their thundering responses.

Here again were the choices that defined the tragedy: *Are you with Cuba, or against it? For the fatherland, or the mercenary scum? Our people, or the imperial beast?*

Either or. Zero sum. The denial of any middle ground, or compromise, or choice. *Which standard?*

In the midst of the speech, with everyone caught in the bond between solitary leader and massed followers, Castro made a comment that went almost unnoticed by the crowd. He said that the Revolution had a 'character', and then explained that it was this character which so infuriated the exiles and the imperialist powers of the world. They 'cannot forgive our being right here under their very noses, or to see how we have made a revolution, a socialist revolution, right here under the very nose of the United States.' He moved on quickly, but that was it. He had blurted out the word for the first time: socialist.

While fighting in the Sierra Maestra, Fidel had denied a hundred times that he was red. The Revolution was democratic, built on a platform of constitutional rule and elections. He had openly mocked the Communist Party of Cuba, calling it a debating club for old men. The Communists, Castro said, had spent the war 'under the bed'. In at least three speeches during his first weeks in power, Castro had denied being a Communist or being influenced by them. Che Guevara called the same allegations 'absurd', and vowed democratic rule, liberal principles and multiparty elections within 18 months of coming to power.

The denials had been countered by rumour, and by code words within the new argot of the Revolution. Castro and Guevara both surrounded themselves with aides who were Communist, and they themselves already talked in the language of socialism: the rebels were 'a vanguard', the new government was engaged in 'struggle' against class and capitalist enemies, and there would be solidarity with 'people's regimes' in the Third World and in Eastern Europe. But through 1959 and 1960, and well into 1961, the denials continued, if ever weaker and more evasive. Everyone had strained to hear any direct words of intent from the man known in the street as Fidel, and in the dispatches as 'Maximum Leader'.

Finally, here were the words everyone had been listening for: 'a socialist revolution'. Castro had made his intent explicit. The declaration was a milestone; the spot where Castro spoke is today marked with a bronze plaque marking 16 April 1961 as the birth date of 'socialist' Cuba.

People may have been listening for it, but that doesn't mean they heard it. Elizardo Sánchez was a student in Havana in 1961, and a member of a small student group devoted to socialist politics. Since the Revolution had gone to enormous lengths to deny that it was actually socialist, actual socialists like Sánchez and his friends were a problem. They had to 'creep about like four cats' in Havana. The last thing they expected was an open admission, from Castro himself, that they had been right all along.

At the back blocks from Castro, it wasn't even possible to hear the speech clearly over the excited hum of the big crowd. People simply responded to cues. When the militiamen lifted their guns and cheered something Castro had said, the front of the crowd cheered too, and then the back of the crowd picked it up. The cheering wasn't fake. There was still overwhelming public support in Cuba for the Revolution, but consent wasn't the issue. Even Castro's strongest supporters had to learn their parts by rote. So people went to the rally and, as one participant of that day recalled, unable to conceal his mirth, they shouted: *Long live Cuba! Long live Fidel! Long live socialism!* And then they all looked around at each other and asked, *What did he just say?*

That was the other thing born in this April of discontent: *doble cara*, the loyalty of the moment. Whether you'd heard Castro or not, whether you liked the idea of socialism or not, you still had to applaud the new laws under which you would be arrested.

About the only place they heard him clearly was in Washington. America was already in an advanced state of fear about Castro, and Washington needed no more justifications. As far as the Kennedy brain trust was concerned, Castro was as red as a baboon's ass. The 16 April speech only confirmed what they wanted to believe.

That very night, President Kennedy signed the final order to launch the invasion. When the ink was dry, a brigade of 1,300 Cuban exiles, already afloat on freighters escorted by US navy ships, closed on the southern coast of Cuba.

TWO DOLORES BOYS, Roberto Mancebo, 18, and his younger brother Jorge, just 17, were in the invasion fleet. They were assigned to the exile army's 2nd Battalion, one of the best trained and best equipped in the larger force, which was called the 2506 Brigade. Mancebo, when I found him, was living in South Florida, a social worker for the state. He was reluctant to discuss his role in the invasion, avoiding my calls for months, but finally spent a morning detailing how he had arrived at the beach.

Mancebo had been an early convert to the anti-Communist cause. In the fall of 1959, the same year he graduated from Dolores, he had enrolled in the chemistry department at the University of Oriente. About 15 boys in the department were alumni of Dolores. There was a lot of rash anti-Castro talking, but during the fall term a dozen of the boys decided to scare the authorities. They started with Molotov cocktails, which they set alight and left in trash cans. Then they made a kind of weak plastic explosive, which they used to blow up some mailboxes and park benches in the middle of the night. Betrayed by their own bragging, the boy saboteurs were called in by the police. Nobody had been killed or even injured, and the prankish nature of the small devices was obvious even to the Revolutionary militia. They gave Mancebo a lecture on politics and then set him free.

Mancebo fled Cuba and turned pro. In January of 1961 he'd gone to Guatemala with the 2506 Brigade, eager to help overthrow Castro. The men had trained hard, building their own camps. Mancebo recalled that the CIA worked them relentlessly, and in the jungle they were given realistic combat lessons from US army veterans. As each month of 1961 passed the equipment improved. M3 rifles from the Korean War. Plenty of machine guns, both light and heavy. Massive .81 mm mortars. The best bazookas. Two kinds of recoilless rifles, especially the .75 mm version that could slice through any armour. More men began arriving, and they got a second base in Nicaragua to launch the actual operation.

The men were divided up into five battalions, three of infantry, one for heavy weapons, and another for headquarters. But there were still only about 1,500 men in the brigade, about half the number called for in the CIA plan. The manpower was so low that a squad of men would be labelled a platoon, a platoon a company, and so on up the chart, creating a kind of hollow army. There was plenty of equipment, however. The stuff kept piling in: a whole rented fleet of supply ships, plus fuel, food and ammo, an entire second fleet of landing craft, scuba gear for commandos, rocket-launchers, a squad of heavy American tanks and plenty of trucks. By March their air force of B-26s arrived, once again the most up-to-date model of American equipment. In almost every case, Mancebo noted, the exiles had superior weapons to the Cuban troops they would be facing – vital since they were to be heavily outnumbered.

The 2nd Battalion would be charged with holding the left flank of the invasion. When the fleet moved into the Bay of Pigs at around 11 pm on the 16th, most of the ships stopped about a mile off shore from the main invasion site. The 2nd Battalion continued on, almost alone, much farther into the bay.

The Bay of Pigs is 800 feet deep in some places, which made it impossible for the troop and supply ships to anchor. And because the beaches were lined with coral reefs, the fleet could not come close to the shore. Mancebo and the other members of the 2nd Battalion had to climb down into small landing boats and make a circuitous approach to their target, the beach at a village called Playa Larga. But the engines on many landing boats would not run; a CIA officer had insisted on using the wrong fuel. Eventually a few boats sputtered to life, and began towing others behind them, but many could not be used at all, others had trouble finding a way through the reefs, and it wasn't until 2 am on the 17th that the bulk of the 2nd Battalion finally headed for the beach.

Meanwhile a CIA officer named Grayston L. Lynch decided to go ahead and scout the route. Lynch was one of just two CIA agents who set foot in Cuba during the invasion, and will have to stand in for all the other Americans, the hundreds and hundreds of agents and operatives in Florida and Washington who conceived, planned and carried out this legendary disaster. Lynch and a team of Cuban frogmen made a quiet approach to the beach at Playa Larga, in a rubber boat, but here they made a cataclysmic and ludicrous mistake. While still a hundred yards offshore, someone – Lynch declined to say who – accidentally switched on the searchlight they were carrying. A bright beam of light shot up, illuminating the boat and the frogmen in it. Even worse, Lynch couldn't figure out how to turn off the huge light, which was meant to guide in the subsequent landing craft. As desperate seconds went by, and Lynch fumbled, the frogmen tried to smother the glowing lens with their bodies. Lynch finally turned the light off, but then, miraculously, someone, somehow, knocked it back on again. A second blast of light flooded the boat, the men and the sky.

Great events have small beginnings. On shore, some Cuban coastguardsmen saw the double flash. Assuming a fishing boat was in trouble, they drove a jeep down to the waterline, and aimed their headlights out to sea. Lynch decided this was the moment to get his war on. He fired the first shots of the invasion, pouring three clips of ammunition into the jeep. He succeeded in knocking out the headlights, and chased off the Coast Guardsmen, at the cost of alerting the entire coastline to the invasion.

By the time the 2nd Battalion began trickling in, almost an hour later, the coastguard had been able to organize a hasty defence. Mancebo recalled running across the beach under light fire. 'Dozens' of policemen and some men from a local militia were holed up in a house, fighting back. The defenders were driven out quickly and then Mancebo and the 2nd Battalion swept through the small village, facing only the occasional stray shot. Their beachhead was secure. They were in Cuba.

Searching the town, the exiles discovered bad news: the village had a microwave transmitter. The CIA's intelligence and planning were off. The main advantage of the Bay of Pigs site for an invasion was its isolation. It had neither phone service nor any radio stations, and the Agency was expecting to have at least hours, and possibly days, before the Cuban government even knew there was an invasion. But here was a microwave transmitter, and it was still warm to the touch. Someone had sent word to Havana.

The invasion was now exposed, and behind schedule. By dawn many exile troops were still not ashore. The beachhead all along the bay was secure, but many of the troops were disorganized, or poorly led, and hunkered down to wait for supplies. It was common knowledge that American power would decide things, somehow, so there was little initiative on the battlefield. The 2nd Battalion moved inland, but not much. Rather hopefully, the Americans and the exile leaders believed that the war would be over before it started. Once the landings occurred, Cuban army officers would supposedly defect to the exile cause. Secret armies would rise up to greet them. The army would stage a coup, short-circuiting the resistance. Castro himself might be chased off by exaggerated reports of an enemy attack, like the president of Guatemala had been in 1954.

But the reverse happened. From the first seconds of the attack, ordinary soldiers and militiamen, policemen and civilians all rallied to Cuba, and therefore to the Revolution, and therefore, ultimately, to Castro. Coast Guardsmen and militiamen fought back at once. There was a group of about 30 literacy teachers working at the head of the bay who forted up inside their school house, fighting with rifles until their blackboard was riddled with bullets. Only one teacher, Patria Silva, was captured alive by the exile attackers. At the same time, on the far left flank of the invasion, there was an aggressive attack by about 150 construction workers, who had been living nearby while building a resort. Equipped with only rifles, the labourers were cut to pieces, but their quick and determined rally signalled that the exile army would face resistance, not welcome. Loyalty – the strong bond of Cuban to Cuba, the weak bond of America to Cubans – would decide this battle.

The worst-case scenario considered by the CIA always assumed that even if something went wrong, and the invaders could not advance, they could sit tight. With dominance of the air, superior weapons, and steady resupply from the sea, the 2506 Brigade could hold a defensive line for weeks or even months. A new civilian leadership for Cuba had already been selected (by the CIA), and once put ashore, these men would declare themselves the provisional government of the free territory of Cuba. If necessary, these politicians could then invite US troops ashore to finish the job.

By dawn on the 17th, Robert Mancebo and his comrades in the 2nd Battalion had moved out of town and advanced toward Havana about as far as any troops in the invasion would ever reach – a mile. They stopped there, about 120 men holding the left flank, and waited. The 5th Battalion was supposed to have landed behind them, reinforcing and expanding their lines, but there was no sign of those men. Headquarters sent them a heavy mortar squad as a crucial stiffening.

There were some air raids elsewhere that morning by the B–26s of the real Cuban air force, which turned out to have survived the prepatory air strikes by the fake Cuban air force. Yet the 2nd Battalion itself wasn't attacked. In relative quiet they worked all morning, digging fox holes and trenches on both sides of a road, setting up overlapping fields of fire for their heavy weapons, and sighting the mortars. They were staring out along the only road in their sector, which ran through the thick mangrove swamp called Zapata, and straight toward a big Cuban army base. They knew the main counter-attack would come here.

It appeared before noon, in the form of a single truck, packed full of lightly armed militiamen. Troops on foot were scouting the sides of the road, but they were searching quickly, almost jogging, and they didn't spot the camouflaged positions of the 2nd Battalion until they were just 75 yards away. Mancebo and other exiles opened up with everything they had; he shredded the trucks with his 30-calibre machine gun. Riflemen cut down the militiamen on foot.

Some survivors crawled into the swamp. Now a pair of exile

B-26s appeared overhead to support the 2nd Battalion. These friendly B-26s pounced on another truck that was farther down the road, and then returned to weave overhead, strafing any Cuban militiamen who were foolish enough to clump together visibly in the muck of the swamp. The battle lasted 25 minutes.

That was too long. The B-26s had used up the last of their ammunition, and Mancebo recalled how they even made a pass over the 2nd Battalion, wiggling their wings in a victory salute. The men on the ground gave a cheer that died in their throats. There was terrible ripping sound, and then a bright flash of silver over the beachhead. The unknown had arrived.

It was a fighter jet. Cuba did not possess fighter jets. The whole exile invasion plan had been predicated on the sure knowledge, intensely cultivated by the CIA, that Cuba had no fighter jets. Cuba had only a handful of B-26 bombers and a few British Sea Furies, obsolete, propeller-driven fighter planes. But what came overhead was a jet.

The CIA knew that the Cubans had two American T-33 jets, unarmed training planes which the CIA had written off. But desperation is the mother of invention, and the Cuban air force had bolted machine guns on to the wings of their 'unarmed' jets. An improvised ammo feeding system was set up, and the Revolution suddenly had two crude but functional jet fighters.

Now the men in the 2nd Battalion watched in disbelief as the enemy's non-existent jet, with an almost casual display of speed and power, pawed an exile B-26 out of the sky, sending it spiralling into the swamp right in front of the battalion. Even worse, the jet easily caught up to the second plane as it tried to flee, mauled its propeller engines, and sent it gliding down into the Caribbean Sea.

The enemy jet was disturbing. But quiet quickly returned at Playa Larga. Mancebo spent the rest of the day preparing for a fight. They advanced their positions a hundred yards and dug in again. Some Cuban troops appeared at the far end of the road, beyond range, but when they saw the bodies of their comrades they fell back. The 5th Battalion still hadn't appeared, so the exiles were reinforced by some men from the main landings farther down the beach.

That night, in Santiago, David de Jongh listened to his radio in disbelief. His guns were hidden at the lab. His friends, his fellow Castro-haters, his co-conspirators in a hundred imagined uprisings, had been caught completely by surprise. No warning at all. They'd even been in contact with an American from the old consulate, hoping for some sort of encouragement.

But nothing. No warning. The people ready to rise up had been given no hint of when the uprising would come. *Why didn't they tell us?* he wailed.

Tuning through the AM dial, he came across the voice of the invasion, a propaganda station which was already reporting the virtual defeat of Castro. The next day, a few hours after hearing the exile radio report that 'Santiago de Cuba has been liberated', David saw Raúl Castro himself driving through the Parque Céspedes in a jeep.

Raúl, recognizing his old schoolmate, gave a relaxed wave, and went on.

THE BIGGEST FIGHT OF THE INVASION started just before midnight. On the road in front of Mancebo, a real Cuban infantry battalion, the 339th, appeared. Not lightly armed militiamen, but a fully equipped force more than twice their size, supported with tanks and artillery. They came up the road very slowly, probing, covered by a crawling barrage from guns in the rear. But the exiles were in new positions, again carefully camouflaged. The barrage passed over, and the attackers (the 339th Battalion) came forward. Bazookas stabbed out in the darkness to meet them, piercing a Cuban T-34 tank. Machine guns scattered the infantry. A second T-34 clattered forward and was destroyed.

Ten minutes later they were attacked again. Again, two tanks were destroyed by bazooka, with heavy losses for the Cuban infantry. And then 15 minutes later, a third attack. This time Mancebo was frightened because the sound of the battle had changed. There was something much bigger coming up the road, the evil grinding noise dreaded by infantry everywhere. Heavy armour. Stalin tanks, in fact. *Osos*, Mancebo called them. Bears.

The fighting became desperate and almost continuous, with about ten tanks trying to storm forward on top of each other. 'Hell,' was all Mancebo said, to summarize what that moment had been like. He made a joke about wetting his 'soldier pants', and then said, 'There was nothing to do but keep shooting. There were tanks in front, and soldiers coming up both sides. We lost many good, young Cuban men. After 44 years I am almost crying.' Then he did start crying.

The swamp favoured the defenders. Machine guns swept away the infantry; and first one and then another tank was damaged or destroyed, until the next ones had to turn off the road to get past. But off the road it was swamp. Soft ground or no ground, treacherous, full of trees. The heavy Stalin tanks slowed down, and became vulnerable as they turned. In the trench next to Mancebo a man popped up, took careful aim with a bazooka, and destroyed one tank as it manoeuvred, only to be killed by a shot from the next tank in line. But the exiles were dug in, camouflaged, and familiar with the terrain. The tank attack faltered, and then the exiles' own M41 tank came forward and blasted another T-34, cracking it open.

There was a lull in the fighting around 3 am, which was broken 15 minutes later by a large infantry attack. Now a machine gunner like Mancebo could fight, and the exiles held their line, calling in mortars. The Cuban infantry attacked for about two hours, but suffered tremendously. The 2nd Battalion had lost only a few dozen killed or injured. After the attacking infantry pulled back, there was another lull, and then a single T-34 tried to push forward at 5.30 am, in the last minutes of darkness. Again, it was destroyed by the exile M41.

The night battle concluded on a ludicrous note when yet another Cuban tank raced forward, only to stop short. A hatch opened and the commander climbed out, thinking that he had reached his *own* infantry. The tank and crew were both taken. And because this was Cuba, the tank commander turned out to be an old army buddy of the 2nd Battalion's own commander.

The quick dawn of 18 April meant they saw everything at once. Smoke poured from more than a dozen shattered tanks, and hundreds of dead bodies littered the road, with more in the swamp. As many as 700–900 men in an attacking force of 2,000 were killed or injured during the night, all by an exile force totalling about 180. The 339th became known as 'the Lost Battalion'. But Mancebo did not gloat over this slaughter. The nighttime attack was a necessity, a sacrifice by soldiers pushing for a weakness. It failed, but it bought time for the Cuban forces to rally elsewhere and rout the invaders.

In the flush of victory, Mancebo learned that the war had already been lost. During the previous day, the Cuban jets and propeller planes had wrought havoc on the invasion elsewhere, shooting down many of the exile aircraft, and then strafing the ships. Their reinforcements, the 5th Battalion, had been shot up while trying to land behind schedule in daylight. Many of the landing boats had been destroyed. Now one of their big supply ships was sinking; another, the *Houston*, still carrying their reinforcements, had been hit so hard that it was taking on water, and the captain deliberately ran it aground to save it.

The 5th Battalion reinforcements crawled ashore, following ropes from the damaged *Houston* to the beach, but they had landed in the wrong place, without their heavy weapons, and hours later, when they finally tried to move up the bay to the 2nd Battalion, they met resistance. Six Cuban sailors, acting on their own, had dismounted the machine gun from a patrol boat, dragged it inland, and set it up in a house beside the coastal road. The 5th Battalion – a hundred men – was stopped and turned back by a scratch force of six.

Now the Cuban air force returned, blasting those few support boats still operating in the Bay of Pigs. More were sunk or damaged; others fled hundreds of miles out to sea, scattering under continuous air assault. After the long night of fighting, the 2nd Battalion learned that most of the ammunition and supplies they needed were either over the horizon or at the bottom of the sea. Counter-attacks were occurring, including strafing by aircraft, but once again Mancebo's experience was atypical. The air attacks were down on the right flank, where there were more roads into the beachhead, and more room for infantry to man-oeuvre.

But soon enough the artillery shells hitting around Mancebo began to increase. Word came down that more tanks and infantry were seen massing ahead of the 2nd Battalion. The Cuban reinforcements were supposed to be delayed by small groups of exile parachutists, but the commandos had mostly missed their targets. And then, as Mancebo waited in the midday heat for what looked to be a huge fight, the trenches were swept with a wild rumour: the beachheads in the south of the bay, the main exile position, were in trouble. This was followed quickly by the shocking news that the rumour was true: the infantry in the south were being overrun. Even the headquarters battalion was under attack. FIGHTING ON BEACH was one of the last radio commu-nications that reached the 2nd Battalion.

The 2nd, alone at the top of the bay, was ordered to fall back on these lower units. Mancebo jumped into a truck, and the battalion rolled down the beach road in a convoy of seven vehicles, trying to find the rest of the 2506 Brigade. The *Houston* was visible in the distance, burning and aground, keeled over. Mancebo was witness then to something that has been written out of history: US navy jets suddenly passed over the beachhead. The Americans were here!

American forces were not supposed to participate directly in the battle. At least not at first. The Kennedy brothers were still hoping for some thin veneer of deniability. The American navy was ordered to stay in international waters, and personal accounts stress that the Cuban exiles did the fighting. It is routinely claimed by brigade veterans that they would have won if they'd had air cover.

But the American jets did appear. They came twice, hunting for Castro's airplanes and raiding the Cuban formations. The first sweep, which Mancebo saw, was by four US navy jets who passed over the beach in a combat air patrol, but they didn't encounter any Cuban aircraft. The American pilots dipped their wings in salute, and then passed on. Within minutes of their departure, the planes of the Cuban air force had returned to blow up another supply ship. And then, when it was too late in the day to matter, the US jets returned once more, this time making a ground attack on a column of advancing Cuban troops. Huge explosions spiralled up from the site of the attack, and Castro himself later said the American jets had caused many deaths.

Two missions wasn't enough to change anything. But as Mancebo, Castro and the CIA all agree, there *was* American air cover that day.

Castro had raced down from Havana, but he had spent the 17th commanding his forces by radio, from the rear, like a sensible general. Now, on the second full day, he put some theatre into the theatre of operations. With the enemy lines collapsing, Castro jumped into a car and moved forward, a photographer in tow. Here was the confrontation he had been waiting for, the spectacular assault by his hated Yankee enemy. Yet by the time he arrived at the beach, the third Dolores boy to touch those sands, the fighting was effectively over. He perched on a tank for the photographer, and then climbed inside it. From there he took some pot shots at the motionless *Houston*, already bombed to pieces, deliberately grounded, abandoned, on fire, and listed over. That particular tank now sits in Havana, with a plaque explaining that Castro himself sank the *Houston*.

Slowly, all day on the 19th, the wheels fell off the invasion. The exile forces were broken up, isolated and pushed into the sea. Their few surviving planes made a final effort (flown by CIA officers this time) but were swatted out of the sky by the Cuban jets.

As the fighting sputtered to a confused end, various evacuation plans were proposed, and two American destroyers surged into the bay that afternoon, successfully bluffing the Cuban army into stalling its advance for a few hours. Some exile infantry jumped on to the last landing boats as they fled the beach; others just swam out, toward the horizon, hoping to be picked up. Those who could find something that floated made for the sea – in rubber life rafts, leaky dinghies and stolen fishing boats. Of these, some were picked up by the US navy within a day, others in five days, but one group wandered the ocean in a sail boat for two weeks, starving, without water, covered in infected scrapes from the mangrove swamps.

All told, some 1,114 members of the 2506 Brigade were captured. Mancebo was one of them. Late on the 18th, the little convoy of the 2nd Battalion trucks had ground to a stop on the road. There was no longer a headquarters to find. Some men waited in the trucks for the end, the obvious surrender that was occurring all around them, but Mancebo was one of dozens who jumped down and ran in to the swamp. With no particular plan, he thrashed his way westward, away from the battlefield, in a diminishing band, eaten by mosquitoes, rubbing his legs raw while clambering over mangrove roots. Occasionally they flushed crocodiles from the murky water. After three days only six men remained, and they had covered some 30 miles. They worked their way to the coast again, and waded out to a tiny island, hoping to spot a passing ship. But that night, as they slept, they were surprised by Cuban troops and arrested.

The officer leading the Revolutionary soldiers asked one question. It was the same one they had been asking themselves for three days: Where were the Americans?

The survivors of the assault were shoved into makeshift prisons, and interrogated individually by the G2, Cuba's military intelligence unit. Although about 600 'counter-revolutionaries' were executed, these were mostly civilians caught in the pre-invasion round-ups, people with records of violence. Only a few of the worst members of the Brigade were sent to the wall, for previous crimes under Batista. Instead, Mancebo and the Brigadistas were subjected to a television trial that summer, a long ritual of humiliation in which they were lectured on their crimes as mercenaries and terrorists. Cuban prosecutors showed (more or less accurately) that the men had been creatures of a foreign power. Each man was interrogated on television, scrutinized for his ties to the Batista army, and even his family tree dissected to reveal ties to the old elite, its institutions, even its schools. Cuban photographers even emphasized the presence of blond men among the prisoners, as if to say, these aren't really Cubans. The class status of the 'mercenary brigade' was detailed, precisely:

100 big landowners
24 important property-owners
67 apartment house-owners
112 big businessmen
194 ex-military men and associates of the Batista tyranny
179 economically well off
135 industrial magnates
112 lumpen and others

(When I aksed Mancebo which of these categories described his own family, he circled the first four.)

At his trial, Mancebo's history of making explosives in Santiago was cited against him. But it didn't matter: everyone was guilty, and they got the same sentence. The prisoners were sent to Los Pinos, the most infamous of Cuban jails, and later distributed to various other stops along the *cordillera* of prisons. After almost two years they were traded back to America for a humiliatingly large shipment of tractors and medicines.

Mancebo had avoided talking to me for months, and after hearing him cry twice while recalling the Bay of Pigs, I couldn't blame him. It was the lowest moment in the history for the Cuban exiles.

After the fiasco, President Kennedy said, 'Victory has a hundred fathers, but defeat is an orphan.' Surely this disaster had a hundred fathers, too: both Kennedy brothers, and the CIA, for its deranged and amateurish plan to attack a swamp, and also Eisenhower, who assumed that the way to deal with Cuba was to invade it. And then, also, the Wise Men of Washington, the Best and Brightest, who drew their conclusions about the Cuban Revolution by meeting with the heads of American corporations in New York hotel rooms.

A folly. A delusion of the exile mind married to American group think. The trick fell apart when exposed to daylight, and Fidel Castro was the only winner.

VICTORY IS A DANGEROUS THING. Speaking to Herbert
Matthews later that year, Kennedy admitted that a victory at the
Bay of Pigs might have had disastrous consequences for the US,
encouraging him to engage in more violent gambles, like making
war in Laos or the Taiwan Strait. Defeat is a better teacher than
triumph.

And sober lessons were in short supply in Havana. The
initial weeks after the April invasion were busy ones, consolidating the victory, and disposing of the 2506 Brigade
survivors, and it wasn't until May Day that Castro began to
publicly revel in his triumph. At a speech that day he
announced that: 'The revolution has no time for elections.
There is no more democratic government in Latin America
than the revolutionary government.' He announced another
fait accompli: although Dolores and Belén were both already
shuttered, Castro declared that all remaining Catholic and
private schools in the country would be shuttered, and all
foreign-born Roman Catholic priests would be expelled.

For the first time since 1952, Castro knew he was secure in his
position. Thanks to the victory of David over Goliath, he no
longer needed anyone. No more puppet presidents or coalition
partners, no more diverse voices or divergent sectors.

Cabrera Infante found the first hints of the new order in
language. Castro had always been prone to long speeches,
especially ones about his own victimhood. His most famous
oration, 'History Will Absolve Me', from his trial in 1952, is
chiefly taken up with repeated assertions that no one in the entire
history of the world has ever faced as much repression or difficulty
as Fidel Castro. But after the Bay of Pigs, Castro sank to a new
low of pettiness-per-hour. On 5 July 1961, Castro – introduced as
'Prime Minister, Dr Fidel Castro, the highest leader of the
Revolution' – gave a speech on the shortages the island was
facing. These included food of every kind, equipment like cars,
tractors and buses, necessities like medicines and clothing, and
everyday items like appliances and toys. Some of these things had
been imported from the US, and the trade embargo was slowly
claiming them, a piecemeal process of closing off one commodity

at a time in an effort to punish Cuba. Earlier in the year it had been the turn of the molasses industry to be added to the trade embargo. Then in summertime it was lard.

Castro entitled his speech on 5 July, 'The Lard Problem and Imperialism'. There was a real lard problem: with Cuba's own food production in free fall, the supply of lard – rendered pig fat – had tumbled. This had triggered rising imports from the US, which in turn led someone in Washington to seize on blocking the lucrative trade in lard as the next step in fighting Communism in the Americas.

Cubans will fry anything. Lard was the poor person's oil, a gooey necessity for making *tostones* and enriching beans, and when it ran short the grumbling could be heard even in Havana. Castro's TV appearance was billed as addressing the crucial 'question of supply' for lard.

But Castro barely mentioned lard, or even food. Instead he digressed into an hours-long description of international relations, detailing the solidarity of the Soviets and the perfidy of the Americans. Shortages, he explained, were not what they seemed. There were only two kinds of shortages in Cuba. The first category were those imposed on Cuba by the imperialists. This was where lard came in for its mention: the Americans were to blame if Cuba had no pig fat. And then there was a second type of shortage, which wasn't really a shortage at all. These items – Castro refrained from specifying just which ones – were actually missing from Cuba as part of a deliberate choice by the Revolution, their absence the fruition of a careful and long-sighted policy of self-restraint. Cuba was freely choosing not to import 'luxuries', Castro said. The so-called shortages were in fact evidence that Cuba's economic power was focused on new priorities, and that the economy was actually stronger, and headed for greater production than ever before.

'The Lard Problem and Imperialism' wasn't bad as Castro's speeches go. It wasn't one of the six- or seven-hour events that tortured people, and it was full of the typical fireworks of the 'highest leader's' thinking, the elaborate reversals of logic that Castro deployed so skilfully, making problems vanish, aportioning blame and identifying villains, all the small thrills of nationalism and victimhood.

But it didn't put any lard on the table. And it didn't answer burning questions. Where were the fruit vendors? Had the coal carts been silenced by imperialism? Who had taken away all the avocados?

What about all the things that had never come from America in the first place? Who took the plantain?

ACTING ON CHE GUEVARA'S ORDERS, Pepín Bou and some colleagues, including José Batlle from Dolores, made the arduous journey back to the mine at Moa Bay. It took two days in a heavy truck to get there, stopping once in a while to pull the truck out the mud with a winch.

Batlle had been watching over the decommissioned plant and it didn't take too long to get the plant running again. They cleaned and checked the reactor chambers, refilled them with sulphuric acid, regreased the conveyor belts, and fired it up.

But they were back on the 11-day shifts. The isolation was unnerving. They had an AM radio, but no way to talk back to the world. In April the Bay of Pigs invasion was over before they even found out about it at Moa Bay. Momentous swings in national life were taking place, all at the indifferent remove of a crackling radio set. On their short stays in Santiago the men struggled to learn and judge what was going on, all while wrestling with a heightened craziness in day-to-day life.

Then a flight back to Moa Bay. During the 11 days, the DC-3 pilots would often be the only source of news from the outside world. They carried messages from family members back in Santiago, and even delivered care packages, tossing them down from the airplane.

Still living in isolation at the remote Moa mine, Bou plotted a new way to leave the country. Even though armed militiamen had been stationed at the mine to keep the engineers working and on site, they had little idea what the engineers really thought. When Pepín Bou had heard Fidel Castro on the radio, listing American companies to be nationalized, pass through the 'F's and come to Freeport Sulfur Company, he had blanched. But it wasn't until later, when Castro announced that *Cuban* companies were also being nationalized, that Pepín voiced what he had not yet admitted. When he heard Castro list Bacardí, a symbol of Cuban talent and initiative, as one of the exploiters, a company that had to be 'intervened', then Pepín had said it, for the first time, to himself: *we have to get out of here*. Then he said it later, in serious and hushed tones, to Celia: 'We have to get out of here.'

They quickly made reservations on an obscure flight, a KLM route from Camagüey to Kingston, Jamaica. No one in Camagüey knew who they were; they could slip out before anyone noticed. But the Bay of Pigs put an end to that, as to so many things. Following the attack, and the internal crackdown that accompanied it, the exodus of Cubans had become a true flood. Airlines were suddenly overwhelmed. That summer, in an abrupt effort to stem the departures, the government in Havana announced a temporary cancellation of outbound flights, and then a new system for regulating departures. There would be much more scrutiny of who was leaving and why. It was still legal to leave, in theory, but the paperwork was suddenly much more complicated.

Pepín was in no position to organize a departure. Planning an escape from Moa Bay was impossible. Celia would have to do it.

They had one hope left: one of their daughters had been born during the two years in New Orleans. That meant she could become an American citizen. And an American citizen could get out. If the American citizen were in fact a small child, then the parents might be able to accompany her by rights.

They arranged to signal each other in code; when Celia had something ready, she would summon him to a cousin's wedding. There would be a lot of paperwork to arrange, so Celia packed up her Santiago household and moved it to Havana, near the decision-makers. In a sign of how little the expectations of the old Cuba had faded, she travelled to Havana with 18 suitcases, her maid and her sister-in-law.

All June Pepín listened for the sound of the DC-3s. Whenever he heard the daily plane arriving from Santiago, he jumped into a company pickup truck and raced to the air field. He couldn't trust anyone, so he lingered around nervously at first, trying to find the pilots and engage them in casual talk. He was waiting for them to say, 'Pepín, your wife says there is some good news.'

Nothing. Day by day he checked. Gradually the pilots got to know him. He flew with them a few times. By late July, whenever they landed they would look for him.

'Pepín,' they called out. 'Don't worry. There's no news about the wedding yet.'

A week later a DC-3 came in. This time the pilot finally smiled when he saw Pepín. He gave a thumbs up. Word had come through – the cousin was getting married, and soon. Pepín's heart was in his throat, but the pilot explained that he didn't have news of an exact date. Just that it was going to be soon. What Celia was trying to say was that she had arranged to get tourist visas to America.

And then a sharp turn. 'There's no wedding,' the very next pilot told Pepín. It felt like a *engaño*, a cheap trick. This message from Celia meant that the 'engagement' had fallen through. The American government had cancelled all tourist visas for Cubans.

In Havana, Celia got rid of most of the suitcases. She practised loading the remaining four. She made piles, counting out the permitted number of socks, of underwear, of every item, filling each bag to the exact capacity. To make sure, she practised loading each of the four suitcases, and then carried them, one by one, to a scale down the block. Nothing would be left to chance.

THE BERET WAS INVENTED for shepherds in the cold hills of the Pyrenees, and the heavy wool and lack of any brim make it uniquely unsuited for the tropics. But when Che Guevara arrived in Moa Bay for an inspection tour of his international nickel trading scheme, he wore his signature black beret. So did the men around him: in the crowd that followed Guevara, there were a half dozen functionaries in uniforms and the useless berets. After two years in power, living in cities, more and more of the *barbudos* were clean-shaven, and the black beret seemed to replace the beard, a sartorial shift, perhaps, from symbolic allegiance to the wildly hirsute Castro toward emotional loyalty to the harder but more dapper man, the impatient Che.

Guevara was also followed that day by his wife, and by the photographer Alberto Korda. Korda would later become famous for his iconic image of the Argentine guerrilla commander, the famous shot of Che peering out from under his beret, his eyes full of fire, his rebellious locks flaring. But today Korda was shooting something prosaic, not heroic. A muddy inspection tour of the Moa Bay plant. No glory, just confirmation of the futility of all inspection tours. The photographs Korda took show Che surrounded by flunkies in berets, men who knew nothing of nickel mining. You could see in the background men in tin construction hats – the kind worn by the engineers and actual workers at the plant. But Korda wasn't aiming at them.

Bou was desperate to avoid Guevara. He was afraid of somehow betraying himself, even if only by a guilty look. But he couldn't avoid his duties, and was tasked with giving Guevara a brief display of the leaching process at work. He took Guevara and the crowd of followers to one of the four 'trains', or production lines. He showed off the 70-foot-high reaction chambers, each 12 feet across, four tanks per train. He showed off the water reservoir, a muddy pond beyond the parking lot. They peered at the conveyor belts, which carried the raw laterite ore in huge quantities. It looked like plain red earth as it marched down the belt, and in a sense it was. Cuban nickel deposits were unusually pure, but that meant just 1.5 per cent of the ore was nickel; 98.5 per cent was wasted soil. It went into the so-and-so, was transported here-and-there, and this-and-that. Pepín went through the motions, frozen.

Guevara was an amateur scientist, but even he found this too much. 'Are you on schedule?' he asked Pepín.

'Everything is fine,' Pepín said, nodding. That was it.

A DC-3 came in the very next day. 'The wedding is set,' the pilot told him, grinning. 'Two days.'

NOW, OR NEVER. Without cleaning his hands, or changing out of his coveralls, Bou climbed up into the airplane.

He left behind all his clothes and possessions at the mine, a snake starting to shed his old skin. Even the jeep: he just left it sitting by the runway. A few minutes later they were airborne. The flight was sold out, so as they flew to Santiago, Pepín sat on the floor of the cockpit and kept up a front, smiling and chatting with the pilots about the wedding. Everything was great. He was giving away his cousin at her ceremony. The party would have plenty of rum. What good times they would all have.

In Santiago he changed his clothes, and then went to see his grandmother. 'I'm leaving,' was all he could say, and that was enough. They both began to cry. Pepín never saw her again.

The Santiago airport, and even the main highway out of town, was often scrutinized by militia. Even the Santiago bus station was out as Pepín thought someone might recognize him. A friend drove him to the bus station in Palma Soriano, a town 30 miles away, where he was an unknown. After reaching Camagüey, where there was much less chance of being questioned at the airport, he flew to the capital and found Celia and their three children. The American paperwork was ready, handled by Swiss diplomats.

On 30 June, they went to Havana's airport with one-way tickets for a special charter carrying Cubans and some resident foreigners out of the country. Before boarding, Cuban officials confiscated all his cash, and the gold band from his wristwatch. Just as the plane was starting to taxi, a jeep carrying four militiamen stopped it. They boarded. They came down the aisle, walked right past Pepín, and removed another passenger. He took the first tranquillizer of his life.

In the air, calmed by the drug and the noisy, draughty reality of movement, he dared to look ahead. He needed to reach his sister, who already lived in Miami with her husband, Alberto Casas.

The passenger at his side, an Englishman, gave Pepín a 1960 American dime. The price of that first call.

The only thing Bou remembered about landing in Miami was the sight of pay phones, banks of them, set up specially for the emigrants. As many calls as you needed, free. He called his sister.

By nightfall he had a roof over his head and his family around him.

In the next few weeks, even when he had money in his pocket, Pepín had trouble paying for anything. He had to stop his hand, and search it; was he paying with that dime? He removed it, time and again, from his hand, putting it back.

Through July and August, he couldn't spend any dime, anywhere. In the fall he finally covered it in tape, to give it a different feeling, and tried going back to spending other dimes, but it was nerve-wracking to go through your hand, looking to make sure you weren't spending the special one. He liked carrying it: sometimes he took it out and showed it to people. By 1962, when the US was having Cuba kicked out of the Organization of American States, the tape on the dime was dark with fingering. He started carrying it in his wallet, handy through the brinksmanship of the October missile crisis that year, the humiliating end to the Heroic Years. By then the dime was a fixture, as familiar to his hand as Cuba to his mind. He replaced the tape sometimes, the metal under it tarnished, filthy. It wasn't until 1966 or 1967 that Celia finally insisted.

She confiscated the coin, setting it aside in a safe place. She eventually had it encased in Lucite. She made sure it was a big block of plastic, too – 8 inches across, several pounds. Too heavy to throw out by accident. Too big to jump into somebody's pocket and wander off, in search of a pay phone.

IT SOUNDED LIKE MAGNANIMITY when Castro started talking about the importance of Cuban culture. He suggested that, among its victories, the Revolution could also create cultural triumphs. Dance troupes, not just militias. Great architectural commissions, not just shortages. There should be a deepening of culture, and also a broadening of it, and more people making it, and more people having access to it. The Revolution had talked about this from the beginning, and Lundy Aguilar had even spent his seven months of 1959 at the new National Institute of Culture. Everyone was for culture. The only thing Castro didn't say, at first, was what he exactly meant by the word.

The signs appeared slowly, in a new vocabulary of power. In the government paper *Juventud Rebelde*, aimed at Cuba's youth, Cabrera Infante noticed a word he had not seen before: *tramps*. This was a reference to some new kind of enemy in Cuba, a warning about unspecified people, traitors who were trying to bring down the Revolution. A polemic was normal; but the word *tramps* bothered him. There was a kind of Puritanism at work within the Revolution, a symptom of a rising fever.

Into this sudden fever for cleaning up culture dropped the little experimental film that Orlando Leal had assembled from his shaky footage of the bars and street scenes that January. He called the short film *PM*, or *Pasado Meridiano*. There was no voice-over, no obvious plot, no agenda, nor any real point other than to embody the style made possible by the light cameras, which had let Leal wind himself intimately inside his subject. In the United States and Europe this kind of *cinéma vérité* was all the rage, but in Cuba there was already one *avant garde*, the vanguard, and they weren't interested in a film-maker's existential self-creation. *PM* – a 20-minute student film with no dialogue – became what Cabrera Infante called 'the beginning of the end . . . the lever of a whole upheaval in the annals of culture under Castro'.

Thanks to Cabrera Infante's influence, *PM* was scheduled to show at a small Havana theatre in June. But the theatre-owner had to receive permission from Cuba's board of censorship before he could run the film. Film censorship was nothing new, but in the past it had been overheated kissing, or un-Catholic dialogue which faced scrutiny.

In the summer of 1961 the censors of the Cuban Film Institute were following new criteria, invisible even to them. Enemies were now within. They were revealed by their failure to conform to the norms of the Revolution. One look at *PM* and the censors panicked: they denied permission, ordered the theatre to cancel the screening, banned the film being shown anywhere, and confiscated the review copy.

Leal thought the film had been banned because it had been made outside of government control. 'It was a crack in the wall,' he told me, in a New York City coffee shop, 43 years after the events. Already in 1961 there had been two big new government feature films, *Esta Tierra Nuestra* and *Venceremos*, that were sleekly shot, boldly propagandistic films about landless peasants and sacrifices. But *PM* showed no New Men: it was a glimpse of ordinary life, squalid and unchanged, full of Vat 69 bottles, people in fancy clothes, drunks, all of it in a seedy neighbourhood of Regla. It was antiheroic, full of people shouting, dancing, quarrelling and generally acting as if there had been no Revolution at all. And the film touched a racist nerve, the film-maker suggested, because of the Afro-Cuban ambiance in Regla. One (white) official said to Leal at the time, 'We are not like that.'

But it is more likely that the ban, and everything that sprang from it, had nothing at all to do with the film itself, and everything to do with who had sponsored it. The Revolution was seeking enemies, and found them in whoever dared to criticize, or declined to offer support and loyalty. The real problem was the film's association with *Lunes*, the literary magazine. *Lunes* was publishing a wide array of radical thinkers – authors like Trotsky and Jefferson, Sartre and Neruda – and it had criticized well-known writers, and the middle-class poets who failed to grasp that history had turned a corner into a new era of freedom and rebirth. By championing Trotsky, the standard-bearer for disobedient Communists, the magazine had offended some of the hard-line Stalinists in Cuba. That wouldn't have mattered in 1959, or 1960, but after the Bay of Pigs these men – the ones Castro had once mocked for spending the war under their beds – were suddenly wielding greater power. The magazine had also accumulated a long list of enemies, often running harsh reviews of the new 'Revolutionary' authors, whose mediocre work belied their enormous self-importance. There were many writers and artists who wanted to see *Lunes* brought down, and since Cabrera Infante had helped Leal get the equipment, the film, the camera and the screening for his film, *PM* became the stalking horse for larger issues. The magazine staff had already been accused of left-wing

infantilism, decadent avant-gardism, and bourgeois cosmopo-
litism; even worse, there were known homosexuals on the
staff. It was time to put a stop to the whole thing.

Sitting in the Manhattan restaurant, discussing all this with Leal,
it was remarkable how little he had changed in 43 years. Though
he had filled out somewhat, he was still boyish-looking, still the
wunderkind, with smooth skin, a wide but cautious smile, and a
bristling head of hair barely touched with silver. He grew sad as he
remembered what had happened next. He had been at home in
Havana one day in late July of '61, still thinking that the worst had
passed, that the banning of his film was all that would happen,
when the telephone rang. Leal heard his wife answer, and he
remembered how nervous she had sounded as she summoned
him to the phone.

'The President of the Republic,' a voice said, 'wants you at the
National Library on Friday.'

He thought it was a joke. A crank caller. He expelled a gust of
disbelieving air and simply put the phone back on its cradle.
That's what Leal remembered, decades later. The way he had just
hung up the phone.

As if you can hang up on Zeus. Or his attendants, who called
right back, furious. This was no joke. He was told to be at the
National Library, the night of 30 July.

'1961 was when they shut down the party,' Leal said.

IT WAS REALLY AN HONOUR, in one sense, to be summoned to the library. There was to be a great assembly of the
nation's leading intellectuals, and being ranked in their number
would, under other circumstances, be a great prize for a 19-year-
old film-maker. The most prominent writers, academics, film and
television directors, painters, sculptors and journalists in Cuba all
received the same call. They were told to assemble for the event,
which would supposedly focus on Cuba's new policies to support
culture.

Support culture. That sounded so harmless that it should have
been a warning. This great meeting of great minds would occur in
the great hall of the National Library. The building was a much

maligned construction in Havana, a monstrosity that Leal called 'a fascist, Mussolini building'.

Or maybe it wasn't the architecture. On the designated Friday night, Leal and his champion, Cabrera Infante, met in the lobby of the library, full of fear and uncertainty. The writer Nestor Almendros joined them in a hushed conversation. The lobby filled up with other intellectuals. Alfredo Guevara, then as now the head of the film industry, collected a small circle of whispering acolytes. Finally Castro swept in and, as he passed, called out to Guevara: 'Alfredo, I've come to smite you with the light.' By speaking this way to the head of Cuba's film production, the Commander was indicating something of his real target.

'And it was just the opposite, of course,' Leal sighed now, recollecting. It was not the light of justice that would smite them, but the beam of a searchlight, coming from a guard tower.

They knew they were in trouble, but it was a question of how much. The year before, everyone had watched as the satirical magazine *Zig Zag* had been shut down after making fun of Castro. In their whispered conversations in the library lobby, the talk was about what wasn't being said: no more government promises about elections. Newspapers were being shut down, and the society increasingly militarized, given to mass spectacles of marching militias. Five hundred thousand people had been enrolled in block committees to 'monitor' their fellow citizens. When Lundy Aguilar had written about the totalitarian trends in Cuba, he was mocked as paranoid, but now the conditions were occurring: dismissal of all forms of constitutional balance and democratic consultation, the rise of one-man rule, and the construction of a personality cult around a 'maximum leader' and 'guide'. The new government films were, even if well done, propaganda. Then there were darker, whispered rumours: talk of the first purges, of the arrest of homosexuals and other distrusted elements, reports of the arrest, or flight of prominent figures who were supposedly involved in conspiracies against Castro. The country had become stifled in the last months, the assault from without now matched by an attack from within. The area of hope was shrinking. There was a sense, Leal recalled, of the 'culture closing in, the pressure building'.

At the appointed hour that Friday in July, the crowd went into the hall in an atmosphere of uncertainty and fear. They left four hours later with much greater certainty, and much greater fear.

The government leadership was spread out behind a long table on a stage. ('It was like the Last Supper,' Leal said.) Castro was in the middle; Armando Hart, minister of education then and minister of culture later, was at stage right. Since the evening was billed as a discussion with 'the intellectuals', different writers and artists were invited to give comments on the benefit of culture for the masses, and an hour or so was taken up with praise for the new *cinevans,* which toured remote hamlets. There was also a lot of talk about *Lunes,* but not about shutting it down: instead, pro-government speakers emphasized the need to increase the number of such magazines. There were plans to diversify and expand and deepen culture, to break the 'monopoly on ideas' held by *Lunes.* It might be necessary, as a temporary matter, to curtail the magazine, but that was only so that its resources could be spread among a wider variety of voices. There would be many new magazines, and a broader, diversified, more democratic culture of criticism.

The words were fine, but the speakers were not. Whatever they said, one after another, the intellectuals sounded nervous. They larded their statements with claims of ardent admiration for the Revolution. After proposing something, they apologized for not serving society more perfectly. As more writers rose to speak, they began to confess to vague errors of judgement. They could not be specific because they didn't themselves know what they had done wrong. They sensed only a general accusation. Guilt stank up the room.

A bootlicker rose and suggested kicking out film-makers who were ungrateful for the Revolution. At this, someone in the back rows shouted out a protest: 'That's what they did to Eisenstein in Russia!' There was laughter, and applause, but the heckler had scored a useless point, and the tide was flowing in the other direction.

Finally one of the poets rose and, almost stuttering, said something so obvious that no one had dared to say it: *I am afraid*. That was his only point. He didn't know why, he confessed. He couldn't think of what he had done wrong. But there was something menacing at work in the National Library. He named the fear, but again, it did no good. Poets could tremble, but they were faced by men who no longer had any fears.

When Castro finally rose to speak, there wasn't a word out of his mouth before he made a gesture that has become legendary in Cuba: he took off his pistol. Orlando Leal remembered the moment one way, describing how Castro removed his entire gun belt and then coiled it up on the desk. It was, Leal thought, a gesture of disarming, of 'deference to intellectuals'. But Cabrera Infante described it as just the opposite: he recalled Castro pulling a Browning pistol out of his holster, and then laying it on the table with a heavy thud. The gun was a reminder, Cabrera Infante said, of where real power lay.

Having set his stage, the old Dolores debater gave a talk that has been kept in print, and sold in Cuban bookstores to this day, and which is still issued as required reading to the cadres. Known as 'Words to the Intellectuals', the speech went into detail, but in the end only a single phrase mattered. After the Bay of Pigs, Castro was both confident and aggrieved, and in the mood to separate his enemies from his friends. To that end, he spelled out a new guideline for artistic expression in Cuba, a standard originally meant to control culture, but which has since become the ideological knife cutting through Cuban life. The simple phrase has spread to govern all forms of thought, from painting and film-making to political ideas and even military obedience. What Castro said that night was strikingly simple: *Within the Revolution, everything is permitted*, he told the upturned faces in the National Library. *Outside the Revolution, nothing is permitted*.

With its absolute sweep, the phrase neatly divided the world into two camps. Those who were loyal and those who were not. Those 'within' the Revolution would have the right to express themselves in art, writing and film, even to criticize and to participate in the political system. But those 'outside' the system would have no rights.

Loyalty was now the declared standard of the land. Loyalty meant loyalty to the Revolution, and therefore the Communist Party, but ultimately, loyalty meant loyalty to one man, personally. There could only be two groups: those for him, and those against him.

That night at the National Library was the end for Leal. The door had swung shut. Castro, of all people, had been his Prophet, the one to tip his own hand. 'People saw, for the first time, the face of absolute power,' Leal said. 'It was the first time we understood the repercussions. To be outside the Revolution was to be outside of the Church. There was no space for thinking, no space for reason. There was only one truth, a Revolutionary truth. It was religious. If you are not for me, you are against me.'

Castro did not invent this idea, or formula, or even phrase. Mussolini had used the same language in the 1930s, while Castro was at Dolores, reading Il Duce's speeches, marinating in an atmosphere of Jesuit sympathy for Catholic strongmen. In Spain, Franco had demanded similar loyalties. The idea has a long pedigree, and a universal appeal to men of authority.

For all its absoluteness, the inside/outside standard was maddeningly vague. The same poem or film or book could be deemed acceptable or unacceptable, loyal or disloyal, depending on the political alignment of its author, the mood of the authorities, the atmosphere in the country, the degree of international scrutiny, and the personal connections between the writer and Cuban leaders. The difference between constructive criticism and serving the enemies of the Revolution lay not in specific words, thoughts or actions, but in how these words, thoughts or actions were perceived by the system, by Fidel Castro or his stand-ins. The idea has endured at the heart of the Revolution, and the same phrasing appears in Cuban newspapers today, four decades later, as the necessary justification for the repression and censorship that have followed ever since. Only the loyal have rights.

The authority to decide where the line lay between the

loyalists and the traitors, between those who had rights and those who lost them, was drawn at the very top of society. As Raúl Castro once summarized it, while silencing a heckler, 'There is freedom of speech in Cuba, and I'm talking here.'

The meeting at the National Library concluded in the only way it could. *PM* was banned permanently, and *Lunes* was closed within a few issues, buried with a raft of promises that of course many new magazines would soon replace it. In August the government announced that a new organization, UNEAC, or the Union of Writers and Artists, would hold exclusive control over 'literary production' in Cuba. Control of all printing presses, publishing budgets, even the supply of paper, would be centralized by UNEAC. Only those who were registered members of the union, who submitted their manuscripts for review, and who published with UNEAC's approval, would be considered as legitimate authors.

Within the Revolution, everything. Against the Revolution, nothing. Anything was permitted unless it wasn't. By the end of 1961, out of Cuba's roughly 200 private newspapers, magazines and newsletters, every single one was placed under state control, along with the country's seven television stations. The costs for violating these rules could be staggering. Cabrera Infante eventually took the advice of his prophet, the Turk, defecting from Cuba and publishing his masterwork, *Three Trapped Tigers*, abroad. The book is a Joycean revel through pre-Revolutionary Havana, a complex narrative full of tricks and insight, deeply critical of the decadent, corrupt and unjust society of the 1950s. But regardless of its merits, Cabrera Infante was in exile, a *gusano*, and his work was therefore automatically unacceptable within Cuba. In a fit of honesty, however, the Cuban poet Herberto Padilla, one of the brightest stars in Cuba's new literary culture, wrote a positive review of *Three Trapped Tigers*. Padilla was immediately arrested, and then simply vanished, without a rumour or trace of his fate, for years. Finally, in 1970, he reappeared as the star of a humiliating show trial, where the poet – beaten and cowed – was forced to confess to a laundry list of imaginary crimes against the Revolution. The only thing not included in his confession was his real crime: a positive book review for an author who lay on the wrong side of Castro's loyalty line.

The principle still applies. In the early 1990s, the poet Maria Elena Cruz Varela was attacked and beaten by her neighbourhood block committee, simply because she wrote a poem which declared:

No
I don't believe in slogans like 'fatherland or death'.

Her own neighbours tore up the poem and, with security men watching, stuffed the offending lines down her throat, forcing her to eat her own words.

That was the legacy of the Year of Literacy. More than 700,000 hungry minds were added to the ranks of readers, but there was less and less to feed them. The National Library was turned into a forum for banning books. Cuba became, in Jacobo Timmerman's phrase, 'a gilded cage', where everyone could read but the shelves of bookstores were empty. Of course, that isn't literally true: the bookstores still carry the works of Che Guevara and the speeches of Fidel Castro. One of the few volumes that is always available, everywhere, is the white-bound text of 'Words to the Intellectuals'.

MIGUEL LLIVINA HADN'T BELIEVED it back in January when he heard the first rumour that Cuba and the United States were breaking off diplomatic relations. 'Everyone thought this was unthinkable,' Miguel said, and so he had allowed himself not to think it. But his sister was more sceptical. She had wisely gotten herself a visa to the US back in 1960, when only the paranoid were doing so. She had wanted to be ready, just in case. She urged Miguel to do the same, but he was busy, doubtful and patient, so he put it off. Eventually he did walk the four or five blocks to the American consulate in Santiago, which was located then in Vista Alegre, and he did apply for his whole family: himself, his wife and his two boys, the elder almost two, the younger just six months. But the visas hadn't been processed by the time diplomatic relations were cut off. The consulate in Santiago closed, and the application was lost. It was still possible to reapply, via Havana, but the complications and the increasing restrictions dissuaded him from trying, since he had no real plans to leave, nor any thought that it might become necessary.

After April, everything that had been difficult became much harder. 'After the Bay of Pigs,' he said, 'I made so many efforts. So many.' He managed to buy a ticket out of Cuba on Pan Am, but the earliest available seat was months away, on 10 August. August 10 came and went, and he was told it would be September. Then October.

Meanwhile, paperwork. There were so many requests for US visas that Washington authorized Cubans to enter the country with only a waiver. But getting this visa waiver required sponsors. Miguel's uncle was already in America, and agreed to handle their paperwork. But the first application was denied. Miguel couldn't recall why, but now assumed that, because he had dabbled in opposition to Batista, the Americans had his name on 'some list from the Revolution'.

Miguel's father had known a British resident in Cuba, a Mr McCormick who 'owned a factory'. McCormick was in Miami working with the Americans who were resettling Cuban exiles. McCormick advised Miguel to apply for another visa waiver, and be patient. But again, nothing happened.

In those days telegrams were delivered by messenger boys who blew a whistle as they approached a house. You could hear them going through Vista Alegre, tooting their whistles. Miguel spent the summer waiting for his whistle, the announcement of the news that everything had been set up. They were so eager to go that the family packed its bags (lightly, with just the minimum allowed to exiles) and kept them in the front room. At one point, encouraged by his uncle to believe that the waivers were imminent, Miguel actually loaded the suitcases into the car and drove everyone to Havana. Once there, a friend serving in the intelligence apparatus of the new government told him the permission to leave was imminent, but to go back to Santiago and wait there.

'We had everything ready,' Miguel recalled. 'At night, every-body waited, listening for the telegram whistle. You knew it was the last sound you would hear in Cuba.'

They did hear the whistle, occasionally, but it was always far away, a signal for someone else. Another block. Another street. Days went by, then months. They grew tired of looking up when they heard the distant *wheeeet-wheeet*, only to hear it fading away. No one came up the walkway to the mesh house.

Reluctantly, Miguel came to realize that there was no waiver. His uncle had filed for the application in Miami, while himself residing in St Louis. It was a jurisdictional mistake, a slip-up. 'They gave thousands and thousands of visa waivers,' Miguel said. 'But we didn't get one.'

All around Santiago, Miguel's friends and colleagues were hearing that whistle, and disappearing. The Heroic Year was rolling past. August 10 came and went without a visa waiver. In St Louis, his uncle now applied to a Missouri senator's office for help, and this time it worked: a visa waiver quickly appeared. But it was for Miguel alone, without his family. He wouldn't abandon his wife and children in Cuba.

In his sheaf of old papers, Miguel came across the waivers, which had finally arrived in 1962, for the whole family. 'Permis-sion to travel without passport,' they read, 'March 30 1962.'

But it was too late. The refugee flights had already been halted. Pan American wasn't flying to Miami any more, and the ticket was useless. Increasingly desperate plans were proposed for transporting people out of the country, like putting them in the holds of cargo ships. John Kennedy had put this idea in motion by arranging to buy out the prisoners captured at the Bay of Pigs. In exchange for shipments of tractors and Gerber baby food, Cuba would release the prisoners. These 'baby food ships' began arriving in late 1962, and the Cubans of the 2506 Brigade were sent back to Miami.

'I tried to get on the baby food ships,' Miguel said. He applied for a spot, and was given a berth – a bit of cargo hold – for the last of the ships. He resigned from his job at the refinery. A govern-ment inspector visited the house and made an inventory of everything which would belong to the Revolution once they left. But in October the last ship was cancelled. It was actually 'suspended' for 'temporary' reasons, but in Cuba everything was temporary, forever. The ship never sailed.

That wasn't the last time they tried. In the intervening decades, Miguel's brother had put him on a list for entry to the United States, but when Miguel applied for a Cuban exit visa he was denied, and suffered the usual consequence. 'They kicked me out of my job, just for asking,' he said.

IN THE HEAT OF THE LATE SUMMER of the Heroic Year, Santiago was set afire with a new rumour, which started among the mariners in the harbour, and within hours had spread to the stevedores, and then the warehousemen, and by night their families. The rumour climbed the hills of Santiago with these people, and in a day or two it had reached the middle class in the city centre, and even the rarefied heights of Vista Alegre. The whisper was that a ship full of money had arrived.

The ship was anchored in the long thin bay, and heavily guarded. It was said to have a cargo of seven tons of money. Not Cuban pesos, or US dollars, or even Soviet roubles, but something new. Although it had been printed in Czechoslovakia, the currency said CUBA on it, and it bore the signature of Che Guevara. A new money for a new country. The old Republican peso, the rock solid peso that had been pegged to the US dollar and was good worldwide, was about to be phased out.

When the rumour first reached him, David de Jongh had gone to his father's *Encyclopaedia Britannica*. The 1911 edition, comprehensive, the world's knowledge pressed into volumes of translucent bible paper. Bound in a leather so soft that each volume could be rolled up, and so flexible that the collected encyclopaedia had to be stacked on their sides because they would not stand on their own. In the De Jongh household the alphabet flowed upwards.

David looked under G, for gold. He read about 20 carat and 18 carat gold, about how to verify the purity, about touchstones, and aqua regia, and the various methods for dissolving gold in solution. Then he went quickly to see one of Santiago's best known jewellers, a man who normally trafficked in baubles and stones.

'I want gold,' David said.

'Oh, yes,' the jeweller replied. He understood, with the situation the way it was. 'I can maybe find an ounce for you,' he offered.

'I'm not buying ounces,' David replied. 'I want pounds.'

He passed on the rumour about the seven tons of new money floating in the harbour. The jeweller was sceptical: Cuba had always had a strong peso, tied to the dollar, stable for decades. Nobody would dare touch the peso, a symbol of Cuba's wealth and solvency. Nobody needed pounds of gold.

David did. He insisted. The jeweller smiled at this crazy man, nodded, and was noncommittal.

But a week later, he called back. 'Doctor,' he said, addressing de Jongh with a new tone of respect.

He had found some gold, he said. A good amount. And more important, he had found that David might be right. The rumour about the currency in the harbour was true. The jeweller had himself already switched some of his money into gold. Out of gratitude for David's warning, he had secured a bit for David too. He'd wanted pounds, and the jeweller had found seven of them.

It didn't look like much when David came to see it: just a quarter of a gold bar. But seven pounds, at the market price of about US $35 an ounce came to about $4,000. That wasn't a lot of money, but it is equivalent to more than $25,000 according to 2006 values. A lot more money than slower-acting people were going to have soon.

Once he had the lump of gold, David didn't know what to do with it. How to get it out? Those allowed to leave the country were being searched. You couldn't just walk out with gold: even gold watch bands were being confiscated at the airports. David thought of burying it under the back lawn somewhere, but that was exactly what everyone would expect: rich people buried their valuables in the back yard. Anyone could examine the ground, looking for signs of disturbance.

David was standing in the back yard with seven pounds of gold in his hand, asking himself, What do I do? He decided to put it in the trash.

At the de Jongh house, family servants burned the household trash ever other day in a bin, right there in the back yard. The bin was always full of ashes and half-burned trash, and David just dropped the gold in, letting it sink to the bottom. He stirred some ashes over it and burned papers.

Weeks later David de Jongh – *Médico* de Jongh – was in Havana on business when he was woken up in his room at the Havana Hilton by a friend. It was 7 am on 4 August.

'Are you standing up?' his friend asked.

'Yes.'

'Well sit down.'

The news was simple: law number 963 had been announced publicly just minutes before. It invalidated all money in circulation. With the stroke of *diktat*, the old currency had been rendered valueless, effective immediately. There would be new, Revolutionary money, just as the rumour in Santiago had predicted. All bank accounts were also closed, although any account-holder could receive 200 of the new pesos, of unknown value, and was promised access to another 1,000 new pesos soon, and another 10,000 pesos at an unspecified point in the future. But in the meantime bank accounts had already been sealed, and automatically converted to a new currency. All of the old cash of the Cuban Republic was to be turned in by Monday, exchanged at a rate set by the government. Otherwise, all the money in every wallet in Cuba would be toilet paper by Tuesday.

Despite the promise of a new currency, David wasn't fooled. It wasn't the replacement of one money with another that was happening. It was the abolition of money itself. The suspicious, dubious, capitalistic *uno-por-uno* peso of the old Republic was taken out and shot at dawn. The Revolution was in an impossible position: it could not live with money, nor without it. Another Cuban cycle of spite-filled self-destruction was occurring. The economy had been shrinking for two years. The rich were fleeing and the middle class was beginning to unravel. More and more people were leaving, and taking their money with them. The confiscation of businesses produced shortages, which produced rationing, which inevitably produced black markets. The nationalization of banks left all financial controls in the hands of the government, and the suspicious population began to withdraw even more money from their banks, hoarding it for the black market or changing it into dollars. Government reserves plummeted. The economy was spiralling downward, clipped from both sides by the chaos of nationalization and the shortages of cash in circulation. And now the government feared that private stockpiles of money were being used to finance counter-revolutionary activities. Money was another one of those things that was dangerous outside the control of the government. People holding on to large amounts of cash, to long-numbered bank accounts, to tinkling piles of silver coins and secret ounces of gold, were people who were independent, beyond control, capable of causing trouble.

The first attempts to control the situation – laws against hoarding and 'unlawful trading' – were pitifully ineffective. The solution was the same one as always: the Revolution would take what it needed. With a stroke of the pen this law 963 seized all money on the island, subsuming all private financial resources under government control. This actual wealth was going to be replaced with a scrip that, thanks to Che Guevara's jaunty signature, was soon worth more as a souvenir sold to tourists than in any market.

Law 963 paralyzed Cuba, at least for the weekend. Individuals were allowed to posses $500-worth of the old cash to tide them over, and businesses could keep more. But even that money was almost useless: the entire country was shutting down. In Havana that morning, the stores simply closed, unwilling to take the old currency, which was about to become valueless, while the new currency had not been introduced yet. The restaurants around the Hilton didn't bother to open that morning. Out in Santiago the port, and even the lighthouse to guide ships to safety, were shut down.

David stood in front of the Hilton overlooking a long sweep of Havana and its ocean, the sinuous stretch of the Malecón, hugging azure waves all the way down to Regla, and the Morro castle beyond. David saw, somewhere out the window, the sign he had been waiting for.

Make a permanent memory of this, he said to himself. *Don't forget this.* He photographed the scene into his mind.

I want to see this because I am leaving Cuba.

Because I am leaving.

I am leaving, he said to himself, for the first time.

NOT SO FAST. He raced the Buick to the airport, on the outskirts of the city, but first all flights to Santiago were cancelled, and then the airport itself shut down. On the way back into town he stopped at the bus station. Not a bus moving. They had no idea when service would resume. It all depended on the new currency.

So the Buick it was. At the Hilton again, he raced upstairs and threw his things into bags. He was right to hurry: his old pesos were dying in his pocket. Every business in the country was shutting down. There would be massive disruption for days, possibly weeks.

The phone rang: it was a friend from Santiago, the governor of the local Lions Club. 'I want to go with you,' he said.

David agreed to take him, with one caveat. 'I'm not getting out of the car,' he said. They were friends, but there were limits to friendship. 'I will drive by your house,' he told the man. 'You be there in the street with your things. You jump in. If you don't jump fast, you stay in Havana.'

When David pulled up minutes later, the Lions Club governor was there, ready, and he jumped in.

'David,' the man's brother called out to de Jongh, 'come have some coffee.' They were waving him in. The world was ending, and they wanted to sit down and drink coffee. He gunned it.

They left Havana and drove east for two or three hours fast, before encountering any trouble. There was suddenly a lot of traffic, and then all the cars ahead were moving into the right lane.

They could see a line of cars stretching ahead in the right lane, a line about a kilometre long. The cars were barely crawling toward a checkpoint of some kind. Militiamen were up there, looking over the passengers for anti-Revolutionary 'elements', and apparently searching the cars for any big stashes of currency.

The left lane, however, was wide open. Without thinking what he was doing, David swerved left and accelerated. The waiting cars ticked by. He rolled steadily down the line, closing on the militiamen. He didn't have an idea in his head, only the impulse. 'If I don't stop,' he told the Lions governor, 'they will shoot us.'

As they approached the militia, David kept accelerating compulsively, and the governor rolled down his window, leaned out and, as they passed without slowing down, he stuck his fist into the air and screamed, with full authority, *'PATRIA O MUERTE!'* (Fatherland or death!).

Fidel's own slogan. The militiamen threw their fists in the air and answered, as one: *'VENCEREMOS!'* We will win!

David's foot felt locked in place. He stormed on, and nothing happened. Eventually they had to stop for gas. They found one of the last stations still open, far enough out from Havana that either they didn't know about the new currency, or didn't know what else to do, because they accepted the old money. The two men filled the tank, and then spent everything they could on sandwiches and drinks, before racing onward, eating from their laps as they took turns driving.

They arrived in Santiago at 1 am, rolling down out of the cool hills into the swampy night of the bay city. Two hours after they arrived, militias closed the roads into and out of Santiago.

GETTING HOME WAS ONLY A WAY OF LEAVING. David had scientific habits: you examined evidence, you measured, you laid out a course of deductions, you made a thesis, and then you followed the trail of logical steps, one by one. Denial has no place in the lab.

His deduction had been correct, The new money heralded a complete takeover of the economy, of the mechanisms of trade.

The process that began with land reforms and the breaking up of big estates was not an end sufficient to itself.

At the house David called Kiki out to the back yard and, acting casually, stirred a stick in the ashes of the trash burner until he hit something solid. 'That is about seven pounds of gold,' he said. Kiki did not show any surprise. David told him to keep the servants from any sudden impulse to clean out the bin, and told him to be ready to move the gold soon. They would need it on the outside.

Kiki was the youngest, and he listened. David got an exit visa later in the year, and went out like anybody. Arturo followed. But Kiki stayed, following his elder brother's instructions to be the last to go. When it was time, and David had everything arranged, Kiki dug the gold out of the ashes. It looked like a filthy fragment of brick, until he wiped it down. It gleamed. Gold cannot tarnish.

Kiki delivered the block to a man at a foreign consulate in Santiago. He was a 'friend' of David. The diplomat carried the gold out of Cuba in a diplomatic pouch. It landed in Florida, where David, and then Arturo, were waiting for it, and for Kiki.

The gold, that little survivor of the family fortunes, made it out. As the months went by, Kiki reported that he himself was delayed.

ON 10 SEPTEMBER, A SUNDAY, Catholics in Havana gathered for the traditional procession of the Virgin of La Caridad, the patroness of Cuba. Thousands of regular Catholics were joined at the march by some anti-Castro activists. The police denied permission to march, then granted it, and by the time the march actually began, hundreds of government loyalists had been brought to the scene to stage an act of repudiation. As the Virgin left the church, someone began shooting. A young man named Arnaldo Socorro fell dead.

The crowd fled; the police arrested several Catholic leaders. The next day the ministry of the interior denounced the Catholic Church as a whole, labelling it a tool of the counter-revolution. Just a day later, 12 September, the police began putting under house arrest all Catholic priests who were deemed unreliable, which was almost all of them. The rival orders – Dominicans, Franciscans, Carmelites, Christian Brothers, Ursulines and the Jesuits – were treated exactly the same. An order of expulsion came down: all foreign priests must leave, and the great majority of priests were foreign. From across Cuba, 132 of these men, almost all Spaniards, were put on board a Spanish-registered ship, the *Covadonga*, and on 17 September it sailed from Havana harbour with virtually all the Jesuits from the Colegio de Dolores on board. They had been thrown out of many countries before. It was part of being a Jesuit. History taught that they would return some day.

Lundy Aguilar's 'El Profeta' featured a man sailing out of Havana harbour in despair. Exile was a normal metaphor for Cuban life. By the end of December, 67,000 Cubans had fled to the United States. Others had gone to Spain, the Dominican Republic and Mexico.

TWO DOZEN LITERACY WORKERS had been killed during 1961 by the sputtering anti-Castro resistance. The last of them, a 16-year-old volunteer, killed just as the year wound down and the spectacle wound up. December 22 was declared the Day of Education, with a massive victory rally in Havana for the teaching volunteers. Their once improvised and enthusiastic effort had become a powerful, institutional structure now, with a huge bureaucracy, a special anthem and a spiral of flow charts communicating in an acronymic language – ORI, AJR, STE, MINFAR, ME, CTC(R), ANAP, FMC, CDR – which could dissuade anyone from reading.

On the day of the great rally in Havana, Castro was introduced with his ornate new titles, including 'our Maximum Leader, the Commander in Chief'. Statistics poured forth: 566,817 persons had been taught to read, although later the number was upgraded to precisely 730,212, and still later, the government said 'a million' had become literate. According to the UN, general illiteracy dropped from 23.6 per cent to 3.9 per cent during a span of 12 months. The stiffest declines were among the rural poor, where 42.7 per cent had been illiterate. Whatever the real numbers, it was a colossal achievement: Cuba had jumped overnight into the ranks of the best-educated nations. *Fidel, how great you are.*

Tens of thousands of teachers marched up the Malecón in Havana that day.

As they passed the reviewing stand at the Hotel Riviera the battalions chanted what they themselves had learned:

FIDEL!
FIDEL!
TELL US WHAT TO DO!

NOT EVERYONE MADE IT OUT in December, or ever, but even as 1961 expired in a frenzy of chanting, it still wasn't too late.

Roca had applied for permission to leave the country much earlier in 1961, but without any result. He'd spent the whole year jumping the hurdles of the new bureaucracy of departure: the health permits and visas and separate certifications of houses, bank accounts and cars, an inventory of all personal property, and, because he was a dentist, permission from the new state association for dentists. The web of rules was tightening, but many of the old assumptions about rights and civil procedures still lingered, at least in a shadow form. And the government simply lacked experience in enforcing its new rules. That meant there had to be loopholes.

Since the Bay of Pigs, Roca had assumed that, no matter how it happened, he and his family would be leaving. He had turned his mind to practical questions. The most obvious of these was how to get out some money, or possessions. Roca found a crack in the system at Guantánamo, the huge American base near Santiago. It hadn't been fenced off completely, yet: Cubans who worked for the American military were allowed to commute into the US base every morning. One of his employees at the dental clinic had a relative who worked at the base, and so effectively left Cuba every day. For a price, this man agreed to help.

Base employees had been a conduit for back-and-forth smuggling of various kinds, and were kept under scrutiny. But Roca used his dental drills to hollow out the heels on several pairs of shoes. Each day he would give a pair of shoes to the worker, who strolled into Guantánamo on top of a piece of jewellery, or a tightly wadded bundle of US dollars, or bits of the gold that dentists kept for making fillings. It didn't add up to much, but there was satisfaction in knowing that they had beaten the system.

The Roca assets went via Guantánamo, and the family itself via Havana. Not one to wait passively for the play, Roca took his family to the capital and checked into the Hotel Capri, the one with the swimming pool on top. When their exit permit proved elusive, and weeks dragged by, they switched to living in the houses of various friends to save money. The bureaucracy would not budge, right through December and the end of the Year of Literacy. Since those who left Cuba were by definition tainted, risk-averse bureaucrats in Havana were stalling. Even approved exit permits would sit unsigned for weeks. Roca struggled with one evasive bureaucrat, who insisted that he simply had no time to handle the family's application. Finally José Antonio went to his house at 5 am, waiting patiently in the street for the man to emerge for work. He presented him with the paper right there, on the sidewalk, and the man rubbed sleep from his eyes and signed it.

In late December, José Antonio, Carmelina and their first child, a daughter, were finally given seats on a flight. They would leave on the sixth day of the new year, 1962. When they arrived at the airport, their luggage was searched to the usual stringent standards, and a policeman confiscated a gold chain from around Carmelina's neck. They walked out of the fishbowl, crossed the tarmac, and climbed the mobile stairs to take their seats.

The flight was brief, an hour passing over the hues of the ocean, tropical green and North Atlantic blue, and then the muddy coastal waters of Florida, and finally the black runway in Miami. Such a short trip, José Antonio recalled, but in that one crowded hour, 'winter gave way to spring'.

6

AVENUE OF THE PRESIDENTS

GRANDMOTHER was in favour of Fidel Castro. Since its first issue in 1965, Cuba's one and only daily newspaper had been full of enthusiastic praise for the Leader, and despite all the decades and misadventures, the editors had never found space for a single word against him. Fidel, known in the streets as the Horse, the Beard, Crazy, This Fellow, the Boss, Him, or just Uncle So-And-So, was identified in the pages of *Grandmother* by a variety of titles:

Leader
Maximum Leader
Major
Doctor
First Vice Minister
President
Prime Minister
President and Prime Minister
First Secretary
Head of the National and International Public Health
    Programme
Head of the National and International Education Programme
Head of Cuba's National Energy Revolution Programme
Commander
Commander in Chief
Invincible Marshal of the Republic

They wrote about Castro every day, most pages of every issue. He was mentioned in about a third of the articles, including the sports page, and even theatre reviews.

The most shocking thing about *Grandmother* was the paper it was printed on, a grey and faintly greasy newsprint with strange bits of fibre and black spots dotting the page. The red ink in the big headlines ('Raúl meets with Italian Foreign Minister') was prone to bleeding out, and the smaller black-type paeans to the State Visit by the President of Burundi, or the Comments by the Chief of the North Korean Armed Forces, tended to smudge on your fingers. It was a tactile experience. The photographs were flat, developed in old chemicals and printed with diluted ink. A front-page smudge on Castro's face could set off an orgy of speculation in Miami (Wasn't it deliberate? A signal from Cuban dissidents in the photo lab?) Smudges everywhere else in the paper drew no such attention.

The headlines were the usual:

The Struggle Continues and Will Continue
The Force of the Revolution Must Be Expressed
An Atomized Society Can Have No Force For Anything
We Have Begun to See the First Fruits
For Development, For Progress, for Justice
For Caribbean Integration
Emulation Among Combines Will Increase Efficiency

Reinaldo Arenas described *Grandmother* as the 'first wonder' of Cuban socialism:

[I]t's the only newspaper in the world in which the events that the newspaper report on have nothing whatsoever to do with reality. It is the most optimistic newspaper in the world, and among the most frequent verbs you will find in its headlines are *inspire, conquer, overthrow, achieve, optimize* . . . It's also the newspaper with the largest potato and sugar harvests in all the world, although we ourselves never see those products any-where. It has no obituaries, and when somebody is shot by the firing squad the newspaper says that the person died in a state of grace, proclaiming the virtues of the newspaper editor who had the person shot.

The 'newspaper editor' was of course the one man, the Horse himself, who appointed the men who chose the men who directed the men who actually wrote, edited and printed *Grandmother*. You could also buy the little grey throwaway, called *Juventud Rebelde* which had caught Cabrera Infante's attention, or you might see a man carrying a paper called *Worker's Daily*, but these were all written and edited by the same staff as *Grandmother*, in the same building, and printed on the same machine.

It was 18 days since the rooftop New Year's party, on the day known as '18 JANUARY YEAR OF THE GLORIOUS AN-NIVERSARIES OF MARTÍ AND OF THE MONCADA.' *Grandmother* was full of exciting news. Castro had called a snap election. Elections occurred at random intervals in Cuba, every five or seven years, always for something new. The emphasis in Cuba was not on who was elected – a foregone conclusion – but on the elaboration and perfection of the system which elected them. Form was substance: this January election, a direct vote for provincial delegates and national deputies, would supposedly give Cubans a chance to improve the 'organization of electoral roundtables' and 'the functioning of the system of communications'.

But the election itself was actually small news, at the bottom of the front page. A much larger and lavishly illustrated article with red headlines and bullet points covered the top front of the paper, and this was, of course, a lovingly detailed account of Castro's latest statements on a variety of topics, taken from a long television appearance the night before. Castro had sat in a TV studio with two men from the electoral commission, discussing the elections. The other men were like the straight men in a comedy routine: their job was to start things off, and then intervene with gentle questions only when one of Fidel's 25-minute monologues petered out into a digression that not even Fidel could fathom. Otherwise they sat quietly.

The night before my arrival, Castro had spoken at length, extemporaneously, wagging his finger in the air, reciting the astonishing array of statistics he kept memorized for this purpose, his superb memory for page numbers and citations as useful today as in 1941. On TV he used standard language about the sanctity, sovereignty, independence, justice, efficiency and morality of the Cuban system. But then he had explained that the logic of his argument had been expressed once before, on the occasion of another election. He picked up some pages and began reading aloud. The television programme now consisted of Castro sitting in a chair reading a speech from the early nineties as two men watched. Then, the next morning, here he was in the nation's leading newspaper describing the television show.

Cuba had to conserve everything in the Special Period, even words. The Cuban system concentrated on delivering the same clear messages again and again, a set of themes derived from official principles, couched in approved language. These messages were delivered steadily, a drumbeat to the Revolution's march.

The very first of these themes was always and ever the same: unity. On 18 January 2004, *Grandmother* called for 'unity against those who want to divide us, weaken us, demoralize us'. Unity was mentioned in the first and second paragraphs of this article, and most of the other articles. At the bottom of the page there was an entire article devoted to unity. This one exhorted the people to vote with unity, and various key phrases were put in all caps (VOTE UNITED!) or in bold (**Make the United Vote a Reality!**).

In 1997 there had been local elections, and Cubans had been allowed to choose loyal Revolutionaries from slates approved by the Party and its many organisms. But the 1997 elections had now been discovered to contain a vital weakness. The candidates were competing against each other, *Grandmother* explained, and competition was inefficient, a wasted replication of talent and effort. In this new election, candidates would no longer vie for the attention of the voter. This time it was a matter of simple ratification: the government had a position for every single candidate. All the voter had to do was put a check mark next to the eight or nine names. It was a plebiscite, not an election, with abstention as the only alternative to saying yes.

But Cuban democracy had been improved even beyond this.

At the bottom of the ballot for the 2004 election, there was a large circle, next to the words 'ALL OF THE ABOVE'. You could put one check mark there, and let the Revolution do all the hard work of picking the right people. Any form of individual choice – anything less than complete conformity – was, in the words of *Grandmother*, an opening to 'imperialism' and 'traitors'. Even showing up late at the polling station was a form of weakness. Vote early, *Grandmother* said, and vote united.

The second theme, in *Grandmother* and everywhere, was equally blunt: patriotism. 'The fatherland needs you,' the newspaper said. Nationalism, hyperbole and false pride marched in step. Cubans were not merely free, the minister of information and communications said, but 'the freest people on earth'. The candidates for office were not merely good, *Grandmother* said, they were the 'most modest and humble of candidates'. The election was not merely democratic, it was, the paper continued, 'the most democratic that has ever been employed in the world', with 'new and creative methods' unknown in the darkness beyond Cuba. No other election had ever been so well prepared and organized. The ceaseless tolling of these achievements, records and improvements was a part of building an alternative universe, what Czeslaw Milosz called the 'Captive Mind' of universal deceit and loyalty rituals.

A cartoon inside the paper reinforced the unity message. There was a four-panel strip that showed friendly Cubans discussing the election while they waited for a *camello*, one of the huge, double-humped buses that Cuba relies on. The punch line was, 'The best thing is to vote united to advance and defend the Revolution!'

Posters about the candidates were soon posted all over the neighbourhoods of Havana, listing their names and résumés. Among thousands of local candidates around the island, only three were not Communists. These were all Protestant preachers, who worked with the government and were urging their flocks to cooperate with the socialist system.

Castro insisted on television and then in the newspaper that there was absolutely 'no intervention by the Party' in the election. The masses themselves had spontaneously nominated

Communists for 98 per cent of the openings. This point was so important that he repeated it again later, almost verbatim, and then veered off into comparisons. By contrast with Cuba, other countries were false democracies, where the the candidates were chosen by political parties, he explained.

Money was 'the great elector', Castro said. Politicians in the US were bought and sold 'in the same manner used to sell soda, beer, or cars . . . any of the millions of articles that are sold in the market'.

True enough, in its way. But maybe it was bad taste to mention that other countries had millions of articles for sale in the market.

THE REVOLUTION EXISTED in the present tense. Other eras were just panoramas, held up for orientation. The actual past and the potential future had ceased to matter. There was only today, the moment, the crisis, the emergency. The Revolution was itself a permanent institution, ceaseless, an island in a world of change. All problems were the result of temporary conditions, as were all retreats, defeats and failures. Like the weather, these difficulties were predicted to change soon ('We Are Beginning to See the Fruits'), without ever changing completely. If there was a shortage, it was the result of imperialism. If a light bulb blew out in Cárdenas, it was imperialism. Every day was the Bay of Pigs. Well into the twenty-first century, the daily news briefs on Radio Reloj were salted with reports of sabotage, spies uncovered and terrorist plots thwarted, enemy agents and mercenaries hunted all over Cuba.

In 1961, the militias marched along the Malecón in Havana, manning anti-aircraft trenches. And in 2004, Castro still ordered tens of thousands of university students across Cuba to spend the weekend digging anti-aircraft trenches and foxholes. Civilians were sent to practise their marksmanship that same weekend and practised donning gas masks as mock air raid sirens sounded in the distance. Castro was shown on TV standing in front of an electrified map of Cuba, teleconferencing with regional authorities, authorizing mock deployments, and getting status reports from fake emergencies. According to *Grandmother*, this demonstrated the Revolution's 'capacity to resist and overcome an imperialist aggression'. It looked more like a mesmeric project, the casting of spells to delude people. And all the while Cyclops, like the Wizard of Oz, insisting that Cubans pay no attention to the man behind the curtain.

When he announced that an American invasion was imminent and that 'the risks of an aggression are real', this was true, in a sense.

On the radio, there was a revolutionary ballad, 'Siempre 26' which played endlessly. *It is always the 26th of July*, the voices sang. It is 26 July 1952, the day of the Moncada attack. Or it is 1961, at the Bay of Pigs, or 1962 during the 'October Crisis'. The past is now. The future is now. *Always the 26th.*

Time itself had surrendered. Cuba was in what a scientist would call a steady state, a self-replicating condition. For the majority of Cubans who were born after 1959, Castro's rule had literally always been. It was only a small step to believe that in any practical sense Castro's rule would always be.

This indelible timelessness was not like a work of fiction, it was one. *The Autumn of the Patriarch* that I had left with Palácios' library was more than just a parable by García Márquez about a green-fatigued Caribbean dictator who rules his collapsing country for 200 years straight. The text had been composed (in the original Spanish edition) as a single run-on sentence, a torrent that poured onward for hundreds of pages without pause, as never-ending as the tyrant himself. There had only ever been one ruler, one moment, one thought, one sentence. The past and the future were today. Dead, ill, alive – it could all be true, and without effect. Castro's shadow will linger long after the man.

THE BASEBALL STADIUM is in a neighbourhood of Havana called El Cerro, or The Peak. In the nineteenth century, a series of plagues drove the rich to flee the miasmic gutters of Old Havana, and many built airy second homes on the small rise of El Cerro, just a couple of miles away. A century later the houses are decayed, rotten and lovely, like so much in Cuba: hundreds of them line a long avenue, more than a mile of colonnaded porches, rococo pediments and rusted ironwork. El Cerro was countryside then; now it is swallowed by the city, but only just. Cuban cities just do not grow: Havana's last era of expansion was the 'American' phase, the first half of the twentieth century, when suburbs like Miramar sprang up. In the 1930s, forties and fifties, hotels and art deco apartment blocks filled in some of the sections of the city, like Nuevo Vedado. But Havana, like Santiago, is a small place and since the Revolution, the capital has hardly expanded at all. Socialist planners have thrown up some suburban colonies, the apartment blocks out on the eastern beaches like Alamar, but most of this 'East Havana' is still empty land, designated for military use, with open beaches and fallow fields. A 20-minute drive from the city centre can put you in a horse pasture. Farm fields seem to be advancing toward the city, rather than the other way around.

Half a dozen people had assured me that there was definitely no baseball in El Cerro this weekend. Both of Havana's teams, the Industriales and the Metropolitanos, were on the road. No baseball. Definitely not. Cab drivers, neighbours, hotel concierges, old friends and strangers had all informed me there was definitely no baseball. But come Saturday night, the TV in F's kitchen was blaring a pregame show, transmitted from a baseball stadium. I could see an Industriales pitcher warming up in the bullpen, and asked F where they were playing. 'Right here,' he said. 'That is the Estadio Latinoamericano, in El Cerro.'

I went out in the street, flagged down a black-market cab, and was at the stadium in under 15 minutes. I paid a dollar for my ticket – Cubans paid 7 cents – and stormed inside, helping myself to one of the many available seats behind home plate. The bleachers were only a quarter full. I managed to catch, live, the last warm-up pitches by the same Industriales hurler I had seen on TV.

I was looking forward to a little nostalgic baseball, the old-time game for which Cuba was famous. Players were paid nothing, rode their bikes to work, and batted and fielded with the desperate heart of true talent. Just five years before, I had such an evening right here in the Estadio Latino. The Industriales had suffered a mind-numbing display of talent by Omar Linares, a

Piñar del Rio infielder. He had brought home the gold from the Atlanta Olympics of 1996, raining hits on the Americans and finally crushing the Japanese with an impossible batting average of .487. Linares was the Satchel Paige of our day, a legendary talent kept out of the big leagues by politics. He was famous for refusing all offers to defect to the US, where he could have earned millions. Instead he had always chosen to stay in Cuba, where he served in the National Assembly, preaching the virtues of loyalty to the Revolution and hard work.

Linares had started that memorable night off with a display of his most famous quality – his blinding speed on the baselines. As the first batter up, he'd been walked by a clumsy starter. Then Linares had somehow disappeared, only to reappear at second base a half second later. After just a few more pitches he rematerialized at third without anyone having seen a thing. Then he'd blown home on a wild pitch, accompanied by the roar of the crowd.

Not tonight. Linares the idealist had finally 'retired early', to take a lucrative contract with the Chunichi Dragons in Japan. Like all loyal Cuban athletes, artists and musicians – the ones who went abroad only with permission – the money Linares earned while overseas didn't go to him. It went to the Cuban Sports Federation, which arranged the contracts and received the hard currency. The government kept up to 80 per cent of the money that a performer, like the late Rubén González of the Buena Vista Social Club, earned. The prize money won by Cuban runners at the Los Angeles marathon was also passed directly to the state. Thus Linares' yen were turned into lead.

When the game started, it was obvious that the generation of Linares had passed. The Industriales pitcher threw three stinkers, all three of which were clocked for bases. Two runs got in before some fans had even noticed that the game had started.

The cold front was still here. Night winds blew into the stadium. The Cuban players weren't used to this kind of weather, the very coldest it ever got in Havana. Their game was stiff, clumsy, almost amateurish. Both teams began smacking singles, doubles, home runs, more singles. It was raining baseballs in the

outfield, but stupid errors abounded, and the sides came and
went. Shivering first basemen dropped everything that bounced
their way. Both teams burned through their bullpens, changing
pitchers after each new disaster, as the game slid toward absurdity.
The weather was miserable, and the crowd became increasingly
surly as the score ran up. About 4,000 people cheered or booed,
depending. Most of them were teenagers, and since cans of beer
cost a *fula* each, they couldn't afford to get even a little drunk.
And a bored teenager is dangerous.

Béisbol goes so deep into Cuba that it can't be dug out. It
arrived in the 1860s brought in by Cuban students returning from
the US, and played by American sailors loading sugar. By the
1890s, *béisbol* had become a Cuban game, a point of nationalist
pride in their struggle against the alien nature of Spanish identity
and rule. Cuban exiles had then carried the game to the Dominican Republic and the rest of the Caribbean. But *béisbol* still
entwined Cuba and America like two tongues in one mouth. As I
sat on a sticky, cold seat of metal, there was *un squeezeplay,*
followed by a *flai* to the outfield, which was caught by a *fildeador*
for an *aut*. The Industriales could barely *pitchear* at all, so that
jonrón followed a *tubey* ('two base'), which followed a *tribey*.
Inning after inning I waited in vain for that supreme display of
competence, *el double play*.

Two Cuban big shots who somehow had tickets right behind
home plate spent the entirety of each inning yelling at the
players. *Fag fag fag you homo you fucking monkey you fag*. They did
this in front of their children, getting more and more furious as
the game ground down into farce. They weren't for either side:
they were against both. *You fag*, they yelled. *I'm going to fuck your
wife just like I fucked your sister you cocksucking fag you fag fag fag*.
They had plenty of money for beer. They were getting red-
eyed, sloppy on their feet. When the Industriales came in from
the field at the end of the inning, both men leaned out to taunt
them. One of the Industriales fielders held out his hand, in a
gesture of reconciliation, and when the drunkard took it, all the
while saying, *You are shit you fag*, the ballplayer gave one clean
jerk and flipped him headfirst over the wall. The drunkard

landed on his head, sprayed with beer, and the ballplayer was gone.

The visiting team, from Santiago de Cuba, had a surprising number of fans behind its dugout – almost a thousand, it seemed. The Industriales still had a strong home advantage, but this was the Yankees-Red Sox rivalry of Cuba and only the Orientales seemed to be enjoying it. During the sixth inning (an cascade of grounders that amounted to nothing) a small fight broke out in the bleachers behind the Santiago bench. I could see windmill punches and a half dozen teenagers battling, and then the blue and grey police wading into the fight.

The crowd around me, on the Havana side of the stadium, began to hoot, and gradually the people behind me began to raise a steady, orchestrated chant, which spread slowly through our section of the bleachers, and finally built up to quite a roar. The fight over on the Santiago side had finally given hundreds of bored people something to get excited about: *PAL-E-STI-NO! PAL-E-STI-NO! PAL-E-STI-NO!*

'Palestinian' was an insulting nickname for illegal immigrants in Havana. Across Cuba, every single person has an assigned residence. Cubans cannot simply pick up and move when they want, where they want; the jobs and dollars might be in Havana, but if you were from Holguín or Santiago de Cuba you had to stay there.

During the Special Period, Havana's population had been swollen by people illegally searching for work or food. Tens of thousands, possibly hundreds of thousands, of easterners had moved to the capital without permission, without residency permits, without ration cards. They were said to be stateless, i.e. Palestinians.

And since there was never enough money for new housing, or social services, or even food, Habaneros liked to blame the Palestinos for crowding, for the shortages, for the lack of jobs, for social problems, for crime, and for starting fights in the Estadio Latinoamericano.

A thousand people now: *PAL-E-STI-NO! PAL-E-STI-NO!*

PAL-E-STI-NO! The drunkard had quickly regained his seat and now he and his friend were on their feet, turned toward the crowd, inciting them. They waved their arms, ordering people to stand up. A minute ago they'd been heaping insults on their own team; now they couldn't assault the visitors fast enough. The usual atavistic accusation: *Them. Outsiders. The Palestinos. They are the source of the problems. Them.* For the average person, less vicious, maybe it was just the ancient rivalry between Cuba's two cities. But the massed voice was a force, a message. *This is our town. We decide things here.*

A dozen police officers were needed to break up the fight. They finally dragged away five or six young men. The chant died out slowly, and the bullies turned their attention back to insulting the sexuality of the players.

A couple of cold, boring innings later, I got curious about the Palestinos, and walked over to the far side of the stadium, shooting pictures, snooping, eavesdropping, and taking notes on everything with my eyes, as Lundy would say. But I made the mistake of wandering too long. I don't worry about safety much in Cuba. Crime is low, weapons rare. Philip Agee, the former CIA spy who had become a turncoat, and exposed many of America's worst plots to murder Castro, had recently opened a travel agency in Havana. He'd boasted that the island was a stress-free travel destination. 'Take a break from anxiety and tension and come to Cuba,' he advised tourists. The island was 'well known for having the safest streets in the western hemisphere'.

Crime had been low. But it was rising and precedent and experience were a poor guide. While I was bent over, composing a shot of the deserted bleachers, something tingled quietly in my subconscious. I whipped around to find that two gangly teenage boys were now sitting right behind me. They were pressed too close together, and looking furiously at the baseball, as if they'd had no thought in the world except to watch the game from ten inches behind my ass. One of the buckles on my camera bag was now open.

'Look, asshole. I have eyes, I can see,' I blurted at the closer one. I jabbed a finger at him, and he fell back, rolling his eyes, insisting he wasn't doing anything. They both got up and walked away.

Grab them? They were young, strong and mean. Two of them. There was no need to debate who could get away with what. Call the police? For what? I hadn't seen anything. Better to leave it alone. I dropped down a level, and walked fast across the stadium, to my seat. I rebuckled the camera bag.

I spotted them watching me, from new seats, much closer. They flicked their heads back to the baseball game.

Fear makes me physically ill so I often deny what is happening to me. I don't like being chased out of places, and decided to leave when I was ready to leave. Stay until midnight, just to prove that I could.

Seventh inning, top and then bottom. More hits. Top of the eighth. More hits. The pitchers were throwing wild, the batters laughed, and the crowd was restive. At the bottom of the eighth, three minutes to midnight, the Industriales were up 14–11, and I went for the exit tunnel.

No taxis, no buses. Just the usual Cuba at midnight. A trickle of baseball fans walked off, heading into the dark streets of El Cerro. I asked the staff where to find a cab at midnight, but I already knew their answer: nowhere. There were never any taxis at the stadium, because Cubans couldn't afford them and foreigners arrived and left in special tour buses. And, one elderly attendant confessed, there wasn't a single working phone anywhere in the stadium from which to call for a cab.

This was no surprise; I'd been here in this place, in this situation, at this time of night. The only hope for a ride was up on a major avenue, four blocks away. You could just make out the cars up there, passing by in a whizz. The only way to find a ride was to walk up there, and then hold a dollar bill in your hand until someone pulled over. The deaf old comrade manning the stadium gate pointed his finger up the street.

Halfway up I stopped to tie my shoe, even though it was well tied. Three boys stopped and watched me. *They are definitely not following me.* I ignored them, tightened up my camera bag and went on, faster. More people ahead of me, also boys. Up at the avenue, everything was fine. *There will be a car soon.*

I stood in plain sight, waiting for cars. In the empty intersection the boys felt too close, so I turned back toward the stadium, but found another six teenagers coming up the alley, animated, spread out, faces open to possibility. Somebody behind me called out in a burst of encrypted street Spanish. The new group called out to the old group, in gruff bursts that bounced off my ears.

Nothing is wrong. I went back across the avenue. *There will be a car soon.* I moved down the road a dozen yards. *Soon.* It was quiet for a long time, four or maybe ten seconds. Perception was beginning to squeeze into a narrow tube with only one exit. The shortest of all the boys, maybe 12, walked up. He asked if I needed a cab. 'No,' I said. *Well yes you do.*

'Actually,' I told him, 'yes, I do.'

He hesitated. 'So . . .' he said, and unable to think, he asked again. Did I need a cab? His clumsy little lie now broke, like a fever. He'd repeated himself because it was a script. A set-up. They were – *three coming fast.* I saw it now but restrained myself from doing anything. Do it one way and play it another. Fast on the inside, slow on the outside. Muttering to the kid, I put my back to a column and looked right. *Four and big.*

They were smiling, walking in quickly. Left, right, and also ahead. All the adrenaline in my body released at once, taking only about one second to tighten all my muscles and speed my heart, dilate my eyes and lungs, flood my bloodstream with clotting agents and cover my face in sweat. *Two in front.*

That was it then. No need to discuss who could get away with what. Someone on the left jumped a railing, to get behind me and my column, and I rocketed forward, looked a skinny boy in the eyes and asked, loudly, 'Can you tell me something?' He froze.

I juked around him, faked a punch at the second kid, and broke into a run, slamming away another hand that grabbed the camera bag, and breaking into the open. Even as I ran I could not accept what was happening. *They aren't chasing me*, I thought, despite the quick slapping of sneakers that came from behind.

I looked. Halfway down the first block, I looked over my

shoulder. It was much worse than I feared. Amazing what your eye can record in a quarter-second. The sallow yellow of his palm, reaching out to grab, the hand just a foot away, so close I can see the dirt under his nails. The Hawaiian shirt, open over a T-shirt. Shorts. A jaunty fade for a haircut, with a fake part on the right, buzzed into the nappy hair with clippers. Behind him, a half dozen other forms, running in.

Now I ran. Huge strides with my long legs, arms pumping, straight as an arrow down the middle of the street. The sound of shoes on asphalt fell in half. I could see the stadium, which looked to be three kilometres away, not three blocks.

'*AYÚDAME*,' I bellowed, running hard and screaming it again. '*AYÚDAME AYÚDAME AYÚDAME!!!*'

In the middle of the second intersection the slapping of sneakers stopped. I sprinted a half block more, just to be sure, and looked back in time to see the boys disappearing around the far corner, on to the avenue where we had started.

The short, determined kid in the Hawaiian shirt was the last to vanish, and did not look back. If they were caught assaulting a tourist they were likely to get severe jail terms. Six, eight, ten years in crowded, harsh conditions. More if they had a record.

Run, assholes. I was bent over, gasping for breath, almost blacked out. *Fuck you fuck you fuck you fuck you you fucking shiteaters*. I wanted to hurt them, to see them afraid. I wanted to split their fucking skulls open in the street.

Fuck you, and your fucked up city. Your shitty neighbourhood. Your arrogant, rotten, evil little selves.

Your turn to run, assholes.

Run.

BY THE TIME I WOKE UP the election was over. I had gone to bed at 1 am in a state of nervous disbelief, which gradually deteriorated with the passing hours into a fevered paranoia. I tossed on the polyester sheets, bundled up against the unfamiliar cold, agonized by the war between exhaustion and jittery energy that was fought out on the field of my endocrine system.

Whenever sleep began to close over me, a hand reached out of the darkness, a hand connected to a cruel, delighted face. The face was connected to a yellow Hawaiian shirt. But it was not fear that coursed through me; it was rage.

I wanted to smash them. To crush them. I imagined flying slowly over the city like a god, hunting down the boys as they fled before me, helpless and terrified. I imagined slaughtering them with knives, with rocks, with sticks, my feet and fists, anything. How quickly I reached for that live wire, the mastery over life and death. Just a few seconds in an alley, and I was full of hatred and the lust for power, my own little dictator.

I kept jolting out of bed, unable to sleep. I tried sitting up, or pacing the dark hall of the house. At four am, trembling in my sheets, I heard the roosters of Havana crowing to each other. One was next door, and others responded from many blocks away. The last time I checked my watch it was 4.30 am. I drifted in the foggy realm of semiconsciousness for the next few hours.

I rose at 10, only because I had to find aspirin. For some reason I could barely move my neck. I couldn't recall suffering any injury during the attack. Had I forgotten something? Had they yanked the camera bag hard enough to sprain my neck? Had I twisted it while slinking out of someone's reach? Did my fake punch really pack that much theatre?

At breakfast, my neck was so stiff that I could barely tip my head back to drink the coffee that F served me. When I told him what had happened in the alley, he looked at me with a kind of deep fear. Foreigners brought trouble, first on themselves, and then on those around them. The money was always balanced against this.

It was Sunday, election day. F brought the television into the kitchen, put it on the counter, plugged it in, turned it on, and a figure in green appeared. Him. Here he was, live, voting in a small city in eastern Cuba, trailed by cameras and hordes of election officials.

Fidel was being watched by a group of journalists, who were described as the 'international press'. Mostly they were Cuban reporters, with just one or two from other Latin American countries. There was a long delay, and several staged discussions between the Commander and the election officials about how exactly one filled out the ballot. All the empty rituals of a meaningless democracy. Then He made His mark, folded over the paper, and inserted it halfway into a ballot box.

He paused there, looking up expectantly. This was stagecraft he knew well: as he waited, dozens of cameras flashed, and sound men shoved in closer for position. He waited for the media, and when the substance was done – not the voting but the display of voting – he pushed the paper into the box like an afterthought.

F was clutching the breakfast table like a drowning man. 'What a farce,' he said. 'It's like Galileo Galilei. The Pope made him say one thing, but he knew it was another.'

I asked F if he was going to vote. 'I voted hours ago,' he said.

He'd gone up the street at dawn, like all his neighbours, and put a check mark in the 'all of the above' circle, just as *Grandmother* requested. He went on with his day. You could still say, as F did, *but it moves*. But you had to whisper it.

Although the vote today was nominally secret, recorded on a folded piece of paper, F was convinced that the government knew exactly how he had voted. He pointed out that the 'secret' ballots had individual serial numbers. And as each voter entered the station, his name and the number from his ID card were noted down. Couldn't these factors be cross-indexed somehow? Maybe they had other ways of knowing. For every real secret policeman there were 99 imaginary ones. You had to be safe, and do what you were told: vote early, vote united. Support the system or face the consequences. The populace ratified the leadership.

Half an hour ahead of the midday sun, I walked up the street one block. The polling station for this neighbourhood was in a television studio. The résumés of the five candidates were taped to the inside of the glass by the front door. Each sheet read roughly the same: a name in bold letters, a photo, the details of age and residence, and then the official organization that the candidate 'pertained' to: PCC, CDR, CTC, MTT, ACRC and so on. The groups were listed in order of importance. PCC was the Communist Party of Cuba; CDR was the acronym for the Committees in Defence of the Revolution, the famous block committees. There were more than 130,000 CDRs around the island, one for every large building or residential block in urban Cuba, and they were scattered in most rural areas. Although Castro liked to claim that 91 per cent of the population was enrolled in the CDR system, that was actually the number of people who were monitored *by* it. The active participants in running it numbered over 2 million. Directed by block captains, these people were responsible for watching every person and residence on the island, entering and evaluating homes for their Revolutionary atmosphere, and tracking their neighbours' participation in the proper Revolutionary activities. Non-participation was a serious problem, and was enforced by unarmed vigilante groups ('popular revolutionary vigilance detachments') who coordinated with the police to ensure compliance. The most ardent members of these CDR detachments were promoted to the notorious 'Rapid Action Brigades', who could be mobilized at a moment's notice to control public events, or stage 'acts of repudiation' against dissidents. And the most devoted members of the Rapid Action Brigades were in turn promoted to the Special Brigades, elite units who specialized in beating square pegs into round holes.

The block committee was required to verify that each youngster was being taught proper 'Marxist-Leninist values' inside the home; parents who insisted, for religious or political reasons, on teaching their children anti-Communist beliefs, could and had lost custody. The children were sent off to boarding schools. But block committees were as varied as the blocks they represented; some were staffed by hard core supporters of the system, who, motivated by the basest forms of envy and resentment, snitched on their neighbours, denouncing those who bought black market food or muttered petty criticisms of the regime. Others CDRs were composed of time-serving retirees who looked the other way, tolerated all sorts of dissent, refused to rat out private enterprise, and put up with unrevolutionary citizens. It simply depended on the people within the system.

Then there was the CTC, the Confederation of Cuban Workers, which was an overarching, state-run labour organization that claimed to be a union for the workers, but which answered to the government and allowed neither strikes nor independent voices. Those few – very few – candidates who were not members of the Communist Party were always members of several affiliates, like the Federation of Cuban Women.

Each candidate offered a biography, of which this one from under the glass was typical: he'd been a member of his local block committee for 42 years, had volunteered on 20 sugar harvests and helped pick 18 coffee crops; had a long career as a driver for state enterprises; had participated in 'various' May Day events; had served an 'international mission' in Angola for three years, and been sent to the Soviet Union in 1984; had 'participated actively in the battle of ideas which liberates our people', and had signed a declaration that socialism was 'untouchable', as well as organized rallies demanding the return of Elián González. He had earned the 'Internationalist Combatant Medal first class' as well as three other non-military medals, five certificates for attending various anniversaries and congresses, two 'distinctions' for meritorious labours, and the Order of Lázaro Peña Heroic Workers of the Republic of Cuba in both second and third classes.

The balloting room was still. Four people sat on chairs. The ballot box was on an end table. The ballot forms were stacked next to a clipboard to check off the names of the neighbourhood voters as they came in. A red, white and blue flag (for Cuba) and a red and black one (for the Revolutionary July 26th Movement) were the only decor.

No one was voting. The election was over. By noon, 154 of the 194 registered voters in the ward had already appeared. When I came back five hours later the same four officials were still sitting there, and the total was still 154 of 194.

The results were a sweep for socialism: all five candidates had been elected. The people of CDR 3/2/2 had, like those in every neighbourhood across Cuba, voted early, and together. Of those 154 voters, 151 had voted straight down the party line for all of the above.

Only three people in the whole district had defied the instruction to vote that way: picking and choosing, they affirmed three candidates but rejected a fourth. It might be someone they disliked, since the candidates were usually the party hacks from the local nomenclature. Or they might have rejected one candidate as a kind of minimal protest, a gesture of abstaining, without running the risks associated with failing to show up at all. A small but impressive number of people had run that very risk. This district, with 194 registered voters, had cast only 154 votes, an extremely low turnout by Cuban standards.

Elizardo Sánchez and a dozen other Cubans had fanned out during election day to observe the vote. Working in pairs, using preprinted tally forms, they had dropped in unannounced during the vote in several places and collected the end-of-day tallies. They weren't well received – within 20 minutes, Sánchez had been joined at his local polling place by more than 20 men with walkie-talkies – but (as Sánchez reminded them) it was legal for Cubans to enter and observe the voting process, *Grandmother* had said so right on the front page, and Fidel had stood on TV and invited the world to come watch a Cuban election. The dissidents were allowed to collect their data and leave without being detained.

Sánchez described the process as generally accurate at the level of the polling places – the totals were posted openly at day's end, and added up correctly at the lower levels of the tally process, where the votes were counted at neighbourhood levels. But somewhere higher up the chain – at the provincial level – the tallies began to look suspicious.

Most of the neighbourhood polling places they checked had the same number of voters as mine – across the city, it was almost always just under 200 per CDR, with only a couple carrying 201 or 189. (One rare exception was Sánchez' own CDR, which had been gerrymandered to include more than 1,300 members; this was to dilute his dissent in a sea of statistical loyalty, he claimed.) In a typical district, the 180-something voters had shown up, out of 190-something. The half-dozen abstainers in the typical district were 'almost heroic', Sánchez said. That made CDR 3 Colegio 2 District 2 look like a land of Solzhenitsyns: more than 30 locals hadn't bothered to say yes to the system. The difference might be political, but it was more likely economic: F's voting place was in a once-posh neighbourhood in the centre of Havana. As it had been half a century ago, it was disproportionately white, middle-class, and therefore more likely to have a good home to rent out, or a relative in Miami sending cash, or a memory of having lost something due to the Revolution. These people could afford the little risks of abstaining.

BY THE TIME I GOT TO KIKI DE JONGH'S neighbour-hood it was dark. A beautiful Caribbean night, cool and windy, the moist ocean air brushing softly over skin. The sky had finally cleared after weeks of cloud, fog, haze, cold and rain. Havana throws up less light during the night than other cities; a dense field of stars stood out like pinpricks on black velvet. The moon would be in its last quarter, but hadn't slipped into sight yet.

I felt sick, standing on the dark street, looking for his address. Some Cubans came down the sidewalk, making my spine tingle, but it was just two young couples, deep in conversation. I held myself steady as their little group split around me and passed downhill, still talking.

The cab driver had dropped me at the wrong intersection, off by four blocks. I headed downhill, counting houses. I ticked off the addresses and studied the avenue, a short, steep one which I'd never visited before. It was luxurious beyond anything I had encountered in Cuba. The roadway was divided, with a man-icured park running down the middle. The trees were in excellent shape, the bushes carved into precise topiary. At least the sidewalks were Cuban: they were broken up, with occasional sink holes and unfinished repair jobs. But there were nice benches, and no disastrous piles of garbage, or rusting equipment. Too nice. This was the Avenue of the Presidents, classier even than Fifth Avenue in Miramar. I'd never seen topiary in Cuba.

The houses were set back from the road, behind chain link fences and high screens of trimmed bushes. Pre-Revolutionary houses, with Spanish tiles and ornate bric-a-brac. There were a few tall apartment buildings, I walked down, passing the first tower and coming to the second, which was finally the address

Kiki had given me when he had asked me to stop by and pick something up. The building was 20 storeys tall, well maintained, each floor made from a slab of white cement that extended to form balconies. It was dramatic, and self-conscious. The home of an architect. The single elevator refused to appear, and eventually I walked up.

Kiki greeted me in the dark, and led me through nine rooms to his study. (There were more rooms; I only saw nine.) The floors were marble, but the walls were made of little more than air. Some of the outside walls consisted entirely of wood louvres, while the rooms were separated from each other with grilles. It wasn't a rich household by the standards of somewhere else. But in Cuba it was a palace, not just large but elegant, neat and glamorous.

'I'm very concerned about your project,' Kiki announced, once we had taken seats in the study. He had never agreed to give me an interview at all, and now explained that there were several things he could not discuss. The first was Fidel Castro himself: Kiki would not breathe one word about Fidel, the human being.

Kiki would only talk about history. It was important, he said, to not misrepresent things. Not to misinterpret them. He explained again that the boys from Dolores were nobody, and meant nothing. The Revolution was made by history, by huge currents. It was vast, a product of the impersonal masses, not something that could be traced back to 'a group of boys'. I nodded my agreement but this did not allay him.

'You Americans are the best in the world at making a small thing stand for a big thing,' Kiki warned. 'It's just like *Time* magazine. They always focus on one thing, and make it stand for everything.

'It's not these people,' he said. He tapped the picture of 238 boys for emphasis. He picked it up, turned it to the light, and fondled the page, squinting through his glasses, adjusting them, searching for faces. 'It's not these people,' he repeated.

The Jesuit system at Dolores had produced few of what Kiki called 'extremists', the radicals of all striptes who appeared in history books.

If the boys in the photo had not become extremists, I asked, then what had they become?

Kiki paused, and then said, 'The majority of these people are professional.' He was guessing, extrapolating from youth to predict adulthood. 'Serious,' he said. 'Cultured. Well placed. A fundamentally religious group. Or at least with elements of religion. They educated their children, and are defined by their families. I'll bet they are, as a group, the least divorced, the least damaged, the least involved in drugs or alcohol. They contribute enormously to the economy of the US. I'm sure these are the most stable families, the honest types. Working people. Well-behaved, with a huge role in the economy, aiding the United States. Most of them went broke [leaving Cuba], and have done very well with their skills, their work.'

It pleased him to predict. To speculate, so that I could go to Miami and see myself.

'A few have stayed,' he said, almost defensively. 'Not many.'

Did he miss them?

He nodded. 'Logically,' he said.

His little studio office was covered with lithographs of Viking ships and Spanish caravelles, and a wall displayed a scale model of his latest architectural project. It looked like a *bohio* at first glance, the traditional Cuban hut. But it was in fact a *cabaña* for a tourist hotel in western Cuba. It was meant to be part of his larger renovation of a hotel complex in Piñar del Rio, but in the end only the little *cabaña* had been built. He had other designs in his folder, sketches of apartment blocks, high-rise hotels, a modern version of the traditional tobacco drying shed. But none of these had ever been constructed: the tourist *cabaña* was the total of his architectural work for the Revolution.

There had been big dreams, at the beginning. Castro had authorized a burst of progressive building in the 1960s and 1970s. The Revolution had put up many new school campuses, most famously converting a golf course into a set of domed buildings for dance students and other artists. That school had been abandoned now, and creepers grew down through the shattered skylights. Kiki's own apartment building, on the Avenue of the

Presidents, had fared better. Built in 1968, it was a rare surviving example of Revolutionary ambition, full of rationed commodities: space, airy, good views. Kiki had been here since it was built; given the housing shortage he would be here until the end.

He felt around in the dark, past his Acer computer and drew one of his portfolios close. He presented me with a drawing. It was a conceptual sketch for a modern Cuban house, white, low and long. The drawing had been given a light colour wash of azure windows and green lawn. The lines of the house added up to the horizontal minimalism common in the 'new' parts of Cuba, that is the mid-century modern buildings. It looked like a house on the Avenue of the Presidents, or the cracked home of Balbino Rodríguez above Santiago. This was why he had asked me to his house.

This was Kiki's own work. For the entrance, he had designed a curtain wall of glass – swirling Fiestaware reds and yellows – so that the house would light up at night like a party beacon. The landscaping details were faint lines, but it looked like there was a swimming pool in back. The legend read, 'PLAN FOR BOU FAMILY HOUSE, 1958'. He put it in an envelope and asked me to send it to Pepín Bou. How long had it been, I asked, since they talked? 'Oh,' he said, and made a gesture as if washing his hands. 'I imagine it was '58. But he is a magnificent person, first quality, just like José Antonio Roca and Lundy Aguilar.'

Near the door, I touched the envelope and asked if the house had ever been built. Kiki laughed. 'No,' he said. 'That's when the Commander came along.'

I walked home. It was about a mile, in the darkness, and it seemed to take an hour. Climbing the avenue, watching for trouble, crossing the back streets of Vedado, and drawing the usual curious stares. It was lit up in some places, but in the darkness along the forbidding walls of the University of Havana, a lean and powerful drunk wheeled toward me, howling and demanding money when he saw I was a foreigner. My heart kept beating. I held tightly to the reins of my inner tyrant; no war tonight.

Eventually I slid past the front steps of the university. The steps, now vast and empty, had been the stage for much of Castro's life. In the late 1940s José Antonio Roca had seen him here, a pistol tucked into his waistband as insurance in the days of 'happy trigger' student gangs. In the 1990s I'd come closer to Cyclops here than anywhere else, standing 30 feet away as he addressed another rally. His voice was surprisingly soft and high, and his way of speaking so clear, so un-Cuban in its precise diction that even a child could understand him. He'd been led away that day, his trembling gait supported by foreign minister Ramón Felipe Pérez Roque, and like so many of the boys from Dolores, time would steal him away with all his secrets. So close, and I'd never touched him. I went down past the silent and shuttered polling station, toward F's place. This had been my eleventh visit to Cuba. Now that I knew I was leaving, maybe for the last time, I felt easy, and I slept hard.

7

WINTER

THE GLACIERS of the last ice age pressed down on New York State for a hundred thousand years, flattening it, taking topsoil off the bedrock in the north and then slowly shoving the dirt and gravel southward, carrying it to the sea, piling up terminal moraines like Long Island, and squeezing mountains of mud into flaky schist, like Washington Heights, the northernmost and tallest extension of the island of Manhattan. The neighbourhood is narrow, taking the north-south shape that survived the passing ice, and peers down on Harlem and the domes of Columbia University. The taller apartment buildings propped on the very top of the ridge face west toward the Hudson, over the shockingly green vista of New Jersey. Peregrine falcons live on the tallest buildings, and Dominican people inside them. They call the neighbourhood Santo Domingo Norte, but Puerto Ricans, Hassidic Jews and African Muslims are sprinkled on the avenues, and even the occasional Cuban.

When I arrived at 187th Street it was mid-afternoon but already as dark as the urban evenings ever get here. Snow was falling, thick and fat flakes. There was already seven inches of powder. The black of asphalt was gone. Parked cars and iron railings were cartoon shapes. The sidewalks were white; the yards white; even the few people in the streets had small accumulations of snow on their hats and shoulders, as did I, and we moved as slowly, as silently, as snowmen. The hush was broken by the shriek of a Dominican boy shooting down 187th Street on a garbage bag.

José Antonio Cubeñas came slowly to the front door of his nine-storey building. He took a full minute to cover the distance of just 20 feet across the lobby. He wasn't feeble or injured; his progress was slowed because he hesitated, stopping to look behind him, unsure of something, occasionally backtracking a few steps, pausing to listen and look. Finally he reached the glass door, let me into the lobby, shook my hand quickly, and then told me to shake off the snow. He hurried back toward his apartment, the very closest one on the ground floor, just around the corner.

'My wife has Alzheimer's,' he called over his shoulder, as he tuned out of sight.

Once inside his apartment, I stomped my boots on another mat, shedding a second layer. The apartment and the building shared a hard-to-define quality, a studied normalcy. The building was red brick and unadorned, all right-angles and straight lines. The apartment was one of many identical units, which themselves sat in a sea of similar blocks, all from the postwar boom, everything made from plain brick, glass, steel, aluminium and cement, never trying to look like anything fancy. José Antonio's apartment was on the ground floor, the windows covered with heavy curtains against street noise and other intrusions.

Of the many *antiguos alumnos* I had now met, few could claim to know Fidel Castro as Cubeñas did. He had gone beyond Dolores with Castro, in nearly continuous contact through the 1940s and 1950s, even in the maw of the war against Batista. Everything about Cubeñas looked, as Pedro Haber had said, *superinteligente*. He was rail thin, and his hair had receded back across his forehead, which exaggerated the size of his skull. Cubeñas was a tall, bony man, 80 years old, but it was not hard to see the strength that had been in him. He had thick fingers and large hands, which were covered with bulging blue-green veins that snaked down his wrists. The veins disappeared under the cuffs of his cardigan, which he wore over a tan, long-sleeved *guayabera*. His fine hair was black on what remained of the top, and white on the sides.

Like his comrades in Cuba, he did not have to leave the room to locate the stash of yearbooks, letters and photographs from the Oriente days. An end table and a larger coffee table were both covered with letters in Spanish, obscure pamphlets on Cuban projects, and heavy pages curled up at the edges with age.

José had been more guarded than anyone else when I first called, reluctant and protected. How had I learned his name and number? Where was I calling from? Who had I talked to? Why? Now, as he settled on to a love seat, facing the armchair carefully prepared for me, he apologized.

'Coming from Cuba, you have apprehension when someone comes looking for you,' he said. He leaned way back, with his hands up in a theatrical gesture of scepticism. He apologized, calling it a Miami reaction that was not appropriate in New York.

Indeed, it was Pedro Haber in Miami who had given me the phone digits, correctly warning that Cubeñas would be afraid. Haber insisted that I speak to Cubeñas 'in strictest confidence', as if we were discussing an invasion plan. I wasn't to disclose who had given me the phone number. Exile was a long catalogue of bitter encounters with journalists, officials, rivals and accusers, and the distrust of outsiders was fundamental at this point.

Cubeñas kept his own jaundiced view of the world at a slow bubble throughout our interviews. As soon as we sat down he began to describe the old Cuba, and he explained that the rise of Batista in the 1930s was really part of a conspiracy by Americans. American companies were behind this, and other things, he said. Nobody knew the real story because deceptions and lies had supplanted the true history of Cuba.

He cited one famous incident from the 1940s, often described in books, in which the sight of American sailors pissing on a statue of José Martí in Havana had sparked a nationalist uprising. This, Cubeñas explained, had never happened – the incident was all an elaborate fabrication, orchestrated by Castro, who had paid the American sailors, and then provided the photographer. 'I know for a fact that the government is listening to all my phone calls,' he told me.

He didn't specify which government. It didn't matter. Larger forces were at work. It is hard to be Cuban and not believe in conspiracies. Cubeñas had been born into an era when the American role in Cuba was not one of occasional meddling and sabotage, but rather outright control of politics and the economy. American domination was so widespread in his youth it was 'a moral and economic scandal', he said.

From the very beginning in 1898, American officials had pushed an agricultural 'reform' that made it easy for American corporations to buy up huge tracts of land. They promptly turned Cuba 'into a giant cane field', Cubeñas said, making the island totally dependent on the annual US sugar quota for economic survival. This was when the Americans had tried to secularize the school system along American lines, appointing a Jew to run the education system. 'A Cuban, but a Jew,' he clarified. Even worse, an atheist. 'That is not what the people wanted.'

Like Lundy Aguilar, Cubeñas was a lawyer who'd dedicated his life to writing, another Cuban pamphleteer who'd spent decades churning out articles, columns and booklets, his mind filled with plans for new parties and constitutions, reforms to Cuba and the exile movement, revised frameworks for speculative transitions, and manifestos and essays on preserving Castilian language, republican values and Catholic influence. Most were self-published, circulated within the little Philadelphia of Cuban intellectuals.

I'd been told that Cubeñas was a member of the Royal Academy of Spain. He reached behind him and drew from the pile of papers on the end table an impressively thick sheet of actual parchment, which was from the Academy in Madrid. Cubeñas was a corresponding member, a distinction he made little of.

'Class of '45, same as Him,' Cubeñas said, abruptly. 'I'm not going to say His name. I'm talking about the Big Chief down there.' He kept this promise, mostly. He talked instead of 'Him' or 'that fellow'. 'Once that fellow is gone, Cuba will recover in three years, you'll see.'

His wife Elsie came into the room now. Her hair was white, and she moved at a slow pace, picking her way through the furniture, distracted, not speaking or looking up. 'She's not that bad,' José Antonio said, 'but she forgets almost everything.' She was aware that something was missing, so she looked for it. If the front door was open she would walk out, sure at some level that it could be out there. She knew all the rooms, but did not know them, and tapped the walls as she moved about, surprised to see furniture. She was on her own island without memory or expectation.

The TV in the apartment was turned to Univision. The screen showed a soap opera, but the sound was off. Cubeñas helped Elsie sit on the sofa across from us, turned her to face the screen, and she watched it, fighting off sleep. Her head nodded, bobbed, fell, and lifted up again. When I looked over minutes later she was wide awake, and rose to walk around the room. As José Antonio and I spoke, going over documents, she opened the door to the coat closet, then closed it, tried the locked front door, and gradually worked around the four walls of the room. She came back and tried the closet again. Then she sat down and began weeping.

José spoke to her softly, in a quiet Oriente accent. *Calma, calma mi amor, que quieres, estoy aquí mi vida.* He fetched a glass of orange juice from the kitchen, and put her hand around the glass until she sensed it and drank. She was a pretty woman, her hair and clothing neat, even her gestures with the glass graceful.

'She is diabetic,' he explained. The sugar made an instant improvement in her mood, and she sat motionless in her chair now, watching the soap. José Antonio's patience and gentle manner never varied, but there was a translucent dried-out pain in him, the kind that can never be relieved. Even with someone at hand, he was alone. Cubeñas and Fidel were not merely class-mates and *internos* at Dolores. They had gone on to the University of Havana together, and then on to law school, both of them graduating in 1950. They had been student cohorts for a dozen years altogether, but the time at Dolores was indelible. It was the shared experience of being boarders that made for their intense and ultimately explosive relationship.

'We were 22 *internos* living in the school,' Cubeñas said. Another 20 were on half-board. Because these students stayed for lunch every day, during the long two-hour break when most students went home, they were considered part of the *interno* group. They were present for not just the meal, but for recess, when the pecking order at the school was established with contests and games. Cubeñas referred to 'all 40 of us together' as the core group at the school. The three Cubeñas brothers shared a small room, catty-corner from the room of the Castros. The relationship between José Antonio and Fidel had started off well, and they often sat on opposite sides of a long table at lunch or dinner so they could talk better.

Cubeñas rattled off the names of the other boys who sat with him, typically: José Antonio Roca, David de Jongh, the class clown Enrique Hechevaria, and sometimes the annoying Raúl Castro too. According to Cubeñas, the young Raúl was interested in Communism, but Fidel was intrigued by the Nazis. He read the speeches of Mussolini from the balcony at Dolores, waving his hands stiffly in imitation of the dictator at a rally.

Castro also read *Mein Kampf*, Cubeñas said. He even recalled Castro going to sleep with the book, then waking up and starting right in reading it again. A few days after Poland was invaded, Fidel marched into the patio, holding over his head a newspaper that read 'NOT ONE POLISH AIRPLANE REMAINS'. 'Our first victory,' Fidel said. But these were mere flirtations, part of a fascination with power that was common enough in 1939, when half the world was convinced that strongmen of one stripe or another – Hitler, Mussolini, Franco, Stalin – were the future. Castro was interested in global events, in the rise of the war, in Europe and Hitler, in the Danzig Corridor and the Molotov-Ribbentrop Pact, but he was chiefly concerned with how these events affected Cuba.

He was never an ideological fascist, Cubeñas said, and was definitely not an anti-Semite. Fidel had explained at the time that he could not be 'with' the fascists because they were against the Jews, and he could not be against the Jews for the simple reason that he was one. He volunteered that he was descended, through his grandmother, from Jews. Fidel was Catholic, not Jewish, and Cuban, not European, but he told anyone who would listen that the Jews were his own people.

I asked Cubeñas what was the single most striking characteristic of the young Castro.

'He was very dirty,' Cubeñas said. 'We called him *bola de churde*, ball of filth.' Raúl's nickname was also bad. 'We called him *la pulga, pulguita,*' he said. The Flea. It came from the way Raúl buzzed around his brothers, sticking his nose in the business of the older boys.

Raúl wasn't as dim as Ramón, the eldest Castro, but he wasn't a Fidel, either. 'He only used his head to keep his cap warm,' Cubeñas said.

Fidel was the academic leader. He wasn't the very best student at Dolores – Lundy got better grades – but Fidel seemed to inhale books on any and all topics, devouring not just what was assigned, but anything else he could get his hands on. With a combination of natural ability and trained discipline, he developed a phenomenal memory, one that gave him a nearly photographic recall of details. When they studied at night, Cubeñas would hold a textbook and ask drill questions. Fidel would answer, easily and quickly, showing his usual mastery of the subject. But what Cubeñas remembered was that Fidel would finish his answers by casually mentioning the page number that Cubeñas was looking at.

'There were many more intelligent than Fidel,' Cubeñas said. 'What Fidel had was memory.' Fidel seemed to feel some pressure. Something was driving him, something he needed to overcome. And Cubeñas – along with most everyone else – knew what it was.

'Fidel had a *gravísimo* problem,' he said. 'It was that he was a bastard. He was the only known bastard who came to the school.'

Fidel had indeed been a literal bastard. His father had not been married to Lina Ruz, a servant girl half Ángel's age, at the time that both Ramón and Fidel were born. Even so, their legal status as Ángel's heirs wasn't confirmed until Fidel was perhaps 16 or 17, and the rumour of their unconventional origins spread from the farm in Birán to the town of Banes, and followed them to Santiago. Out in the countryside of Oriente, even in a busy town like Banes, such casual family arrangements could be ignored, even tolerated. But in a big and pretentious city like Santiago, among boys from elite families with ancient Spanish surnames, legitimacy still had its prerogatives. *Hijo de puta* (bastard) was one of the most routine insults in Cuba, and Cubeñas remembered hearing boys taunt Fidel.

Denied one kind of legitimacy, he sought another, making himself the leader in all things, the organizer, the prima donna, the orchestrator of games, trips and entertainments. He would announce there was going to be a baseball game; assign the boys to teams himself; then insist on pitching, umpiring, keeping score and calling the game like a radio announcer. When he came to bat he would make his own decision about whether a pitch had been a strike or a ball. If he got a hit, it was the best hit of the game. If he swung and missed, it was lousy pitching. He acted as if he ran the the school, rather than attended it.

Cubeñas called Fidel a *gallito*, a little rooster. He puffed himself up, and would never back down, at least in public. He was a bully, brave on the outside but 'always a coward, inside'. Cubeñas loved retelling the story of their famous fight at the railing above the cistern. By his account he had given Fidel a thrashing. He was probably the only person alive who could say that. Cubeñas called him a coward, but not every boy would have marched up the circular staircase into the face of an enemy.

According to Cubeñas, the next year when Fidel went home for the summer vacation he had a chance to hone his skills at beating up the weak. This would have been in 1941 or perhaps 1942. In the midst of World War Two the demand for sugar and the shortage of labour had driven Cubans to import a lot of *macheteros* from Haiti. And back in Birán, Ángel Castro was one of those who had hired the migrant workers. The black Haitians were generally treated with racist contempt by white Cubans, and were allotted even worse pay and food than Cuban *macheteros*. The Haitians refused to work in these conditions, and soon there was an informal strike in progress. Ángel didn't like rebels. He sent in Fidel to break the strike. 'He broke it on horseback,' Cubeñas said. Riding in among the strikers, Fidel beat them with the flat of a machete and ordered them back to work. The horse was intimidating enough; the rider, wielding a sharp blade and backed by the power of a whole system, was even more instructive. The Haitians were driven back into the fields, and took up their work again.

The breaking of the strike was news all the way back in Santiago. The whole harvest across Oriente could have been affected by labour troubles in Banes. So the *Diario de Cuba*, Santiago's main paper, carried an item marking the good news. Sugar would be harvested on schedule in the heart of the agricultural belt, thanks to the promising middle son of citizen Ángel Castro.

During the final exams, Fidel and Cubeñas had studied together for a history exam, the subject that they and the majority of the boys took most seriously. The test consisted of four questions requiring short answers and then an essay on a surprise topic.

After so much studying with Fidel, Cubeñas was confident, and during the exam he raced through the first four questions and came to the essay section. They were invited to make the case for either Frederick the Great of Prussia or Peter the Great of Russia as the more influential leader. Cubeñas was the first to finish. He dropped his pencil, turned in his exam, and nervously waited outside the classroom. Fidel was the next student out.

'Cubeñas,' he said. 'Which did you answer? I answered Frederick.'

'Well, I answered Peter.'

When the scores came back, Fidel was second only to Cubeñas. Both had been rated *sobresaliente*, excellent, the highest. But on a numerical score, Cubeñas received a perfect 100, with Fidel just a few points behind. The Jesuits encouraged this kind of intellectual rivalry, the natural desire to compete, but Fidel didn't like being second, and kept silent for a while.

The world of Dolores began to break up. After the 1942 school year, Fidel was transferred to Belén in Havana. Lundy and at least half the boys in each graduating class went on to Belén. It was the best way to get the new fifth year of high school required by the educational reforms, and also the best way to get some polish and social contacts in the capital. But Cubeñas still preferred to see Fidel's departure as a result of losing that fight. 'He tried to impose himself on me. I fought him and won in front of 45 boys. That was why he left Dolores and went to Havana.'

Fidel may have left, but he and Cubeñas were far from done. Both boys arrived at the University of Havana as freshmen together, and overlapped on that bustling campus in the centre of Havana for most of the 1940s, until winning their law school degrees in 1950. After that, they finally went their separate ways, at least for a few years. Cubeñas went home, setting up a law practice in Manzanillo and supervising his father's farm.

'Our farm was in the first foothills of the Sierra Maestra,' Cubeñas told me. It was a big spread, 150 *caballerías*, or about a thousand acres. It lay on the inland, or north side, of the mountain range, and was separated from Santiago de Cuba by a long range of steep hills that, for a hundred miles west of the city, were not crossed by a single road. The Sierra Maestra are the tallest mountains in Cuba, where the Jesuits had often taken Fidel and other students into their depths, lecturing on botany as they hiked.

Castro had been an enthusiast for these explorations, often their leader. ('They goaded us into sports, excursions to the mountains,' Castro recalled in his interview with Frei Betto. 'All of that exerted a great attraction over me.') In December 1956 he brought his guerrilla fighters here, where they could ambush, flee, regroup, hide and fight again, using the convoluted terrain to evade their powerful enemies. But to do that, they needed Cubeñas.

'There were only two roads into the Sierra in this region,' Cubeñas explained, 'and both of them passed through our land.' Immediately upon landing, the guerrillas began to need things – bullets, guns, medicine, food, money, clothing, boots and information. 'All the supplies had to go down those roads. Everybody knew it. The Batista government knew it, but they didn't do anything about it because the soldiers were afraid they'd get shot if they came down the roads. So they declared them open roads.'

Cubeñas had a small legal practice in Manzanillo, serving as a notary and dealing with people from all walks of life. He travelled back and forth between Manzanillo and the farm, which he managed for his father. Between his practice in the city, where he heard gossip all day, and his house on the farm, where he could see everyone who came and went from the mountains passing just 50 yards away, he knew more than most people.

In January 1957, messengers from the guerrillas descended from the hills for the first time, and passed through the farm at night. Recruits from Santiago and the rest of the country went the other way, joining up with Fidel. Marijuana growers were among the only people who regularly took motor vehicles up the tiny, rutted tracks in the Sierra Maestra. They packed their crop into the big metal cracker tins then in use, and drove their sagging vehicles into Manzanillo. The smugglers were willing to bring supplies back uphill, and Castro allegedly declared, in these first desperate months, that 'if the marijuana ends, the Revolution ends'.

Fidel and Raúl were operating from a series of camps, most of them only an hour away from the Cubeñas farm by horse. But in the next two years of fighting Cubeñas never went to see his schoolmates once. Not that he wasn't invited: in February 1957, just three months into the war, Raúl wrote him a long letter, pleading for support, money and supplies, and warmly recalling their friendship. He urged Cubeñas to come to the Sierra, and signed off dramatically, vowing that 'if the bullets respect me' he would give Cubeñas a hug 'after the triumph'. His older brother added a postscript, scratching out, 'A hug for everyone, Fidel.'

The fist-fighting antagonists had been reconciled over that salt cellar before leaving Dolores; they had gone through law school together; they came from similar backgrounds, rural boys with wealthy fathers holding big lands. Both men hated Batista. The one thing they did not share was real friendship. Castro was uneasy with anyone who could and did challenge him. Cubeñas was afraid that Fidel's ambition, his need to dominate, would burn all around him. Cubeñas was invited to join the movement, to visit the camps, to take up various clandestine and finally overt positions in the Revolution, but he always declined, made excuses, pretended not to have received the letters, stalled, feigned illness, or went travelling. He made small financial contributions, but otherwise he said 'neither yes nor no' to anything Fidel and Raúl asked him to do personally.

This was the Cuban art of passive survival. Squeezed between two opposing forces, he said nothing as the guerrillas trafficked weapons, supplies and recruits up the road right past his house, and pretended to know nothing as the army launched counter-offensives in the area. Neither side was fooled. Caridad Fernández, the army chief in Manzanillo, came to visit Cubeñas's law practice one day. Caridad had a woman's name but he was a vicious soldier, a trusted crony of Batista, sent to Manzanillo to crush the festering insurgency. Caridad accused Cubeñas of being involved with his old friend Castro. Cubeñas heard everything on his farm. He knew the guerrillas' plans, the locations of their camps. As a notary, he was in touch with the poor of Manzanillo, and could learn which Batista official might be assassinated next. Cubeñas would have to become an informer for the government.

Cubeñas did not deny anything. 'Yes,' he said. 'You know that I do speak to everyone. I do know all the conspiracies.' But he served neither side, and was valuable right where he was, in the middle. 'If I hear that something is going to happen to you, specifically,' he promised Caridad, 'then I will seek you out right away and tell you. And the same is true for Fidel. If I hear a specific conspiracy against him, I'll warn him.'

Caridad measured the utility of this – a lot of Batista officers were being assassinated – and left Cubeñas alone for the rest of the war. But having connections was as dangerous as it was useful. Any association with the guerrillas could be fatal.

In February of 1958 the American journalist Herbert Matthews, working for the *New York Times*, came to Oriente looking for Castro and his guerrilla army. After an exchange of messages, Matthews was given permission to join the guerrillas, and a guide brought him up to the Sierra. Like everyone else, he had to pass through the Cubeñas farm to reach the rebel camps. Cubeñas played no direct role in the assignation, but one of his employees acted as a guide, showing Matthews the way to his rendezvous. The resulting article, appearing on the front page of the *Times*, put the lie to government claims that Fidel Castro had been killed, and caused a sensation.

The interview's fallout was felt in Havana and foreign capitals, but what José Antonio Cubeñas remembered was the local reaction. Matthews had been careful not to reveal how he had reached the guerrillas, but *Bohemia*, Cuba's premier magazine, casually printed the name of the guide.

'It was a death sentence,' Cubeñas said. The many agents of SIM would not hesitate to arrest, torture and assassinate the guide. Even Cubeñas, who carefully avoided ever going up to the camps, could be arrested. At the very least his quiet neutrality would be shattered.

But *Bohemia* was printed in Havana, and arrived only slowly throughout Oriente, carried by local bus services. Tipped off by a phone call from Santiago, José Antonio realized he could still intercept the incriminating issue before it reached Manzanillo, the closest military headquarters.

Cubeñas jumped into his car and rushed to the nearest town, where he didn't have to wait long before a La Cubeña bus from Santiago appeared. He tried to convince the driver to hand over the entire stack of *Bohemia*s in the cargo hold, but the driver wouldn't consider it: the magazines belonged to the news vendors. He unloaded some for local use, but he wouldn't sell the ones for Manzanillo. Cubeñas had to wait there in the bus terminal for the newsboys to show up, and then he bought every local copy of *Bohemia*. This was enough to buy a few hours, perhaps half a day. Cubeñas warned the guide, who went uphill at a fast clip. Cubeñas pleaded ignorance when the police arrived. Nothing happened.

PEOPLE OFTEN SAY that Castro came to power on 1 January 1959, but that is wrong. He came to Santiago on 1 January 1959. Power was in Havana, eight days away. It was Che Guevara who rushed toward the capital, while Fidel stayed in his tent. He had not left Oriente with their advancing columns; only now, with the battle won elsewhere, did he do what armies always did in Cuba, which was march into Santiago. The city surrendered joyfully to the rebels, a day of ecstatic revels that fully confirmed the population's belief that they sat at the centre of world history. Castro gave his first address to the nation from the radio station on Enramada, declaring the city the 'moral capital' of Cuba.

Arturo de Jongh, Kiki's youngest brother, had the pleasure of liberating the city himself. He had joined the guerrillas just two weeks before the end of the war, part of the last-minute flood of support for Castro that made Batista fold his hand and bolt the country with a million dollars and one hundred friends. Arturo hadn't even received a weapon by the time the war ended, and woke up that last morning among a big group of other recruits. They'd bunked in El Cobre, on the far side of Santiago Bay, just outside the city proper. The guerrillas had Santiago surrounded, but the police and the army had held out successfully. Now, with dawn, there was no Batista for them to defend.

The defeated and the victorious alike lost all discipline. The worst of Batista's torturers and cronies scattered into hiding that morning, and the rebels in El Cobre made a sudden rush for the city. Arturo jumped on to an overloaded jeep that had been commandeered by a 26th of July officer, and then covered with Cuban flags and rebel banners. They sputtered toward the city with no idea what to expect. They crested the high point of the Carretera Central, which gives spectacular views over the bay and Santiago. Directly in front of them was the Rancho Club, one of Arturo's old hangouts. They rolled down, parading into the avenues amid the disbelief and cheers of surging crowds. Cuban flags had sprung out like daisies. Thousands of civilians appeared in hand-made red and black armbands, the colours of the 26th of July Movement. The officer drove around, honking the horn, looking at the city, trying to find other officers, and at one point Arturo just stepped off the jeep and went home. He had never picked up a weapon. Arturo slept in his own bed that night.

Cubeñas wasn't one of those who rushed into Santiago. He remained his withdrawn self. It wasn't for six months that he stirred, until he was finally rousted out by a letter from Celia Sánchez, the effective head of Fidel's operations. Six months in, the euphoria over, the rebels needed to staff a government, and were drawing on old friends. Even Lundy Aguilar had taken a temporary job at the institute of culture. Everyone was needed, good will was at a high, and Cubeñas went to see Calixto García, the newly appointed governor in Oriente. Cubeñas still had the letter of introduction he carried that day, written in a feminine hand on official 'Rebel Army' stationery from the 'General Command':

Havana
Dear Calixto,
The carrier of this note is Dr José Antonio Cubeñas, a great friend and comrade of ours. It serves you two, and Oriente, to know each other. Work together. Talk to him, he can help you now greatly.
Hugs,
Celia Sánchez
6/18/59

That was six months into power. They still styled themselves the Rebel Army, but Castro was living in the presidential suite of the Hilton and the task at hand was not fighting, but politics. The non-rebel army – the defeated and demoralized Batista army – had already been purged, re-educated, and put under the command of rebel officers. New governors, men loyal to Castro himself, had been appointed to run the provinces.

Discerning the future tyrant didn't require a seer, or a prophet, Cubeñas said. 'All who knew Fidel Castro knew what he was going to do. All his intimate friends knew. No one who was close to him stayed with him. He was always amoral. Not immoral, but amoral. He couldn't be loyal to anything.'

Cubeñas said he would help Calixto any way possible, and then went back to the farm, and did nothing. During the long afternoon we talked, that was one of the few times he broke his rule: he actually allowed himself to say the words 'Fidel' and 'Castro'. His wife was looking agitated again, and we had already talked for hours. Outside it was night. I left, struggling through the snow and then descending to the subway system, using an elevator because the tunnel was so deeply buried.

I returned to Washington Heights in other seasons. Cubeñas was always ready to talk, but he kept his arms tightly bound around his papers, his letters and pamphlets. He was going to publish them himself. He hinted at secrets held back, and would wave old letters in front of my face, refusing to let me read them. But he would grow tired, and leave them lying on the table as he went for water, and they would turn out to be more old letters, cryptic, secondary, dim photocopies of ordinary communications.

One he did show me, from the late 1940s, was a note from Fidel encouraging Cubeñas to come back to Havana to study for a law school exam. Cubeñas insisted that Castro was really proposing that they cheat on the test. The phrasing was ambiguous, but not to Cubeñas. 'You see?' he said. 'You see?' A cheater.

To me it was more interesting that Castro had used a sheet of stationery from the Cuban Senate. He'd probably stolen it while visiting some politician. The young Fidel was on the move in the capital, spending time in political circles, dropping in on government, helping, arranging, building, pushing and filching. All these papers were a historic trove, Cubeñas told me. He was going to publish them. Make his name, show the world, reveal secrets, and maybe even get some money. The world would see.

In Miami a year later, I ran into him while visiting with some Dolores people. He was on his own. His wife had deteriorated to the point where he could not care for her, he explained. She was in a home in Miami now, which meant he was spending much more time in Florida. It was an improvement for both of them. He was looking brighter, relieved. The friends around him appreciated the talk of the old days. Dressed up in a blue blazer, with a pin in his lapel, he managed to smile.

IT TOOK ME ALL THAT SAME YEAR to find the other José Antonio. That was José Antonio Roca, the dentist. A chain of phone calls led to an apartment complex in Bailey's Crossroads, Virginia. When I tucked the borrowed station wagon into a huge featureless parking lot on the bright morning before Christmas, I was early and sat in the car, looking up for a while. I had grown up seven miles from here. My mother still lived in the same house. For my whole life I'd been passing right by these buildings, residential towers so generic that dominated the crossroads. I'd never noticed them before. There were three nearly identical slabs of brown, and Roca lived on the twentieth floor of the

middle one. That is about as high as one can live in the
Washington area.

Bailey's Crossroads is less a suburb of Washington than a
coordinate, defined by its transport opportunities. Most people
know it by numbers: it is squeezed between 395 and 66, exactly
where 7 crosses 244, with 50 passing close by. Amid the asphalt
are retail outlets with deliberately generic names (The Chicken
Place, Total Value Shopping, City Diner) to make them seem
both everywhere and anywhere. A very American place, with
only a few traces remaining of the old Virginia, mostly in pockets
of federal red brick housing thrown up during World War Two.

Driving here I had passed a Central American neighbourhood,
then the largest mosque in the Washington area, and come finally
to the big apartment complexes like this one, which were full of
modestly successful middle-class people. Some were the rising
young apparatchiks of the Beltway-Industrial complex, who liked
easy parking. Other inhabitants were often elderly people who
had downscaled from bigger houses, looking for something well
maintained.

The three towers didn't block the hard winter wind. Architecture instead channelled the air, accelerating it. The station
wagon shook and whispered in its parking place, and I saw ice in
the storm drains. Underdressed, I struggled upwind to the sidewalk, battled my way around to various wrong entrances, and
finally found the building number Roca had given me on the
phone. In the lobby I had to collect a parking pass, then go back
to the car, leave the pass, and return through the arctic insult to
the building and elevators.

José Antonio Roca was dead centre in the 1941 photo, the
second row from the top, almost shoulder to shoulder with
Lundy Aguilar. Roca held the enormous standard of Santiago,
topped with a gilded halberd, and Lundy stood with a smaller flag
of Cuba. José Antonio Cubeñas was directly below them. Pepín
Bou was four spaces down to Roca's left, Fidel Castro one row
down and six spots over.

Alberto Casas had written 'VA/Spain' next to Roca in the
list. This modest condo was the VA. And in the summer they

went to a house they owned in Spain for a few months. And they were leaving in a few days for Miami, to be with their children for a month. As we sat down in the white living room, Roca asked to see the photo. Unlike Pepín, Lundy, or Casas, he didn't own a copy.

The survivors always mentioned Roca. He was tall, a flag-bearer, a good student, a leader, but that wasn't why they remembered him. It was because of the basketball team.

Now here he was, a retired dentist, thick around the middle, with a full head of grey hair. He wore a plaid shirt, with a Mont Blanc pen tucked in the pocket, black corduroy pants, and slippers. Roca sat in an armchair, beside a table covered with a huge crèche, a whole manger-in-Bethlehem extravaganza of miniature buildings, Wise Men, lambs and donkeys, dozens of human figures in cloaks and sandals, all of it laid out across a big stretch of burlap sack, which, Roca informed me, made it look more like the Middle East. He'd done well enough in life, and as he started to talk he had the easy manner of a man recalling a shipwreck from the vantage of a warm hearth. He bubbled over with enthusiasm showing me pictures of his six children, all but the last born in Cuba, and detailing their successful careers. He introduced his wife, Carmelina, when she came in with a tray of sharp Cuban coffee, by saying that she was far more interesting than he was. And he presented me with a copy of his self-published autobiography, bound in a lovely cream buff cover with a picture of him and Carmelina. He had called it *Recuerdos* (*Memories*). Pepín Bou had already lent me his copy, saying, 'He wrote it for his family. It's not the greatest book ever written, but it tells his story with great feeling.'

True enough. The short text, loaded with family photos, rushed through his youth, Dolores, and the time of the Revolution. Most of the book was about his good times with family and friends, either in Cuba or later in America.

In reality his arrival in the US had been tough. After landing he, like other Cubans, was told that his professional accreditation was worthless in America. Only West Virginia would give him a one-year waiver to practise. So they moved to Welch, West Virginia.

There were plenty of difficulties that year – a cold winter, a new language, and a small home they struggled to keep heated – but José Antonio drilled a lot of teeth and looking back, he couldn't contain his gratitude to the people in Welch, who 'were magnificent, they couldn't have been better'. Carmelina, dressed in a house coat and slippers, bobbed her curls in agreement. Looking for a way to requalify as a dentist, José Antonio's eyes fell on Washington DC. The city had a large Jesuit university, Georgetown, with a dental school. Through a Jesuit in West Virginia, José Antonio arranged introductions, and drove to Washington eight times that year to take necessary exams. The school then allowed him to skip directly into the second year of their dental programme. They moved to Arlington, Virginia, the next fall, and for three years José Antonio studied by day and worked at night as a waiter at Blackie's House of Beef, while Carmelina drove a school bus.

José Antonio's memoir was long on the Virginias, but short on Dolores, and I prompted him to tell the story of what Lundy Aguilar had called 'the Night', meaning the night he had scored more points than anyone. 'I scored 62 points once, a record,' he conceded, throwing up his hands. But he didn't seem to care about basketball. Not like some people. 'Fidel was a fanatic supporter of the team,' Roca recalled, 'fanatic.'

Despite his reputation as a baseball lover, basketball was Castro's favourite sport, and Fidel couldn't get enough of it. But he couldn't make the team, either. He was good, but he wasn't one of the best five players at Dolores, and warming the bench was not for Fidel. Instead, he invented a kind of fan club for the team, declaring himself president. At the last game of the season, Roca came off the floor, sweaty and exhausted, to find Castro confronting him. 'José Antonio,' he called out. 'Look how many votes I'm getting for you.' Fidel flashed a handful of tickets discarded by fans leaving the gym. You were supposed to write your pick for Most Valuable Player of the season on the back, but some people forgot, or didn't care, and Fidel had rifled through the bleachers as they emptied out, and worked the crowd as it exited. 'Fidel stood by the door, asking them for their tickets.

Some of them didn't have any opinion, and so . . .' He didn't finish the sentence. Castro turned each one over and wrote José Antonio Roca. It was in the bag.

Roca became MVP, of course. He could never understand why Fidel did it. Roca probably would have won anyway, and he didn't even care that much about the MVP. So why? Why try so hard? What did this kid need from José Antonio Roca so badly?

JOSÉ ANTONIO ROCA'S GLORY DAYS at Dolores ended abruptly when his family ran short of money. Not everyone at the Colegio de Dolores came from wealth, or even the middle class. The school actively sought out talented boys from families of modest means. 'The Jesuits,' Roca said, 'if someone had qualities, they wanted him. So there were the sons of Bacardís, of industrialists, but also of barbers, and of tailors.' His own father had worked for a department store. It wasn't just any store, but El Encanto, the best department store in Cuba, which of course had a branch in Santiago, right on Enramada. Dolores families strolled into the store to examine the latest cosmetics and clothing from the capital and abroad, as well as to be seen seeing them.

But José Antonio's father wasn't walking in the front door, he was using the back. He was El Encanto's *cobrador*, a collection agent. He was paid a commission to walk around the city all day, visiting the store's clientele, and collecting their small payments against an instalment plan. The year after José Antonio posed in the Dolores photograph holding the flag, El Encanto introduced a pay-by-mail scheme, and the instalment system, and with it the family's finances, collapsed. The family could no longer afford Dolores but was too proud to accept when the Jesuits offered to waive their fees for José Antonio's senior year. At the age of 17 he abruptly dropped out of school, moved to Las Tunas, six hours from Santiago, and tried his hand at peddling life insurance to strangers. He made almost no money, and finally suffered an emotional realization while meeting with his boss: the man's shoes were worn out, his jacket ratty. Suddenly high school looked better than the insurance business.

Back in Santiago after 12 months, with his family finances starting to recover, he enrolled in the fourth and fifth years of high school simultaneously. He attended one of the city's public high schools as a fourth-year student, but took a job at Dolores coaching his old basketball team, and the Jesuits allowed him to attend fifth-year classes. By doubling up, he was able to graduate with a Dolores diploma alongside his original classmates. José Antonio continued rushing toward middle-class stability, racing through dental school in a year less than normal, and setting up a practice in Santiago by the age of 24. Soon he was president of the association for Santiago dentists, and then also of the association of Dolores alumni. His memoir was thick with tales of the good times had at the Ciudamar Yacht Club in Santiago, where he played dominoes with friends and appeared at formal events, presenting or receiving awards in a white suit, in a room full of white suits.

The Moncada attack of 1953 interrupted the good times. Roca had been woken up at dawn by the sound of gunfire, as surprised as everyone else in Cuba. Even Castro's old friends had no idea of the mission. Fidel had been in touch, writing letters about how they would play basketball together some day, but he didn't want anyone that he already knew involved in the attack, José Antonio suggested.

'He didn't want anybody from Dolores. He was afraid we wouldn't follow him. All the boys he looked for when preparing his coup were much younger, of little preparation, of very little culture.' By culture he meant personal character, or backbone.

The only Dolores boy in the attack (aside from Fidel and Raúl) was the almost beardless Renato Guitart, the 22-year-old commemorated on the walls of the small museum at Dolores today where he was depicted as the 'right-hand' of Fidel, a key player in the attack, although no specifics were offered. Renato never met Castro at Dolores, and never shared a meal or a fist fight with him. He was Carmelina's distant cousin.

'He was very impressionable,' she said, a romantic young man who was carried off by the idea of making history. He was a 'follower', she said, 'not a boy who could act as an equal to Fidel.'

The subsequent 1956 attack was less of a surprise. Castro was in Mexico with a big group of anti-Batista men, preparing to overthrow the government. This was no secret: Fidel had announced to journalists that he was about to invade the island. The government knew he was coming, and so did a wide network of supporters. On 27 November 1956, using a fake name, Castro sent a telegram to Santiago which read, in its entirety: OBRA PEDIDA AGOTADA. The three words themselves were meaningless. Three words was a code meaning three days. It was the signal for sympathizers in Santiago to rise up in three days, with another Moncada-style assault in the city centre. This time the *subterráneo* network was well prepared, and they didn't attempt to topple Batista, only to distract the security forces while Castro landed several battalions of men far to the west on the morning of 30 November.

The invasion was a success, of course, but as successes go, this one was highly Cuban. Castro's boat, the *Granma*, turned out to hold only 80 men, and more than half the troops were left behind in Mexico. Slowed by a storm, they fell behind schedule. Taking on water, they had to throw away some of their heavy weapons and ammunition.

On 30 November, Roca was woken up before dawn by the sound of gunfire. ('Once again,' as he put it.) The Santiago underground staged its big effort, and rebels, led by men like Jorge Sotus, shot up several police posts around town, and even fired a few mortar rounds into the Moncada. But the distraction they created was wasted, and so were the lives of the men who fell. Castro was still roaming the ocean, and the attack was crushed. It only served to alert the army to watch for Castro. Two days behind schedule, the *Granma* ground ashore in a swamp, lost. The men were soon spotted by airplanes. Castro lost most of his force in the first two days. Only a mythological dozen guerrillas survived to actually reach their rendezvous point in the Sierra Maestra.

Roca was 34 then, a dentist, fully engaged in civic life, a regular visitor at the American naval base. No rebel, in other words. But he discovered that several men he knew, at least by name, were participants in the uprising in Santiago. The survivors of that failed attack were now scattered in the city, hunted. It was just like 1953 all over again, and everyone knew how the police and the army had hunted down and murdered the rebels that time. But what could a dentist do? The next night he found out. As Roca was smoking his nightly cigar, a friend stopped by and mentioned a curious thing. He'd heard that a certain someone was reported to be hiding in a certain garden in the back of a certain house. Nobody knew who this person was, really. But it was obvious what he had done, because the police and the army were looking for him. Somebody had to go get him. The 'somebody', Roca learned, was him.

He didn't have to go alone, they would do it together. In fact, they had to go together. Roca's friend revealed that he had been given a special recognition signal, a few notes to whistle so that the fugitive would recognize that these strangers could be trusted. And here was the problem. Roca's friend couldn't whistle.

They drove over to the address, and then stood in the street, nervous and obvious, unsure what to do. They peered into the dark area beside the house, still blinded by their own headlights, unable to see. Roca tried to whistle the notes, but his mouth was dry. He tried again, but it was pathetic. This wasn't his line of work.

The man came out anyway. Everything was very businesslike. He got in back of the car, gave them an address, and the three of them drove through a Santiago teeming with nervous police officers and army troops. They did not talk. The address was a building right in the city centre. They climbed up to a second-floor apartment, together for appearances' sake, and then the man closed the blinds and told them to leave.

The underground gradually recovered from the failed uprising. Castro and his motley band were established in the mountains, and opened communication with the city. By December of 1956 Castro was directing his first attacks, and recruits from Santiago were starting to filter up into the hills near the farm of the other José Antonio, Cubeñas.

Roca tried to stay out of it. He knew people who sympathized. He remembered his old Dolores classmates. But after that first night, he thought he could still stay out of it. He had just helped one person, that was all. He went home and lit a new cigar. His hand trembled as he held the match.

UNFORTUNATELY FOR ROCA'S PLAN, the People's Revolution needed a friend with a car. He had succeeded in staying out of things for a while, but during 1957, as the guerrilla group in the mountains spread out, sparring with the Cuban army, the urban underground began to braid itself through Santiago. Roca was one of many people who made small financial donations to the movement, even as his career was blossoming, and he regularly filled his dental chair with some of the top people in Santiago. By early 1958, the urban underground was both far larger and far riskier than Fidel's guerrilla group in the mountains. Even at its very largest peak, the guerrilla force never held more than 800 or 900 full-time fighters in the Sierra. But now thousands of Cubans were joining clandestine militias in the towns and cities of Cuba. In the Sierra, Fidel had a chef, a mistress and bodyguards, and the incompetent and demoralized government troops never once succeeded in dislodging him from his principal strongholds. After the first few skirmishes, Castro himself didn't even participate directly in the fighting, preferring to take symbolic potshots at retreating soldiers in the distance, using a sniper's rifle with a telescopic sight.

By contrast the covert war in the cities was brutal, and its leaders highly vulnerable. Good men began to disappear. Batista became serious about the war, in his fashion. He replaced the honest army chief for all of Oriente with a corrupt man who demanded kickbacks from legitimate businesses, and who soon controlled all the illegal ones, from smuggling to whorehouses, and even the numbers game in the poor streets of Santiago. This money was then used to buy loyalty, and pay thousands of informers to rat out the urban rebels. The official branch of SIM, the military intelligence men, was expanded, staffed with killers, and complemented with civilians who could do the very dirtiest work. Batista brought in a notorious gangster-politician named Rolando Masferrer – an old rival of Castro's from Havana days – to head a kind of death squad that roamed around different parts of Oriente at night, killing anyone suspected of ties to the rebel movement.

Newspapers were afraid to report the assassinations, but so many corpses were turning up on the outskirts of Santiago, often showing signs of torture, with mutilated faces and tied hands, that the papers began to use a euphemism, describing the victims as Vertillon 166, an autopsy code which was understood to mean 'assassinated'.

In Santiago itself, the *subterráneo* leaned heavily on its wealthy and powerful supporters, both for money and for the crucial safe houses. Roca started with money. Aside from his own contributions, he volunteered in 1958 to be a sort of *cobrador* for the rebels, collecting donations from ten of his own friends and contacts, and then turning the money over. The dental practice was perfect cover, because anyone could make an appointment, come in, and have privacy to sit in the chair and hand over money, take money, give names, or leave a message for another one of these fake clients. Then Roca would clean their teeth just so it looked like something had been done. But the money grew, exponentially. At the start of 1958 it was just the donations of his ten friends. But he was soon entrusted with the donation of other circles of friends, too. Now he was regularly carrying bags of cash for the rebels.

By spring he was dealing directly with Celia Sánchez, Fidel's most trusted assistant. He became a kind of local treasurer for the guerrillas, bringing Sánchez $10,000 at a time. Then in quick succession, the two men above him in the finance system were killed. Roca was promoted by default and supervising a dozen clandestine fundraisers and shaking down prominent industrialists (many of them, like the Bacardís, friends from Dolores). As the amounts of money grew larger, the rebels had to issue receipts. These came in the form of bonds, in denominations of 1, 10 and 100 pesos. Roca wasn't even an official member of the 26th of July Movement (although 'Practically speaking, I was') but he held the engraved lead stamps that the movement used to print the bonds – essentially, the guerrilla mint. If he were caught with them it would be impossible to survive.

But he was more than a bag man. People smuggling was a regular business. He moved Lester Rodréguez, the number two leader of the urban underground, to a safe house, and then to a boat. And in July, he moved Frank País, the number one leader, from house to house in Santiago on several occasions. José Antonio knew places to put people. Someone from the dentists' association had a disused summer house on Cayo Smith. A friend from Dolores had an uncle who was a rabid *Fidelista*, with a small farm he could lend out. Week after week that summer, he roamed around the city picking up men.

If one safe house was 'burned', meaning exposed to suspicion in some way, then he would swoop in with the car and evacuate somebody. Usually the passenger sat in the back, with a gun concealed beneath a newspaper, in case they were stopped by the police. Carmelina began to accompany José on the drives and was particularly cool. One morning they had two men with submachine guns in the back of the car when José Antonio turned a corner and was abruptly stopped by police. Carmelina leaned out, flashed a big smile, and explained they were taking some patients to the dental office for an emergency. The police waved them along. The *subterráneo* had moved more than a hundred men so far, mostly passing them into the Sierra, but sometimes helping them out of it, either back to Santiago, or to other parts of Cuba, or even to the US.

In July, Roca once again moved Frank País, taking him from one safe house in Vista Alegre to another in the city centre. País had changed identities, taking the code name David, and had to change locations too, because the police, backed by intelligence agents from SIM and their criminal allies in the Masferrer gang, were searching whole districts of the city now, house by house. Roca dropped off 'David' in Santiago's downtown, and went home. With experience he had grown calmer.

A couple of days later Roca was working on a patient when he was interrupted, and told there was an urgent call. The receptionist said it was someone named David, so he thought it might be País, in an emergency. But it was another David: David de Jongh, the eldest of the three brothers. They'd known each other at Dolores, and David was a doctor now. This David knew that Roca was in the underground, and had called because he had just heard a burst of gunfire. Something was happening. De Jongh could see out the window that police were moving around.

Roca realized that de Jongh's office was near to the house where he had left País. That house had been used by numerous people in the movement before. Although it was well hidden, tucked behind another house, it was stocked with obvious giveaways, like 50 pairs of boots and a collection of Coleman stoves. The neighbours had recently seen a man shuttling two dozen rifles from the house to a car, the guns badly concealed under a single sheet of newspaper. Frank País was doomed to become the hero everyone wanted.

Deeply religious, idealistic and democratic-minded, the alternate Fidel, País had spent his final days reorganizing the rebel forces, putting the clandestine militias on an equal footing with the guerrilla fighters in the hills. The militias were more and more active all over Cuba; they had sacrificed as much as the rural guerrillas. But the rise to equality of this *llano* (plains, or lowlands) was an implicit challenge to the *sierra* (mountains). Fidel had staked the Revolution to the idea of a heroic guerrilla in camouflage climbing through the forests. A conflict between these two views was inevitable, and in one of his last acts, Frank País warned that the rebel movement as a whole had to avoid sliding into gangsterism, the war of personalities and rival leaders.

Amid all this drafting of memos, dispatching of letters, discussions of plans, and bullets-and-beans logistics, conducted in the safe house, Frank proposed marriage to his sweetheart, a member of the movement named América. (For a honeymoon, he proposed hiking into the mountains to see Castro.)

País knew his time was running out. He had already escaped out the back door of a safe house as the police came in the front, and his brother had been killed. On 30 July police and SIM agents began registering houses on a cross street near the hideout. Frank dawdled a few critical minutes, sending others to safety but neglecting to put on the priest's robes that he carried for exactly this purpose. The first two men to leave the house climbed into a car, and then calmly asked permission from the police to drive the wrong way down the street, against traffic, to reach the corner. This theatre of misdirection worked and they were sent on their way. But when Frank stepped outside and got in a car, a SIM officer said, loudly, 'Colonel, do you know who that is? It's Frank País.' They dragged him between two houses, beat him, and then shot him dead with a sub-machine gun. Afterwards, the officer in charge made all the SIM men fire a shot into the corpse. That way, everyone was equally guilty. This was the cascade of shots that David de Jongh had heard.

WITH PAÍS DEAD, the conflict between the *llano* and the *sierra* was over. Frank's successor, code named Daniel, tried to preserve the independence of the underground, and told José Antonio (who was his dentist) of a private fear that Castro might actually be a Communist. But Roca, like most people, 'never suspected' such a thing, and dismissed Daniel's worries. And soon Daniel was killed. Castro then reorganized the militias and insisted, stridently, vehemently, repeatedly, that they surrender all their weapons, delivering them to the *sierra* for distribution to his guerrilla troops. The urban network was being weakened from both sides. Roca tried to lie low for a while, but too many people knew who his friends were.

Early one morning in November an American appeared at the clinic. He was particularly huge, sweaty and improbable. He arrived at Roca's office claiming, in crude Spanish, that he had a toothache that needed emergency treatment, and wouldn't take no for an answer. After nearly forcing his way into the dental chair, he looked around conspiratorially, and then took off one of his shoes. Inside it was a letter. It was an introduction from a mutual acquaintance, asking for help sending the American up to the mountains, to join Fidel. The shoe trick was strange. That wasn't how the rebels did things. And although Roca knew the 'mutual acquaintance', he didn't know him well, and had never seen his handwriting. How could he tell if it was real? And this guy, this huge, sweating, clueless monstrosity from abroad, was going to become a guerrilla, running around in the mountains? Roca stalled, pretending not to know what it was all about. The mutual friend was mistaken. The American must have been looking for a different dentist. The Sierra Maestra? He didn't know anything about the rebels, or the mountains. After a few awkward minutes, the American left.

Roca went right to a phone and called a neighbour named Basilio, an American who worked at the US consulate. José Antonio knew that his name wasn't really Basilio, and that the American was actually the CIA man in the city. He asked Basilio if he knew of some big, crazy American who was in Santiago, looking for the guerrillas. Basilio checked, and someone at the consulate had in fact heard about an American in town, talking too loudly about joining the movement. He'd apparently been talking loudly in Miami too. Basilio called back to suggest that Roca be very careful, but it was November of 1958 now, and the season of amateurs was over. They were still on the phone, discussing what to do, when SIM agents rushed the door of the clinic and arrested José Antonio. He noticed that they blindfolded him with a handkerchief when they took him out. That was a very bad sign.

IT WAS ONLY MIDMORNING, but instead of a short drive to a police station, there was a long drive, up, out of town, many turns, and then a long ride, ending with a very slow drive on dirt. When Roca, blind but attuned to other senses, felt the asphalt give way to dirt, he grew even more afraid. The car stopped, somewhere. They took him out of the car and put him on his knees in a sugar cane field. He heard voices in the distance, and then a couple of shots. The longest minutes of his life passed by. This was going to be a Vertillon 166 in the papers. The sugar cane smelled incredibly strong. Then cold metal pressed against the back of his head. They didn't beat him, or torture him. They didn't touch him. They just put the gun barrel where he could feel it, and then someone spoke in the tone of a man with nothing to lose. If Roca didn't immediately name all his contacts in the

26th of July Movement, they would kill him right now. A bullet through the head. He wouldn't. They pulled the trigger. Click. The gun wasn't loaded. Just the click of the hammer falling on an empty chamber.

He was taken back into the city. Still blindfolded, Roca listened to the sounds of the car, felts its turns and speeds, recognizing the descent into the centre of Santiago. There was a sudden turn off a fast street, and then he was out. The voices were now those of sentries, and of command. This had to be Moncada, the main barracks. They took off the blindfold. Although the facade of the building had been spattered with bullet holes during the 1953 attack, the holes had already been filled in and painted over. It wasn't very well done: you could still see where some of the shots had struck. A cosmetic gesture for a hollow regime.

Roca was in a different situation now. He was led inside, processed by police officers, and then interrogated by men who seemed to have learned their technique from a Hollywood film. They shone bright lights in his eyes, hiding themselves from view while asking the same questions again and again. He gave no answers, or diverted them with stories of his innocence, his loyalty and his quiet life as the dentist to various people they might have heard of. He did not know what they were talking about. The Sierra? Fidel Castro? Sure, they'd been at Dolores together, but that was it. He wasn't involved in the underground. The questioners did not touch him, not even once, and gave up after a couple of hours. They locked José Antonio in a room with another prisoner. A woman. They didn't know each other, but she was some kind of rebel supporter who had been picked up. They were kept under observation, and ordered not to move from their chairs, and not to speak to each other, or even look at each other. Roca sat, motionless, perfectly silent, recalling the smell of the sugar cane. Maybe 11 hours went by like that. Just sitting. No questions. No beatings. No food or water. No bathroom trips. No sound. Not even movement. He never spoke to the woman, or learned who she was. Power was restraining itself or being restrained.

AS SOON AS CARMELINA heard the news she called everyone she knew, which was a lot of people. She came from a large
and prestigious clan herself, and knew her husband's social
contacts as well. Carmelina told everyone the same thing: her
husband was in the hands of SIM.

The revolution against Batista was largely a phenomenon of
class. Their class: the middle class, the professionals and techno-
crats, the engineers and lawyers. People like Fidel Castro. It was a
revolution of lawyers, and of dentists. These were the people in
Cuba who could literally afford to rebel, to risk things in pursuit
of the better instincts of Cuban nationalism and democracy.

Kiki de Jongh had insisted that Frank País and the poor boys
around him were more important than any group of Dolores
alumni, but the poor were the disposable ones, the ones who did
the dying, and the killing. Many of Che Guevara's best soldiers
were street urchins, barely into their teens. The most famous
assassin in the 26th of July Movement was a 14-year-old boy from
the slums of Havana. But the Revolution was made overwhelmingly by people from the big middle of Cuban society. The
Revolution was made for the proletariat, not by it. Until 1961,
when it became unfashionable, the Revolution itself had conceded this point. Castro called himself 'a son of the oppressor
class', and his followers bragged that socialist Revolution had
occurred in Cuba, before anywhere else in Latin America, not
because Cuba was poor or backward, but because it was more
advanced, with a larger, stronger middle class, better educated
professionals, a complete bourgeoisie ready to throw off Batista.

Lundy Aguilar had argued in one of his books that people at the
bottom of Cuban society – blacks in particular – had been
disinclined to support Castro because they feared all revolutions
equally, and repressions fell on them first and heaviest. The poor
filled Castro's ranks, the rich filled his coffers, but it was the
middle, rejecting the cruelty of Batista, which made revolution
possible.

They tried politics, new constitutions, civil resistance and
general strikes. When they saw, in 1958, that nothing peaceful
could stop Batista, that torture and assassination were now going

to be the rule, even for dentists, they threw their support to Castro. It didn't hurt Roca's case that he also knew the mayor, and the archbishop of Santiago.

After Carmelina raised an alarm, both of those men called Moncada to insist that José be freed. Within hours the newspapers also heard what was happening, and made inquiries. At what must have been nearly midnight, the army commander at Moncada suddenly appeared in Roca's room. They had met before, in other circumstances (he was 'a good man', according to José Antonio).

'Dentist,' the officer said, 'don't be afraid. The whole city is up, clamouring for your freedom.' After the commander left, another officer came in. It was Lieutenant Heredia, a notorious enforcer. He was said to have killed a long list of men in the underground. Killed them personally. 'Doctor,' Heredia told him, 'you have many friends. But you are lying to us. You have the face of a shiteater. We know who you know. Some day we will catch you.' And then Heredia set him free.

He walked out, called Carmelina, and went home. Which is how it worked in Batista's Cuba. The old Cuba, where flags rippled at sunset against blue seas and palm trees. A poor boy would be found stiff and cold in the sugar cane fields the morning after his arrest and listed as Vertillon 166. A boy from Dolores would go home, with a warning, and sit in his usual chair, and smoke a *puro*.

Roca was done. He ended his fundraising, told Celia Sánchez that he was resigning as treasurer, and surrendered the lead seals for the guerrilla bonds to another supporter. Fidel himself sent down word that Roca should flee into the mountains, and become the dentist to his troops, but that wasn't the point for Roca. José Antonio wanted to get out, not go deeper in. He had never intended to do anything more than whistle once, in the dark, or maybe give some money. 'I had a mortgage, and my family,' he said. 'I wasn't like Fidel or Che Guevara, who renounced everything. I always loved my family.' He made sure that everyone in Santiago knew that he had quit the movement, completely. Before it was too late, he would become a dentist again.

But it was later than that. The Masferrer death squads didn't care who he knew, or whether he had resigned from the rebel movement. As José Antonio was sitting at home one night with Carmelina, they heard the roar of a car engine in the street. Just as they looked up, whoever was driving past unleashed a volley of shots from a sub-machine gun. Like a lot of Santiago houses, theirs was made of very thin wood, with louvres everywhere. The bullets punched holes through the louvres in front, passed through the interior walls of the house, and then exited out the back. Neither they nor their kids were hurt. And then a few weeks later it happened again. A slower car. A more carefully aimed, sustained burst of gunfire into the house. They were sleeping this time, and once again the bullets passed over them, through the house, without striking anyone. The bullets just flew off into the night.

WHEN IT WAS TIME TO LEAVE for my mother's house again, I told Roca that I'd been in El Encanto, his father's store. Enramada wasn't much of a place to be seen any more. The Foto Mexicana studio was gone; El Ten Cent was shabby and shuttered. But El Encanto was still open, sort of. It was a state store, but there was almost nothing to sell. The marble floor was still lovely, and the old glass showcases were there, empty but for a museum-like display of Warsaw Pact engineering books. The whole sales floor was dark and cool. The only real business in the place came from a few standup racks right by the front door, where they sold notepaper and cheap pens.

'I haven't been back since the day I left,' Roca said, his big hands – basketball-sized hands, too big for a dentist – resting flat on the armrests of his chair. 'I always thought I would go back when Fidel was out, but I don't believe it now. And anyway, his brother Raúl is strong.' He meant Raúl was tough, as iron-hard as Fidel. Roca illustrated this by making a muscle with his bicep, pounding on it with the other hand, but the blow wasn't a hard one, like Alberto Casas would have done. It was just a symbolic tap on the sleeve of his cardigan.

The view out the window behind him was strange and

captivating to me. We towered over the asphalt crossroads of shopping malls and highways. It was the first time in my life I had seen the geostrategic sprawl of the city from above. Behind and around us was the suburban belt of government, that began near the CIA in Langley and ran in, toward the Pentagon. Straight out ahead was Arlington, the Potomac, and then Washington. The highways all around us fed bridges – Chain, Key, Memorial, Fourteenth Street, then the railroad trestles – that served the federal city. Then there was the great oblong Mall, lined by the State Department and the monuments of this new Rome, all in their rows.

The last thing Roca told me was that he had run into Basilio once. The CIA man from the consulate. He was a legend among people in the Santiago underground, because he'd helped get visas for some of them, saving their lives. Basilio had been seen in Panama, and was rumoured to have been involved in bringing down Manuel Noriega there. And then about a decade ago, Roca had gone to a party, a random evening in Washington where the accidental round of drinks, dinners and picnics always meant running into government types. The party was at a private house, and José Antonio immediately recognized Basilio, standing in the kitchen. He hadn't set eyes on the CIA man in decades. Roca reintroduced himself, reminding Basilio how they had met. The man looked at him with no expression at all. Standing in the kitchen, he said his name wasn't Basilio. They hadn't met before. It was a mistake. Then he left the party.

8

KEY BISCAYNE

WHEN I FLEW OUT of Havana the last time I carried four
envelopes. Jorge Segura had given me two of them. One was
for his brother, Carlos Segura, who lived in South Florida. Jorge
had wanted me to stamp and mail it inside the US, so that it
would arrive quickly, and he wanted me to follow it up with a
call as well. I was supposed to put the touch on the brother.
The goal was to make Jorge sound needy, but not too needy, so
that the brother would support him, but not think Jorge was
lying.

The second letter was to Pedro Haber, the reunion organizer in
Miami, and described an annual meeting for Dolorínos in
Santiago, an alumni group that Jorge called the Family of Dolores:

Santiago de Cuba

Pedro Haber
Florida, USA

Dear Brother Pedro:

I'm taking advantage of a friend who is traveling to the
USA to send you these lines. I hope you have received my
letter of December 20. I inform you of the following
activities:

A mass the previous Sunday the 5th, in the church of the
Sacred Family of Vista Alegre, officiated by our spiritual
leader RP Jorge Contelles SJ; We commemorated the second
return of the Company of Jesus to Cuba, 1854, and the Saint
Mary Mother of God. A good quantity of Dolorinos attended, 16, the Dead were remembered (7), and then a few

words from P. Contelles, with 40 for very modest refreshments and drinks.

I am putting together a calendar of the activities of the [new] year, I will send you a copy. We will probably celebrate on the first of June an activity to commemorate the fifth anniversary of the creation of the Family of Dolores. In reality it was May 31, but as that fell on a Saturday we opted to celebrate it on Sunday. I will send you the program.

Once again I insist that you send us a copy of the alumni magazine, receiving it would bring us a huge spiritual delight.

If you have a chance to send a ribbon for a typewriter, I would thank you.

My affections to all the brothers from Dolores, I always include them in my prayers.

We are brothers in Christ,

Hugs,

CP Jorge R. Segura

Everybody had a title in Cuban letters. Dear Brother. P for Padre. Or RP and SJ, the Reverend Padre, Society of Jesus. Even Jorge was 'CP Jorge,' or a Certified Public Accountant.

The third letter was given to me by a man in a Havana street. Having known me for two minutes, he asked me to wait, and then went inside and dashed off a paragraph to his uncle in 'Oonion City' New Jersey. He left the envelope open, just as Jorge did, on the theory that it was best to show you had nothing to hide.

In theory, there is normal service for letters between Cuba and the US but letters mailed from the island to America can take six weeks, or six days, or four months, and some just disappeared. Mail heading the other way, into Cuba, is even less likely to arrive. In Virginia, José Antonio Roca had talked about mailing four letters to Segura in Santiago, none of which had arrived. He blamed Segura's 'situation with the government', but it seems unlikely that the MinInt agents are combing the mail of an elderly accountant whose greatest concern is an annual high school reunion. Thievery could account for some

of the letters disappearing, since Cuban postal workers cut open
many envelopes from abroad, looking for money. But there is
also the mere ineptness of Cuban government services. I once
sent a letter, wrapped around a $20 note, to a friend in Havana.
Six months later the envelope was returned, unopened, with a
notation in perfect cursive: *Returned due to death of addressee.*
Two years later the dead man wrote me from the same address,
asking why I never sent him $20 bills any more. So hand
delivery is best, especially for the larger envelope which contained Kiki de Jongh's sketch addressed to Pepín. I called the
(305) phone number on the envelope, for South Florida, to try
the brother. 'He hardly ever gives me any help,' Jorge had told
me. 'Just a pair of pants one time, and $100 many years ago.
Call and tell him how difficult things are for me. Make it sound
bad, but not too bad.'

I called the brother, Carlos. He spoke fine English, but was
gruff. He himself had graduated from Dolores in 'I think it was
'42, or '43', but he hadn't seen the photograph of all of them
together, and didn't care to. Despite overlapping with the Castro
brothers, he said he hadn't known them, 'and I don't think I
missed anything there'.

I tried to begin the your-brother-is-bad-but-not-too-bad
speech, but he cut me off. 'Nothing about those people interests
me,' he said. 'I left Cuba 33 years ago. I got a hard time leaving
the island, whoo. Like the Yews say, never again.'

He paused, as if remembering something. 'I don't want anything to do with those people,' he finally said.

'So thank you,' he said. And then hung up.

I put a stamp on Jorge's letter and sent it to him anyway.

PEPÍN BOU LAUGHED, and smiled and shook his head, when
I handed him the envelope from Kiki de Jongh and he saw what
slid out. A colourful little sketch of a house that never would be.
The house the Bou family would have lived in now. It was like a
postcard from some alternate reality.

'A lot of time gone by,' Pepín said, holding the sketch and
smiling. 'A lot of time gone by.'

He didn't need the sketch to remember the plan for the house. He leaned back and described it, waving over his wife. 'That was for a beautiful spot outside the city, with a tremendous view over the bay,' he said, handing her the sketch. 'Oh, that was a beautiful spot. It was going to be the family house. But it was 1958, and it was never built.'

Pepín had moved many times in his life. Just now he had moved, for what he hoped was the last time. He'd given up the house with the swimming pool for a condo in a tower, near where the crabgrass touched the ocean. It was just a mile away from the old home, still on the familiar Key Biscayne. Instead of no view and some crossed palms, he had a wide sweep of glass looking out to sea in two directions. The lobby of the building was a concoction of white gilding, buffed brass rails, glass and dappled marble, but their new apartment was soothing, with white sofas, wall-to-wall carpeting, and pictures and photographs in gold frames around the walls. It was more manageable than a house.

A sea breeze rattled the windows. It was a hazy day, and the winds were shifting around, unsure. One moment they were battering the windows on the east, then they were striking the south. Then they fell silent. The barometer was changing, one weather system giving way to another.

It wasn't the quietest time of the year, but someone tries to leave Cuba in a boat almost every day of the year, regardless of conditions, and today was no exception. It was a Saturday, and tonight, near midnight, a group of six people would slip off a beach in Cuba, in a small boat with a worn outboard, trusting themselves to the pilot and the gods. Possibly a storm was coming, but they didn't wait. The US Coast Guard intercepted about 1,500 Cubans a year at sea, so a bit of foul weather could help their small boat hide. If you had a telescope, you might see them coming over the horizon from up here.

We looked over the house sketch. It was 'very moderniste, very 1950s Cuban', Bou said. The house looked very American to me, but that was part of the point. It had been a time of intense connection between the two countries. With his wife standing behind him, pressing down on his shoulders, Pepín recalled all the tourists in Santiago then. The whole world was flooding into Cuba, bringing money and something intangible.

'To think in 1960 they had the ASTA convention, or whatever you call it, the association of all the travel agents, in Havana. Fidel boycotted it. He said he didn't want tourism. He didn't want prostitution either, but now everyone is a prostitute. He didn't want tourism. Now everyone is a tourist. He didn't want arms. *Armas¿ para qué?* That was his favourite speech. Why would we need arms? Everybody was brothers. Now they are armed to the teeth.

'All the world has its history,' he said, without further explanation.

He inquired about Kiki. They hadn't seen each other since 1958, and Pepín wasn't expecting that to change. When we had started all this, two years before, he told me that no Dolorinos remained in Cuba. Then he'd admitted that there had to be some. Finally he'd concluded that 'even if I did know someone who was still there, I wouldn't know him.' That's how he felt about Kiki.

'I thank him for the drawing,' Pepín said. 'But I don't want to talk to him. That's bullshit. I respect him, but I don't agree with him.'

I'd known for a while that Lundy and Vera were going to sell their house. Now Pepín mentioned that they had already bought a condo right here, in the same building. Two floors down.

High school all over again. A permanent reunion. They'd started out as kids in the same city and same building. Now they would end that way. The old remade, again, in foreign climes.

KENDAL IS A NEIGHBOURHOOD that would only be considered a neighbourhood in Miami. It lies south of Little Havana and its Cuban kitsch, west of Coral Gables, with its absurd bridal shops and *quinceañera* extravaganzas, and had none of the exclusion of Key Biscayne out in the ocean. Kendal was the flat, fecund stretch of green and asphalt that you passed as you shot south out of the city, on an elevated expressway, peering down from Rt. 826 at 90 miles an hour. It was cut into pieces by 826, and the South Dixie Highway, and crosscut by 878, and divided by drainage canals, a railroad, and unexpected wild corners. Cement and stoplights in one direction, verdant saw grass and vines in another. The telephone lines and the stop signs were in the grip of creepers, and all the streets the same, so that reaching David de Jongh meant telling 85th Street from 85th Place, which were both found off 85th Avenue. I drove around a cul-de-sac of modest ranches, and stopped the car. There was a spatter of rain, and I was early, so I sat and waited. The house had nice ornamentation – cut glass lanterns in front, a heavy knocker, bits of brass, spur stones, the usual Cuban love of too much.

Up north when you read about Miami it was all about alligators stealing the family dog out of the back yard, or picnics that were interrupted by indian pythons that had slithered off cargo ships, or five-foot-long monitor lizards that were released into the canals by panicked pet-owners. Miami was where old men went out for their daily swim and were yanked under by bull sharks. It was a tropical freak show of crooked politicians, fraudulent elections, and lowbrow dingbats running pyramid schemes and self-improvement rackets. You could get the antenna and mirrors ripped off your rental car by gangs of macaques. Everyone was here to party except the immigrants, the Haitians and Cubans.

Out on the ocean now, a full day into their journey, some-where deep in the Caribbean, the six would-be immigrants from Cuba were in the grip of the Gulf Stream, the dark blue conveyor belt water. Even the best boat could be swamped here. The rain from the straits was brief and intermittent, but it looked to be coming in hard.

Of the de Jongh brothers, only the youngest had stayed behind. This was the house of David, the eldest. It was the kind of paradise that looks like hell to some people: they were surrounded by roaring freeways and swamps full of invaders, but the block was quiet, handsome and clean, the house trim, the paint good. It was all good enough. You would never need to leave.

David's wife Elena let me inside, and had me wait alone at a glass table, under a glass roof, on the glassed-in porch. On the way through the house I'd only had time to glimpse the shelves, the end tables and the mantelpiece, all crowded with art, with collectibles, figurines, books, knickkacks, souvenirs. Everything bright, accumulated, a feast for the eye. After a few minutes David came out to the porch, tall, grave, slow-moving, his hands and scalp dotted with liver spots. Despite recent surgery, he moved with a kind of physical authority. He didn't bother to shake my hand or say much. He just sat down at the table and said, 'Yes?'

I showed him the photo. He tried to act unimpressed, but after a minute he was fingering it, hungry. He ran his eyes over it. 'Echevaria!' he said, stopping abruptly over a face. He whistled, twice. Elena appeared. 'Guess who that is,' he said, and grew frustrated when she didn't have an answer. 'Echevaria,' he said. 'It's Echevaria!' She wasn't as excited. He looked cross. I noted that whenever he wanted something – a glass of water, a coffee, or help remembering a name – he whistled like that.

I flipped over the picture, ran through Alberto Casas' list of names and pointed out himself and his brothers in different rows.

Elena sat down at the table now. Like all the wives of the boys from Dolores that I had met, she seemed ten or 15 years younger than her husband, although they were both 79. Her hair was a perfect copper suspension, hairspray and willpower. David, by contrast, had missed a big spot while shaving his throat. A fringe of thin white hair surrounded the pate. He was similar to Kiki in many ways: the same compact head and thin lips, the very precise manner of speaking.

Elena visited Dolores, and remembered the people in the boyish faces. She herself was from one of the oldest families in Santiago, she said: the Portuondos. She led me into the living room, to where the Portuondo arms and crest were displayed on a wood plaque. Many of the paintings on the walls were her own work. These were consistently good oil landscapes of Cuba. Not any Cuba that had or did exist, but an elemental Cuba, an island of resonances. She showed me one of Santiago Bay, the blue water dotted with sailboats.

'It was wonderful,' she said. 'A paradise. Every summer day was wonderful. People went for three-month vacations. Almost everybody had a boat, a small boat to go around in the bay at five o'clock in the afternoon, just calling out, Hi, hello, how are you.' She stood in the living room, waving graciously at those other boaters, floating in the golden sunshine. Paradise was just childhood, in the end.

Back on the porch I punctured the atmosphere by asking about Kiki's recent visit. After I'd interviewed him in Havana, Kiki had made his first visit to America. It was always a monumental thing for a family to be reunited across the Straits, and the brothers hadn't seen each other in decades. But the visit hadn't been terrific. Kiki hadn't even told his brothers he was coming. They only found out from Radio Bemba, when a friend of a friend mentioned that Kiki's wife was coming to see family in America. When they found out Kiki was coming too, they still didn't communicate, and nobody arranged anything. Only at the last minute, when Kiki was about to leave for the airport, did the three brothers come together at this house. After embracing they sat down and avoided discussing anything even remotely contentious.

'We didn't talk about Cuba,' David said. 'Or the house. Nothing.'

'Just family,' Elena added, grimly. 'How is your brother-in-law, and so on.'

No discussion of 'the house', that most symbolic of all exile obsessions, with its promise of restoration and return. No mention of Him, Cyclops, the Horse. Their old friend. No talk of ration books, nor of dubious elections. After an hour, Kiki went back to Havana, willingly. To the very thing that David abhorred.

How could David explain that?

'I don't know,' he replied. 'There is a saying in Spanish, *al pan, pan, y al vino, vino*. Wine is wine, bread is bread. I would say to him, to me, you are a mystery.' The mystery was how Kiki could still believe. Cuba was an unmitigated disaster to David. 'I

understand some people believe in Mohammed. Some people
believe in Buddha. But 30, 40 years on? You have seen what it is.
There is no way you could be fooled.'

David and Kiki now spoke of politics, through me. I read back
some of Kiki's comments and explanations. How he had called
the Revolution 'a necessity', for example. 'The Revolution was
something necessary, yes,' David agreed, nodding. 'But Communism, no.'

Kiki had argued that the rich had fled Cuba because the
Revolution took away their wealth. They had fled because it
was in their economic interest to do so.

'We don't care about money,' Elena said, curtly.

David nodded slowly. 'I left nothing behind,' he added after a
moment.

Nothing of value, he meant. All the things that he and Elena
had abandoned in Cuba were just things, and not important in the
long run. Things could be replaced. What mattered was freedom.
Having room to breathe, to make their own lives. 'We can't live
like that,' David said, of Kiki's Cuba.

David told a story about keys. So many Cuban exiles
remembered the keys: the keys to homes, to automobiles,
to workplaces. Keys were intimate, personal, portable, bound
up with ideas of security and control, or one's own place in
life. They were symbols of the Enlightenment, and manifesta-
tion of Eleggua, the opener of doors and pathways. So many
exiles came out clutching a key to a house, holding fast to that
metal, dreaming of returning, of opening those doors once
again.

'I used to carry all my keys on a key ring here on my belt,'
David said, touching his right side. The de Jongh family was rich,
he said, with many properties and buildings. As the eldest son, and
a medical doctor, David had a lot of keys.

By 1959 he had built up a successful laboratory and blood
bank in Santiago. 'You don't just build a laboratory,' David
said. Kiki had been his partner, the architect on the project.
First they studied building plans in the Sears Roebuck catalogue, and then together they drove 'all over the Republic',

looking at laboratories and hospitals, seeing how they were built, the way they were laid out to collect northern light, with a soft floor to protect the feet of the weak and ill. 'We visited every place we could find,' David said. 'Every building, every laboratory. We studied every instrument. We did everything ourselves. We even produced our own reagents for the lab work, too. It was a dedicated effort on my part. It took many months, a year.'

The lab and clinic that Kiki designed became David's little domain, and the keys on that key chain – for the company cars, the different doors of the different buildings – were always at his side. He could identify each key, just by fingertip, without thinking or looking. 'I was very *dexterous*, very *agile*, in picking out a key,' he said, mixing precise English words into his Spanish. He mimed the action of reaching down and whipping a key off the ring without looking, a blur of motion.

Then the Revolution. In 1959 the economy began to fall apart. In 1960 the confiscations began. In 1961, the militias began rounding up people like him, who were known to be against Castro. He was his own prophet, hiding his gold in the ashes and telling his staff that the end was near.

'I remember the staff were all there once, and I said to them, One day you will see me leaving Cuba. They said, No, this is your life, your laboratory, you can't leave them. But I said, Yes, I'll take my keys and when I go out the door for the last time, I'll throw them behind me.'

This was exactly what David had done. When he left the laboratory for the last time, he threw the key ring over his shoulder. 'I told them, wherever I go, I'll build a new blood bank. I'll build a new laboratory. And I'll be a free man.' Now, he said, he didn't miss the keys, or the things they opened. Not the cars. Not the labs. Not the house. Not the stamp collection he had built up carefully, over many years, and then left in a drawer. Those things could be replaced. In America, after much struggle, he had forged his life over. A new blood bank. A new laboratory. A new house. A new car. A new set of keys. 'We would give it away again ten times over, if we had to,' he said, as Elena nodded.

What made David angry was the loss of something entirely different. He fell into an unsolicited rant about the decline in American culture. The United States, he said, was now hated all over the world not for our foreign policy or economic power, but because we mocked our own symbols of authority. David blamed it on television. It had all started with *McHale's Navy*, and *F Troop*. These were 1950s shows, in black and white, that had been the basest, most obsolete reruns in my youth. They outraged David because they encouraged people to laugh at the flag, the military uniform, all 'the emblems of the country. Those things are sacred.'

Next thing you knew, Rosanne was mocking the national anthem, spitting on the ground. He was speaking faster and faster. Roseanne *infuriated* him. 'If Fidel was out and I was in,' he said, jabbing two fingers into the table, 'she would be shot by sunset. I would shoot her. When the sun came up in the morning she would *not . . . be . . . alive.*' Jab, jab, jab.

Once he was done shooting comedians David was ready for Fidel himself. David was 'absolutely sure' that Castro had directed the September 11 attacks on New York and Washington. The hijackers had trained in Florida. And absolutely nothing could happen in Florida without the knowledge of Castro's spy networks. Therefore it was 'not possible' that Castro was *not* involved. I challenged him for evidence, but David had the only evidence he needed: Castro's character. He picked up the photo. 'I'm here,' he said. 'Fidel is here.' He dragged a nail across the picture. 'For many years we were together. We played baseball many times. I know him from a child –'

He came to an abrupt halt. 'My God,' he said, staring at the spot where his fingertip had landed. 'It's Santangello!'

Now it began to rain. Not just rain, but the sudden onset of a tropical storm. The wind blew up and a minute later the downpour was so loud on the glass roof that David and I could not hear each other. It grew dark, and palm fronds scattered down everywhere, along with seed pods and sticks. Kendal was getting hit.

Out at sea a squall like this would throw up crisscrossing swells that slammed at little boats, shook loose the screws in their motors, pried at the their amateur seams and crudely constructed equipment. The storm would look for a way to break a small boat. Six people, wet and cold would begin to doubt. The storm would slow them, too. Rafters sometimes ended up in the Bahamas, or as far north as the Carolinas. It was 200 miles from Cuba to Miami, and a storm could double or even triple the miles covered, while dragging out the trip for days. About 950 Cubans a year landed successfully in Southern Florida.

WHEN THE RAIN RETREATED, I mentioned the *Encyclopaedia Britannica* to David. His face changed. 'Kiki has it?' he asked.

No. Kiki had reminisced about the *Britannica*, but he didn't have it any more.

'Oh, it was magnificent,' David said. 'And that edition!'

Another de Jongh family lecture on the genius of the 1911 edition. All the knowledge of the world in one package, David said. All about *aqua regia* and touchstones. About gold. David brushed his hands over the memory of those soft leather covers, and mimed rolling a whole volume up into a tube. Then he slashed his hand horizontally through the air, recalling, like his brother, the way his father piled them in upright stacks, rather than linear rows, so that the thin paper and leather wouldn't bend.

Arturo de Jongh now came into the house. The middle of the three, he introduced himself, but immediately fled into the kitchen, where he talked quietly with David's wife. He was the least assertive of the brothers. Arturo was the one who had joined the guerrillas for the last two weeks of the war, liberating Santiago without a weapon. Arturo had always been hard for me to interview, because in his late sixties he was always flying or driving somewhere in Florida to broker a new real estate deal. His corporate masters had big money at stake, so he could never get away to talk with me. There was a fantastic frenzy of real estate speculation under way, so there was always another shopping mall or housing development to push.

Now that I had seen all three brothers, I asked David to try once more to explain the differences among them. How did he and Arturo end up here, and Kiki there?

'Explain Kiki,' David said. He wasn't repeating my earlier question. He was ordering me to answer it. He tapped the photo, lying on the glass table. 'Same father. Same mother. Same city. Same school. Same university.'

Same but for the result. The conclusions they drew from their own lives were diametrically opposed. Not just contradictory, but a negation of the other's very existence. They were like one of David's laboratory projects, two reagents cultured in the same petri dish and then put to utterly different purposes.

And that was it. Explain Kiki? There was no explanation. When nations sink, people make life rafts from a flotsam of ideas and stories, old keys and dimes blackened by age. Life was held together with ideology, loyalty, ambition. We are all drowning, slowly. But like the Jews, the Cubans understand in a deep way how to stay afloat.

On the way out, David left me in the living room for a while. Going to the bathroom takes a long time when you are old. I studied Elena's paintings. Voluptuous green hills. The elderly city that she called by its full name, Santiago de Cuba. The bay dotted with sails. The water was calm. Everybody had a boat.

David let me out a moment later, just after I'd finished inventorying the walking sticks in his umbrella stand. There was something he and Kiki had in common. Back in Havana, Kiki had a walking stick. And here in Miami, David had nine.

THE NEXT NIGHT, many of the most important figures in *El Exílio* were gathering in the Biltmore Hotel in Coral Gables. The event was a cocktail party and fundraising dinner in honour of Václav Havel, the former dissident and now outgoing president of Czechoslovakia. Cubans were paying $1,000 a table to sit near Havel's halo, and hear his anti-Communist philosophy.

The Biltmore is an embarrassing Moorish fantasy from 1926, with a big central tower in yellow, and long wings on each side containing vaulted banquet and meeting rooms. The idea was that Havel would appear first at a cocktail party in one wing, where he could embrace former political prisoners from Cuba in a public display of solidarity. But the room could contain only about 200 people in a city where more than 20,000 describe themselves as former political prisoners of Castro. The organizers had been forced to pick carefully, and had focused on the usual names.

Ileana Ros-Lehtinen, the Republican congresswoman from Miami, was one of the first faces I recognized when I came into the room. There were also players from the major Cuban-American lobbying organizations, including the Cuban-American National Foundation (CANF). In the 1980s the group had held a kind of monopoly in Washington on Cuban issues, but their strident leader, Jorge Más Canosa, had died abruptly in 1997. (Though Jorge Más was from Santiago, and one of his brothers had gone to Dolores, he wasn't himself a Jesuit product.)

CANF had been weakened in recent years. Hardline supporters defecting to the Cuban Liberty Council, moderates falling away to the left. The room was full of the *plantados*, the hardest of the hardline men who had come out of Castro's prisons. The *plantados* were known for the length of their sentences and were rejectionists by nature, proudly to the right of Genghis Khan. In Castro's jails, they had refused to recognize his authority, starving themselves, refusing all instructions, even going naked rather than wear Castro's clothing. In exile, they were the refuseniks, opposed to any compromise, dialogue, contact, or commercial opening to Havana, under any conditions.

The *plantados* wore name tags that listed their sentences. Havel, who endured four years under arrest, waded into the crowd and was embraced by Huber Matos ('20 Years in Jail'). The Velvet Revolution and Operation Mongoose were together at last. Matos has been a soldier his whole life, first as an army major for Batista, then as a *comandante* against him, as one of Fidel's most trusted commanders. Then Matos had tried to overthrow Castro, served 20 years, mostly in the notorious Isle of Pines prison. Now Matos was was one of the most ardent advocates of violence against Cuba.

No sooner had Havel, the apostle of peaceful transition, moved on to shake more hands ('Luis Gonzales Infante, 16 Years in Prison'), then Matos spoke up for more violence. He praised Havel as 'one of our own', but then told me that the Czech was just plain wrong when it came to Cuba. Matos offered his plan: *militarismo*. The Cuban army had a long tradition of overthrowing leaders, he said, approvingly. Officers within the Revolutionary armed forces could be convinced to toss out Castro. The *plantado* answer for the future was the same as the one offered for centuries. Force.

I asked Matos why a Velvet Revolution wasn't possible in Cuba. 'The difference,' Matos said, 'is the Czech Republic is in the heart of Europe. They had contact with other countries all around. But Cuba is an island.' But it was the *plantados* themselves who demanded isolation. They wanted maximum hostility and minimal contact. Anyone who stayed behind in Cuba was useless. They denigrated people like Elizardo Sánchez and Palácios. These *inxiles* speaking of electoral reform and human rights were naive, hopelessly compromised, even collaborators.

Behind Matos, 'Mr 16 Years in Prison' nodded, and then condemned the internal dissidents. 'Václav Havel considers it correct. But we see it as not the correct line to free Cuba.' The next government in Havana would have to come from Miami, he said, because there could be absolutely no participation by '*corruptos*', which meant anyone involved in the old system at all.

Not surprisingly, those who had been forced to live within the old system were quick to disagree. Most Cuban-Americans were younger than the *plantados*, or of more recent vintage as exiles. Right behind Matos were two recent arrivals, younger dissidents named Maritza Lugo and Marco Torres, who had both come to America within the last year. Torres had served five years in Cuban jails, and Lugo had been arrested more than 30 times. Torres, wearing a long-sleeved *guayabera* and staring intently at his glass of white wine, had left Havana just two months before. 'There are a lot of political differences in this room,' he said quietly. 'We want concessions. The *Exílio* is not putting the interests of Cuba first.'

Lugo, who had had left the island eight months before, added, 'I'm not *plantado*.' Wearing a new gold dress and matching shoes, she surveyed the high-ceilinged room with the eyes of a woman watching a fundraiser for the first time. 'There are a lot of groups within the exile,' she said. 'There are some discrepancies of opinion, but that's Cuban.' She herself supported Havel, and his nonviolent approach. The older generation of *plantados* 'struggled for so many years, was jailed for so long, saw their families killed, their friends executed. These people don't know another route to power except through force.

'Miami is very different,' Lugo mused. 'It's a radical change, so different from Cuba.' She pointed to a vast centrepiece of grapes, cascading down on to a serving table covered with cheese and crackers. 'The food is very different,' she said, politely. 'But there's a lot of it.'

Havel's dinner speech disappointed the *plantados*. At an event that raised about $100,000 for Havel, they got only two sentences in English. At dinner, he returned again and again to the theme of nonviolence, to the moral authority that comes from embracing the enemy.

Cuban-Americans should push for maximum opening and contact with Cuba, not just because it would strengthen the *inxiles*, but because it would change the exiles. They were the ones who needed to adjust to the reality of the internal dissidents, Havel said.

The only thing that could confront and shatter a state built on lies was acting on principle. 'The mysterious, radiant energy that comes from free speech and free actions turns out to be more powerful,' he concluded, 'than the strongest army.' He called this 'the power of the powerless'.

I wanted Havel to be right, but my dreams didn't believe him. That night, falling asleep in the Holiday Inn in Little Havana, I saw visions of a dystopian Cuba, richer and freer in all the wrong ways, divided, filled with crime and vainglorious wealth. Where would the infant mortality rate go when businessmen and politicians divided up the spoils? What would happen to the boys outside the Estadio Latinoamericano? It was enough to make me miss the hand that throttled me. Once Cyclops was gone, everyone would miss his fist.

There was no real plan in Miami, nor in Havana either. The only formal plan in Cuba was for a succession, not a transition. In 2006, when Castro was abruptly sidelined by intestinal surgery, he wrote a letter turning over not just his duties but also his titles (First Secretary, Commander-in-Chief, President of the Council of State and head of the health, education and 'Energy Revolution' programmes) to his younger brother. For the first time in half a century Fidel was at a distance from the public eye. He soon posed for photographs where he was shown reading *Grandmother* in his pajamas, or getting a hug from Venezuela's Hugo Chávez, or a courtesy call from Kofi Annan. But Castro was missing the Movement of Non-Aligned Nations meeting right there in Havana – a favourite forum. He was alive but mute.

It can't last, but Cuba's best hope for the future is something just like this. If Fidel Castro fades away slowly, it may force Cubans everywhere to make realistic plans. All the desperately needed economic reforms that Castro always blocked could be slipped into place slowly, right under his nose; the old man wheeled out for annual rallies as the men around him begin their negotiation with reality. Certainly, whenever and however Castro goes, his funeral will be among the most spectacular events in Latin American history. I fully expect to see even his enemies crying crocodile tears down both sides of their *doblecaras*.

And then? Then Raúl. Raúl was head of the armed forces, the man who invented MinInt, either an inflexible, charmless, and violent ideologue responsible for more deaths than Fidel, or a warm family man depending on whom you listened to. The truth is that nobody knows him, or what he will do. In the streets Raúl was known as *el chino* for his Chinese eyes, a nickname that conveys a certain hope: Cuba's own Communists have broached the idea of the 'Chinese model', or opening the economy to profit with everything managed by a dictatorship of the party and the military. If the average person benefited, the Chinese model might be possible.

But what new Cuba could be born from this rotten thing, this crumbling island of dashed expectations, surrounded by vultures? There can be no *Fidelismo* without Fidel.

Cuba could easily unravel. Economic changes would produce wealth, but also disparity; then social tension, increasing crime, factionalism, and the collapse of some parts of Cuban society. After half a century, there is something dark and messianic at the bottom of the Cuban experience, an unplumbed depth of resentment, salted with the will to power. The *plantados* and thousands of other exiles vowed to leap into boats as soon as possible, heading back to Cuba to reclaim their old houses by force. This would probably spark a civil war, perhaps a deeply cruel one. Cuba has fought itself before.

The filing cabinets of Miami are stuffed with plans for personal revenge and radical, free market reforms, for franchise opportunities and offshore havens. The best preview of democracy in Havana is democracy in Miami. That isn't Havel's picture, but it isn't entirely hopeless either.

Strange and little reported events were occurring in far parts of the country, especially the traditionally rebellious towns of Villa Clara. Spontaneous acts of dissent. Even disorganized demonstrations. A new group appeared suddenly in Havana, calling itself the Mothers in White, marching to the Malecón to commemorate loved ones who died while trying to flee the island. They went to the water and threw in wreaths. This was something out of Václav Havel's speech, a small event with unseen ramifications.

But Castro, and the system he has built, will not go quietly. Within minutes of their appearance on the Malecón, the Mothers in White were under surveillance. The police arrived. Soon a dial-a-mob was mobilized from local block committees, and confronted the Mothers in White, surrounding them, shouting insults, tossing trash and chanting: FIDEL, FIDEL, THIS NEIGHBOURHOOD BELONGS TO FIDEL.

About 50 of the women in white were detained. Castro's personal reaction came a few days later, when he thundered that there would be no more tolerance of 'traitors and mercenaries'.

Opponents would not be allowed to go 'one millimetre' beyond what 'the people' would tolerate. Then Cyclops, the Horse, Him, the *bola de churda*, turned on a Jesuitical dime, and denied that there even was an opposition in Cuba.

'The much-publicized dissidence, or alleged opposition in Cuba, exists only in the fevered minds of the Cuban-American mafia and the bureaucrats in the White House,' he said, to cheering and applause. The big theatre was full, every seat taken by government staffers, military officers and a large contingent of American solidarity activists.

'You would think that the Revolution only had a few hours left,' he added, to laughter.

THE NEXT DAY, out on the Key again, the Aguilar household was upended. Lundy and Vera were moving. There were decades of accumulated material, a household of carefully constructed identity, to be moved for the last time into smaller quarters. Old age was its own exile, a stripping-away of the self. Life became a regression, from the sufficiency at birth to the emptiness of even the fullest old age.

His son Lou met me in the driveway. He was named Luis too. He wore a blue T-shirt and jeans. We chatted in the driveway and he gave me the same warning.

'He has Alzheimer's,' Lou said. 'He's lost it. It's over.'

How did Lou know it was Alzheimer's?

'He keeps repeating himself,' he said.

The prophecy of Alzheimer's was coming true. When he talked of the raider boat back in 1961, describing what powerful motors it had, what a marvellous boat it was, the superb handling, and the crack of cannon fire from a Cuban frigate, his mind was clear. The old memories were good. But tangles of proteins were slowly grabbing at his brain cells. When I called him on the phone now, he sometimes stopped abruptly, losing track of the conversation. 'Who is this?' he said to me, astonished. 'What do you want?'

There was little sign of this when I found him inside the house. Vera always arranged my visits for late morning, when Lundy was at his best. We would talk, and then finish with lunch. Lundy was worried about the deep divisions within the United States, where politics increasingly consisted of opposed groups who denied the legitimacy and even language of the opposition. The future of Cuba was also hard to see. Civil war was possible, he acknowledged. 'It will take generations to restore the society,' he said, glumly. Lundy had learned from Castro himself to be 'a peaceful revolutionary', he said. Violent overthrows could only produce new governments built on force and the strongman. 'I never argue with someone who has a gun,' he said.

'Maybe the future is here,' Lundy suggested. It was a radical idea for a Cuban. It was heresy to acknowledge that there would be no satisfying end to this story. There would be no *reconquista*, no triumphant re-entry, no fitting of old keys into the houses of memory. Cuban-Americans could 'go back to the island slowly, over time', Lundy suggested. 'Over time' meant over decades, generations, centuries. Cubans could become like the Jews, he suggested, defined by their floating state, their recitation of what was left behind in an ancient homeland.

I left the old house for the last time, steering around the lizards and stopping back on the main drag, Crandon Boulevard. Key Biscayne only had one of everything, but that was all you needed. I bought a coffee at the standup window of La Carreta, and a *Miami Herald*. The coffee was good Cuban stuff, espresso with the sugar mixed right into the grounds. The steam caramelized the sugar, and the black honey that emerged was smothered in a froth of hot milk.

The *Herald* carried a small item. Yesterday, before dawn, right here on Key Biscayne, six Cubans had come ashore. Their pilot must have been good. He'd sailed through two Coast Guards and a storm, and brought them right into Biscayne Bay, to a point where they could see the purple neon towers of downtown Miami in the distance. Then the smuggler had turned left and aimed for the first beach he saw. Just outside the surf line, he'd tossed his six passengers overboard, and then motored off to fend for himself. The money was so good that many smugglers went back and forth.

The six had staggered ashore and found themselves on Crandon Park Beach, half a mile from here. Standing in the crab grass,
beneath the baobabs, their feet were wet, but officially dry. In
accordance with American law, the six were taken by police to a
detention centre, processed, and released. They would have legal
residency a day later – today sometime – and, if history was any
guide, would be connected with family members and working at
jobs within the week. I passed by the landing spot on the way out.

I went back to Key Biscayne several times. Lundy and Vera
moved to the new apartment, and it was a good spot. Their other
son George, a film producer, had bought the house from them,
keeping it in the family. In the new condo, two floors below
Pepín, they had a simpler life. Someone was always vacuuming
the hallways, polishing the elevator, or clipping the grass. It was
smaller than the house, but Lundy had still found room for
battalions of Saxons, Cuban irregulars and Waterloo victors on
shelves in the bedroom, and his crazy swords and polished
muskets were hanging on a wall.

Lundy paid less and less attention to these things. He was
increasingly captivated by the view, by the wall of glass in the
living room. The vista wasn't as lofty as in Pepín's place but was
intimate, a tree-level view right into a thick grove of Malay and
Panama Tall palm. There were a few baobabs off to the left,
imitating the great Ceibas of Cuba, the holy trees where Santería
spirits gathered. Out ahead were mangroves, some of the last
stands in Miami. Aside from the mangroves, all the trees were
imports from somewhere else. And aside from the green, all you
could see was the washed out sky.

'I love these trees,' Lundy told me. 'You can't see any buses, or
streets.'

Just trees, swaying and waving their arms in silence.

THE LAST THING I HAD TO SEE WAS BELÉN, which
stands to the west of Miami. It had been in Havana until 1961,
and then was refounded in Miami in 1963 by and for Cubans
fleeing Castro. Several of the Jesuit priests from Dolores joined
the staff, but most teachers were from the other Jesuit schools, in

Cienfuegos and Havana. Like their teachers, the students from Dolores had been subsumed into the larger school on arrival in Miami. Dolores had, in this sense, disappeared.

The new campus was in West Miami, near Palmetto Express-way, facing the humid interior of Florida. Here, finally, was the facility the old Jesuits had always dreamed of. They had drawn up blueprints for new, updated campuses in both Santiago and Havana, but the real Belén that had risen up instead, in Miami, was like a college campus, a collection of connected buildings backed with playing fields.

In the lobby of Belén, right where you walked in, there was a photo mural of the old Belén in Havana. You had to show what you had lost. The could-have-been. And across the lobby, in the middle of another wall, was a school photograph. Not the entire school body this time – with more than a thousand students, the boys of Belén would not fit in any viewfinder. This was the senior class, which had just graduated, in 2004. Instead of a group portrait, it was a pointillist composition of several hundred individual shots in tight columns. The boys were wearing neck-ties. The class was not all Cuban – there were Colombians, Dominicans, Venezuelans, even Mexicans – but it was over-whelmingly a class of second- or even third-generation Cuban-Americans, fluent in Spanish but at home in America. The boys of Belén were 17 and 18, and the only Cuba they knew was a story. In the whole class of 2004 there was not one black face.

The school had an inner courtyard, a *patio* in the old verna-cular. But this was a vast oval in poured concrete. Efficient, cost-effective, the Florida way. There were good playing fields out back, a theatre, modern science labs, and well-equipped class-rooms, with a wide variety of extracurricular programmes, espe-cially the sports teams.

Out front, cars started appearing at about 2.45 pm. The first few filled in the parking lot, but more kept coming. They filled the kerbs, then double-parked in long rows. By 3.10 a traffic jam of 60 spilled out the driveway and into the street. One man drove a flashy BMW convertible, another sat reading the paper in a battered Honda Civic. Some listened to the radio. Women were doing their hair or talking on the phone, sometimes both. The majority were driving boat-sized Lincoln Navigators and Chevy Suburbans, the huge SUVs and gleaming status brands. Two people arrived separately in Hummer H2s, swathed in dark windows, one of the wagons topped with extra banks of fog lights and accessories from stem to stern.

At 3.15 the students came pouring out, a sea of boys, some in what passed for formal outfits. That meant white, collared shirts and baggy, low-riding blue trousers. Nobody wore a tie, and many, who were heading for the practice fields or gym, were already in the sweat pants or gym shorts of the Belén teams, the Wolverines. Everything was coloured Colegio de Belén blue.

SELECT BIBLIOGRAPHY

Adams, Charles et al., *Social Change in Latin America Today*, Random House, New York, 1960.

Aguilar, Luis, *De Como Murieron Las Palabras*, Editorial Playor, Madrid, 1984.

Arnaz, Desi, *A Book,* William Morrow and Co., New York, 1976.

Asus, Moises and Levine, Robert M., *Cuban Miami*, Rutgers University Press, New Jersey, 2000.

Bardach, Ann Louise, *Cuba Confidential*, Random House, New York, 2002.

Bellville, Bill, *Deep Cuba*, University of Georgia, Georgia, 2002.

Bonachea, Ramon L. and Martin, Marta San, *The Cuban Insurrection 1952–59*, New Brunswick, New Jersey, 1974.

Calvo, Hernando and Declercq, Katlijn, *The Cuban Exile Movement: Dissidents or Mercenaries*, Ocean Press, Melbourne, 2000.

Cameron, Sarah, *Footprint Cuba Handbook*, Footprint, Suffolk, 1998.

Canizares, Raul, *Cuban Santiera*, Destiny Books, Rochester, Vermont, 1999.

Canto, Jay, *The Death of Che Guevara*, Random House, New York, 1984.

Cushing, Lincoln, *Revolucion!: Cuban Poster Art*, Chronicle Books, San Francisco, 2003.

Eckstein, Susan Eva, *Back from the Future: Cuba under Castro*, Princeton University Press, New Jersey, 1995.

Eire, Carlos, *Waiting for Snow in Havana*, The Free Press, New York, 2003.

Foehr, Stephen, *Dancing with Fidel*, Butler and Tanner, London, 2001.

Freire, Joaquin, *Historia de Los Municipios de Cuba*, La Moderna Poesia Inc., Santo Domingo, Dominican Republic, 1985.

Fuentes, Leonardo Padura, *Mascaras*, Tusquets Editores, Barcelona, 2001.

Gimbel, Wendy, *Havana Dreams: A Story of a Cuban Family*, Knopf, New York, 1998.

Halstead, Murat, *The Story of Cuba: Her Struggles for Liberty*, Franklin Square Bible House, Chicago, 1898.

Human Rights Watch, *Cuba's Repressive Machinery: Human Rights Forty Years After the Revolution*, New York, 1999.

Hyde, Lewis, *Trickster Makes This World: Mischief, Myth and Art*, Farrar, Straus and Giroux, New York, 1998.

Infante, Guillermo Cabrera, *Three Trapped Tigers*, Hurst Books, New York, 1971.

Infante, Guillermo Cabrera, *Mea Culpa*, Farrar, Straus and Giroux, New York, 1994.

Iyer, Pico, *Cuba and the Night: A Novel*, Knopf, New York, 1995.

Korda, Alberto, *Diario de una Revolucion*, Ediciones Aurelia, Panama, 2000.

Krich, John, *A Totally Free Man: An Unauthorized Autobiography of Fidel Castro*, Simon and Schuster, New York, 1988.

Miller, Tom, *Trading with the Enemy: A Yankee Travels Through Castro's Cuba*, Macmillan, New York, 1996.

Oppenheimer, Andres, *Castro's Final Hour: The Secret Story Behind the Coming Downfall of Communist Cuba*, Simon and Schuster, New York, 1992.

Perez, Louis A, *The War of 1898: The United States and Cuba in History and Historiography*, University of North Carolina Press, 1998.

Sayles, John, *Los Gusanos,* HarperCollins, New York, 1991.

Schneider, Ronald M. and Kingsbury, Robert C., *An Atlas of Latin American Affairs*, Methuen, London, 1966.

Suarez, Virgil and Van Cleave, Ryan G. (eds), *American Diaspora: Poetry of Displacement*, University of Iowa Press, Iowa, 2001.

Sweig, Julia A., *Inside the Cuban Revolution: Fidel Castro and the Urban Underground*, Harvard University Press, Cambridge Mass., 2002.

Tattlin, Isadora, *Cuba Diaries: An American Housewife in Havana*, Algonquin Books, North Carolina, 2002.

Wendell, Tim, *Castro's Curveball*, Ballantine, New York, 1999.

INDEX